THE INNER CITY

THE INNER CITY

A Handbook for Renewal

Edited by ROGER L. KEMP

McFarland & Company, Inc., Publishers
Jefferson, North Carolina, and London

Library of Congress Cataloguing-in-Publication Data

The inner city : a handbook for renewal / edited
by Roger L. Kemp.
p.   cm.
Includes bibliographical references and index.
ISBN 0-7864-1015-9 (library binding : 50# alkaline paper) ∞
1. Urban renewal — United States.
2. Inner cities — United States.
3. Urban policy — United States.
4. Community development, Urban — United States.
I. Kemp, Roger L.
HT175.I55   2001   307.3'416'0973 — dc21   2001032652

British Library cataloguing data are available

Manufactured in the United States of America

McFarland & Company, Inc., Publishers
Box 611, Jefferson, North Carolina 28640
www.mcfarlandpub.com

Jonathan and Wendy
May you always reach for the stars

ACKNOWLEDGMENTS

Grateful acknowledgment is made to the following organizations and publishers for granting permission to reprint the material contained in this volume.

American Economic Development Council
American Planning Association
American Society for Public Administration
Committee for Economic Development
Congressional Quarterly, Inc.
FCW Government Technology Group
Government Finance Officers Association
International City/County Management
    Association
Intertec Publishing Corporation

League of California Cities
Maryland Municipal League
National Academy of Sciences
National Civic League
National League of Cities
Nolan Media, LLC
Partners for Livable Communities
University of Texas at Austin
Urban Economic Development Council
Urban Land Institute

TABLE OF CONTENTS

PART IV. CASE STUDIES

PART V. THE FUTURE

PREFACE

Our inner-city areas, located in the hearts of our urban metropolitan centers throughout America, typically flourished in their earlier years. They were places that attracted commerce and industry, manufactured those goods and services needed by our society, and created the jobs and economy necessary to make the surrounding neighborhoods survive.

As America's network of roadways expanded, both in number and size, the jobs and houses relocated to the suburbs, and millions of people followed. Even when jobs remained in our metropolitan areas, the distances to reach them from outlying areas seemed to shrink because of the increased speed allowed by these automobile expressways. As the flight from the core areas of our cities continued throughout the years, it left functionally obsolete buildings and antiquated streets in its path.

Our public leaders in these urban areas have learned to cope, even make considerable progress, in rebuilding our nation's inner cities. As our society enters the 21st century, the state of our inner cities and the quality of life they provide to citizens have, in many cases, improved dramatically. While we cannot change our roadway networks, many companies and citizens are relocating to our metropolitan areas in record numbers. While the number and size of suburban shopping malls

will not diminish, selected commercial establishments and residential neighborhoods not only exist but are starting to flourish in our inner-city areas. Many of our inner-city metropolitan areas have been retrofitted with multiple large municipal parking garages to accommodate our main mode of transportation, the automobile. In some cases aging streets have been closed to vehicular traffic and remade as attractive pedestrian walkways. Public officials in our metropolitan areas are focusing their attention on restoring an outdated public infrastructure and creating more civic open space for citizens to enjoy. Some residential areas are even undergoing a renaissance.

In recent years, particularly the past decade or so, citizens have demanded that their inner-city areas be brought back to life for current and future generations to enjoy. Our municipal officials have responded to this challenge in a number of different and creative ways. Numerous tactics have evolved in recent years to revitalize these urban core areas, including the use of selected economic development incentives.

While municipal officials can ensure the public's safety by hiring more police officers and fire fighters, and they can rebuild the public infrastructure, other measures are needed to attract merchants and professionals to fill up vacant space in

1

these areas. Over the past decade, the tools available to rebuild our downtowns have evolved from a loose assortment of inducements to the use of many diverse, yet highly focused, incentive programs. In many cases, these incentives can be tailored to achieve the specific goals desired by public officials and citizens as they rebuild these urban inner-city core neighborhoods.

Part I of this volume includes an introduction into the state of our nation's metropolitan cities and their urban problems as they exist today, focuses on creative approaches to the many issues associated with these problems, and examines practices to create globally competitive communities in the information age. The author of one chapter suggests that in the new world economy, cities must have an educated workforce in order to economically compete with other communities in the state, nation, even the world. Cities that are globally competitive will thrive economically in the new millennium. Lastly, this section looks at the different roles of economic developers and planners, focusing on the different skills needed by these two entirely different types of urban professionals. Taken together, the chapters in this section provide readers with insight into the evolving field of inner-city renewal, and set the stage for a discussion of the numerous processes available to public officials and citizens to help them bring their inner cities back to life in the years ahead.

Part II examines how public officials and metropolitan governments must mobilize their resources and focus their attention on inner-city renewal. New approaches to managing urban growth are emerging, and are discussed in these chapters. How to manage and revitalize downtowns by district is also examined. Ways to strengthen inner-city businesses, as well as ways to create and mobilize social capital,

are also topics of this section, along with two new issues that merit close attention. These issues are, first, consideration of when a municipal government and its public officials should consider the use of economic incentives; and, second, how to calculate the costs and benefits associated with the use of these incentives. Public officials should keep in mind that taxpayers are footing the bill for most economic development incentives, and that the value of these incentives, in the aggregate, should not exceed or even equal the anticipated economic return to the community in terms of jobs and revenues. This is a very politically sensitive issue, one that requires the use of incentives to be compared against the collective-help values in each community. Overall, Part II builds a solid foundation upon which to examine the numerous tools available for our inner-city communities to tackle their economic problems.

Part III is devoted to the tools available for inner-city renewal. Some 16 different practical tools are examined in detail. These tools, discussed in alphabetical order for ease of reference, include public investment strategies, the use of special zones and districts, links between development and available public services, and the creation of more attractive urban areas through curbs on growth and improvements in both the quantity and appearance of public spaces. A chapter on self-evaluation and benchmarking will help officials in cities recognize available resources, set appropriate goals, and properly plan for their future.

Most of the tools discussed in Part III are already available for cities, such as the use of community-based development organizations. Only two of the tools discussed, federal empowerment zones and historical preservation tax incentives, are made available by higher levels of government.

A discussion of these tools would not be complete without showing how they have been successfully applied in other urban inner-city areas throughout America. For this reason, Part IV consists of sixteen case studies showing real-life examples of public officials' efforts to revitalize their inner-city commercial areas and residential neighborhoods. These case studies include the use of special zones and districts, historic preservation and restoration programs, the creation of inner-city parks and open spaces, and the rebuilding and refurbishing of older residential neighborhoods. Some cities have used new inner-city malls, museums, performing arts centers, and riverfront developments to revitalize their aging commercial buildings and residential neighborhood dwellings. One city even revised its old zoning ordinance in order to attract more creative development proposals. Historical preservation and restoration programs for older buildings are at the forefront of the inner-city revitalization movement. Such programs invariably include retrofitting urban core areas with public spaces, as well as enhancing the size and quality of existing inner-city parks and open spaces. These trends will continue well into the new century.

The cities examined in this volume are typically larger ones, ranging in size from about 125,000, like Hartford and Lancaster, to several million inhabitants, such as New York, Los Angeles, and Chicago. While most of our nation's cities are not large, those communities facing urban problems tend to be large-sized, older cities with aging central urban core areas, and to have experienced an outmigration of their population over the years due to expanding vehicular transportation networks and new housing markets. Geographically, the municipal metropolitan areas examined range from the west (Lancaster, Los Angeles, and Portland) to the east (Balti-more, Boston, Cambridge, Hartford, Newark, New York, Philadelphia, and Washington, D.C.), and from the north (Chicago and Minneapolis) to the south (Chattanooga and Memphis), as well as the midwest (Kansas City). The reason there are a larger number of eastern cities in this work is because this corner of the nation contains many of its largest and oldest urban cities. Nevertheless, the cities examined in this volume represent a mix of municipalities in virtually every geographic region of the United States. They also represent a diversity of political structures.

Part V examines the future of inner-city renewal. This section is intended to provide critical thinking about how our urban economic development programs will be designed and conducted in the 21st century. It is essential that public officials in both cities and suburbs work closely together to improve the quality of life for the citizens they serve. In this final section, a study by the National League of Cities proves that a positive linkage exists between urban center cities and the suburban towns and communities that surround them. Next, ten traditional myths about downtown revitalization are highlighted, along with seven secrets for inner-city renewal. The two final selections focus on creating sustainable development and ways to end unsightly urban sprawl. These chapters examine new practices for building environmentally sensitive developments and preventing those patterns of urban sprawl that have plagued both urban and suburban residents in recent decades.

A detailed listing of organizational resources is also provided, along with a comprehensive bibliography on inner-city renewal. The resource directory provides information on professional membership associations, research organizations, and educational centers and institutes that focus on various topics related to inner-city renewal. Information is provided on nearly 40 major resource organizations, including names, addresses, telephone and FAX numbers, and website addresses. Some of these entries include general city-related membership organizations, such as the International City/County Management Association and the National League of Cities, but have resources and produce publications relating to the revitalization and renewal of our urban communities. The bibliography includes a comprehensive listing of nearly 270 books, monographs, articles, and other sources in the field of inner-city renewal. Most of the material collected has been published since 1990, with rare exceptions of classic works in the field, which have been included regardless of their age.

The use of inner-city renewal tools and incentive programs has evolved primarily over the past few decades. They are typically applied in a piecemeal and incremental fashion by public officials from city to city. While federal and state laws may limit the types of incentives that can be provided by cities, the need exists to codify the available information concerning the best practices of inner-city renewal. This information must be made available to our local elected leaders, our municipal public officials, and most importantly, to the citizens they serve and represent. It has been the goal of this volume to provide the best available literature, featuring the best practices that can be used in other urban cities as they grapple with the issues and problems relating to inner-city renewal.

Roger L. Kemp
Meriden, Connecticut
June 2001

PART I

Cities and Renewal: An Introduction

1. REBUILDING THE AMERICAN CITY

John T. Marshall

Between 1954 and 1974, the federal government's urban renewal and federal highway programs radically changed the appearance and residential character of American cities. From the core of cities spring wide ribbons of multi-lane expressways and areas of concentrated public development, including hotels, office buildings, university campuses, and civic centers. In just twenty years, freeways and building projects reshaped cityscapes that had evolved slowly over the course of the nineteenth and the first half of the twentieth century.

The urban renewal and federal highway programs were designed to increase the domestic security of the nation by creating jobs, increasing commerce, rebuilding old or decaying structures, and establishing a fast and efficient means of intercity travel. The formulation and implementation of these initiatives resulted in a comprehensive response to specific economic problems, but the effect that these revitalization programs would have on the overall stability of the political community

escaped attention during the legislative process.

Two legislative programs—The Federal-Aid Highway Act of 1956 and the urban renewal title of the Housing Act of 1954—were intended to bolster the economic resources of urban communities, but actually destabilized the social and political character of the communities they were intended to protect. The concerns addressed by these initiatives show that lawmakers were most attuned to the relationship between a city's tax base and its ability to provide services for businesses and residents. An analysis of the federal highway and urban renewal programs reveals that legislators did not understand the role that urban residential communities play in promoting the vitality and safety of the inner city. Legislators failed to appreciate that urban communities nurture friendship bonds and social networks which are the foundation of a political community, and that these interpersonal ties are of value to the state. In their haste to lay the physical foundations for more attractive and

Originally published as "Rebuilding the American City: Bonds of Friendship as Bricks and Mortar," Planning Forum, *Vol. Spring, 1995. Published by the Community and Regional Planning Program, School of Architecture, University of Texas, Austin, Texas. Reprinted with permission of the publisher.*

productive cities, they did not consider the psychological effect that their actions would have on the people who lived in the inner city. Legislators failed to see that friendships are the bricks and mortar of the political community.

Had the federal legislators of the 1950s and 1960s shared the views expressed in Aristotle's writings, the renewal and highway programs might have taken a different course. Aristotle wrote for legislators, and in so doing, stressed that laws should transcend particular needs and promote the public welfarc. Richard Bodeus asserts:

> [T]he entirety of Aristotle's reflections on human things (the study of ethical matters and of matters relating to the organization of cities) is addressed to legislators, who he regards as responsible for education and thus as artisans of human happiness.[1]

Aristotle believed that lawmakers had a twofold responsibility: first, to address matters of common concern; and second, to ensure the well-being of the regime. These two commitments are particularly pertinent to an examination of the federal government's urban revitalization programs. Aristotle reminds lawmakers that, as "experts in politics" or physicians of the body politic, they are charged with treating the particular ailments of the political community in a way that respects the special needs and constitution of the state. Legislators must have an idea of which remedies will "create, support, preserve, or destroy [regimes]."[2] The remedies applied by federal lawmakers, and by the planners and policy makers who implemented the federal highway and urban renewal programs achieved the immediate objectives of slum clearance and an improved transportation infrastructure connecting all cities of more than 50,000 people. The objectives of these laws make clear that legislators perceived the welfare of the political community as being engendered by

measures that would promote commercial activity and economic growth. To the contrary, the government's goals of faster transportation, national security, and commerce at worst subverted and, at best, ignored the welfare of the members of the political community.

Of the many factors that contribute to the welfare of the political community, Aristotle suggests that friendship is among the most important. Friendship, of course, does not receive explicit attention in the founding documents of the United States as a vital element of the constitutional order. Aristotle's formulation of friendship, however, has tacit significance for any regime, for friends, like family, are the essential associations that compose the larger association of the political community. The State is realized as a partnership of partnerships.

As new initiatives such as the Clinton administration's Urban Empowerment Zones or the National Urban League's call for a domestic Marshall Plan are considered and implemented, it will be helpful to stake out a new vantage point from which the scope and content of programs may be evaluated. The time is ripe to examine urban programs not only with thought to how they propose to solve urban problems, but more importantly how they will protect the interest of the entire political community. This article focuses on the importance of friendship to the political community and the necessity of its consideration in the formulation of laws that direct urban initiatives.

The Federal Highway and Urban Renewal Programs: Fragmented Communities

The end of the Second World War both invited and demanded development in the United States. The return of millions of military personnel to civilian life and the need to secure the economic prosperity lost in the Great Depression led federal lawmakers to initiate several major projects that would put Government Issues (GIs) back to work and stir economic productivity. Legislators worked to formulate programs that would address the most acute areas of concern, including the need for fast and safe means of transportation between urban centers and the challenge of creating cultural attractions and jobs in the midst of a decaying urban core.

The federal highway system stands out as the most extensive and visible product of post–World War II projects. Signed into law as the Federal-Aid Highway Act of 1956, and later expanded under the Federal-Aid Highway Act of 1958, the nation's network of interstate highways grew to include 43,000 miles of multi-lane highways by 1974.[3] The interstate network may be credited with at least three important accomplishments: it facilitated the unification of the continental United States through a network of direct and safe freeways; it bolstered national security; and, it triggered a period of major economic expansion.

The federal highway system immediately changed the lives of many Americans. The expressways opened the possibility of traveling quickly and safely to and from work and to every corner of the country. Chicago's Dan Ryan Expressway, Boston's Southeast Expressway, and Washington's Beltway gave families who could afford the price of a home in suburban towns an incentive to move out of the city to safer neighborhoods with better schools and more stable property values. The new highways also made intercity travel quick and feasible. By connecting major cities, the federal highways encouraged travel to every state and region of the country. Indeed, one of the federal government's major accomplishments in constructing the highway system was drawing the country together

so as to encourage the free flow of people and ideas.

The interstate highway network also succeeded in boosting economic and military security. Over a period of twenty years, a significant portion of the government's $76 billion in expenditures flowed into highway construction jobs.[4] "Interstates" also led to direct national transportation routes which sparked increases in tourism and the transportation of commercial goods. In addition, the highway network established a quick and reliable means of transporting military supplies and personnel in a time of crisis, as federal highways tied together airports, cities, seaports, and other strategic locations.

Many Americans perceive only the positive and not the negative effects of these programs. Indeed, the negative effects are not easy to identify if you live outside the city, but for those who live in the city, those whose communities were divided or leveled to make way for the interstates, the construction of highways left an ugly imprint. The federal highways divided cities by erecting insurmountable physical barriers.

Lawmakers drafted the federal highway legislation with the goal of making the city more accessible to outlying areas. Little thought was given to the effect this might have on the lives of "the insiders," or urban residents. The effort to open the city to travelers from all directions — north, south, east, and west — often required that it be carved into quarters or lesser segments. Convenience and expedience drove the design decisions of politicians and, later, engineers. The welfare of the residential communities that occupied the urban core was not a primary concern in the lawmakers' deliberations. For this reason, it is not surprising that legislators observed little restraint in leveling inner-city neighborhoods. As Leland Roth claims, they could not "resist cutting broad new thoroughfares through whole sections of the urban core deemed 'deteriorated.'"[5]

Concurrent with the federal highway program, the urban renewal program established under Title III of The Housing Act of 1954, attempted to infuse new life into the nation's downtowns and depressed neighborhoods. In order to draw businesses, tourists, and families back into the city, the new law encouraged removing urban eyesores, such as deteriorated housing and storefronts, and replacing them with civic centers, office buildings, parks, and hotels. To this end, lawmakers crafted the renewal legislation to "encourage public agencies to experiment with new methods and techniques of preventing and eliminating slums and urban blight."[6] The government believed that by providing the initial stimulus it could encourage the private sector to redevelop inner city neighborhoods. Its motivation stemmed from the belief that the physical poverty of the city could be eradicated through the construction of new buildings and attractions. Politicians, developers, and planners in Pittsburgh, for example, worked to transform a downtown area that was dominated by unused train yards and "run-down" housing into a thriving urban environment by creating "The Igloo," a major sports arena, public office buildings, and a large park at the confluence of the Allegheny and Monongahela Rivers. Many similar parks and sports arenas are part of the positive legacy of the urban renewal movement.

While the urban renewal movement may have enriched or transformed the physical environment of the city, these advances came at the expense of poor inner-city communities. Although the urban renewal movement may be credited with cosmetic changes, any advances are counter-balanced by the fact that, in many cases, "renewal" compromised the character and communities of the city. For example, the urban renewal movement fell short on its commitment to inner-city communities by failing to meet pre-set targets for affordable housing. Developers did not find a way to replace the low-cost housing units that were typical of inner-city residential communities. Even the downwardly adjusted projections for the Housing Act of 1954 fell short of the goal of 35,000 to 40,000 units.[7] The reason for this shortfall is that affordable housing was not profitable to build. As Martin Anderson explains, old inner-city housing units were not replaced because "private developers have decided that rents obtainable from new construction in certain areas of cities would not be sufficient to recover their total investment."[8]

The urban renewal movement was formulated to modernize and reshape the physical character of the city. The welfare of urban neighborhoods and their residents was seen as a function of whether people had access to new community centers or schools. As a result, the government emphasized reconstructing the physical or built environment of cities rather than preserving the ethnic or family character of neighborhoods.

One of the chief results of the massive physical restructuring of cities was the displacement of more than one million poor families and thousands of small neighborhood businesses.[9] Though the government made efforts to compensate and relocate both families and businesses, the urban renewal movement ultimately resulted in fewer opportunities for poor families, destabilizing them and yielding only inadequate living conditions. Martin Anderson comments in his 1964 study of the federal urban renewal projects,

… privately sponsored studies [on the displacement of families] generally indicate that the people displaced by urban renewal tend to move into housing of approximately the same quality as the housing they move from; in addition, they pay higher monthly rents.

In most cases their predicament is compounded not alleviated.[10]

The fate of small businesses is even more disturbing. Again, Anderson notes that "the 'death rate' experience of 21 urban renewal projects in 14 cities covered by this study reveals that 756 of the 2,946 firms involved either went out of business or disappeared."[11]

These inner-city neighborhoods had thrived on a tight network of friendships that supported personal and commercial endeavors. When banks would not extend credit to recent immigrants for home improvements or business start-up costs, it was common for friends and local merchants to underwrite their neighbor's expenses. The political value of such friendships is discussed by Aristotle in *Ethics* and *Politics*.

Friendships and the Welfare of the State

The challenge of addressing specific policy problems and pursuing the overarching goal of maintaining the values of the political community is not new to lawmakers. Solving specific public problems while remaining mindful of the core values of the political community is one of Aristotle's principle concerns. Carnes Lord maintains that Aristotle's *Politics* may have been written to rebuke the sophists "whose approach to legislation was characterized by an over-concentration on the laws as such — laws abstracted from the context of the regime."[12] Among the main concerns expressed by Aristotle in the *Politics* is that legislative "experts" or rulers should know how to maintain the existing regime order. In other words, the people crafting laws must inform themselves of both the central principles of government and the goods which are necessary to make the nation function effectively.

It is Aristotle's observation that a particular, yet universal, requirement for a state's continued welfare is the strength of the friendships that bind each household and the city together. For Aristotle, friendships represent the "basic necessity of conjunction of persons who cannot exist without one another."[13] Friendships encourage people to pursue the good, and in so doing are necessary to the formation of a healthy political community. Indeed, friendships are primary relationships by which individuals pursue the good, and the city represents an association of these primary associations. Aristotle's opinion of friendship is based on what he considers to be the two important contributions of friendship to the city or political community. First, friendships maintain cohesive communities and second, friendships, along with households, are among the fundamental associations which form the building blocks of the political community.

Aristotle considers friendships to be central to the welfare of the city because they nurture and sustain every stage of human development. Early in life, friendships between family members or teachers and children establish important moral principles, and as Aristotle notes, "help the young avoid error."[14] As children grow into adults, friendships offer a sense of security by expanding the sphere of people on whom individuals can rely for help. The elderly are sustained and brought into the affairs of the community by their neighbors and other longtime friends who keep their company and are concerned for their emotional and physical welfare. And for those often marginalized in the city — the poor, the destitute, and the elderly — Aristotle notes that friendships offer hope, sustenance, and a connection to the larger community. Friendships check despair and isolation, for as Aristotle reasons, "in poverty and all other kinds of misfortune men believe that the only refuge consists in their friends."[15] Friendships offer many benefits to the state and, for this reason, Aristotle observes that "[f]riendship ... seems to hold states together, and lawgivers apparently devote more attention to it than to justice."[16]

Aristotle's consideration of prevailing or common opinions about friendship at the beginning of Book Eight of the *Ethics* reveals that life's pursuits are nearly impossible without friends. His discussion of the connection between friendship and individual welfare is doubly revealing; it shows a clear connection between friendship and the common good. Aristotle's account of how friendships provide for the care of the young, the old, and the disadvantaged members of the community points to the key function that friendships play in sustaining the health and welfare of the community. In so doing, Aristotle demonstrates how friendships serve as building blocks of the city.

In the *Politics*, Aristotle poses the fundamental question "what constitutes a political community?" He explores whether the state is founded on "geographical contiguity, a set of common laws, trade, or the social division of labor." Ultimately, as George McCarthy notes, "Aristotle argues that the state is founded on friendship."[17] The strongest friendships within a city or neighborhood recognize a common understanding of the fundamental principles of right action. Friends share a view of what is just. Friendships represent agreement on "goods," or shared values, for friendships crystallize a notion of what individuals believe to be "goods." These shared "goods," which include integrity, justice, responsibility, and caring, shape the individual's public pursuits and, in turn, the character of the public sphere or political community.

Thus, Aristotle recognizes that friendship embodies the best aims of the state, for "when people are friends they have no need of justice...."[18] Aristotle appreciates that friendship is the union of ethics, the study of the pursuit of the individual good, and politics, the study of the pursuit of the good of the entire city. Politics is a broad science which governs the collective pursuit of the good, and ethics is a constituent science of politics instructing people on the individual activities of living well, living a life of right action. For Aristotle, friendship occupies the point at which a person's individual pursuit of the good overlaps with the political community's goal of living well, or politics.

Aristotle's discourse on the nature of friendship and its role in shaping urban communities underscores the profound implications that the destruction of urban communities may have on the welfare of the city. Subverting the welfare of communities solely to the goals of economic revitalization squanders the ties of friendship. This decision making results not only in personal and emotional loss, but also in fragmentation of the public sphere. When people are forced to move because the local streets, public square, shops, and park have been destroyed, the friendships that motivated and animated their public actions are dissolved. The network of people whose assurances and kind gestures gave shape to a supportive community loses its constituent members and ceases to function.

Friendships do not occur spontaneously. A common neighborhood or business affiliation provides a fundamental experience resulting in a group of individuals sharing a world view. Frequent contact over long periods of time and a common interest in the affairs of a neighborhood or business kindle friendships. These friendships are squandered when individuals are displaced from their place of work or residence. A bond established by riding the same bus to work or joining together to petition the city because of poor trash collection services dissolves. An activity that engendered a developing interest in the life of another individual is no longer shared.

When neighborhoods that support friendship networks dissolve, the cost is not merely emotional or personal. It is profoundly political. The collapse of friendships destablizes an individual's life, and also removes some of the predictability and security which allow neighborhoods, and therefore cities, to function more smoothly and efficiently. There are three ways in which friendship networks help neighborhoods and cities function more efficiently as political communities: friendship frees people from the rigid calculations of "partial justice" connected with public and private transactions; friendship associations form a social safety net for the disadvantaged members of the community; and, friendship networks give people incentives to enter into relationships in which they would not otherwise receive due recognition or remuneration for their kind and generous actions.

First, the trust and good will which pervade the community help to supplant the formal obligations of justice, making friendship networks valuable to the political community. In particular, Aristotle maintains that friendship takes the place of the sphere of "partial justice" which concerns reciprocal exchange in the transaction of material goods.[19] The "motive" for this type of justice is "the pleasure that comes from profit."[20] Friends, however, are not ordinarily interested in securing profit through exchanges with one another. They are more interested in securing their mutual advantage than their individual advantage. The local baker, for instance, may not demand prior payment for the delivery of cakes and pastries to a nearby merchant or a local wedding because neighborhood clients are friends. Consequently, the baker is more concerned with making a sump-

tuous wedding cake than winning business because he sells fine desserts. At the same time, the local merchant's close relationship with the baker makes the merchant especially eager to support the baker's endeavors by paying for goods promptly and in full. And, in the case of the wedding, not only might the baker be invited, but the bride and groom might honor the chef with timely payment in light of the particularly beautiful cake that he crafted for their wedding.

So, what is there to gain from sharing a view of justice with one's neighbors? The advantage is a community tied together by a shared notion of right and wrong. These beliefs, when held in common by a group of people, serve to promote stability and order in urban life. Such friendships foster the trust that leads to thriving commerce without the undue burden of legal restrictions. In a community that supports a strong network of friendships, Aristotle claims that transactions do not need to be mediated by the threat of law or police powers. The best friendships are based on a mutual interest in the welfare of the other. Although neither party in a strong friendship would entertain the thought of undercompensating a friend, each would trust the other to fulfill any outstanding obligation that might have been incurred. The special capacity of friendship to transcend the formal dynamics and compensation of business transactions means that individuals and merchants can focus their energies on efforts that enhance the productivity and stability of a community.

The second way in which networks of friends have an explicit political value is the way in which friendships weave a mesh of relationships that ensure the economic, emotional, and moral welfare of a community. Aristotle's account of the attendant goods and benefits of friendship reveals that they are the silent movers and unifiers of neighborhoods and cities.

The concept of friendship networks and their value to the political community might best be described in similar terms to Adam Smith's "invisible hand." In *The Wealth of Nations*, Smith uses the concept of "the invisible hand" to describe how the actions and interests of eager (labor-hungry) capitalists actually help meet the needs of the people who have fallen through the cracks in the capitalist system of production. The efforts of individuals to form friendships could be said to establish the same sort of safety net for those who are less fortunate. The members of the community who have the time, and the necessary social and financial resources, are able to cultivate a broad network of friends. A network that makes up a neighborhood may, through the ethnic, professional, or religious bonds that form the basis of relationships, create a spirit of good will. This spirit of good will engenders a common notion of justice, familiarity with and affection for one's neighbors, and a shared sense of place, creating a sense of belonging, caring, and stability that motivates individuals to perpetuate the welfare of the community. These building blocks of community vary in their form and function. Some friendships serve to nurture the young, others to provide companionship to the old. The invisible hand of friendship establishes a support network for the most vulnerable members of the community. Friendships bolster the moral development of the young, provide for the needs of the elderly, and supply relief from misfortune.

The third way in which friendship networks contribute to the welfare of the political community is by promoting noble and selfless actions. Friendship networks enable cities and neighborhoods to operate more efficiently and compassionately by encouraging individuals to engage in supportive relationships that they otherwise would have avoided. Business owners and individuals enter into relationships with people who may not be able to return their kindness or monetary contributions because they expect to receive recognition from their friends.

As a practical matter, Aristotle realizes that not all friendships arise out of mutual interest in the good of another person. Many friendships are motivated wholly by the benefits that one expects to receive from relationships. In particular, Aristotle recognizes that some relationships are based on the honor which a person expects to receive should he give more than that for which he can be compensated. Aristotle notes that these friendships are imperfect but he acknowledges that such charitable exchanges will not go unacknowledged in the context of a community of friends. Praise from a peer group, acknowledging a person's generosity or magnanimity, is a significant benefit of committing to a relationship from which one cannot expect to receive fair compensation. Friendships between unequals— rich and poor, learned and unschooled — are often stimulated by the realization that an individual will receive public recognition. Aristotle states:

> A person who contributes nothing good to the common interest is not held in honor. For what belongs to the community is given to him who works for the common good, and this common possession is honor.... Therefore if a man sustains a financial loss, honor is his reward.... For a return proportionate to merit restores equality and preserves the friendship.[21]

By supplying approval and honor to deserving individuals, Aristotle notes that the network of friends which composes the political community encourages ties between people who would otherwise not come in contact with one another. The urban community serves as a catalyst for friendships that benefit those who are disadvantaged or marginalized. Friendships establish a foundation that supports the concerns of a broad range of people — old and young, rich and poor, merchant and artisan, strong and weak.

Aristotle's thoughts on the importance of friendship to the social order or regime remain valid in contemporary urban communities. Many of Aristotle's observations find explicit validation in analyses of post–World War II urban revitalization programs.

The Case of Boston's West End: Studies of Friendship and the Urban Environment

It has been observed that friendships and neighborhood relationships were among the most destabilizing casualties of the federal government's urban renewal programs. Those who have reviewed the federal government's urban efforts of the 1950s and 1960s bring the issue of the destruction of friendships and social networks to the fore of their analyses. They make no estimation, however, of the political implications of the loss of friendships. Little thought has been devoted to understanding how sweeping changes wrought by the federal highway and urban renewal programs might have compromised the ability of cities to function as communities where people could "live well." Studies produced by a broad range of sociologists, political scientists, physicians, and urban analysts indicate that the complete or partial destruction of city neighborhoods resulted in the loss of communities that had previously fostered social interaction and sustained poor, sick, or aging members.

Two prominent researchers, Herbert Gans and Edward Ryan, lived and/or worked in Boston's West End. They both constructed convincing cases that neighborhood relationships are building blocks on which the stability of a community is based. Their assessments of the impact of urban revitalization programs contain empirical observations that confirm Aristotle's account of the interplay between friendship and the urban environment. However, Gans and Ryan could have offered more penetrating analyses of the implications of friendship for the political community. Both Gans and Ryan emphasize that the residents of the West End placed a high value on the friendship bonds that united their community. They observe that the urban renewal program destroyed communities and, consequently, friendships. But, they do not appreciate that by destroying these friendships, the federal laws failed to maintain, and in fact eliminated, the political community.

Although their respective studies yield observations that have special significance for the welfare of the political community, Gans and Ryan do not attempt to evaluate the political implications of the West End's redevelopment. Their research shows how friendship bonds animated and united this urban community. They point out that when the West End ceased to exist, so too did the support networks, the sense of self, and the sense of community distilled by West Enders over the course of their lives in that neighborhood.

In the case of the West End, friendships served to give individuals who lived in a poor urban community a sense of importance and belonging. Ryan notes that the friendships among West Enders:

> ... [were] effective in providing the individual with an alternative structure upon which his sense of personal worth and certainty of identity could be maintained, even though challenged. Wealth, education, high status occupations, and social power, as it were, could be given their due recognition; but at the same time it was possible to affirm implicitly, and at times overtly, the superiority of West End morality.[22]

As is the case for many working class

communities, an address in Boston's West End signified more than just a geographic location. Limits on financial resources and mobility meant that the majority of West Enders considered their neighborhood the full extent of their social community. As Ryan's research reflects, the West End neighborhood did not function like a suburban bedroom community. Residence in a West End neighborhood denoted membership in the West End social network. When Ryan asked West Enders what made the surrounding streets and buildings a neighborhood,

> Forty-three percent mentioned only their feeling of attachment to people there, 17 percent referred to the general atmosphere of friendliness without indicating specific ties and another 20 percent mentioned close personal ties and friendly people. In total, 80 percent of West Enders made reference to friendship as a central value and central characteristic of neighborhoods.

And when Ryan inquired,

> which they would prefer to be, an auto mechanic who had many friends and who was contented, or a general manager who was to become a leading businessman, but who had little time for friends, 64 percent chose the auto mechanic.[23]

The importance that West Enders accorded to friendship echoes Aristotle's own dictum that "no person would choose to live without friends." Belonging to a close-knit network of friends was so crucial to residents that an overwhelming majority would forego significant prestige and wealth to retain their places in the community among friends.

Though friendships were considered by West End residents to be important personal assets, friendships were most valued because they established an environment of common concern. Ryan notes that when

West Enders referred to the spirit of the West End community, they characterized relationships as being about "helping others." More specifically, when Ryan asked residents "what they would expect of friends that they would not expect of someone else," his research revealed that "giving or receiving assistance [was] either the only response or a prominent theme in 60 percent of the replies."[24]

The demolition of the West End separated neighbors, isolated the old, dissolved church organizations, and rendered business associations meaningless. For tenants, owners, and businessmen, the destruction of the neighborhood exacted social and psychological losses. The clearance destroyed not only buildings, but also a functioning social system. The scattering of family units and friends was especially harmful to the many older people.[25]

As Gans asserts, the destruction of Boston's West End left the residents of this neighborhood without the support networks that gave them a sense of identity and security. However, the severed bonds of friendship represent a loss whose importance transcends the practical and emotional value of neighborhood relationships. As fundamental political associations, friendships undergird the stability of an entire city, not just a single neighborhood.

Learning from Aristotle: Cities Built on Friendship

Herbert Gans and Edward Ryan echo Aristotle's basic observations about the connection between the welfare of the urban community and the presence of neighborhood friendships. Their research shows that when the West End and other urban communities like it are demolished, neighborhood residents lose both their sense of identity and their support networks. Instead of revitalization, the urban environment undergoes a sort of spiritual death. Corner store chats among parents, card games among the elderly, and stickball and street hockey games between teams of neighborhood children are silenced under the foundations of new office and apartment buildings.

Sociologists, political scientists, psychologists, and other students of the urban environment recognize that friendships have emotional value, and they mourn their loss for that reason. What they do not see is that friendship binds the political community together in the ways described. The massive restructuring of the cities through urban revitalization and the federal highway program did not merely destroy friendship networks, but according to Aristotle's teachings, these programs destroyed the fiber of the political community. Although Gans, Ryan, and others note the obvious costs of efforts to revitalize the city — the separation of immigrant families and the struggle of elderly city dwellers who have no immediate neighbors to look after them — they fail to see the full political significance of the loss of friendships. They do not appreciate that every torn friendship is another broken bond in the political association. Gans and Ryan document that when the bulldozers arrived, people were forcibly isolated and separated. Aristotle understood that breaking these bonds of friendship destroys the life of the political community.

Recognition of the profound destruction wrought by urban renewal on the political community is facilitated by an Aristotelian understanding of the city. "Every city is some sort of partnership," Aristotle states, "and every partnership is constituted for the sake of some good."[26] The subversion of friendship — one of the most basic partnerships in the city — leads to the subversion of the political community. The dissolution of the bonds that unite friends,

families, and neighborhoods atomizes the city. Cities continue to grow in population, but without neighborhood environments where friendships are nurtured. The result is an undeveloped political community. The city becomes an increasingly private place to live. A lack of connection with neighbors means more strangers and increased suspicion, in turn encouraging the proliferation of laws, security guards, fences, and neglect of those in need. The city is more rigid, less trusting, and less efficient.

The ancient thinker Aristotle offers a new perspective to the planners and legislators whose desks and drafting boards are piled high with proposals for urban initiatives. He emphasizes that, unlike cities, political communities are not built vertically — from the ground up — but instead horizontally — through the interconnection of individuals.

Notes

1. Richard Bodeus. 1991. "Law and Regime in Aristotle." *Essays on the Foundations of Aristotelian Political Science*. ed. Carnes Lord and David K. O'Connor. Berkeley: University of California Press.

2. Aristotle. 1984 ed. *Politics*. Introduction by Carnes Lord. Chicago: University of Chicago Press, 21. Lord uses the term "regime" to connote Aristotle's use of the Greek word politeia. This term may be defined as constitution, government, social order, or state.

3. Leland M. Roth. 1983. *America Builds*. New York: Harper & Row, 517.

4. Roth, 517.

5. Roth, 517.

6. Mel Scott. 1969. *American City Planning*. Berkeley: University of California Press, 497.

7. Scott, 503.

8. Martin Anderson. 1964. *The Federal Bulldozer*. Cambridge: MIT Press, 23.

9. Anderson, 54.

10. Anderson, 60.

11. Anderson, 69.

12. *Politics*, Introduction by Carnes Lord, 21.

13. *Politics* (35–36) 1252a26–28.

14. *Politics* (215) 1155a12–13.

15. *Politics* (215) 1155a12–14.

16. Aristotle. 1962. *Nicomachean Ethics.* Trans. Martin Oswald. New York: Macmillan Publishing Company: 215, 1155a23–28. Aristotle citations are from two different sources.

17. George E. McCarthy. 1990. *Marx and the Ancients*. Savage, Maryland: Rowman & Littlefield Publishers, Inc., 76.

18. Aristotle. *Nicomachean Ethics.* (215) 1155a22–25.

19. Aristotle's discussion of partial justice can be found in Book Five, Chapter Two, of the *Nicomachean Ethics.*

20. Aristotle, *Nicomachean Ethics* (116) 1130b4–5.

21. Aristotle, *Nicomachean Ethics* (244) 1163b5–14.

22. Edward Ryan. 1963. "Personal Identity in an Urban Slum," in *The Urban Condition*, ed. Leonard J. Duhl. New York: Basic Books, 149.

23. Ryan, 142.

24. Ryan, 145.

25. Herbert Gans. 1962. *Urban Villagers.* New York: The Free Press, 320.

26. Aristotle. *Politics.* (35) 1252a1–3.

2. RETHINKING THE NATION'S URBAN PROBLEMS

Josh S. Weston

America's inner cities have not wanted for attention. From turn-of-the-century settlement houses for immigrants through the Model Cities program of the 1960s, the Urban Development Action Grants of the 1970s, the enterprise zones of the 1980s, and the empowerment zones of the 1990s, the nation has poured much earnest hope and billions of dollars into urban improvement.

Yet, significant portions of our cities continue to decay. In these neighborhoods, the prevailing environment is often one of fear and despair. The sound of gunshots and the threat of violent victimization are everyday realities. Children aspire not to be doctors or lawyers but only to live to adulthood. Unemployment regularly surpasses 40 percent, and high school dropout rates may approach 80 percent. Less than 20 percent of households include two parents, a third are dependent on public assistance, and half live below the poverty line. Daily life is consumed by mere survival, and opportunities for a better future appear inaccessible.

The failure of past efforts at urban revitalization has so discouraged leaders of the public and private sectors that many have turned their attention elsewhere. But while most of the nation has been looking away, residents and grassroots institutions in many decaying neighborhoods have quietly begun to turn their communities around. Community development corporations (CDCs) in Miami's Liberty City and Newark's Central Ward have built their neighborhoods' first supermarkets in over a decade. Community patrols in Washington, D.C., have closed open-air drug markets. An employment program in San Antonio has connected poor and welfare-dependent residents to high-quality jobs. Thousands of low-income families have moved into decent housing. Such community-based successes offer new hope that the complex problems of the inner cities *can* be solved. *Something is working.*

These little-heralded efforts must now be recognized and amplified through the support of powerful government, business, and philanthropic institutions. *Community*

Originally published as Chapter 1 of Rebuilding Inner-City Communities: A New Approach to the Nation's Urban Crisis, 1995. Published by the Committee for Economic Development, New York, New York. Reprinted with permission of the publisher.*

groups offer indispensable institutional and human resources, a knowledge of neighborhoods and their problems, and the trust and participation of residents. *Outside institutions* possess financial resources, technical knowledge and skills, and political power. *Partnerships* between these two complementary sources of strength represent the nation's best hope for revitalizing inner-city communities.

This policy statement does not address in detail each of the problems crushing inner-city communities today. Violence and crime, drugs, unemployment, teen pregnancy, welfare dependency, domestic violence, welfare dependency, domestic violence, inadequate housing, crumbling infrastructure, inefficient municipal governance, deficient transportation, fiscal shortfalls, and limited health care and family planning pose their own difficult policy dilemmas, and each must be addressed in its own right.

Instead of pursuing those subjects, however, this statement argues that unless we invent in the *community* prerequisites for inner-city revitalization, no effort to solve any of these problems will have more than marginal impact. On this premise, the statement proposes a watershed change in how the public, private, and philanthropic sectors approach each problem in inner-city neighborhoods. **Community building alone will not revitalize distressed communities, but no initiative will succeed without it.** This is the core of this statement's approach to the nation's urban problems.

The Nation's Stake in Its Inner Cities

Our nation's continuing failure to bring its distressed neighborhoods into the national mainstream imperils the American dream for residents of the inner city *and* for the country as a whole. As Henry Cisneros, Secretary of the Department of Housing and Urban Development (HUD), has observed, this nation and its cities have "interwoven destinies."[1]

Inner-city distress presents an urgent challenge to the nation. Within America's 100 largest cities, distressed and at-risk areas account for between 11 percent and 33 percent of all neighborhoods and between six million and 17 million residents. Many other urban neighborhoods remain viable and attractive places to live; however, if urban decay is left unchecked, it threatens to spread to them as well.

For many urban Americans, the primary "solution" to inner-city decay has been to flee. As middle-class residents and businesses have moved toward the suburbs, policy makers and others have hoped that the problems left behind, if not solvable, were at least containable. But as the size, tax burden, and violence of distressed neighborhoods have continued to grow, the futility of containment has become increasingly apparent. The problems of the inner city cannot be isolated. They reach and damage the larger society in at least five ways:

• **Inner-city blight undermines the fiscal and operational health of major cities.** Distressed neighborhoods contribute little to a city's tax base yet impose heavy demands on public services. This imbalance undermines the fiscal and operational integrity of virtually all the nation's major cities. The resultant physical decay, crime and fear, and declining quality of life are contagious. As they spill out of distressed neighbors into surrounding areas, they replicate the same imbalance, accelerating the exodus of businesses and residents and further diminishing property values. The erosion of city governments' financial and operational capacities becomes dangerously self-accelerating.

• **Inner-city distress threatens important economic assets.** Even in an era of dramatic changes in information and communications technology, the nation's large cities and their downtown business districts continue to offer unique environments for many economic and social activities. Central cities contain huge investments in immobile, productivity-enhancing infrastructure and unique cultural institutions, and they anchor the economic growth proliferating in their suburbs.[2] Our national economic prosperity depends in no small part on these threatened assets.

• **Inner-city distress weakens the nation's human resources.** Demographic trends dictate that American employers increasingly rely for their workforce on members of minority groups and recent immigrants, groups heavily represented in inner-city communities. Nearly 40 percent of the nation's African-American children, 32 percent of its Latino children, and 36 percent of its students with limited English proficiency are being educated in only 47 large-city school systems.[3] Many of these future adults emerge from inner-city schools with inadequate educational preparation, reflected in staggering rates of functional illiteracy and school dropout rates as high as 80 percent. The implications for a productive workforce are troubling; the implications for a well-informed citizenry are dire.

• **The costs of inner-city problems fall on taxpayers wherever they reside.** All the nation's taxpayers pay for the problems of distressed inner cities through government expenditures for welfare, law enforcement, social services, and remedial education. Additional costs accrue to all consumers informs such as insurance and security costs, tuition for private education, and prices for goods and services that reflect firms' increased costs of doing business. One estimate of the damage to large urban economies from crime alone is $50 billion annually; special federal expenditures for inner cities add another $75 billion.[4]

• **The isolation of distressed urban neighborhoods conflicts with our national ideals.** Equality of opportunity is a fundamental principle of American society and a right of all Americans. Extreme differences in the range of life chances between persons in one segment of American society and another, one racial or ethnic group and another, or one part of an urban area and another conflict harshly with this ethical standard.

For all these reasons, the persistence of distressed urban areas is dangerous to America's future. The nation should renew its commitment to addressing the serious social and economic problems concentrated in its distressed inner-city neighborhoods.

A New Understanding of Inner-City Distress

This new commitment must not, however, result in more programs shaped as they have traditionally been shaped, more dollars spent as they have traditionally been spent. Renewed efforts should reflect a new understanding of the nature of distressed communities and a sea change in the way their problems are addressed.

This new understanding begins with observations about *nondistressed* communities, communities that foster rather than inhibit positive outcomes among residents. Such communities encompass many relationships and institutions by which residents share information, work toward common goals, and acquire needed support. They are not isolated from the society outside their borders, and residents maintain and utilize resources and contacts from across their metropolitan areas. Through these mechanisms, formal and informal, healthy communities identify and address problems, reinforce social norms, and promote productive lives for individuals and their families.

In recognition of the importance of these processes, this statement focuses on the *community* as a crucial but neglected resource for inner-city revitalization. Specifically, Chapter 3 calls attention to *social capital*, the attitudinal, behavioral, and communal glue that holds society together through relationships among individuals, families, and organizations. **Without social capital to sustain problem solving within distressed communities and to link community residents to the broader society, efforts to address specific problems of individuals, families, and neighborhoods will make little progress.**

Inattention to community is evident throughout traditional approaches to the economic and social ills of distressed neighborhoods. Over the years, numerous public and philanthropic initiatives have addressed such concerns as poverty, welfare, unemployment, inadequate education, substandard housing, and crime. But past efforts have tended to consider these problems one at a time. That approach ignores the crucial fact that the co-existence of problems within a neighborhood creates a *mutually reinforcing* process of decay that limits the effectiveness of each narrowly focused initiative.

In a related fashion, most past efforts have viewed residents of distressed neighborhoods as passive recipients of treatment. Many efforts to renovate housing, control crime and drugs, or increase employment have been developed and implemented with little participation from the individuals whose problems they are trying to solve and little regard for how they live and interact. They emphasize individuals' deficiencies rather than their problem-solving skills and promote dependency rather than self-sufficiency. Failure to enlist local

institutions and citizens as *partners in problem solving* leaves essential resources untapped, ignores local priorities, and misses opportunities to strengthen communities' own problem-solving capacities.

In part, such failures reflect a belief that the appropriate way to address the problems of distressed neighborhoods is to have residents move to more desirable locations. Our focus on stabilizing and revitalizing troubled neighborhoods is not intended to denigrate opportunities for inner-city residents to reside in other localities throughout central cities or suburbs. Such mobility has been traditional for generations of Americans moving up the economic and social ladder, and each year some inner-city residents follow in their footsteps. However, for most inhabitants of distressed inner cities, such mobility is only a distant dream. Limited incomes, ties to friends and family, racial discrimination, and other factors effectively prevent many from leaving their neighborhoods, however dangerous and deficient. Realistically, millions of Americans will either find their way out of poverty and disadvantage within their inner-city communities or not at all.

Solving Problems by Rebuilding Communities

Reflecting these considerations, CED (Committee for Economic Development) concludes that the nation should invest in the community fabric of inner-city neighborhoods where local resources are overwhelmed by concentrated problems. Past efforts have tried to solve the social and economic problems of neighborhoods and their residents without the community prerequisites for these initiatives' success. Instead, when addressing the problems of distressed inner-city neighborhoods, the public and private sectors should consistently adopt a community-building style of problem solving.

Chapter 8 (page 84) presents impressive examples of community-building efforts that work: training and employing inner-city workers, developing retail services, developing and managing quality low-income housing, cutting crime and fear, and solving other inner-city problems. These examples define what the community-building style of problem solving means in practice:

• **Neighborhood residents participate in efforts to identify and resolve neighborhood problems.** As with current efforts within corporations to decentralize management and empower workers, grassroots participation improves the effectiveness of initiatives. Simultaneously, it develops residents' networks, norms, and skills that become resources for addressing other problems. In this sense, community building is not a single event but an ongoing process.

• **Community-based institutions —community development corporations, schools, churches, and others — are frontline service deliverers for public and private initiatives within their neighborhoods.** Again, the goal is dual: to enhance the effectiveness of individual programs and to strengthen these institutions for further community building.

• **Problem-solving efforts are comprehensive.** The multiple, mutually reinforcing problems within distressed neighborhoods and families will quickly overwhelm narrowly focused efforts.

• Some neighborhoods may be too distressed for community building to succeed unless accompanied by major changes in the physical and social environment. **Community building reflects a realistic understanding of neighborhood circumstances, conditions, and resources. When this understanding suggests that basic** social or physical changes in the neighborhood are necessary for community building to succeed, these changes are part of the community-building process.

Significant community-building initiatives are now under way in many of America's inner cities. However, these efforts are too often isolated and modest in scale. As Chapter 15 discusses, the challenge facing the nation is to provide the resources and commitment to "scale up" these exemplary endeavors into a sustained national movement. The key to this process is to expand the financial, technical, and political support for local initiatives from citywide, regional, and national sources.

Summary of Recommendations

THE GOVERNMENT ROLE

No effort to revitalize distressed inner cities will proceed very far or very fast without the support of the federal, state, and local governments. The public sector must be an active partner in community-building efforts, aggressively implementing policies that support community building and removing those that impede it.

• **Federal, state, and local governments should control the weapons that disrupt community life.** Some neighborhoods in this nation are so violent and menacing that terms such as *community building* and *shared civic values* are meaningless. No community organization can thrive on streets where children murder each other without remorse and where gangs, drugs, and violence have replaced family, work, and the rule of law. No social capital can burgeon in neighborhoods where residents are afraid to leave their homes to go to the grocery store, recreational programs, or community meetings. No enhanced connections between inner-city neighborhoods and the mainstream society are realistic when outsiders refuse to enter the neighborhoods and fear is the dominant emotion many Americans feel toward their residents. Where civil order has broken down, local, state, and national governments must restore a basic level of safety and a sense of security.

The proliferation and easy availability of weapons for criminal purposes is a significant contributor to civil instability within inner-city neighborhoods and the fear-based separation between these neighborhoods and the broader society. The most important precondition for community building that federal, state, and local governments can provide is to eliminate the national plague of cheap handguns and assault weapons and to take firearms out of the hands of juveniles and criminals. Such efforts have been advanced by recent federal legislation mandating waiting periods for the purchase of weapons, banning selected assault weapons, and enhancing data systems tracking weapons purchases. At the federal, state, and local levels, such efforts should be continued through vigorous enforcement of existing gun control laws and expanded through legislation imposing substantially broader restrictions on weapons and ammunition.

• **A second major disrupter of inner-city communities is the traffic in illegal drugs.** This pernicious trade leaves shocking numbers of inner-city young people dead or scarred by criminal records; addicts unable to function as learners, earners, parents, or community members; and community interaction disabled by the fear and reality of violence.

Current antidrug efforts rely primarily on interdiction to prevent drugs entering the country and incarceration to deter drug distribution and abuse. These efforts do not effectively reduce the trade in illegal drugs in inner cities. Moreover, the incarceration of drug abusers removes them from the community and scars them with criminal records without addressing their fundamental problem of addiction. In contrast, a community-building approach to the drug issue would emphasize community supports and opportunities for residents, especially young people, to avoid drug use. In addition, rather than sending drug abusers to prison, it would help them overcome their addiction so that they may become productive members of their communities. Federal, state, and local governments should reduce the adverse impact of illegal drugs on community life. In particular, they should shift resources from the current incarceration-oriented approach to preventing drug abuse through education and other means and rehabilitating addicted individuals.

• **Across all programs and policies that have an impact on inner cities — housing, criminal justice, environmental management, social services, and others — federal, state, and local governments should review and modify policies that concentrate social and economic problems in distressed communities.** Through a range of explicit and implicit decisions, the public sector has often promoted the concentration of distressed populations and undesirable facilities in small geographic areas, overwhelming the resiliency of many inner-city communities. For example, in public housing, the criteria used to locate housing sites and select tenants have tended to collocate large numbers of severely troubled families in already-distressed or threatened neighborhoods. Instead, *de*concentration should be promoted through scattered-site public housing and housing mobility programs and recruiting two-parent, employed families as public housing tenants.

• **Federal, state, and local governments should continue to eliminate racial,** ethnic, and other forms of discrimination in employment, credit, and housing. Discrimination in many aspects of daily life continues to deny many inner-city residents opportunities to improve their lives, to perpetuate and concentrate poverty in inner-city communities, and to thwart connections between inner-city communities and mainstream society. Public agencies should vigorously enforce antidiscrimination laws targeting redlining in lending and discrimination in employment, housing, and public accommodations. At the federal level, these laws include the Civil Rights Act of 1965, the Community Reinvestment Act, the Fair Housing Act, and the Equal Credit Opportunity Act. Additional legislation should extend data gathering on credit practices to sectors of the financial services industry not covered under the Community Reinvestment Act.

• **Federal, state, and local governments should encourage and participate in partnerships that link inner-city residents and their community-based organizations to support from the philanthropic sector, government, and the business community.** Community-based initiatives within distressed neighborhoods will not achieve substantial scale without partnerships with powerful public and private actors from outside their neighborhoods to provide financial, technical, and political support. To promote these partnerships, the public sector should routinely consult community-based organizations on decisions affecting their neighborhoods; join ad hoc coalitions with community groups to implement specific projects; participate in ongoing partnerships that bring together the public, business, philanthropic, and community sectors; and require collaborative planning and nongovernment matching for publicly funded initiatives. Through such means, local, state, and federal governments can make such partnerships important institutions and can make

the partnership approach standard in addressing the problems of distressed inner-city communities.

• **Federal, state, and local governments should expand their use of community-based organizations to implement programs and deliver services in inner-city communities.** Community-based organizations are often particularly effective at delivering services because of their relationships and reputation within the community, understanding of community needs, ability to coordinate multiple programs into comprehensive packages, and employment of local residents. They may be willing to operate in neighborhoods where other organizations are not. At the same time, the revenues and experience community organizations gain through such roles can strengthen them as resources for addressing other community problems. The federal, state, and local governments should aggressively seek opportunities to employ community-based organizations as frontline implementers of public initiatives. For example, government agencies should increasingly contract with community-based organizations to deliver publicly funded services.

• **When implementing programs directly rather than through community groups, public agencies should operate in a community-building style.** Currently, public agencies tend to operate in isolation from each other, frustrating community-based attempts to provide comprehensive services to address residents' multiple needs. A hallmark of the community-building style is aggressively to seek opportunities to integrate previously uncoordinated services and deliver comprehensive services to residents by such means as co-location of programs administered by different agencies, case management to integrate assistance to individuals or families with multiple problems, and use of common eligibility criteria for multiple programs. A second hallmark is establishment of administrative boundaries and service areas (such as police precincts) to coincide with neighborhoods.

• **The public sector should invest in strengthening the capacity of community-based organizations.** Sustained community building occurs primarily through ongoing institutions such as community development corporations, schools, and churches. Some distressed inner-city localities enjoy few local leadership institutions. In other communities, such organizations exist but make only limited contributions because of their constant struggle for survival. Public funds from such sources as Community Development Block Grants should be used to enhance the organizational strength of community-based institutions. Typical needs in this regard are staff development, implementation of efficient management systems, and enhancement of organizations' stability through multiyear funding not tied to specific projects.

• **The federal government should expand the Low-Income Housing Tax Credit and enact a parallel mechanism to support commercial and industrial development in distressed communities.** Participation in projects by investors from outside distressed neighborhoods brings capital into the inner city and builds connections between these communities and mainstream society. Each year, the federal Low-Income Housing Tax Credit connects thousands of corporate, individual, and institutional investors and billions of dollars to projects in distressed neighborhoods. A parallel mechanism covering nonhousing projects would have similar community-building benefits while contributing to commercial and industrial development in distressed communities.

• **The public sector should encourage and support research to improve the effectiveness of community-building ac**tivities. These efforts should include evaluation of the impact of community-building efforts, **dissemination** of "best practices" to increase the efficiency of community-building activities, and **measurement** of conditions within inner-city areas.

THE CHALLENGE TO BUSINESS LEADERSHIP

Not all companies have a direct stake in central cities, even in the cities near which they are located. However, all have a stake in the nation's broader economic and social health. Alarmed by the threat to social order, the injustice, and the economic waste in the nation's distressed inner cities, business leaders should be among the nation's most vocal advocates and active participants in urban community building.

The managerial skills, strategic vision, and financial and political resources commanded by senior executives of the nation's major corporations make their participation particularly crucial to these efforts. Diversity among companies dictates that the form of support for community building will vary, and executives should tailor their involvement to reflect the strengths, market position, and resources of their individual companies. Various avenues for business involvement are readily available:

• **Executives should encourage their companies to use emerging inner-city resources in their business activities.** For almost all firms, distressed urban neighborhoods may offer locations for plants or offices, pools of potential employees, or minority-owned subcontractors and suppliers. For some firms, these neighborhoods also offer potential consumer markets. As community-building efforts create more such opportunities and a more hospitable business environment within inner-city areas, mainstream firms outside the neighborhoods should reconsider these commercial possibilities. Unless senior executives lead their firms to rethink these opportunities, many businesses will continue to assume that they do not exist.

• **Executives and their firms should join local and national systems of support for inner-city community building, such as national community development intermediaries and metropolitan-wide housing partnerships.** Like the public sector, the corporate community is an essential member of multisector partnerships to support community building. Historically, business leaders have played prominent roles in civic partnerships to boost downtown development, attract sports franchises, and support cultural institutions. Corporate executives should exercise the same leadership in inner-city projects and institutions, both locally and nationally.

• **As community leaders, business executives should encourage the reshaping of public and nonprofit programs to reflect the community-building approach.** As members of the boards of civic, educational and human service organizations and as political opinion leaders, corporate executives can influence public and nonprofit institutions to allocate increased resources to distressed urban neighborhoods, to enhance the involvement of local residents and community institutions in service delivery, to identify and train community leaders, and to encourage policy changes to remove impediments to community building.

• **Business leaders should guide their corporate charitable activities and community involvement toward inner-city community building.** Current corporate efforts to be good citizens in their operating locations take a variety of forms, from cash grants to employee involvement, for a range of worthy causes. Distressed inner-city neighborhoods should become an in-creasing object of these efforts, and the community-building style should shape the involvement. For example, greater priority might be given to investment in Low-Income Housing Tax Credits targeted to inner-city neighborhoods, financial support that strengthens community leadership institutions, and loaned executives and other efforts that foster personal contact with inner-city residents and organizations.

Social capital, in and of itself, is not sufficient reverse urban decay. Inner-city communities face many specific problems that must be addressed: too few jobs, failing schools, broken families, violence, and drugs. But no effort to provide jobs, control crime, or improve the lives of children will succeed in America's urban environments if poor and disadvantaged Americans live in isolation from the larger national community, from each other, and from shared national values, purpose, and hope. Distressed, isolated urban communities can and must be brought back into the social and economic mainstream. Inner-city community building offers a new, effective way to pursue this vital national goal.

Notes

1. Henry G. Cisneros, ed., *Interwoven Destinies: Cities and the Nation* (New York: The American Assembly, 1993).

2. Larry C. Ledebur, and William R. Barnes, *All in It Together: Cities, Suburbs, and Local Economic Regions* (Washington, D.C.: National League of Cities, February 1993); Richard Voith, *Do Suburbs Need Cities?* (Philadelphia, Penn.: Federal Reserve Bank of Philadelphia, 1994); Charles F. Adams, Howard Fleeter, and Mark Freeman, "Flight from Blight" (Paper presented at the Annual Research Conference, Association for Public Policy Analysis and Management, 1994).

3. *National Urban Education Goals: Baseline Indicators, 1990–91* (Washington, D.C.: Council of Great City Schools, September 1992), p. xi; *Workforce 2000* (Washington, D.C.: U.S. Department of Labor, 1987).

4. Christopher Farrell, "The Economics of Crime," *Business Week*, December 13, 1993, pp. 72–81; Kenneth Labich, "New Hopes for the Inner City," *Fortune*, September 6, 1993, p. 83.

3. INNER-CITY PROBLEMS FROM A FRESH PERSPECTIVE

Josh S. Weston

This chapter reflects an understanding of inner-city distress that differs substantially in emphasis from how these issues are often examined. This different perspective begins with the definition of the problem address.

For many Americans, an intuitive definition of *distressed communities* is revealed in a simple action. Empty stores? Gang graffiti spray-painted on walls? Idle men on street corners? Driving into such a neighborhood, middle-class, suburban dwellers promptly lock their car doors. Right or wrong, this reaction reflects a sense that they have entered a world separate from, and threatening to, "mainstream" America.

What is the source of this sense of social chasm? It does not reflect simply being in a large city, for many urban neighborhoods are pleasant and prosperous. Nor is it associated with low income alone, for many neighborhoods of modest means are orderly and welcoming. Nor is it always derived from the presence of racial and ethnic minorities, for many minority-dominated neighborhoods are middle class and stable.

Instead, the defining characteristic of distressed neighborhoods is the *simultaneous* presence of *multiple* social problems: poverty and joblessness, crime and violence, family instability and welfare dependency, and depressed property values and physical blight. Individually, each of these problems rises to disastrous levels in some inner-city areas. But what triggers fear in a passing stranger and defines the distressed inner-city communities that are the subject of this statement is that these problems coexist, mutually reinforce each other, and cumulatively overwhelm the mechanisms of social control. Thus, **inner-city distress is about more than poverty or individual problems; it is about the collapse of a community's ability to cope with problems.**

To measure this collapse, social scientists often begin with the presence of multiple problems. For example, one research effort defines distressed neighborhoods as those census tracts that are substantially

Originally published as Chapter 2 of Rebuilding Inner-City Communities: A New Approach to the Nation's Urban Crisis, *1995. Published by the Committee for Economic Development, New York, New York. Reprinted with permission of the publisher.*

above the national average simultaneously on four indicators: the proportion of households in poverty, the proportion of households headed by female single parents, the proportion of households receiving public assistance, and the prevalence of joblessness among adult males.

The following reports the results of applying these four criteria to 1990 census data for the 100 largest cities in the nation.[1] These data confirm that not all or even most neighborhoods[2] within these cities are distressed. On average, in these 100 cities, distressed neighborhoods are home to only 11.1 percent of a city's population; that proportion exceeds 25 percent in only eight cities: Detroit (47 percent), Flint (38 percent), Buffalo (33 percent), Cleveland (31 percent), New Orleans (29 percent), Newark (28 percent), Shreveport (27 percent), and St. Louis (25 percent). Nationwide, about 5.7 million persons, or 2.3 percent of the U.S. population, reside in these neighborhoods.

This set of neighborhoods, identified under a stringent definition of distress, represents the most troubled urban areas. Research suggests that for each of these neighborhoods, approximately two additional neighborhoods exhibit many of the same problems to a lower degree.[3] Often, these additional areas are at the margin of decline in both a social and a geographic sense and are likely to complete the process of decay if left unaided. That fate is by no means certain, however, so we distinguish them from *distressed neighborhoods* by referring to them as *threatened neighborhoods*. Whereas distressed areas account for about 11 percent of all neighborhoods in the nation's 100 largest cities, distressed and threatened areas together account for about 33 percent, or about seven percent of the nation's population.

Whether we focus only on neighborhoods that are already distressed or include areas that may become so, these data offer an element of hope: **The nation's seemingly intractable urban problems can be conquered. Many have given up on our cities and turned their backs on these neighborhoods, believing that the problems are too overwhelming. They are wrong. The scale of distressed urban neighborhoods is relatively limited in comparison with the size of the nation and its urban areas. America need not despair about its distressed inner cities.**

However, the nation should be seriously alarmed. At least one distressed neighborhood is present in nine out of 10 of America's 100 largest cities. Distressed and threatened neighborhoods together contain more than 17 million persons, which is more than the total population of Australia or the Netherlands. More than 1.1 million persons in New York City alone and more than 100,000 in each of 13 additional cities are condemned to the living hell of distressed communities.

Even more alarming than these numbers, however, is the fact that these areas, if left to fester, will continue to grow, engulf adjacent communities, and sweep additional Americans into their maelstrom.[4] The distressed-area population that in 1990 totaled 5.7 million had stood at only one million 20 years earlier. This reflects a compound growth rate of approximately nine percent annually. The number of distressed census tracts that in 1990 had grown to 1,850 stood at only 296 in 1970, a compound annual growth rate of almost 10 percent. The fate of America's urban areas hangs in the balance in its distressed and threatened neighborhoods.

The measures of distress cited here are not perfect. On the one hand, they fail to convey the horror of daily life in the very worst neighborhoods, such as the Robert Taylor Homes public housing project in Chicago. On the other hand, any dividing line between distressed and nondistressed is arbitrary at best. Moreover, census tracts, which are the basis for the figures just presented, may correspond to several "neighborhoods" as perceived by the people who live there, some distressed, some not. Nevertheless, these measures provide a reasonable indication of the scale of decay within America's major urban areas today. Throughout this statement, they serve as an operational definition of the problem we are addressing.

The Social Capital Deficit

Although the incidence of multiple problems can be used to identify distressed neighborhoods, these problems are, in an important sense, symptoms of a more fundamental condition. Poverty, unemployment, welfare dependency, physical blight, and crime and violence are not merely serious problems that overlap geographically. An integral — indeed, a defining —

aspect of distressed urban neighborhoods is *mutual reinforcement* or *negative interaction*, in which each problem intensifies other problems and hampers their solution, making the whole worse than the sum of its parts.[5] Here is a highly simplified illustration of this process: Joblessness leads to low incomes, which lead to low rents, which lead to inadequate building maintenance and security, which lead to crime and fear, which lead to middle-class flight, which leads to a decline in school quality, which leads back to joblessness. Challenged to unravel this Gordian knot, the nation might understandably be baffled about where to begin.

The most pernicious consequence of such negative interaction is that these multiple problems themselves weaken the community's mechanisms of social coping needed to address them. Among the most important of these mechanisms is social capital.

FIGURE 1— THE MULTIPLE PROBLEMS THAT BOMBARD DISTRESSED INNER-CITY COMMUNITIES

JOB READINESS AND JOB AVAILABILITY[6]

• In minority-dominated high schools in central cities, the dropout rate may rise as high as 80 percent.

• Even those who graduate are often unprepared for work. One study in Chicago found that 25 percent of high school graduates read at no more than the sixth-grade level.

• In 1990, 81 percent of young dropouts living in distressed urban areas were not employed.

• More than 40 percent of adult men in distressed inner cities did not work in 1990, and many others worked only sporadically or part-time.

CRIME, VIOLENCE, GANGS, AND DRUGS[7]

• America's urban areas suffer a murder every 22 minutes, a robbery every 49 seconds, and an aggravated assault every 30 seconds.

• Between 1979 and 1989, the violent crime rate in central cities increased an average of 33 percent. Chicago's increase was 173 percent. In 1993, one-third of homicides in New Orleans, the city with the highest homicide rate in the country, took place in the city's distressed public housing projects.

• In a survey of first and second graders in Washington, D.C., 31 percent had witnessed shootings, and 39 percent had seen dead bodies.

• Many inner-city residents fear leaving their homes after dark or letting their children play or sleep near windows. Forty percent of low-income urban parents worry "a lot" that their children will be shot, compared with 10 percent of all parents.

• In some distressed public housing projects, more than one resident in ten is a crime victim each year.

• One of every 24 black males in the nation will have his life ended by homicide. Nationwide, on any given day, one in four

(Figure 1, continued)

black men between the ages of 20 and 29 is under the control of the criminal justice system. A study in Baltimore found that 56 percent of black men ages 18 to 35 were under the control of the criminal justice system or being sought on warrants.

• In 22 cities, 60 percent of arrestees for violent crimes tested positive for at least one illegal drug.

• A survey by the U.S. Department of Justice found that 22 percent of high school students in crime-ridden neighborhoods own a gun.

• In inner-city neighborhoods, handguns, military-style rifles, and shotguns are often available for less than $100 on the street, about three hours' wages for a street-level drug dealer.

• Rates of physical and sexual child abuse are six times higher for children in families with income under $15,000 than for other children; adults who were abused as children are significantly more likely to be arrested for a violent offense than those who were not.

POVERTY, FAMILY DISSOLUTION, AND WELFARE DEPENDENCY[8]

• Half of all residents of distressed neighborhoods live below the federally defined poverty threshold (in 1993, $14,763 for a family of four).

• Approximately 60 percent of households with children in distressed inner-city neighborhoods are headed by women; in some public housing projects, this proportion is above 95 percent. Much of this is due to a high rate of out-of-wedlock births. Nationwide, 65 percent of black births are to

unmarried women, about a third of these to teenagers. Of unmarried teenagers who give birth, about half are likely to receive public assistance within four years of the birth.

• Nationally, nearly 50 percent of female-headed families live below the poverty level, almost seven times the rate for two-parent families.

• Approximately 36 percent of households in distressed inner cities received public assistance in 1990, nearly five times the national average.

• Among African-American children under the age of three who live in urban areas, 52 percent lived in poverty in 1990, the great majority in single-parent families.

PHYSICAL BLIGHT AND INADEQUATE HOUSING[9]

• In the Sandtown-Winchester neighborhood of Baltimore, of 5,000 structures in the area, 600 are vacant, and 3,000 need rehabilitation or wrecking. A broader study of 14 cities found rates of building abandonment reaching 20 percent.

• In large metropolitan areas nationwide, there are about two prospective low-income tenants for every low-rent unit. As a result, some lack shelter of any kind; the Urban Institute estimates the number of homeless in America at 600,000 each night. Many others live in overcrowded and substandard housing units.

• In 1989, among 5.1 million low-income renters nationwide, nearly half of them in central cities, 60 percent live in seriously substandard housing or pay more than half their income for rent.

The term *social capital* refers to something most Americans living outside distressed neighborhoods experience in their daily lives: *the resources embedded in social relations among persons and organizations that facilitate cooperation and collaboration in communities.*[10] Like physical and human capital, social capital is a productive resource that makes possible otherwise un-

achievable results and enhances the productivity of other resources. For example, educated parents (human capital) benefit their child if parents and child spend time interacting (social capital).

Social capital exists in three principal forms: First, *information sharing* uses social relations to convey valuable information. Thus, a parent seeking child care may consult friends, relatives, or neighbors who have experience with local child care providers. Second, *trust* engendered through social relations establishes *generalized reciprocity* as a norm within a community: "I'll do this for you now because you (or someone else) will assist me later." This process does not require specific reciprocation; rather, it is a shared expectation that if residents need help, they will receive it. Third, *norms and values that maintain social order*— social expectations such as delaying childbearing until marriage or investing in education — are passed on in families, schools, churches, and other settings. They are reinforced by social support, honors, and rewards, whereas failure to comply with expectations is sanctioned by punishment or loss of status.[11]

Despite its common occurrence, social capital is not easily created. It is most often a by-product of routine living and cooperative activities within communities. People join social clubs for recreation or block associations to prevent crime, not because they want to create networks to facilitate future problem solving. Nevertheless, that is exactly what results. And as is the case with other resources, communities that have more social capital generate more. Successful collaboration in one endeavor builds relationships that can be applied to unrelated tasks. In fact, social capital is depleted if it is *not* used.

Indications of the depletion of social capital in distressed inner-city communities are not hard to find. They can be seen, for example, in the relative absence of, and disconnection of residents from, community institutions and services. Poor urban parents disproportionately report that groups supporting youth development, such as scout troops, organized sports, religious activities, and special classes, are not readily available for their children. Only about one low-income parent in ten belongs to a parent-teacher organization,

and fewer than one-third of those who belong actively attend meetings. Isolation is similarly evident in informal and interpersonal relations. Men and women living in neighborhoods of concentrated poverty, particularly those who are not employed, are especially at risk of isolation from friendship networks, and poor urban parents are more likely than others to have no one to turn to for advice on child rearing. One-third of low-income parents report that they do not talk to their children about their school experiences, and a significant number of urban teenage boys say they have no best friend and no person they trust. Similarly, residents often have limited exposure to personal or occupational role models. In one study of inner-city Boston, less than 30 percent of inner-city teenagers reported that they "know well" persons in professional occupations, and 50 percent reported knowing of no such persons in their neighborhood.[12]

This dearth of social capital exacerbates every one of the problems listed in Figure 1. For example:

• **Educational Achievement.**[13] Absence of parental support for education decreases the likelihood of academic achievement; a high neighborhood dropout rate reduces the stigma attached to dropping out of high school; and the absence of educated, gainfully employed adults in the neighborhood obscures the rewards of graduation. In some inner-city high schools, *negative* social capital develops, in which dropping out is the norm and peer pressure and community sanctions work against academic achievement. Consequently, even after controlling for a student's socioeconomic background and other factors, living in a neighborhood with few high-status workers or a low level of civic engagement significantly increases a student's chance of dropping out of high school.

• **Crime.**[14] Weak social ties and other measures of community disorganization (such as housing density, residential transiency, and the proportion of single-parent families) account for a greater portion of the variation in crime rates among neighborhoods than does poverty alone. This relationship reflects a number of processes at work: Youths are prime perpetrators of crime in many distressed neighborhoods and a breakdown of social networks forces parents to rely only on themselves to monitor and control their children. Distrust and fear discourage residents from venturing outside their homes, limiting participation in community activities and interpersonal relationships and leaving streets deserted and dangerous. And the large proportion of inner-city youths under the control of the justice system dilutes the stigma of arrest and prison.

• **Unemployment.**[15] Many inner-city residents are disconnected from successful, legally employed individuals. As a result, they fail to see the rewards for delaying childbearing, staying in school, and avoiding criminal involvement. Even for those who circumvent such troubles, lack of access to employed persons makes searching for gainful employment more difficult and discouraging. About two-thirds of job vacancies in the American labor market are filled by direct application at the work site, employee referrals, and similar means in which information about job openings is not widely publicized. Successful job seekers often rely on personal networks to learn of openings and to obtain recommendations from someone the employer trusts. If opportunities within a job seeker's neighborhood are limited, if his relatives, friends, and neighbors are not employed, and if he is reluctant to venture into more prosperous communities, the most effective modes of job seeking are closed to him.

Why Has Inner-City Social Capital Declined?

In nondistressed communities, social capital is a by-product of daily life. Healthy communities are more than individuals and families living adjacent to each other; they encompass numerous networks among residents. These associations include formal groups (such as church congregations), informal groups (such as block associations), and casual social gatherings (in restaurants, stores, and other local meeting places), as well as relationships among individuals.

Healthy neighborhoods are also not isolated from the society outside their borders. Both individual residents and community institutions employ contacts and resources from across their urban areas. Information, financial resources, and opportunities flow easily into the community; residents routinely travel outside and move from the neighborhood; and outsiders reciprocate in the opposite direction. Consequently, norms within the community remain consistent with those of the broader society, and social relationships seamlessly extend to encompass many sources of potential assistance.

In distressed inner-city neighborhoods, such processes are hampered at every turn. A shortage of community institutions to serve as meeting places or rallying points, fear of crime and violence that discourages interaction and participation in community events, a reluctance by resource-rich institutions and individuals to venture into the neighborhood, a sense of civic powerlessness in which public agencies are seen as unresponsive to local needs, a reluctance to travel outside a familiar environment — all contribute to this outcome.

One key source of the decline of social capital in many urban neighborhoods has been the suburbanization of the American middle class. When better-educated, employed persons in intact families move from a neighborhood, they take social capital with them. The departure of their political, cultural, social, and financial support weakens community institutions such as churches and schools and prompts a spiral of decline among businesses and properties in a neighborhood.[16]

Among white Americans, suburbanization of the middle class has proceeded steadily since the end of World War II. In many minority-dominated communities, this process was delayed until the 1960s, when changing societal moves and antidiscrimination legislation began to expand employment and residential options. As in nonminority communities, the people who took advantage of these opportunities were generally better educated and more affluent that those who remained behind, and the physical decline and segregated nature of their former neighborhoods discouraged middle-class persons from moving in to replace those who departed. Thus, many minority-dominated urban neighborhoods rapidly converted from segregated but stable, mixed-income environments to communities dominated by people poor in both income and social capital.

A second trend undermining inner-city communities has been the decline of employment within central cities, particularly well-paid jobs with limited educational prerequisites such as those historically provided by manufacturing. For the past several decades, the bulk of job growth in the American economy has been in the nation's suburbs and exurban areas, from which many inner-city residents are physically and socially isolated, and in higher skill categories, for which many inner-city residents lack educational qualifications.[17] As employment opportunities have declined, the proportion of inner-city residents who are employed has fallen, undermining their incomes and reducing financial support of neighborhood institutions, weakening norms favoring employment, and eliminating social contacts for job seeking.

Although suburbanization has put many urban neighborhoods at risk, the decline of such communities is not inevitable. Many city neighborhoods have retained middle-class residents and remained stable and attractive. Others have undergone *gentrification*, in which access to downtown employment and urban amenities attracts affluent, middle-class in-migrants. The difference between these communities and their distressed neighbors is often public and private actions that push endangered neighborhoods over the brink.

In most communities that have gone over the precipice, the divisive issue of race has been at the center of the process.[18] Residents of the distressed neighborhoods are approximately 68 percent African-American, 20 percent Hispanic, and two percent "others"; only 10 percent are white.[19] Since the 1960s, numerous federal, state, and local laws have prohibited discrimination based on race and ethnicity in employment, housing, public accommodations, and other aspects of daily life. Nonetheless, many African-Americans, Hispanics, and other minorities have continued to experience differences in opportunity based on their race or ethnicity.

The consequences have been devastating for the inner-city communities where many of these persons reside:

• **Employment Discrimination.**[20] Over the past 30 years, employment discrimination against minorities has declined but has by no means been eliminated. One study estimates that young black male job seekers today encounter significant discrimination from approximately one employer in four. Other studies document the continued prevalence of negative stereotypes among employers concerning the employers concerning the intelligence, honesty, and work habits of minority job applicants.

Such employment discrimination undermines the financial base of inner-city neighborhoods. Lack of earnings translates into inadequate purchasing power that stunts local businesses, limits the ability of landlords to maintain properties, and thwarts residents' efforts to accumulate assets through home ownership. Limited employment opportunities also undermine community norms of self-reliance and self-respect and send the message to inner-city residents that education and honest work efforts have few payoffs.

• **Residential Segregation.**[21] Numerous studies verify the persistence of practices that keep minority residents out of nonminority neighborhoods. According to Squires, "To this day black and Hispanic homeseekers experience discrimination in over half their encounters with real estate sales and rental agents." Simultaneously, many whites continue to avoid neighborhoods where their neighbors would be minorities. Segregation in America's major urban areas peaked in the 1950s, when it was often reinforced by restrictive covenants. Although such explicit practices have been largely eliminated, segregation has not declined substantially. In 1980, the average African-American in the central city of 30 large metropolitan areas lived in a neighborhood that was 75 percent black. In Chicago, for example, nearly nine out of ten blacks would need to move to white areas for the city to be fully integrated.

Racial segregation is one of the most powerful forces concentrating large numbers of disadvantaged people in distressed communities. Equally important, racial divisions between neighborhoods bifurcate social networks, isolating minority persons from the social capital found in non-minority communities.

• **Redlining in Financial Markets.**[22] *Redlining* is the practice of denying goods, services, or financing to an area's residents based on real or perceived risk associated with the racial, ethnic, or economic background of its residents. Although it is not always easy to distinguish between real risks, perceived risks, and discriminatory intent, redlining by financial institutions and its damage to minority-dominated areas have been widely documented. Appraisers, creditors, real estate agents, and others associated with the housing industry continue to undervalue or avoid property in, and limit the availability of financing for, such neighborhoods.

Redlining hampers the preservation and redevelopment of inner-city communities. Denial of mortgages and the extra cost or unavailability of insurance limits opportunities for potential home buyers, the stability they bring to a neighborhood, and opportunities for them to accumulate assets for purposes such as entrepreneurship. Lack of access to home improvement loans and business loans speeds the decline of residential and commercial properties in the neighborhood, hampers business expansion, lowers property values, and discourages investment.

In parallel with these private-sector practices, policies of federal, state, and local governments have also helped to push many threatened inner-city neighborhoods into distress. In some circumstances, these policies have been discriminatory in intent[23]; in other cases, however, this result is an unintended side effect of the pursuit of legitimate public goals:

• **Excluding the Working Poor from Public Housing.** As shown by Chicago's Robert Taylor Homes, the most severe inner-city distress is often found in the nation's high-rise public housing projects. Central to the unacceptable environment in these projects is the virtual absence of working people and two-parent families.

In some projects, fewer than 10 percent of residents are employed, and as many as 95 percent of households are single mothers with children. Adults and youths live there in virtual isolation from employed role models, personal job contacts, and norms of self-sufficiency.[24]

This overconcentration of persons outside the workforce can be traced in part to well-intentioned policies. To target the nation's limited supply of public housing to those most in need, the federal Brooke Amendment in 1969 limited public housing rents to 25 percent of resident income (now 30 percent), making units less expensive for those with very low incomes than for those with steady earnings. The resultant domination of public housing projects by distressed families was later reinforced by a requirement that at least 90 percent of units be rented to households with "worst-case needs," such as the homeless.[25]

• **Single-Purpose, Crisis-Oriented Service Programs.**[26] A troubled inner-city family might include an unemployed, drug-addicted single mother and an undernourished child who is behind in school. Even if the child receives special tutoring, she is likely to continue to fail because of other adverse circumstances in her family life. Without a *critical mass* of coordinated, integrated services for the entire family, most individual forms of assistance are unlikely to have more than marginal benefit.

A major cause of service fragmentation is categorical funding of public programs to address specific problems; by some counts, programs limited to narrow purposes currently total more than 200 at the federal level alone. This categorical structure allows public decision makers to express their priorities and ensure that funding is used only for intended purposes, reasonable objectives under the sound principle of accountability. However, the resultant conflicts in eligibility requirements and program rules, exacerbated by turf protection by program-specific bureaucracies, often preclude comprehensive assistance to individuals and families with multiple needs.[27]

• **Not in My Back Yard (NIMBY).** Every urban area contains some facilities, from halfway houses for ex-offenders to disposal sites for solid wastes, near which residents prefer not to live. With both the quality of daily life and property values at stake, the location of these facilities is often hotly contested. Affluent neighborhoods often muster zoning restrictions and political power to keep such facilities from their areas and cluster them in distressed neighborhoods.

This pattern of placement may have some logical basis. If the facilities in question harm adjacent properties, economic losses may be minimized by placing them where neighboring properties are already of lower economic value. However, the cumulative consequences for receiving neighborhoods can be disastrous. In communities at the margin of distress, an overload of undesirable facilities may accelerate the process of decline. Furthermore, the politically and economically weakened condition of the receiving neighborhood may tempt authorities to invest less in minimizing the negative effects of the facilities than if they had been placed in more attractive locations.

• **Destruction of the Beat Police System.** Prior to the twentieth century, American law enforcement routinely relied on informal cooperation between police officers and residents. This practice fell into disfavor as concerns over bribery and favoritism rose, and reformers championed a more professional approach to policing. By the 1950s, most urban police departments had centralized control and deliberately reduced police-community linkages. Officers were moved from beats they covered on foot to patrol cars, and radio communication replaced direct interaction with residents for reporting and responding to crime.[28]

This new style of policing was instituted to promote impartial law enforcement and reduce police corruption. However, it destroys trust between police officers and citizens, reduces resident participation in crime prevention, and constructs the informal flow of information needed to prevent crimes and apprehend and prosecute offenders. Moreover, professional policing does little to reduce the fear of crime that powerfully affects the level of insecurity and distrust in a community.

Making Community Building a National Priority

The processes just described illustrate two general points about neighborhood decline: First, public and private decisions and actions outside the inner city contribute to the creation and perpetuation of distressed neighborhoods. Turning these neighborhoods around will require changes by those outside the neighborhoods as well as by those within. Second, neither public nor private decision makers have paid extensive attention to the consequences of their actions on the social capital and community life in inner-city neighborhoods.

The author believes that the problems of the nation's distressed inner-city areas can be addressed only if these past patterns are broken. **A key to reversing the negative processes that predominate within distressed inner-city areas is to rebuild, rather than to destroy, the social capital that differentiates healthy communities from distressed ones. The nation has instituted programs to address specific problems afflicting urban areas and their residents. To achieve sustainable revitalization, it must make parallel efforts to help distressed communities regain and** retain the internal resources to heal themselves.

This principle by no means suggests that current public and private initiatives targeted to the inner city and its residents are unnecessary. Unless the nation significantly reforms its failing educational system and perverse public assistance programs, many of the problems of youths and families in inner-city communities will remain unsolved; and unless the nation generates adequate employment opportunities for inner-city residents and adequate fiscal resources for central-city governments, many of the nation's large cities will remain endangered. **Social capital is not a substitute for effective public policies or for financial and other resources. However, it is a necessary complement for them to be effective, one whose importance has received too little recognition.**

Notes

1. John D. Kasarda, "Inner City Concentrated Poverty and Neighborhood Distress: 1970–1990," *Housing Policy Debate* 3 (1993): 253–302. In this analysis, "substantially above the national average" is defined as one standard deviation above the national average of census tracts in 1980, which corresponds to at least 33 percent of the households with income below the federal poverty threshold, at least 37 percent of households headed by females, at least 18 percent of households receiving public assistance, and at least 45 percent of males over 16 and not enrolled in school employed less than half the year.

2. Here, data limitations force the use of census tracts to represent neighborhoods. In reality, functioning neighborhoods are defined by the perceptions of the people who live there and may encompass only a piece of a census tract or extend to several tracts. Similarly, a census tract may contain some areas that are distressed and others that are not.

3. The ratio of threatened neighborhoods

to distressed neighborhoods is based on research showing that for each neighborhood in severe poverty (defined as more than 40 percent of residents falling below the federal poverty threshold), there are approximately two additional neighborhoods with more moderate levels of poverty (defined as more than 20 percent of residents below the federal poverty threshold); see Kasarda, "Inner City Concentrated Poverty," p. 258.

4. Paul A. Jargowski, "Ghetto Poverty Among Blacks in the 1980s," *Journal of Policy Analysis and Management* 13 (1994): 288–310.

5. Laurence E. Lynn, Jr., and Michael McGeary, eds., *Inner-City Poverty in the United States* (Washington, D.C.: National Academy Press, 1990). To describe this interaction, economists sometimes use the terms *negative externalities* or *negative public goods*.

6. John D. Kasarda, "Inner-City Poverty and Economic Access," in *Rediscovering Urban America: Perspectives on the 1980s*, ed. Jack Sommer and Donald A. Hicks (Washington, D.C.: U.S. Department of Housing and Urban Development, 1993), pp. 4–25; George E. Peterson, *Confronting the Nation's Urban Crisis: From Watts (1965) to South Central Los Angeles (1992)* (Washington, D.C.: The Urban Institute Press, 1992), p. 9; Kasarda, "Inner City Concentrated Poverty," pp. 274, 276–277.

7. *Partnerships in Crime Prevention, Final Summary* (Washington, D.C.: National Commission on Severely Distressed Public Housing, 1992); Rick Bragg, "Where a Child on the Stoop Can Strike Fear," *New York Times*, December 2, 1992, p. A28; Morton Winsberg, "The Mean Streets Get Meaner: City and Suburb," *Population Today* 19 (April 1991): 4–5; Fred M. Hechinger, "Saving Youth from Violence," *Carnegie Quarterly* (Winter 1994): 2; *Speaking of Kids: A National Survey of Children and Parents* (Washington, D.C.: National Commission on Children, 1991), p. 34; *Crime Incidence in Chicago Housing Authority Developments, 1993* (Chicago: Chicago Housing Authority, March 1994), p. 5; National Research Council, *Understanding and Preventing Violence* (Washington, D.C.: National Academy Press, 1993), pp. 10, 62–64, 186, 239; Don Terry, "More Familiar, Life in a Cell Seems Less Terrible," *New York Times*, September 13, 1992, pp.

1, 40; National Institute of Justice, *Gun Acquisition and Possession in Selected Juvenile Samples* (Washington, D.C.: U.S. Department of Justice, December 1993), pp. 4–7.

8. Kasarda, "Inner City Concentrated Poverty," pp. 263–265, 275, 276; *The Final Report of the National Commission on Severely Distressed Public Housing* (Washington, D.C.: The Commission, August 1992), p. 47; *1992 Green Book* (Washington, D.C.: Committee on Ways and Means, U.S. House of Representatives, May 15, 1992), pp. 1074, 1076; *Families on Welfare: Focus on Teenage Mothers Could Enhance Welfare Reform Efforts* (Washington, D.C.: U.S. General Account Office, May 1994), p. 8; *Starting Points: Meeting the Needs of Our Youngest Children* (New York: Carnegie Corporation, April 1994), p. 21; National Center for Children in Poverty, *News and Issues* (Fall 1992): 5.

9. Guy Gugliotta, "Rebuilding a Community from the Bottom Up," *Washington Post*, January 24, 1993, p. A1; Robert Woods, "Standing Ground" (Keynote address to the Conference on New Strategies for Fighting Disinvestment and Reclaiming Urban Neighborhoods, Middletown, Conn., Weslayan University, May 13, 1992), p. 11; Susan Kellam, "Public Housing: Can the Largest Assisted-Housing Program Be Improved?" *Congressional Quarterly Researcher* 3 (September 10, 1993); 800–801; Martha Burt and Barbara Cohen, *America's Homeless: Numbers, Characteristics, and Programs that Serve Them* (Washington, D.C.: The Urban Institute Press, 1989). Other estimates put the number between 700,000 and 2.2 million; see Kasarda, "Inner-City Poverty," pp. 4–18; Carol Steinbach, *A Decent Place to Live Revisited* (Columbia, Md.: The enterprise Foundation, 1992), p. 18.

10. Robert D. Putnam, "The Prosperous Community: Social Capital and Public Life," *The American Prospect* (Spring 1993): 35–36; James S. Coleman, "Social Capital in the Creation of Human Capital," *American Journal of Sociology* 94 (Supplement 1988): S98; Mitchell Sviridoff, "The Seeds of Urban Revival," *Public Interest* 114 (Winter 1994): 82–103; John L. McKnight, "Redefining Community," *Social Policy* 23 (Fall-Winter 1992): 58; Mindy Leiterman and Joseph Stillman, *Building Community: A Report on Social Community Development*

Initiatives (New York: Local Initiatives Support Corporation, June 1993), P. 13. The concept of social capital and its role in American life was noted at least as long ago as Alexis de Tocqueville's famous essay *Democracy in America* (1835). CED has previously recognized the importance of social capital in *Why Child Care Matters: Preparing Young Children for a More Productive America* (1993), p. 4.

11. Nicholas Lemann, "Four Generations in the Projects," *New York Times Magazine*, January 13, 1991, pp. 14, 16–21 (quotation is from p. 14); *Crime Incidence in Chicago Public Housing Authority Developments, 1993*, p. 5; *Statistical Profile 1991–1992* (Chicago: Chicago Housing Authority, November 1992), p. 20.

12. *Speaking of Kids*, pp. 35–36; Paul E. Barton and Richard J. Coley, *America's Smallest School: The Family* (Princeton, N.J.: Educational Testing Service, 1992), p. 37; Roberto M. Fernandez and David Harris, "Social Isolation and the Underclass," in *Drugs, Crime, and Social Isolation*, ed. Adele V. Harrell and George E. Peterson (Washington, D.C.: The Urban Institute Press, 1992), pp. 257–293; Senator Bill Bradley, "Violence in America" (Speech to the National Press Club, Washington, D.C., May 11, 1994), p. 5; Anne C. Case and Lawrence F. Katz, *The Company You Keep: The Effects of Family and Neighborhood on Disadvantaged Youths* (Cambridge, Mass.: National Bureau of Economic Research, 1991), p. 12.

13. Isabel Sawhill, "Young Children and Families," in *Setting Domestic Priorities*, ed. Henry J. Aaron and Charles L. Schultze (Washington, D.C.: The Brookings Institution, 1992), p. 162; Putnam, "The Prosperous Community," p. 37; Signithia Fordham and John Ogbu, "Black Students' School Success: Coping with the Burden of Acting White," *Urban Review* 18 (1986): 176–206.

14. Robert J. Sampson, *Crime and Community Social Disorganization: Implications for Social Policy* (Washington, D.C.: U.S. Department of Housing and Urban Development, 1993), p. 6; National Research Council, *Understanding and Preventing Violence*, p. 15.

15. Marc Bendick, Jr., "Matching Workers and Job Opportunities: What Role for the Federal-State Employment Service?" in *Re-thinking Employment Policy*, ed. D. L. Bawden and Felicity Skidmore (Washington, D.C.: The Urban Institute Press, 1989), pp. 81–108.

16. William Julius Wilson, *The Truly Disadvantaged* (Chicago: University of Chicago Press, 1987); Kasarda, "Inner-City Poverty," pp. 4–12; Marc Bendick Jr., and Mary Lou Egan, "Linking Business Development and Community Development in Inner Cities," *Journal of Planning Literature* 8 (August 1993): 3–19.

17. John D. Kasarda, "The Severely Distressed in Economically Transforming Cities," in *Drugs, Crime, and Social Isolation*, ed. Adele V. Harrell and George E. Peterson (Washington, D.C.: The Urban Institute Press, 1992), pp. 45–97; George E. Peterson and Wayne Vroman, eds., *Urban Labor Markets and Job Opportunity* (Washington, D.C.: The Urban Institute Press, 1992).

18. Douglas S. Massey and Nancy A. Denton, *American Apartheid: Segregation and the Making of the Underclass* (Cambridge, Mass.: Harvard University Press, 1993).

19. Kasarda, "Inner City Concentrated Poverty," p. 263.

20. Marc Bendick, Jr., Charles W. Jackson, and Victor Reinoso, "Measuring Employment Discrimination Through Controlled Experiments," *Review of Black Political Economy* 23 (Summer 1994): 25–48; Raymond Struyk and Michael Fix, eds., *Measurement of Discrimination in America* (Washington, D.C.: The Urban Institute Press, 1992); Jolene Kirschenman and Kathryn M. Neckerman, "We'd Love to Hire Them, But…: The Meaning of Race for Employers," in *The Urban Underclass*, ed. Christopher Jencks and Paul E. Peterson (Washington, D.C.: The Brookings Institution, 1991), pp. 203–232.

21. Gregory D. Squires, ed., *From Redlining to Reinvestment: Community Response to Urban Disinvestment* (Philadelphia, Penn.: Temple University Press, 1992), pp. 4–6 (quotation is from p. 5); Massey and Denton, *American Apartheid*, pp. 46, 68, 71; "To the Promised Land," *The Economist*, July 9, 1994, p. 32.

22. Squires, *From Redlining to Reinvestment*, p. 20; *Housing Policy Debate* 3 (1992); Timothy Bates, *Banking on Black Enterprise: The Potential of Emerging Firms for Revitalizing Urban Economies* (Washington, D.C.: Joint

Center for Political and Economic Studies, 1993).

23. For example, some public housing authorities have maintained separate waiting lists by race and explicitly avoided placing minority-dominated public housing projects in white residential areas. See Kellam, "Public Housing," p. 802.

24. Lewis H. Spence, "Rethinking the Social Role of Public Housing," *Housing Policy Debate* 4 (1993): 355–368.

25. Sandra J. Newman and Ann B. Schnare, "Last in Line: Housing Assistance for Households with Children," *Housing Policy Debate* 3 (1992): 417–456.

26. Martin H. Gerry, *A Joint Enterprise with America's Families to Ensure Student Success* (Washington, D.C.: Council of Chief State School Officers, 1991).

27. Gerry, *A Joint Enterprise*, p. 5.

28. Richard L. Worsnop, "Community Policing: Is It the Answer to the Nation's Crime Problem?" *Congressional Quarterly Researcher* 3 (February 5, 1993): 104–106.

4. CREATING GLOBALLY COMPETITIVE COMMUNITIES

David B. Bowes

Flourishing communities are the foundation of a healthy and prosperous society. Today, a profound convergence is occurring in the planning priorities of American manufacturers and the state and local jurisdictions where they operate. "For the first time since the Industrial Revolution," declares the Washington State Department of Community, Trade and Economic Development, "what now constitutes a good business climate has the same criteria as what constitutes a good quality of life."[1]

Among the important measures of a community's quality of life are its attractiveness, cleanliness, safety, and educational and employment opportunities. Many manufacturers have adopted the concept of total quality management, moving from pollution abatement to waste minimization, to life-cycle engineering, and to "greener" products and markets. Meanwhile, local government managers are daily dealing with improvements to schools, the building and maintaining of roads, ordinance development, land use decisions, and sanitation — issues that affect the com-

munity in both the short and long term. Moreover, local governments are redefining quality of community life to include not only urban amenities but also more and better jobs. The successful communities are those with proactive government managers who strive to improve the community in accordance with its values, needs, and vision.

Today, community life, trade, and economic development are seen as mutually reinforcing. Tomorrow, localities will become more productive and livable not only by meeting employers' needs but also by enhancing the lives of their workers. There's abundant evidence that modern manufacturers, together with employers in industry's growing service component (e.g., spin-off and high-technology companies from which manufacturers buy everything from consulting services to food services), seek much the same atmosphere that communities wish to preserve or recreate.

Global competitiveness ensures a community's strong employment and tax base. But one thing is certain: a community's

From Creating Globally Competitive Communities (Abstract), *1996. Published by Partners for Livable Communities, Washington, D.C. Reprinted with permission of the publisher.*

global competitiveness depends on a balance between a strong business community, a healthy environment, and a good quality of life. Community leaders who try harder to help manufacturers respond to global market challenges are seeking in return more economic security through new job creation, a superior quality of life, a better handle on political stability in times of jarring change, and robust future philanthropy.

Both business owners and local government officials are embracing a vision of the globally competitive community. The means for achieving this vision is . "high-performance" economic development. High-performance economic development impresses companies that are searching for new locations by demonstrating that a locality committed to quality and productivity is already supporting its manufacturing base.

Partners for Livable Communities and The Manufacturing Institute, the education and research affiliate of the National Association of Manufacturers, have spent a year and a half studying the extent to which high-performance, manufacturing-based development figures in local and regional planning. Their findings reveal hesitation as well as activity on the part of local governments.

Some communities still concentrate on wooing the service the distribution sectors, believing that these are supplanting manufacturing. Others assume that the economic pie is shrinking and are more eager to wrest companies from adjacent jurisdictions than to maximize the performance of local manufacturers and hatch new firms.

Some local officials are not aware that since the dark days of the 1980s, when many companies (and communities) fell victim to inefficiency and foreign competition, U.S. manufacturing has had a renaissance. The United States again is the most competitive nation in the world, according to the respected World Economic Forum. America's heartland — a "rust belt" for two decades— is back and is still manufacturing based. Seaboards and Sunbelt are methodically building industrial futures that are less dependent on defense spending.

Meanwhile, other communities, having realized that their employers are now competing globally, are partnering to maximize the performance of local companies. Some school systems are responding to calls for better-educated graduates in the workforce. Put another way, the creation of new wealth that is inherent chiefly in modern manufacturing has become central to formal planning and informal debate in more and more communities.

For example, the city of Springfield and Clark County in Ohio acknowledge in a joint strategic plan that they must and will "provide an environment where manufacturing remains profitable and ... we can diversify with changing times. In order to do so, we must recognize the global issues facing our local industries."

Brevard County, Florida, has a community quality council that has been helping industry and educators instill a combination of quality assurance (Japanese *kaizen*) and new approaches to work training and team building. Brevard 2005 is an ambitious visioning process that sets nine-year goals for making the Melbourne area the nation's best place to learn, work, and play.

Tucson, Arizona, whose rate of manufacturing growth has led the nation, calls itself "a community of small businesses with a strong entrepreneurial spirit, recognizing that the local market is too small and the future lies in linking with the rest of the world."[2] The once-sleepy retirement community hosts visitors from emerging markets such as India to new clusters of high-technology industry.

The process of bringing together community resources and economic policy, along with responsible attention to the environment and community vitality, will take years if not decades. Local leaders must be convinced that competing with a united industrial Europe, the city-states on the Asian rim, and the cheap-labor nations in the Third World has to become for communities what the quest for top quality is for U.S. manufacturers.

Any community that shapes its business climate based on the criteria presented in this report, and that also considers the manufacturing "intersection" of raw materials, energy, and innovative effort as important as any intersection in town, has begun arduous but hopeful process of becoming globally competitive.

The Importance of Manufacturing to Local Economies

Plant Site Locators, an Oklahoma City firm that specializes in matching companies of all sizes with prequalified communities, quotes a survey from the U.S. Bureau of Labor Statistics: 75 new manufacturing jobs can create up to 48 other positions that support the additional economic activity. This triggers $2.6 million in total, first-year spending by employees. Moreover, each new factory job generates, on average, $600 in increased annual sales tax revenues.[3]

Manufacturing employment at large companies declined by 2.4 million between 1967 and 1992, in part because some manufacturing jobs were reclassified as service jobs. By contrast, manufacturing employment at companies with 500 or fewer employees grew by 1.7 million in the same period.

Large companies are "outsourcing" major contracts to these smaller firms. Many small companies become design-and-de-velopment partners of the giants they serve. Because the realistic locus of much future job creation is smaller companies with growth potential, they receive particular attention in this report.

The Research for This Report

To encourage closer local examination of balanced economic growth and the ways to generate it, Partners for Livable Communities and The Manufacturing Institute conducted surveys, focus groups, and interviews with more than 400 private sector chief executive officers (CEOs) nationwide, who responded anonymously. Small and midsize manufacturing companies received special attention. Some of their public sector counterparts— members of the National League of Cities and the International City/County Management Association — also were questioned. The author also reviewed the findings of similar surveys conducted by local chambers of commerce.

The survey's sole question, used in focus groups and interviews as well, was as follows:

> Here is a list of concerns you may or may not have as your company prepares to compete in the 21st century. Please add to the list if you wish, then rank five areas of support you'll need most from local governments, school systems, centers for technology transfer, economic development departments, and other local institutions. The aim is to visualize high-performance industry in a prototype globally competitive community.

The top five responses given by each senior manufacturing executive who participated in the survey were tallied and ranked. The manufacturers' chief concerns as revealed by the survey can be summarized as follows:

• Smaller manufacturers want a stronger work ethic among younger workers. They cite better education and training for community workforces as their second greatest need.

• Small and midsize manufacturers identify regulatory compliance procedures (especially environmental) at every level as the biggest barrier to investment in expansion.

• Principals in smaller manufacturing companies believe the best incentives for business expansion are reserved for larger local companies and for hot prospects from elsewhere.

• Small and midsized manufacturers are responsive to the idea that communities could become more globally competitive in a systematic way.

• Few manufacturers are convinced, however, that communities understand manufacturing well enough to harness its full potential. Many concede that manufacturers haven't told their own story.

• Smaller manufacturers express some interest in starting up on or relocating to abandoned urban land if concerns about security, accessibility, and workforce skills can be addressed.

Many of the local officials interviewed in this study are cautious about shaping economic development strategies to emphasize manufacturing. Some mistrust the motives of private sector firms. When they review the growth policies that smaller manufacturers say will help create additional employment, local officials have two responses. First, they say there is considerably more local and state assistance available to all industry than most manufacturers are aware of. Second, they seem to want the manufacturers to be more willing to trust local government, understand the constraints on local government, and participate in local initiatives.

These findings have important implications for local government economic development programs. Local governments and even chambers of commerce often have surprisingly few regular exchanges of ideas, information, and viewpoints with smaller manufacturers. In California, a government program called the California Supplier Improvement Program broadens the capabilities of the smaller manufacturers with fee-based workshops. Generally, however, small companies poised for growth as vendors to large manufacturers are still just names on lists at city halls. Perhaps the first step toward an improved economic environment is better communication with the private sector.

The Globally Competitive Community

Manufacturers believe farsighted public leadership is essential to meet the challenges of a global economy, but leadership is just the beginning. The rest of this report examines the 15 characteristics of a jurisdiction that approximates manufacturers' optimum operating environment and offers examples from current practice of how some communities are improving their ability to compete for jobs in a global market.

IMPARTS THE WORK ETHIC TO EACH GENERATION

A globally competitive community introduces each new generation to the work ethic, underscoring responsibility, initiative, team participation, pride in workmanship, and other traits central to producing a gross community product of world-class quality.

Even more than they want better schools, smaller manufacturers wish for a turnaround in the declining work ethic among younger employees and job candidates. A recent defense conversion survey by the East county Economic Development Council in La Mesa, California, near San Diego, spoke for manufacturers nearly everywhere:

> Also beyond the control of individual companies is the perceived slackening of the work ethic among younger job applicants. Several of our participants suggested that training per se is less of an issue for them than "trainability." Employers are looking for people who come to work clean, rested and willing to put in a day's labor. They are more often confronted by a labor force with an "attitude"—people who resent having to work and are not motivated to learn new skills and techniques.[4]

Not everyone agrees on precisely how "work ethic" should be defined. Some local officials tie it to wage levels—the better a company pays, the harder employees are motivated to work. Other officials say unwillingness to work at all is the threshold problem, not on-the-job motivation or exertion.

Meanwhile, employer-employee relationships increasingly stress employment development over job security. Veterans workers are newly responsible for their own careers, and the work ethic they grew up with is no longer a fully adequate guide. Training and retraining are now part of "continuing education" on the job. Training authority Anthony Carnevale, vice president for public leadership at the Educational Testing Service, believes that the need to allocate time between performing today's tasks and training for tomorrow's requires society to "rethink what we mean by work ethic."

To date, however, the work ethic apparently has been too big and too sensitive an issue to touch. If some community has stepped up to this pervasive concern, marshaling its best educators, coaches, clergy, youth leaders, and preschool specialists to address it long term, that community is hiding its light under a bushel.

EDUCATES FOR BASICS AND THE SCHOOL-TO-WORK TRANSITION

A globally competitive community augments basic curricula and electives with workplace-focused courses that help students move from classroom to appropriate employment, contribute to the local economy, and engage in ongoing career preparation.

It's the best of times and the worst of times in local education. Scores on seven of the nine trends in the National Assessment of Educational Progress in reading, mathematics, and science are at all-time highs. Yet what the Competitiveness Policy Council concluded in 1993 still rings true: "[America is] producing a substantial cohort of workers with poor basic skills, little understanding of what work demands, and limited grasp of how to find a good job or get good training."[5]

Manufacturers acknowledge some progress in academic achievement, but they want schools to be more productive, efficient, and focused on excellence. They also want a seamless transition from school to work, the kind of transition that Siemens Corporation encourages with outreach to high school "pre-apprentices" at its electronics and electrical plants in Florida, Kentucky, North Carolina, and Georgia.

Year-round education appeals to many manufacturers partial to results-oriented flexibility. Extended schedules are in effect in some 2,400 schools in 34 states. Allowing education to break free from the fixed calendar of an agriculture-based economy, these schedules reinvent education around learning instead of harvests. Year-round education also promotes more intensive use of existing facilities.

The Socorro Independent School District near El Paso, Texas, teaches 20,000 low-income Hispanic students year-round. It's one of the few districts with those demographics that exceeds average statewide test scores. Socorro's assistant superintendent Sue Shook, president of the San Diego-based National Association for Year-Round Education, says the district schedule of 60 weekdays in class, followed by 20 weekdays of "intercession" enrichment and vacation, also reduces failures and discipline cases.

A program in North Branch, Minnesota, delivers a 12-month curriculum to 800 students from several high schools. Motivated students move up to technical training or college after three years; dropouts take courses at an area learning center. In West Virginia, nearly half the pupils at Charleston's Piedmont Elementary School are embarking on a modified year-round calendar on the theory that earlier remediation and shorter breaks will improve content retention. Programs between quarters, presented by citizen volunteers, stress continuous learning.

The transition from classroom to workplace also is receiving more attention. Competitive communities are responding to the fact that local commitment to education reform is beginning to appear among corporate site-selection criteria. For example, smaller manufacturers tell the Arkansas Science and Technology Authority that the lack of trained maintenance people is as large a stumbling block to sustaining improvement as is the cost of new machinery.

In Omaha, Nebraska, the Omaha Work Keys program is profiling the city's 50 top job categories, assessing employment readiness skills, adjusting curricula for a better match, and aiming for a 50 percent increase in high school graduates prepared for work. In Eugene, Oregon, with assistance from the Pew Partnership for Civic Change, Networking for Youth has drawn on local manufacturers and others for career mentors. It offers six-week "reality check" internships for teachers and obtains employer validation of school curricula.

Farther up the educational ladder, Ohio's University of Akron pioneered innovations in continuous learning with the Will-Burt Company, an Orrville, Ohio, firm now owned by its 286 employees. Will-Burt snapped out of a slump, worker attendance went up, and worker compensation costs declined. The company began to deliver such superior advanced metal fabrications that customers paid premiums and signed new contracts. One user stopped inspecting parts, calling the company's quality control "flawless."

The University of Akron's collaboration with a private company is a textbook example of local partnership. What began as a mandatory course in blueprint reading for the firm's employees, taught on Will-Burt time, widened to include statistical process control and geometric dimensioning. Next came a "mini–MBA" program to cross-train production workers who don't know finance, materials control, sales, and other office functions, and office workers who lack production savvy. Employees who earn the mini–MBA at Will-Burt expense, or an "associate degree" in manufacturing, qualify for tuition toward a bachelor's degree.

SUPPORTS HIGH-PERFORMANCE ECONOMIC DEVELOPMENT

A globally competitive community shapes, pursues, and adheres to a comprehensive strategy of balanced growth from high-performance economic development, emphasizing wealth creation through modern manufacturing and the service industries that support it.

Incentives have become "table stakes" if not always decisive factors in industrial relocation decisions. A spokesman for North

Carolina, decrying the sharp escalation in bidding, says companies now interpret a lack of incentives as a no-growth posture by the jurisdiction in question. One hundred economists from Ohio, a winner in the plant relocation races, have recommended ending tax abatements everywhere.

"State and local governments ... assume that states and localities, not businesses, are the competitors," says Stuart A. Rosenfeld in *Competitive Manufacturing: New Strategies for Regional Development.* "As a result, their policies are aimed at competing for new firms rather than helping their existing firms modernize and become more competitive."[6]

The antidote is high-performance economic development — again, economic development in localities whose commitment to quality and productivity is already supporting its manufacturing base to the extent that it impresses other companies to locate there. Since up to half of all U.S. manufacturers embrace flexible, worker-empowering industry, communities should shift away from providing direct assistance and toward creating a "total economic environment" that complements the private sector's efforts to boost performance.[7]

Smaller manufacturers are less likely to share in tax-break bonanzas than larger, more footloose enterprises, so they prefer to see local officials strengthen the broader basics of community competitiveness.

Nurturing the city's established local companies is the first priority in the Campaign for a Greater St. Louis: 1995–2000. The objective of this $10 million, public-private initiative — coordinated by the St. Louis Regional Commerce and Growth Association and the Greater St. Louis Economic Development Council — is to add 100,000 new quality jobs in the city and 12 counties of Missouri and Illinois by the turn of the century.

Responsibility for strengthening mod-

ern manufacturing — one of St. Louis's preferences for clean future growth — is shared by the Critical Technologies Partnership and two of its members organizations. Together, these entities are creating more responsive linkages between universities and industry. Long-term support for manufacturers of all sizes, both current and future, comes from St. Louis's Manufacturing Resources Advisory Board and its Mid-America Manufacturing Technology Center.

To enhance Maryland's competitive posture and help generate 90,000 net new jobs by the year 2000, a state commission of business leaders recommended the following new initiatives: stressing "customer focus" among regulatory and enforcement officials, reducing the personal income tax rate by 15 percent within three years, setting a time frame for issuance of permits and a rapid response unit for resolution of problems, implementing a job creation tax credit, strengthening customized workforce training through community colleges, and expanding international business.

The city of Tupelo and Lee County, Mississippi, have added more than 1,000 new factory jobs a year for the last 10 years — 18,380 in all. This progrowth outlook dates back to 1936, when a local development foundation launched "Balance Agriculture with Industry," a menu of inducements to attract branch plants. Today a trusted community relations agency helps resolve employer-employee issues. Citizens support school construction, retraining programs build local skills, and outside evaluators coach the whole community through future planning every 10 years.

Local governments can make explicit their expectations for a connection between incentives and jobs. For example, the city of Parma, Ohio, insisted on local hiring when it negotiated an agreement with an out-of-state manufacturer interested in making Parma a national distribution center. The firm agreed that at least half of its new hires would be Parma residents and at least half would be people who had been on welfare.

MAKES A SERIOUS COMMITMENT TO EXPORTING

A globally competitive community makes a commitment to becoming outward looking and export oriented. It collaborates with industry to introduce advanced technologies, and it helps smaller employers find expert counsel when they're adjusting to change.

According to a study done in 1994, one-fifth of all firms with fewer than 500 employees were exporting by that year — nearly double the percentage in 1992. Communities have an important stake in this trend. An academically rigorous study of hundreds of exporters of all sizes, released in March 1996 by The Manufacturing Institute and the Institute for International Economics, documents the manifold benefits that exporting companies bring to communities and their tax bases:

• Exporting companies create jobs almost 20 percent faster than comparable, nonexporting firms and are nine percent less likely to go out of business in an average year.

• Workers in companies that export earn from five to 15 percent more than workers in companies that don't; further, their jobs grow 15 to 40 percent faster and are more stable.

• Worker productivity is up to 20 percent higher at exporting plants than at nonexporting plants; total commitment to exporting matters more than export sales volume.

The New Jersey legislature enacted the Export Financing Opportunities Act to help companies and communities foster trade. Agencies in Buffalo, Louisville, Philadelphia, Houston, Tucson, and Spokane collaborate with private sector export promoters. Anniston, Alabama, employs an expert to give free counsel to manufacturers who need ISO 9000 certification to sell inside Europe's Common Market. Brevard Community College and Central Florida Manufacturing Technology Center jointly sponsor briefings on patent protection.

Farsighted communities help local companies increase productivity, improve business practices, step up to unfamiliar technologies, and even dispel denial that there is a need to seek outside help. Organizations that deliver such services typically are led by boards of executives with production credentials. In the case of Cincinnati, these manufacturers are joined by the city manager and the president of the University of Cincinnati.

Dedicated to promoting and measuring continuous industrial improvement, Cincinnati's Institute of Advanced Manufacturing Sciences (IAMS) measures its own success in "key metrics." IAMS's membership rose to 159 companies last year, an increase of 51 from the previous year. A related metric, the ratio of local to state funding, reflects another step ahead: IAMS received three dollars from local industry and from program fees for every two dollars that came from the state.

Still another IAMS metric is customer satisfaction. Initiatives such as PRISM (Program of Regional Improvement Services for Manufacturers) save companies an average of $35,000 the first year after pollution prevention assessments and $225,000 after productivity assessments. For example, from an analysis of just one of its six nozzle assembly lines, a manufacturer of fueling components expects gross first-year savings of more than

$200,000. IAMS helps Cincinnati managers spend precious time and capital most effectively.

In Grand Rapids, Michigan, the center for manufacturing improvement is Performance Place. Opened last year in a renovated factory, Performance Place is home to the Grand Rapids's Manufacturers Council, which promotes improvement of the regional manufacturing economy of West Michigan, and the site of workshops ranging from "Understanding and Eliminating Waste" to "Looking at the Future for Owners and Executives."

Performance Place was created by The Right Place, a program to expand, retain, and attract manufacturing jobs. The facility was designed and furnished by Grand Rapids-based Steelcase, Inc., as a prototype for interactive learning environments. Ameritech brought in the fiber-optic communications network.

Some jurisdictions no longer wait for appeals from beleaguered companies that might go out of business or move away. Washington State's Business and Job Retention Program (BJRP) is a model for communities that want to take preventive action. By publicizing its willingness to help at-risk companies, BJRP hopes to achieve win-win-win solutions for employers, workers, and communities alike.

In a recent five-year period, BJRP retained more than 175 manufacturing companies, 11,800 family wage jobs, and $43 million in tax revenues. County agencies provide cash matches nearly equal to state funding. Local development officers provide "eyes and ears" support. The state saves $23 for every dollar it invests, says program director Howard Levens, formerly a small-business owner.

Because it respects confidentiality, BJRP never looks to accountants or taxing agencies for tips on which firms are in trouble. To identify manufacturers who may need its help, it depends on stories in the local media and a confidential, two-page mail survey sent every two years to appropriate industrial classification (SIC) codes. Levens himself monitors corporate annual reports. Companies that complete and return the survey may be visited by a county-level expert. This early-warning initiative receives calls from out-of-state investors looking for turnaround opportunities.

DEVELOPS LOGICAL CLUSTERS OF INDUSTRY

A globally competitive community knows its indigenous strengths and leverages them to build logical economic clusters. That is, it helps companies maximize their performance so that similar and interdependent firms will come to the area.

The cluster theory of economic development says that large, globally competitive manufacturers in the same industry often situate in clusters with related suppliers. Although the value of this theory is still being debated by academics, local and state governments have nevertheless begun to act on it.

Communities as diverse and livable as the city of San Diego and a dairying county in Vermont have taken a searching look at themselves to define their abilities to attract certain types of jobs. Most strategic plans written in the last ten years show that local governments know who they are and what types of economic development are most logical. The emphasis is on building on current strengths and helping existing local firms grow in the hopes that their success will attract similar kinds of employers.

San Diego's economy may seem dominated by tourism and the Navy, but manufacturing is that city's largest economic sector. Three-fourths of its factory employment, according to the San Diego Economic Development Corporation, is concentrated in the production of innovative, high-value durable goods. Charter companies in the San Diego Technology Incubator include firms developing a vision system for inspecting mass-produced products, an industrial computer systems integrator, "smart" material products that measure structural strain, and data visualization tools for debugging computer software.

"Since we're not going to have a lot of big manufacturers, we have to really foster smaller companies," explains Joan Stepsis of San Diego City College's Center for Applied Competitive Technologies. The center is one node in what the director of the city's economic development services calls "seamless service delivery for the 21st century." A technology council coordinates support. CONNECT at the University of California, San Diego, pulls together "virtual boards" of experts to help firms chart future growth.

Franklin County, Vermont, is leveraging a cluster of food-processing and pharmaceutical companies and support firms into more of the same. The jurisdiction already accounts for nearly three-fourths of Vermont's food industry; adjacent counties in upstate New York augment Vermont's farm output. The companies range from dairies to ice cream manufacturers, bakeries, and labeling and food brokerage firms.

Borrowing food-company research from Washington State University, the Franklin County Industrial Development Corporation is strengthening manufacturing-related services such as product testing, nutrient analysis, and assistance with state and federal food and drug regulations. Seven local firms are collaborating to attain ISO 9000 certification. A projected science and technology center would offer school-to-work learning in microbiology (essential to meat processing), dairy processing, and environmental sciences.

EXTENDS INCENTIVES TO SMALLER FIRMS

A globally competitive community levels the playing field for existing smaller companies and start-ups, declaring them as eligible as large companies for expansion incentives consistent with their potential for creating new jobs over time.

Longmont, Colorado, north of Denver, is happy to welcome new companies and frequently does. But Longmont's leadership thinks that economic growth is more certain and more methodically planned when it's homegrown. Thus the city of 56,000 offers a range of hard and softer development incentives to smaller manufacturers already operating there. In 1995, 70 of the community's 140 primary employers declared their intention to expand, adding 1,026 jobs and 311,000 square feet of industrial space.

The 15 monetary incentives include waiving 75 percent or more of a city development fee collected when permits are issued for manufacturing construction. To date, Longmont has waived nearly $750,000 in such fees. If the city council approves a 100 percent waiver of that development fee, the expanding company can ask the council for an "enhanced waiver" of all sewer, water, and other related infrastructure costs. The enhanced waiver for one recent project totaled $2.2 million.

Longmont's nonmonetary incentives include a fast-track annexation application process for industrial companies needing at least 80 acres of property. In addition, the city has implemented 50 recommendations from a task force that reviewed local regulations and fees for competitiveness. Because overall quality of life is a subjective term and thus a subjective incentive, Longmont benchmarks its housing costs, school expenditures per pupil, student/teacher ratios, and health care availability against those of competing jurisdictions.

Manufacturing jobs are the most solid among the many thousands of jobs that have been created through reuse of jettisoned properties. Rantoul, Illinois, began seeking new employers immediately upon learning that the Pentagon would close 70-year-old Chanute Air Force Base. The city lost a new United Airlines maintenance facility to Indianapolis, but it learned a lot in the process about what an airfield could mean to the community. Today, Chanute's hangars house several small companies. Rantoul Products runs three auto parts production shifts there with 450 employees. A unit of Textron spent $2 million retrofitting a hangar as an injection molding facility to make plastic interiors for Chrysler trucks and minivans. Caradco, a local window-making branch of Aluminum Company of America, jumped into a spacious jet repair building and added 100 jobs. J. B. Hunt Transportation Services of Lowell, Arkansas, found Chanute's runways and dorms ideal for a truck-driving school. Other base residences have been converted into a foster home program called Hope for Children.

Supporting start-up manufacturers until they grow enough to create employment is increasingly common among local strategies. The VisionAire Corporation, a small aviation company, settled on Ames, Iowa, after looking at more than two dozen possible locations for its first aircraft assembly facility. Work ethic, taxes, wage rates, and capital (intellectual and investment, in that order) counted in VisionAire's choice of Ames. Ames Municipal Airport's trump card was its proximity to the Iowa State University departments of aeronautical engineering and composite materials. City and state incentives totaled $3 million, including $100,000 in equity from the Ames Seed Capital Fund for prototype development. Ames's vision is to parlay VisionAire's 150 jobs into a center of business aircraft production.

Baltimore's South Harbor Business Center, Akron's Industrial Incubator Project, and Colorado's Innovation Foundation incubation sites are other examples of support for start-up manufacturers. These incubators offer flexible space and leases, exposure to business and technical consultants, and contacts at financial institutions. The National Business Incubation Association counts 500 such sites, half of them sponsored by governments and non-profits.

Some communities profit from the efforts of private individuals. In Melbourne, Florida, a former employee of a high-tech company who now sells real estate runs his own Innovation Center of Brevard — three in-town incubators with 43,000, 50,000, and 63,000 square feet, respectively. Entrepreneurs who move into one of these spaces get growth counsel from local business leaders over breakfast. These meetings are arranged by their landlords, who feel this help is good for their business, too.

Smaller companies often need help in creating a high-performance factory environment. Many of them lack the resources and know-how to provide cutting-edge training and education to workers. Without this knowledge, which is now common at large companies, it's much harder to become productive enough to qualify as vendors to big companies with global reach. The Washington-based Partnership for a Smarter Workforce, supported by the Pew Charitable Trusts and federal grants, is creating a pilot CEO-to-CEO network in Illinois and Massachusetts to share training information with smaller firms.

AVOIDS AN ADVERSARIAL REGULATORY POSTURE

A globally competitive community strives to avoid adversarial relationships in environmental and other regulations; it understands that mature, public-private partnerships foster a climate of constructive communication, common objectives, and trust.

Initiated by the federal Occupational Safety and Health Administration (OSHA) in Upper New England, the Maine Top 200 Program illustrates the kind of cooperation needed. Noting in 1993 that its backlogged inspection process wasn't reaching companies with the highest worker compensation claims, OSHA confirmed that one percent of Maine employers accounted for 45 percent of workplace injuries, illnesses, and fatalities. OSHA offered the problem firms the choice between an increase in traditional inspections or a voluntary action plan with quarterly reports to OSHA — the Maine Top 200 Program. Most of them chose the action plan. As of last August, these firms had identified 174,331 hazards and corrected 118,671. By striving to create a nonconfrontational partnership between industry and OSHA, the Maine program improves community competitiveness. Singled out for praise by Harvard's Kennedy School of Government, the program keeps economic growth in mind, focuses less on techniques than on outcomes, and cuts red tape.

The Waste Reduction Assistance Program of Florida's Department of Environmental Protection is a free, nonregulatory, confidential service. An example of its work is helping a printed circuit board manufacturer reduce wastewater discharge by 20 million gallons and save $489,000. Under its Blackstone Project, the Massachusetts Department of Environmental Protection moved from narrow, technical inspections to "cross-media" advisory reviews conducted by one inspector. That individual acts as a general practitioner, considering the plant as a whole with pollution prevention in mind.

Washington State's ombudsman saved employers and cities $27 million in 1994 through interventions and by training agency rule writers. Montgomery County, Maryland, expedited the city, county, and state paperwork that Hughes Network Systems needed to build a $7 million plant in six months. Colorado Springs, Colorado, has mobilized its Rapid Response Team to run interference for SCI Systems Inc. and 50 other companies wanting to expand.

A program being discussed at the state level in Colorado would offer both nonfinancial and financial incentives to companies (and governmental jurisdictions) that, under voluntary three-year agreements, "go beyond compliance and improve their environmental performance by reducing their impact on the environment through pollution prevention, resource conservation strategies, and other measures."[8] Nonfinancial incentives for qualified Colorado firms would include official recognition usable in promotion and marketing, the right to self-monitor and self-report current status, accelerated applications and consolidated permits from the state, and an extension of the life of existing permits. Financial incentives could include tax credits and low- or no-cost loans.

ENCOURAGES NEW USES FOR "BROWNFIELDS"

A globally competitive community encourages cleanup of and productive new uses for abandoned and polluted "brownfields." The objective is to make all local resources pull their economic weight and give residents of older urban neighborhoods the opportunity for gainful employment nearby.

Between 1963 and 1987, manufacturing activity in large urban areas declined as urban residents and jobs migrated to the suburbs and rural areas. Left behind in aging cities were block after block, often mile after mile, of what some call TOADS — temporarily obsolete abandoned derelict site — and most call "brownfields."

Missouri is one of a number of states with voluntary brownfield restoration efforts as an alternative to regulatory enforcement. Four barriers have to be overcome:

• Uncertain liability under Superfund law and its state counterparts
• Lack of uniform processes for pollution cleanup
• Unnecessarily stringent standards for new industrial uses
• Lack of creative financing to supplant declining federal support.

For companies that create or retain at least 25 jobs on brownfields, Missouri offers a 100 percent tax credit for up to 20 years on the cost of site remediation to prudent levels. St. Louis plans to reclaim 40 million square feet of abandoned land — one-sixth of the entire city — and return that land to the tax rolls. Typical property is a 29-acre parcel of 12 cleared blocks in the Dr. Martin Luther King Business Park. The U.S. Environmental Protection Agency (EPA) awarded the city a $200,000 grant to assist in recovery efforts. Underground storage tanks have been removed, but potential buyers who still fear liability given the area's history of pollution can apply to the Missouri Department of Natural Resources for insurance. Businesses new to the park are eligible for tax credits if they hire from within that enterprise zone.

The Baltimore (Maryland) Development Corporation, with help from Cornell University and a grant from the U.S. Department of Housing and Urban Development, is creating an "eco-industrial park" in Baltimore's Fairfield Empowerment Zone. The park is patterned after a project in Denmark. At Fairfield, which is on the waterfront, waste from one company will become raw material for another. The goal is a return on assets of 30 to 50 percent above the industry average.

UPGRADES ALL FACETS OF INFRASTRUCTURE

A globally competitive community upgrades its transportation and transit infrastructures, and expands information highway linkage, so that all citizens have access to decentralized modern manufacturing employment as well as mobility for learning, safety, and health.

The changing nature of export-driven manufacturing reinforces traditional needs for infrastructure and creates new ones — from paved highways that move goods to data highways that move information. A factory is no longer just a place; it's a stage in a value-adding process. Employees commute daily to discrete workplaces, but computer and voice technologies link distant production points as never before.

Strengthening infrastructure is a top priority for Shelby County, Tennessee, as the Memphis area begins benchmarking seven "peer cities": Atlanta, Birmingham, Charlotte, Dallas, Indianapolis, Louisville, and Nashville. Already the hub for Federal Express flights, Memphis is developing a comprehensive regional intermodal transportation system. Planned improvements range from expanded freight terminals at the Port of Memphis to a regional bus system for worker use. The goal is to become a logistics center that combines communication technology, all transportation modes, and "just in time" manufacturing. By providing expanded services at lower rates, Memphis hopes to provide an opportunity for every person to be connected to a seamless information utility where they live, learn, work, and play.

To link learning, health care, reclaimed brownfields, and new business investment near transit stations, St. Louis has built a bistate seventeen-mile, nineteen-station light-rail system called MetroLink, at a cost of $19.8 million per mile. Jobless youth among the system's 26,000 daily passengers will learn manufacturing skills almost trackside at an abandoned complex of buildings near a MetroLink station. A program called The Cornerstone Partnership will offer remedial education and technical skills to several hundred youths each year.

New telecommunications infrastructure makes possible distance training for skills, safety, and maintenance in manufacturing. Distance learning and decentralized production networks are especially important where mountainous terrain or distances isolate communities and companies. PMG Combined Manufacturing in Wheeling, West Virginia, is an example of a private entity that incorporates the resources of a number of independently owned industrial manufacturing and service companies. Among the group's competitive strengths are shared technology, team engineering, centralized ordering, minimal outsourcing, and group contract management. Local governments can increase the success of these clusters of coordinated production by looking to their special infrastructure needs.

Encourages Competitive Energy Supplies

A globally competitive community urges utilities to sell power to industry at competitive rates, to broaden incentives for energy conservation, and to continuously improve the quality of power for sophisticated, computerized manufacturing technologies.

Municipal and privately owned utilities play a prominent role in local economic development. Utilities can

• Integrate their energy efficiency and related financial incentives into local business retention strategies

• Encourage expansion of existing local businesses through energy-efficient modernization and diversification

• Promote small businesses and start-ups, and improve the local economic climate by reducing energy costs

• Achieve better demand management which, along with other initiatives, supports development growth.[9]

Communities reap benefits when utilities participate in development outreach. For example, access to plentiful electricity at reasonable rates was a key factor in the decision of IPSCO Steel, Inc., to begin building a $375 million, 300-job mini-mill in Muscatine County, Iowa. The gas and electric utility serving an IPSCO facility in another part of the state helped IPSCO identify the new site and qualify it.

The deregulation of electric power, like that of natural gas before it, will increase competition among both traditional utilities and newer wholesale generators already exempt from restrictive ownership regulations. Once utilities can sell power and transmission services anywhere on the grid, it will be interesting to see whether their own health will remain tied to the fortunes of primary service areas, or whether they will continue to play the same role in community development or serve in a different capacity. Communities that intend to become globally competitive are already tracking the transition.

Concerning conservation, the Electric Power Research Institute estimates that 24 to 38 percent of projected industrial demand by the year 2000 could be eliminated through "efficiency" improvements. Cinergy Corporation has established the Industrial Competitiveness Center, which serves plants in southwest Ohio, southern Indiana, and northern Kentucky. Cinergy pays half the cost (up to $15,000) of customized audits for industrial customers with peak demands of more than 150 kilowatts. Conducted by Cincinnati's Institute of Advanced Manufacturing Sciences, these comprehensive energy audits typically save 10 to 20 percent of a company's annual power bill while reducing unit costs and extending recycling.

Meanwhile, a bill passed by the New York legislature allows two-way meters on solar-powered houses: if these houses send back more electricity to the utility than they purchase, the homeowners get a credit.

Quality of power is increasingly important for advanced manufacturing technologies. Just as a digital clock is more sensitive to power dips and surges, so too is computerized and computer-integrated machinery on the modern factory floor. Memphis's Light, Gas, and Water Division counsels its industrial customers, monitors a range of "reliability indices," and upgrades its own distribution system. Qualified employers who can halt production when the utility faces peak loads owing to weather earn the lowest electric rates.

TEMPERS TAXATION WITH INVESTMENT SUPPORT

A globally competitive community levies taxes, fees, and permit charges with an appropriate balance between legitimate community need for revenue and employers' need to invest continuously in "hard" and "soft" technologies that boost productivity and pay.

The National Association of Manufacturers, which has 14,000 member companies, most of them small, underscores simplicity, elimination of double taxation, and stability in describing the kind of tax system — federal, state, and local — it favors:

The new system should be one that average wage-earners can both understand and believe to be fair.... Income once taxed should not be subjected to multiple taxation just because it is saved or invested rather than consumed.... Business taxes under any new system should be compatible with those of our trading partners so that, for example, American exports are not double-taxed by the U.S. and the destination country.... Present tax laws are both disliked and hard to understand in large part because they are in a constance state of flux.[10]

A business panel to a large, eastern state had this to say about taxation:

Tax burden in an area often received disproportionate emphasis during the site selection process relative to its ultimate impact on total operating costs. However, tax burden is strongly equated with a state's overall business climate.... The primary taxes evaluated during site selection are corporate income taxes, property taxes and personal income taxes. Sales taxes are rarely an important consideration [but] play a role if there is a sales tax on a specific product type that a company sells, or on equipment that a company must buy."[11]

On the basis of an analysis of nine industrial states east of the Mississippi River, those most successful to date in economic development chose one of three tax strategies:

• Spread the tax burden evenly among corporate income taxes, property taxes, and personal income taxes. Don't tax businesses disproportionately relative to taxation in neighboring or competing jurisdictions.

• Place a greater proportion of the burden on individuals than on companies by lowering taxes that influence bottom lines— that is, property and corporate income taxes.

• Eliminate or reduce a specific tax to create a visible competitive advantage. Examples are Delaware's corporate income tax structure and Tennessee's personal income tax structure.[12]

IMPROVES QUALITY OF LIFE FOR CITIZENRY

A globally competitive community pursues and monitors, with local business support, an inclusive vision of quality of life so that citizens of all ages and incomes can participate in educational, recreational, civic, and cultural dimensions of local life.

When a manufacturing company weighs expanding an existing facility or moving to a new plant site, the tie-breaking factors between otherwise equal candidate communities are often

- Cost of living
- Housing
- Crime
- Environment
- Education at all levels
- Climate and geography
- Commuting times and congestion
- Recreation
- Entertainment and cultural offerings.

Taken together, these factors measure a community's livability or quality of life.

Because quality of life is in the eyes of diverse beholders, it's easy for communities to talk the talk without really walking the walk. New Brunswick, New Jersey, reached that conclusion more than 20 years ago, creating nonprofit New Brunswick Tomorrow (NBT) to spur urban revitalization and actually measure its progress. NBT's tenets are summarized here:

- Know our history, in order to deal with the present and plan for the future.
- Maintain the "unity of purpose" to which the public, private and community partners are committed.

- Continue the measurement of our efforts through unique methods such as the biennial ... surveys of community perceptions and concerns.
- Strengthen our holistic model — for only by meeting the needs of the whole person through the entire life cycle will we become a community that is economically strong, socially progressive and caring and healthy.[13]

Rutgers University conducts random-sample telephone surveys to measure New Brunswick's success. The 101-page report from the last sounding covers the downtown business district; housing, parking, and schools; social services and health care; and quality of life generally. It includes graphs reporting answers to such questions as "How much influence does Johnson & Johnson have in what happens in New Brunswick?" ("Too much" crested back in 1988; "Right amount" reached an all-time high in 1994.)

When local manufacturers are responsive to 21st-century environmental standards, older localities can become "walking cities" again. For example, in Laguna West, the "lake community" near Sacramento, residents stroll to Apple's largest Macintosh factory, which is soon to be joined by a consumer electronics plant. To make walking to work a possibility in more communities, the Ohio Housing Research Network recommends amending IRS Code Section 1034 that governs homeseller capital gains. At present, sellers can't move down in price — a benefit of moving back into cities — without incurring a tax penalty.

The Chesapeake Bay Foundation of Annapolis, Maryland, and the Environmental Defense Fund studied ways to reduce sprawl in the Chesapeake Bay watershed. They point out the benefits for residents of improving conditions for walking, bicycling, and taking public transportation, and they also list several benefits for business:

• Businesses in compact communities that are well served by a variety of transportation modes can access large market areas.

• More intensive use of land and building space, greater sharing of common facilities, and more efficient public services can reduce business costs.

• Businesses will need fewer parking spaces if visitors use public transit or walk.

• Employees using public transit will be less affected by highway congestion and inclement weather.

Noting that "trends are not destiny," the study observes that sprawl is the result of a long-term accumulation of public policy decisions. Changing direction will take time and communitywide commitment to two steps. The first is creating an alternative vision of community health based on jobs and housing proximity, a light-rail and busway transit network, travel demand management, growth boundaries, and regional cooperation and coordination. The second step is developing a plan of action for realizing the new vision.

PARTICIPATES IN REGIONAL PLANNING AND CONSOLIDATION

A globally competitive community participates in good faith in regional planning and consolidation initiatives to ensure that jurisdictional boundaries don't inhibit areawide economic growth or the cost-efficient delivery of services to the private sector.

A business alliance in Somerset County, New Jersey, encouraged the county and the 21 municipalities within it to share common services. As of 1994, the jurisdictions had the same database and could begin to share services. The community of Somerville, by hiring the county to provide engineering services, saved money and advanced more projects.

Transportation and land use were the overarching concerns that prompted areawide cooperation in Portland, Oregon. In 1979, Portland area governments banned development outside a boundary ringing the city. Voters established Metro, the country's first elected regional government, and gave it control over planning for three counties and 24 municipalities. Freeway appropriations were channeled into better bus service and a new light-rail system. Since 1979, the number of downtown jobs has doubled without a need to build or widen roads or add parking.

Modern manufacturing depends so much on coordinating decentralized production that manufacturers prize consistency in their operating environment. Nothing dramatizes the importance of regional cooperation better than the mere existence of Silicon Valley Joint Venture. When computer industries began to choose Texas, Oregon, Utah, and Virginia instead of Silicon Valley for newer factories, Joint Venture was formed to keep the region competitive by responding to the needs of high-tech industry. In the words of one CEO, "Without this change, San Jose would not have been chosen as our headquarters site. You have to have the city, the county, the state, and the private sector all singing from the same sheet."[14]

PROMOTES ACCESS TO DEBT/EQUITY CAPITAL

A globally competitive community encourages local and regional sources of capital to assist economic development by making expansion loans to innovative smaller manufacturers and other qualified applicants that are poised for more growth.

Local governments can be more than bystanders when lending decisions retard the pace of job creation. For example, a 1993 survey by the American Bankers Association revealed that 83 percent of smaller banks declined to make loans where there were questions of environmental liability. In a globally competitive community, leadership anticipates this problem and seeks corrective action both legislatively and with technical assistance from an organization like Clean Sites, making it easier for local banks to support growth.

Development strategies that call for methodically building clusters of interrelated companies also can be reassuring to local lenders. Not every jurisdiction can win a huge new manufacturing plant, but an "anchor" facility of any size will authenticate future directions. Such a facility gives banks a context in which to weigh loans to companies that will be part of the anchor's corp of suppliers.

Chicago's South Shore Bank, a national model of community development banking, has created the Austin Enterprise Center and the Austin Labor Force Intermediary (ALFI) in that city's Austin neighborhood. The center provides bank and nonbank capital to smaller manufacturers, of which there are hundreds in the area, along with workshops on procurement and quality. ALFI coordinates the output of local family service and employment training organizations. South Shore's objective is to upgrade the skills of residents so that these employers will want to hire them.

During 1994, South Shore's affiliates in Chicago, Cleveland, Michigan's Upper Peninsula, and elsewhere made 384 enterprise expansion loans totaling $28.4 million. They counseled 160 companies on planning, plant modernization, and financial management. This observation is taken from 24-year-old Shorebank Corporation's annual report: "Sharp cash flow analysis and character judgment are critical supplements to collateral valuation: they enable Shorebankers to convert ensured deposits into investments in the growth of small firms, recognized worldwide as the starting point for successful job creation."[15]

Communities anywhere can learn and spread the word about nonbank sources of capital. "When I needed money two years ago," recalls a small manufacturer in Connecticut, "it was the state of Connecticut that finally provided me a loan. Recent bank failures had dried up the conventional local sources. I'm afraid that if newer businesses must finance their growth only from savings and earnings, they may not be able to add jobs at the stage when that should be possible for them."

The Enterprise Florida Capital Partnership was set up in 1994 to improve the relative availability of private risk capital and commercial lending for the manufacturing sector. The partnership is increasing the flow of debt and equity capital to smaller Florida companies by two means. First, its Florida Development Finance Corporation provides creditworthy manufacturers with financing up to $2.5 million under terms generally difficult for Florida's existing financial service institutions to provide. The loan portfolio is financed through tax-exempt bonds. Second, the partnership's $31 million Cypress Equity Fund provides Florida's most promising technology companies with direct access to national venture capital firms.

Beyond institutional sources of capital there are elusive "self-made, high-networth individuals," according to the University of New Hampshire's Center for Venture Research. Their money and perspective, argues Jeffrey Sohl, director of the Durham-based center, are among America's underused economic resources. Research conducted by the center confirms that "business angels" are interested in pace-setting new technology firms. Drawn to start-up companies close to home, angels "appear to have longer exit horizons and less risk aversion than venture capital funds."[16]

BUILDS PUBLIC SUPPORT
FOR ECONOMIC GROWTH

A globally competitive community cosponsors promotional initiatives to build support for economic growth, entrepreneurship, and careers in manufacturing, and to lay groundwork for "aftercare" attention to the newer employers attracted to the area.

Community competitiveness is a frame of mind as well as a range of incentives. Vision from elected and appointed officials is critical. Yet vision at the top can't prevail if citizens don't support new directions in policy and new priorities in spending. For every jurisdiction that is steadily rebuilding after a military base closure, there's an outwardly identical place still seeking consensus on its economic objectives.

Reshaping community culture is even more challenging than transforming corporate culture. Manufacturers understand this. What helps, they say, is local commitment to a plan for informing citizens about how economic growth occurs. When CEOs were asked about workforce readiness by the National Association of Manufacturers and the U.S. Department of Labor, they said they need a fundamental shift in attitudes toward growth and manufacturing to attract the next generation of talent.[17]

Baltimore's Regional Manufacturing Institute hosts awareness breakfasts for educators and community leaders. The St. Louis Regional Commerce and Growth Association bestows Entrepreneur of the Year awards. The Economic Development Association of Longmont, Colorado, showcases local companies every other month. Georgians for Manufacturing stages an observance reminiscent of Minnesota Manufacturing Week. Florida marks Industry Appreciation Week to acknowledge that job-creating manufacturers also provide funds to meet government priorities such as public health care, criminal justice, and education.

A program called "Esprit" was launched by the Boulder, Colorado, Development Commission a dozen years ago to "celebrate Boulder County's amazing entrepreneurial spirit." Primary criteria for Esprit Entrepreneur of the Year and Esprit Entrepreneurs of Distinction include the founding of a business, that business's current profitability, unusual growth or staying power in adversity, and "vision fraught with risk." There's an awards banquet and media coverage, and the winning founder and CEOs lead plant tours. Boulder's educational initiative makes a point of keeping the media focused on companies that make a difference locally.

Cities need to celebrate "committed companies" as one way of attracting others, says Martha A. O'Mara, professor at Harvard University's Graduate School of Design. O'Mara, who studies how information age corporations select sites, explains that as the pace of competitive change increases, companies want to collocate all core management and technical functions more swiftly than they once did. Because these firms prefer attractive support systems and amenities already in place, "this may help make urban locations more competitive in the future."[18]

Finally, globally competitive communities make provision for "aftercare" and take it seriously. Aftercare is the economic development equivalent of legislative oversight: revisiting agreements to keep them on track. "Deals that are struck must actually be survivable by the parties," notes David L. Johnson of Baker and Daniels, an Indianapolis law firm that represents manufacturers entering communities. For example, don't assume a company knows that when incentive dollars come from public sources there must be public bidding on construction contracts.

Charting Your Community's Course

How can you know whether this list of concerns is valid for your community? A great deal of parallel evidence authenticates the overall thrust of the National Association of Manufacturers/Partners study reported here, but you may wish to replicate this study in your own community.

Community analysis and redirection can seem too big a task to undertake. Should the community start by surveying infrastructure needs, by developing a new industrial park, or by designing a school-to-work program?

It may be helpful to note the following characteristics, which most often influence success in communitywide collaboration:

• Mutual respect, understanding, and trust
• An appropriate cross-section of members
• Open and frequent communication
• Sufficient funding to support the endeavor
• A convener with interpersonal skills and fairness
• A history of collaboration in the community
• Members who see self-interest in collaboration
• Members with a stake in the process and outcome.[19]

Choosing the first steps toward achieving global competitiveness may not be as important as keeping the above principles in mind. A community might even recruit and train volunteer process leaders, and then ask them to fashion a two-way process for addressing economic growth and job creation.

Notes

1. Mike Fitzgerald, "State of Washington Development Strategy," Washington State Department of Community, Trade and Economic Development, 1996.

2. Greater Tucson Economic Council, *Tucson: The Future's Frontier* (Tucson, AZ: Tucson Office of Economic Development, n.d.).

3. "Consumer Expenditure Survey" (Washington, D.C.: U.S. Bureau of Labor Statistics, December 1992).

4. East County Economic Development Council, "The Economic Adjustment of Small Defense-Related Firms in the East County Region of San Diego County: Analysis and Prototype," La Mesa, California, December 1994, p. 13.

5. "Investing in Our Workforce" (Washington, D.C.: Competitiveness Policy Council, 1993), p. 13.

6. Stuart A. Rosenfeld, *Competitive Manufacturing: New Strategies for Regional Development* (Piscataway, NJ: Center for Urban Policy Research, 1992), p. 1.

7. Richard Florida and Timothy McNulty, "High Performance Economic Development: New Strategies for the New Economy," *Economic Development Commentary* (Spring 1995): 22–29.

8. Colorado Health Advisory Network for Governmental Efficiency, Task Force on Incentives for Pollution Reduction/Prevention, "The Change Incentives Task Force's Proposal for a Colorado Environmental Leadership Program," February 12, 1996, pp. 1–10.

9. Charles Bartsch, "The Role of Utilities in Community Development," *Community Economic Development: Building Capacity Through Stronger Partnerships*, ed. Jenny Murphy (Washington, D.C.: National Council for Urban Economic Development Information Service, 1988), pp. 8–10.

10. National Association of Manufacturers Board of Directors, "Resolution on Growth and Taxes," Washington, D.C., February 10, 1996.

11. Maryland Economic Development Commission, *Strategic Directions for Increasing Maryland's Competitiveness*, report to Gov.

Parris H. Glendening, Maryland Department of Business and Economic Development, 1995.

12. Ibid.

13. John L. Heldrich, New Brunswick Today, Annual Report, 1995.

14. Peter Mills, U.S. Display Consortium.

15. Shorebank Corporation, Annual Report, 1994, pp. 10–11.

16. John Freear, Jeffrey E. Sohl, and William B. Wetzel, Jr., "Angels and Non-Angels: Are There Differences?" *Journal of Business Venturing* (1994): 109.

17. "The Smart Workplace: Developing High-Performance Work Systems," a report to the members of the National Association of Manufacturers, Washington, D.C., November 1994.

18. Martha O'Mara, "Strategy, Location and the Changing Corporation: How Information Age Organizations Make Site Selection Decisions," report sponsored by the Real Estate Research Institute, 1996.

19. Partners for Livable Communities, "In Pursuit of Livability: A Strategic Planning Cooperative," preliminary report, Washington, D.C., 1996.

5. THE DIFFERENCE BETWEEN ECONOMIC DEVELOPERS AND PLANNERS

Timothy W. Gubala

The average citizen would think that the purposes and goals of local government for comprehensive planning and economic development are synonymous. In practice, the reverse often seems true. Economic developers complain that planners hold up site plan reviews of industrial projects over trivial matters such as requiring the planting of shrubs for landscaping or screening of dumpsters. Planners charge that economic developers circumvent in areas not envisioned for development. The argument goes on; the sides are drawn and internal department conflicts occur in local government buildings and courthouses across the country.

Planners and economic developers have roles that are in conflict due to basic differences in attitude, perspective and approach to business that perpetuates conflictual relations with each other.

But the picture is not hopeless. There are opportunities for team building that allow both professions to achieve their goals and work together. Out of the conflicts come problem solving techniques that will benefit the community.

Whose Vision of the Community?

A community's Comprehensive or Master Plan sets forth the long range goals and objectives for land use, transportation, housing and public facilities. This plan is prepared either by a planner employed by the local government, a regional planning agency or private consultants. The public reviews the plan during citizen workshops or public hearings. A series of maps and printed reports is prepared that describes the future community. Recommendations for implementation and action are referenced and are given priorities.

The plan may be considered current but most likely, it was prepared more than five years ago. A 1990 Virginia publication

From Economic Development Review, *Vol. 10, No. 2, Summer, 1992. Published by the American Economic Development Council, Rosemont, Illinois. Reprinted with permission of the publisher. Copyright 1992, all rights reserved.*

showed that 73 of 135 (55%) cities and counties had plans that were adopted before 1985.[1] The community's adopted vision lags behind the actual pressures for additional industrial land, roads and public water and sewer improvements.

The adopted plan reflects the attitudes of the community. Public services boundaries may be officially delineated by means of an urban service boundary. Beyond this line, urban activities are discouraged. Economic development areas are depicted by commercial or industrial designations.

To the economic developer, the plan may be a document conceived in the past and out of date with the reality of what the prospect wants.

The local government economic developer has a mission of attracting new business and industry. He may be involved in identifying and developing separate industrial sites as well as parks. All sites identified for industrial use may not be shown on the comprehensive plan. Planners regard this as illogical and irresponsible.

Economic developers see it as a normal procedure to create an inventory of sites and begin the long term process for rezoning, extending utilities or improving access.

The issue is whom, specifically which professional, should make the determination about the designation of land for industrial use. Is this a selfish "turf fight" or a serious question that requires an answer in communities?

What does light industrial mean? If the Comprehensive Plan is the fabric of a community's future, then the zoning ordinance is the structure. Every economic developer wants an inventory of industrial zoned land. Or do we? A study of zoning for cities and counties in Virginia in 1990 showed that 125 of 136 localities (81%) have a zoning ordinance adopted or revised before 1985.[2] Zoning definitions,

standards and requirements reflect the era of the 1950s with "light" and "heavy" industrial districts. Automobile graveyards and petroleum storage are allowed alongside laboratories and electronic assembly facilities. Since most zoning ordinances follow a Euclidean Standard (i.e., each zoning district includes uses allowed in the lesser intense district, such as commercial uses allowed in industrial), a variety of uses may be permitted in the most intense industrial district. Unwanted land uses need to be stated somewhere in the zoning ordinance, and preferably restricted in any zoning district adjacent to a residential area.

When the economic developer brings forward an industrial prospect such as a robotics manufacturer, a thermoplastics company or a maker of ceramic chip capacitors, the planner looks through the schedule of permitted uses in the industrial zoning district to determine if the particular use is permitted. He/she may make an interpretation that would allow these uses to go into one or more industrial districts. He/she may determine that a zoning amendment is needed to allow the use or he/she may refer to a quasi-judicial body such as a Board of Zoning Appeals to make an interpretation. The economic developer would hope that a favorable interpretation could be made to allow these uses rather than face an extended time period for public hearings, review and a determination on a zoning amendment. If the latter occurs, the prospects will be seeking a community that has zoning in place or flexible interpretation procedures.

Planners and economic developers are aware of the Office of Management and Budget guidelines known as the Standard Industrial Classification (SIC) Manual.[3] The entire field of economic activity is included and divided into groups and divisions by means of a numerical designation of two, three and four digit numbers.

The system is more detailed and inclusive than the district uses of the typical zoning ordinance. Economic developers routinely refer to the SIC Manual in targeting and identifying prospects. Planners find the SIC Manual less useful than the economic developer because impact measures such as noise, separation of hazardous waste and traffic cannot be assigned by SIC numerical designations. At best, planners use the SIC Manual as a reference while economic developers may use it more as a "Bible."

Process vs. Product. Planning is a process and not an end in itself. It is continuous, ongoing and dynamic. Concepts such as inventory and analysis, goal setting, and the development of alternatives are indicative of the planning process. The object of preparing a plan and having it adopted is not as important as the process whereby the community is involved and accepts the plan. Once a planning process is established, it is used continuously to review and comment on planning-related issues facing a community, such as a zoning ordinance revision, a controversial rezoning or a capital improvement plan. Planners will use a successful process as a model to review economic development proposals even if economic developers do not agree that this is the best method.

Economic developers are product-oriented. They seek to close the deal, locate the prospect and get going on the next project. Activity is sales-driven. Dollars of new investment, jobs created and acres developed are some of the measures by which economic developers evaluate their success. If there is any emphasis on process for economic developers, it is short-range and aimed at achieving a goal that will improve the product that the local community has to offer.

Product development is a goal that encompasses site development, image enhancement and identification and improvement of the community's quality of life. Local economic developers find themselves viewing the community in a broader sense, focusing on areas that need improvement to make them into assets. In doing so, they cross over into areas traditionally viewed as being in the realm of planning, such as determining priorities for capital improvement projects. The goal of product development comes into conflict with the planning process because of timing and plan compliance issues.

Specificity vs. Flexibility. Daily, planners rely on comprehensive (or master) plans and ordinances to assist them in performing their job. Tasks such as reviewing site plans for building permits and evaluating concept plans for rezonings cause planners to apply standards and policies outlined in ordinances and plans. This review process creates conflict between economic developers and planners. An individual business, flushed with the publicity of a recently announced building expansion or location decision, often faces the realities of its decisions as the company enters the development review process. "Bureaucracy" is the mildest term used to describe the procedures that a business must go through to comply with local government codes, ordinances, and standards. In order to obtain a building permit, applicants must first show "on paper"—on the site plan—provisions for parking (including handicapped spaces), landscaping, screening of dumpsters, location and area of all signs and truck loading/unloading spaces. Innocuous enough, but the interpretation of the regulations by individual planners is as varied as night and day; economic developers each have "horror stories" about planners applying specific regulations to a business location and threatening to withhold the issuance of a Building Permit or Certificate of Occupancy until these regulations are met.

Economic developers want the widest

latitude in interpretation of ordinances and standards. The Comprehensive Plan of the community which shows "long range recommendations for the general development of the jurisdiction"[4] is used to back up zoning ordinance decisions for specific parcels of land. In some jurisdictions, the Comprehensive Plan has become a document "formed in concrete" and is considered inflexible to proposals for change. The plan must be amended by a rezoning applicant. The general document then becomes specific and the focus of planning dwells on the site rather than the community as a whole.

It is becoming commonplace to regard a community planner as that professional who applies ordinances and codes to development proposals. Planners risk becoming so site-specific that they lose their vision of the community. They become truly engrossed in the "shrubs and trees" of a site plan rather than the larger community as a whole.

Incentives. As part of the effort to sell the community, local economic developers continually seek out incentives for businesses to relocate, expand or enlarge their local capital investment. These may take the form of tax abatements, free land, rent-free clauses for industrial buildings or connections to public water and sewer. These may supplement state incentives for industrial training, construction of highway improvements or additional tax abatement and financing programs.

Incentives are committed up front and evolve as a part of the confidential location process. When they become public, these incentives may conflict with existing master plans and capital improvement budgets. An industrial location may cause water and sewer lines to be extended to a site that is not envisioned for growth within the time frame of the plan or capital improvement budget. This would affect the growth potential of adjacent proper-

ties resulting in a conflict between the planners and the master plan, on the one hand, and economic developers and prospect location on the other.

Sometimes commitments for a change in a zoning district, a variance for the height of an accessory use or a promise of an "expedited" building permit are made to a prospect. This infuriates the planner who believes that the process of planning has been violated. The community has no input, no influence on the project, if economic developers make promises ahead of time. Expediting a building permit may be done, but planning staff feel pressured and may more closely scrutinize plans to be certain that everything strictly conforms with codes.

Opportunities for Team Building

With the range of potential roles in conflict between planners and economic developers, it is a wonder that businesses ever locate in a community. The impetus for ending conflicts may come from the public disclosure of internal conflicts from a dissatisfied business owner or from a self-imposed truce. In any case, the economic developer can provide for leadership and take the initial steps to resolve conflicts with planners. There is an opportunity for joint resolution of conflicts and problems between the professionals that will provide opportunities for team building.

The economic development strategy. Economic development planning occurs separately from the Comprehensive/Master Plan process. Many communities today have developed and adopted a strategic plan for economic development. This is the "process by which an organization envisions the future and develops the necessary procedures and operations to achieve that future."[5] (Note that strategic planning is process-oriented.) Further, strategic planning for economic development is the process by which an area's resources are allocated and used in accordance with an overall program designed to maintain, diversify and or expand the economic base of the community.[6]

Given the background of planning in a community, there is an opportunity to develop a strategic plan for economic development that supports the adopted Comprehensive Plan. Consultants and businesses evaluating a community routinely ask for a copy of the Comprehensive/Master Plan and Ordinances. Making a copy of an adopted Economic Development Strategy available as well, demonstrates the community's commitment to economic development.

The ideal team-building scenario would have the economic developer prepare an Economic Development Strategy that references and or complements the adopted community Master Plan. The planner and the economic developer can work together to prepare a document that serves their joint needs and, since the documents will most likely have been adopted at different times, the Strategy may serve as an interim document that points out proposed or recommended changes in the Plan, making it more supportive of local economic development issues.

A Strategic Plan is implemented by means of an annual work plan or action plan that sets forth specific tasks to be accomplished in economic development. Since this action plan may directly conflict with an adopted Comprehensive/Master Plan that is out of date, close coordination with the planner is critical for achieving positive results.

Involvement. Planners pride themselves on their ability to involve various segments of the community in the planning process. The traditional public hearing has become the final formal step before an elected governing body adopts a new Comprehensive Plan. Most of the negotiations, compromise and input occur months before at the staff level, in committee meetings and during community workshops with the citizens. This is the time frame during which economic developers should be involved. Opportunities to change plans, ordinances and standards exist while they are still draft proposals. Later, the adoption and approval process becomes more formalized and opportunities for change become less likely.

The economic developer must rely upon contacts in the business community to assist in influencing the drafting of ordinance proposals. For instance, in communities where separate study committees are used, a proposed sign ordinance should seek outdoor advertising representatives to review the draft. Comprehensive/Master Plan updates may be presented to the local Chamber of Commerce as part of the adoption process. A zoning ordinance revision that affects commercial and industrial uses may be improved by having commercial realtors comment on the draft before its adoption.

Since planning is a public process, the economic developer has a responsibility to ask questions about the changes being proposed and how he/she and the business community can be involved. Local government planners see the entire community as their clientele but do not know how to involve the business community as a specific interest group. Getting the business community involved in the public planning process is both a challenge and opportunity for the local economic developer.

On being an ombudsman. Economic developers recognize that up to 80% of the new jobs in a community are created by existing business. This job creation is not a spontaneous process; it requires conscientious efforts and commitments from community leadership. The role best suited for the local economic developer is that of "ombudsman."[7]

There are difficulties with site development plan approvals, building permits, business licenses, rezonings, variances, utility connections, assessments and taxes and public safety that cause business to be in conflict with local government. The economic developer must learn to cut through the "red tape," to expedite plans and permits and solve problems for business.

Where business expansions are handled in a professional manner by local government, the positive relationship contributes to the business being satisfied with the community. If businesses have a poor opinion of local government, the word travels and the community is labeled as anti-business. That counters efforts by the economic developer to attract out-of-area prospects.

Local economic developers can "take care of business" by becoming problem solvers. They establish an existing industry program firmly seeking out the issues and concerns that business has with local government regulations. Rather than complain about the planners, the economic developer works to understand the codes and ordinances, the standards required and the procedures by which development occurs in the community. He/she builds rapport with the regulatory agencies of local government. Then the economic developer can assist a project by understanding the problem, explaining the procedure to resolve it and or describing the alternatives. He/she will be recognized in the business community as someone who is a problem solver, and in the long run, becomes recognized as the person to handle opportunities.

Public-private partnerships. The ultimate opportunity for team building between economic developers and planners is the formation of a public-private partnership. This concept involves the design of a joint project between the local government and the private sector. A good example is a site development project that involves the extension of public water and sewer and the construction of a new access road to a privately owned industrial site to attract a new company.

The planner and the economic developer must work together to accomplish the project. When both are committed and have ownership in the project, the team concept is strengthened. Public-private partnerships enable the planner, as a public official, to understand the calculated benefits and payback from incentives offered by the developer and apply his/her knowledge of economic impact analysis techniques. By working together, the impact measures and public benefits can be determined and the project supported.

Through his/her contacts with the planners, the local economic developer can gain access to the arena of grants. Even though federal grant programs have decreased, the states have taken over grant administration. Economic developers can apply for the limited grant funds and programs available to support projects that aid product development. For instance, in Virginia, funds for site planning and development are available from the State Community Development Block Grant program.

The economic developer should understand the grant process, the role and support that the planner can lend, and the relationship of these grants to the overall community Comprehensive Plan.

Conclusion

Local government planners and economic developers need not exist as separate office entities. Although conflicts will occur, they must learn to overcome differences and work together to solve problems.

The two professional groups can work together to develop a vision of the community that includes both the long range elements of the Comprehensive or Master Plan and the short range action agenda set forth in the Economic Development Strategy. The two documents can complement each other and present the community in a positive and progressive manner to both prospects and existing businesses.

Regulatory reform can be accomplished with less conflict if the planners and economic developers can openly share observations, concepts and ideas that support the community vision established in the Plan and Economic Development Strategy. Definitions of zoning, descriptions of industrial uses and standards for site plan review can be updated and amended together. An approach of openness and joint problem-solving will more quickly resolve a zoning question than one of conflict and confrontation.

Being an "ombudsman" means that the economic developer becomes a vocal and visible contact within local government for the business community. He/she can use his/her internal contacts to obtain information, route requests for services and resolve issues before they become problems. By working within the governmental structure, the economic developer can be positive force affecting the success of the community's economic development program. The economic developer can find the balance between economic opportunities and regulation of development.

Economic developers are aware of the financing gaps faced by businesses as they seek private financing for building expansions, new construction and purchases of capital equipment. Planners' skills in obtaining grants and loans can be of benefit to the developer who is preparing an application package for state funds or providing supporting documentation for a company's application for financing from a lender. The justifications, impacts and benefits of economic development can be shown by economic developers through public-private partnerships.

The issues of economic development provide opportunities for team building between the two professions. Through the team concept, the goal of improving the community can be achieved. From the diffrent perspectives of the economic developer and planner, the team can achieve the vision of the community.

Notes

1. "Directory of Local Planning in Virginia 1990," Planning Assistance Office, Department of Housing and Community Development, Richmond, Virginia, 1990.

2. Ibid.

3. *Standard Industrial Classification Manual.* Executive Office of the President, Office of Management and Budget, U.S. Government Printing Office, Washington, D.C., 1987.

4. "Local Planning Legislation," Office of Local Development Programs, Department of Housing and Community Development. Reprint from the Code of Virginia of 1950 and 1986 Cumulative Supplement, The Michie Company, Charlottesville, Virginia, 1986.

5. Goodstein, Leonard D., et al. "Applied Strategic Planning: A New Model for Organizational Growth and Vitality." *Strategic Planning: Selected Readings* (San Diego: University Associates, 1986), p. 2.

6. Kolzow, David R., "Strategic Planning for Economic Development," American Economic Development Council, Rosemont, Illinois, 1988.

7. A Swedish word for a government official or representative who investigates complaints, reports, findings and helps achieve an equitable settlement.

PART II

The Process of Renewal

6. A NEW APPROACH TO MANAGING GROWTH

Maryann Froehlich

Competing demands are a daily fact of life for local governments. Simultaneously maintaining great schools and low taxes, good transportation and clean air, rising property values and affordable housing are just a few of the balancing acts that local governments are expected to perform. The field of development embodies these tensions. Development can create a better tax base, provide jobs and amenities for residents, and enhance a community's livability. It also can add to traffic problems, disrupt neighborhoods, and detract from the character of the community. To avoid the pitfalls and to capture development's benefits, local governments are increasingly turning to the policy of "smart growth."

Smart growth invests time, attention, and resources in restoring community and vitality to center cities and older suburbs. New growth is more town-centered and transit- and pedestrian-oriented; includes a greater mix of housing, commercial, and retail users; and preserves open space and other environmental amenities. Examples are springing up in communities across the United States.

Portland, Oregon, with its longstanding urban growth boundary and well-developed transit system, is one of the best-known and most frequently cited examples of smart growth. A recent groundswell of efforts around the country has been changing development patterns for the better. Over the past 18 months, 11 cities in California have enacted urban growth boundaries.

The city of Fort Collins, Colorado, is expediting permitting for exemplary developments with superior environmental performance. Charleston, South Carolina, is creating dispersed affordable housing that actually revitalizes neighborhoods and spurs private investment. Lancaster, California, is encouraging investment in town by reducing development impact fees. And the city of St. Louis, St. Louis County, and the state of Missouri are using their new transit system, Metrolink, as a potential focus for new development.

Originally published as "Smart Growth: Why Local Governments Are Taking a New Approach to Managing Growth in Their Communities," Public Management, *Vol. 80, No. 5, May, 1998. Published by the International City/County Management Association, Washington, D.C. Reprinted with permission of the publisher.*

This movement is not about no-growth, or even slow growth. People want the jobs, tax revenues, and amenities that come with development. But they want these benefits without degrading the environment, raising local taxes, worsening traffic congestion, or busting budgets. More and more local governments are finding that current development patterns and practices often fail to provide this balance.

The Right Time for Smart Growth?

In communities across the nation, there is a growing concern that current development patterns— dominated by what some call "sprawl"— are no longer in the long-term interest of our cities, existing suburbs, small towns, rural communities, or wilderness areas. Though supportive of growth, communities are questioning the economic costs of abandoning infrastructure in the city, only to rebuild it farther out. They are questioning the social costs of the mismatch between new employment locations in the suburbs and the available workforce in the city.

They are questioning the wisdom of abandoning brownfields in older communities, eating up the open space and prime agricultural lands at the suburban fringe, and polluting the air of an entire region by forcing more people to drive to get anywhere. Spurring the movement for smart growth are demographic shifts, a strong environmental ethic, increased fiscal concerns, and more nuanced views of growth than in the past. The result is both a new demand and a new opportunity for smart growth.

Demographics and Preferences

Consumer preferences change as demographics and values change. A demographic study by the marketing firm American LIVES indicates a growing desire for community, open space, and town-centered living, with less reliance on the automobile. Demographic shifts underlie and support these trends. The phrase "typical family"— meaning a married couple with children — described 40 percent of all households a generation ago; it now accounts for only 26 percent.

Homebuyers are getting older, too. A third of the homebuying market is over the age of 45. In surveys published by the National Association of Home Builders, most of this market segment wanted to live in communities with a diversity of ages and thus a diversity of housing sizes and types. Three of their top four location priorities were based on ease of transportation and access— to shopping, family and friends, and medical care.

And most of the mature homebuyers who intend to move will move to smaller houses with smaller yards, to reduce cleanup and yard work. Mature buyers' preferences, in combination with the overall trend in the United States toward smaller households, will mean a greater market for smaller houses on smaller lots, especially where density's perceived problems can be solved through smart design.

Environment

It seems that everywhere you look, from Portland, Oregon, to Portland, Maine, and from Toronto, Canada, to Miami, Florida, people are concerned about vanishing farmland and open space. Yet loss of open space is not an inevitable outcome of growth. Smart growth scenarios such as the New Jersey redevelopment plan show that a 43 percent reduction in the loss of open space can be achieved by better directing growth. Support for plans that preserve open space is evident. Open space initiatives and bond issues fared well on voters' ballots in the last national election and often have won support at the local level.

Water quality concerns also are affecting the development industry. Contaminated urban runoff increases as rainwater pours off newly constructed roofs, driveways, roads, and parking lots and into lakes, rivers, and bays. Increasingly, developers and local governments seek development designs that protect water resources. Town-style developments designed with stream buffers and lots of open space can cut runoff by over 40 percent, reducing contaminants and avoiding potentially costly upgrades at the local treatment plant. Projected treatment-plant cost savings drove New York City and upstate New York to an agreement sharply curtailing development in upstate watersheds.

Time, Air Quality, and Traffic Congestion

Getting stuck in traffic is a ubiquitous phenomenon in America. In fact, Americans lose more than 1.6 million hours a day mired in traffic. And delays only are expected to lengthen, as traffic congestion is projected to get worse. For a suburban mother interviewed by the *Wall Street Journal*, the cost of being stuck in traffic is already high. Asked what social reform would most improve her quality of life, she replied, "Lower the driving age to 10." She had put 40,000 miles on her minivan in the previous 18 months by ferrying her three kids around the suburbs.

Costs to the nation also are high. Traditional fixes—involving building more roads—seem to be less effective. Congestion levels have risen an average of more than 22 percent between 1982 and 1994 (just under two percent per year) according to a 10-year study recently completed

by the Texas Transportation Institute. Many localities have experienced a much greater increase in congestion during this time, including two with greater than three percent increases per year. Of the 50 cities in the study, only two (Houston and Phoenix) had lower congestion levels in 1994 than in 1982. Metropolitan planning organizations like the one in greater Washington, D.C., predict that even massive, costly building programs will only be able to slow the worsening of traffic conditions on area roads.

The connection among development patterns, transportation, and air quality is receiving increased attention. There is a growing recognition that the auto-oriented development patterns of the past 50 years have contributed to the need to drive more and farther. While Americans average 4,485 automobile-miles per person in 1970, this number increased to 6,330 miles per person in 1993, a 41 percent increase.

Between 1983 and 1990, almost every segment of U.S. society increased its trips and mileage. According to the national personal transportation survey conducted by the U.S. Department of Transportation during that time, the average trip for all purposes went from 8.68 to 9.45 miles. EPA's Office of Air and Radiation predicts that by the year 2005, growth in vehicle-miles traveled will begin to overtake the improvements in air quality gained from using cleaner fuels and less-polluting cars. In other words, after 30 years of steady improvement in air quality, we will begin to lose the battle because of burgeoning growth in automobile travel.

These trends are stimulating a search for development alternatives that will provide more choices, better accessibility, and less auto dependence. Advocates for alternative means of transportation believe that air quality, community livability, and transportation choice all can be improved through smart growth and through supporting transportation investments. This means that the traditional opponents of development are increasingly seeing development as part of the solution.

And local governments are agreeing, particularly when they have the opportunity to combine more intense, compact, mixed-use development with access to transit. Rail transit service is a new feature in a dozen cities, including St. Louis, Tampa, Salt Lake City, San Diego, and Dallas. An amazing 100 new transit project startups are currently proposed in the United States.

Fiscal Concerns

Fiscal conservatives and antitax groups have been increasingly vocal players in development debates. They object to the dynamic of subsidizing costly development at the fringe while previous investments in neighborhood infrastructure go underused or unmaintained. This phenomenon can be seen at work in the state of Maine: between 1970 and 1995, the state lost 27,000 students but spent $434 million on new schools in outlying locations. During this same period, school-bus costs rose from $8 million to $54 million, a 65 percent increase in inflation-adjusted dollars.

And in Prince William County, Virginia, officials estimate they collect about $2,100 a year in real estate and other taxes on the average house. That same house, however, costs the county $3,700 a year in services to its occupants.

Scattered development also can bring higher infrastructure and public capital costs as development takes place beyond the local service area. A major source of the higher costs for "leapfrog" developments is the need for longer trunk lines and connecting roads. The Urban Land Institute has reported that for residential de-velopments of three to five dwelling units per acre, which are located 10 miles away from the service area, utility costs are almost $10,000 per unit, compared to less than $5,000 for developments that are five miles away.

Concentrating development along service corridors or in a specific area can reduce costs. A study of the forms of similar land uses and levels of service in Florida, conducted by James Duncan and Associates, showed that public capital costs were between $16,000 and $17,000 per unit for corridor and nodal developments and almost $24,000 for scattered developments.

Another study of two alternative growth patterns in New Jersey conducted by the New Jersey Office of State Planning found that following the dispersed pattern of growth would cost approximately nine percent more in infrastructure capital costs than following a planned development pattern. Other studies have found similar outcomes.

Thus, while previous efforts to redirect growth have often been driven by a desire to protect open space and the environment, the new concern in many communities is increasingly about the fiscal impacts of development patterns.

Local Competition

To relieve fiscal pressures and bring in jobs, virtually every local government pursues what it calls economic development. According to former Pasadena (California) Mayor Rick Cole, in the vast majority of cases, what that essentially boils down to is sales tax development. Cities, particularly those in California, depend on sales tax revenue to pay the bills for police, fire, library, and other basic services.

Unfortunately for local governments, the escalating subsidy war is stealing more and more revenue from these services. For instance, in the past several years, New York City had provided subsidies to corporations to keep them from moving to New Jersey or Connecticut: $235 million to Chase Manhattan Bank, $98 million to the National Broadcasting Company, and $97 million to Citicorp. As long as one jurisdiction offers incentives, others must follow suit.

Local officials know that this type of competition often is a loser for the public. And more and more taxpayers are questioning it, too. Stadium bonds are facing tougher scrutiny, and local jurisdictions are seeking solider assurance that the promised jobs, taxes, and other benefits will materialize. But some jurisdictions have taken steps to make more fundamental change. They are seeing a common interest in ensuring the health of their nearby neighbors.

Minneapolis/St. Paul has an innovative tax base-sharing arrangement. Corporate executives in the Pittsburgh area have proposed a metro-wide sales tax, including the outer suburbs, to finance new riverfront development projects downtown. In greater Cleveland, a regional consortium of older suburbs has joined forces with the city, civic, and business leaders to lobby state officials to stop building new roads and start repairing older ones, and to push for legislation that would encourage families and businesses to reclaim vacant land near the urban center rather than undeveloped farmland farther away.

Projects at Loggerheads

Unease over current growth patterns has spread among suburbanites, environmentalists, fiscal conservatives, alternative-transportation advocates, and civic activists. As a result, pitched battles over approvals of new infrastructure and development projects have become more and more the norm.

Win or lose, developers and local advocates pay a higher and higher toll-in the form of lost time and piecemeal, ad hoc solutions that often fail to satisfy any group. Proposals to stop all growth, to cap property taxes permanently, and to close off schools to new residents have gained currency in some locales, illustrating one extreme of the spectrum of community reactions to growth.

Surprisingly, some good is coming out of this seemingly intractable impasse. Frustrated with the business-as-usual, project-by-project fighting that has prevailed, developers, fiscal conservatives, local governments, environmentalists, and suburbanites are finding common ground in the philosophy of smart growth.

No Special Formula

Smart growth shifts the terms of the debate away from the pro- and antigrowth context of the past. It seeks growth, recognizing the crucial role that development plays in maintaining and improving communities. But smart growth also acknowledges the fiscal, environmental, and other concerns that are dominating current discussions of growth, and it asks the fundamental question, not of whether to grow but of how to grow.

There is no one-size-fits-all formula for smart growth. It takes different forms in different communities. Smart growth, however, shows common features in each of the communities that have adopted it. Wherever it occurs, smart growth:

• Enhances a sense of community.
• Protects investment in existing neighborhoods.
• Provides a greater certainty in the development process.

• Protects environmental quality.
• Rewards developers with profitable products, financing, and flexibility.
• Decreases congestion by providing alternative modes of transportation.
• Makes efficient use of public money.

Following smart growth principles, developers, environmentalists, affordable housing providers, and alternative-transportation advocates are able to agree on a surprising range to development questions. The most consistent agreement occurs over the need to enable development that meets smart growth criteria — to make it easier to permit, easier to finance, and easier to build.

Many local governments have found that they play a crucial role in bringing barriers down and offering incentives for smart growth. For example, some communities have discovered that their zoning ordinances actually raise barriers to the type of growth they want to attract, requiring unnecessarily wide streets, deep setbacks, large lots, and excessive parking.

Ordinances often forbid mixing retail and commercial uses with residential ones. In addition to changing zoning, many local governments have had success in using tax increment financing, public/private partnerships, coordinated transportation and land use policies, and other approaches to encourage smart growth.

Although smart growth is not the answer in every locality, an increasing number of local governments are using it to create good neighborhoods, reduce traffic, and preserve open space. And, these localities are not only finding solutions. By encouraging development that serves the economy, the community, and the environment, they also are helping to build consensus and broad support among key community constituents.

7. MANAGING DOWNTOWN REVITALIZATION BY DISTRICT

Maureen Atkinson and John Williams

No downtown is a single, homogenous entity. Recognition of this simple fact is a key to the success of downtown revitalization efforts. The downtowns of almost all cities, especially those with populations greater than 50,000, are made up of distinct areas, each with its own special character. This character is formed around the specific consumer market segment the district serves. Usually, the tighter the focus, the greater the strength and health of the district.

The nodal character of downtowns allows the problem of "fixing" a declining downtown to be segmented. An apparently overwhelming challenge can be approached in small, manageable portions. Such a piecemeal approach is far preferable to large-scale schemes, which usually never get off the ground. Massive downtown revitalization schemes usually require enormous, unrequited infrastructure expenditures for the pacesetting project, are too large to manage, take too little account of market demand, and fail to enlist individual investors because these investors cannot see where they might fit into the scheme.

Planners, politicians, developers, and downtown business organizations must recognize the diverse nature of their downtowns and support this diversity. Development that is sympathetic to the character of its district helps that district flourish. Development that goes against the character usually suffers along with the district.

Downtown Districts

A typical downtown contains some of the following eight types of districts, and some larger downtowns may encompass them all.

The business district, universally present in cities. Large impressive buildings with entrances and lobbies designed to communicate an aura of strength characterize these precincts. The most successful kind of retail business is banking, and banks dominate the streetscape. Because these districts are unpopulated at night and on weekends, only certain kinds of retailers— personal and business services, vendors of service merchandise, restaurants and fast-food outlets, and occasionally men's wear stores—can do well.

From Urban Land, *Vol. 49, No. 9, September, 1990. Published by the Urban Land Institute, Washington, D.C. Reprinted with permission of the publisher.*

The mainstream shopping area, the old backbone of downtown. These are the districts that have been most affected, often devastated, by competition from suburban shopping centers. Nonetheless, some cities have managed to maintain healthy, competitive shopping districts with active department stores and other retailers. Many cities recognize that these areas will never again be as they were in "the good old days," but that they can be revitalized with a new specialty focus.

The avant-garde arts district, adding true interest and excitement to downtown. Arts districts tend to spring up in low-rent areas where large spaces are available. Often, old warehouse buildings are turned into artists' lofts, galleries, and work space for small, creative businesses. The arts node exhibits a colorful street life, as much because of the characters who frequent it as because of the kinds of businesses that cater to this clientele. The mainstay businesses are restaurants, cafes, secondhand stores, antique stores, and "starving designer" boutiques.

The cultural/entertainment district, usually centered around special attractions. Theaters, museums, or a stadium can anchor such a district, and the better they are related to the street, the better they can support ancillary activities. Restaurants typically do well in a cultural/entertainment district, and gift shops and upscale clothing stores can also thrive in many of these districts.

The visitor district, usually oriented toward a special attraction like a waterfront or a distinctive tourist attraction. The most successful visitor districts offer the tourist an out-of-the-ordinary, yet nonthreatening experience. Mainstay businesses in these districts include hotels, gift shops, fast-food outlets, and restaurants.

The upscale retail district, not found in every city. Its presence depends on the number of upper-income residents in the city, the physical condition of the downtown, and the presence of supporting facilities, such as cultural institutions. The kinds of businesses that tend to locate in an upscale retail district include designer apparel shops, expensive restaurants, antique stores, and interior designers' studios.

The low-end retail district, which may or may not be in run-down condition. Requirements for these bargain store districts include large store spaces, low rents, and good traffic. Pawnshops, discount retailers, and secondhand stores are the mainstay businesses for these areas. Warehouse retailers—of carpets, furniture, and office equipment—may also find these areas good locations, and shelters and social services facilities may be sited here. While often neglected by revitalization efforts, these districts are important to the lower-income shoppers and businesses they serve.

Ethnic districts, which emerge where concentrations of a particular ethnic group are found. Ethnic districts tend to be food-based, with the mainstay businesses being markets and restaurants. In areas with sufficiently large ethnic populations, import retailers will set up shop.

Although each area maintains its own distinct character, these various downtown nodes do not stand in isolation from one another. They relate to each other in different ways, for better or for worse. The best relationships are possible between two districts that serve the same clientele, like a business district and a traditional shopping district, or an arts district and a theater district. If such districts are adjacent, they can work together to expand the shopping, entertainment, and dining selection available to their overlapping customer bases.

Adjacent districts serving different clienteles will not contribute to one another's activity and may even clash. For example, the synergy between a business district and a tourist district will range from weak to nonexistent, because the markets they serve are so different. Also, the basically austere business district, symbolizing power, tends not to relate well physically to the lively, playful, colorful tourist district. Similarly, upscale shopping districts and low-end shopping (and low-income residential) districts relate badly. Their different clienteles feel uncomfortable in one another's territory, so little flow takes place between them.

The ideal configuration for the working-together of all of a downtown's nodes may be one in which the mainstream shopping area, which is able to relate well to most other nodes, occupies a central position with regard to the other districts. Toronto exemplifies such an ideal configuration. Norfolk, on the other hand, suffers some district configuration problems. But it does provide an example of a downtown seeking to revitalize itself step by step, focusing on strengthening one district without sacrificing the assets of others.

Downtown Toronto

Toronto's main shopping district centers on Yonge Street and includes the Eaton Centre, a successful 2.7 million-square-foot mall. When the Eaton Centre was built 10 years ago, many of the retailers on Yonge Street moved in, and the street experienced a decline. Yonge Street has pretty much recovered, but in the process its character has changed dramatically. Now, it focuses on leisure, casual food, and entertainment uses that complement the urban mall.

At the northern end of downtown, an upscale shopping district called Bloor/Yorkville stretches over more than 10 blocks. It is home to every well-known international designer located in the city, and adjacent to upmarket hotels and residential areas.

The Bay Street financial/business precinct, south of the mainstream shopping district, commands some of the highest office rents and enjoys one of the highest office occupancy rates in North America. An extensive underground shopping complex connects with the rapid transit and commuter rail systems. Large office lobbies and banks dominate the streets, which lack the ambience and uses that would attract people outside of office hours.

A theater/entertainment district west of the financial district includes the new Sky Dome, a giant sports stadium with a retractable roof; a 540-square-foot convention center; a 1,500-seat theater; and a 2,800-seat concert hall. The restaurant trade in this district thrives off both the lunchtime office workers' trade and the nighttime theatergoers' trade. An arts district to the north and west of the entertainment district offers residents and visitors off-beat designer fashion stores, restaurants, and nightclubs—an interesting alternative to mainstream shopping.

The working-together of these nodes has helped Toronto win a reputation as an interesting city. Office workers enjoy an attractive variety of choices of restaurants and shops, either along Yonge Street or in the entertainment district, while both retailing areas obtain extra support from the office-worker customer base. Yonge Street, the mainstream shopping and traffic artery that connects these nodes, offers middle-ground alternatives for everyone. The patrons of the destination facilities in the entertainment district often avail themselves of restaurants and cafes in the arts district, augmenting the latter district's customer base. In turn, the refreshing dining alternatives offered by arts district restaurateurs strengthens the appeal of a trip to a concert, a theater, or other facility in the entertainment district.

Downtown Norfolk

Norfolk's mainstream shopping district runs along Granby Street. Its vitality has been eroded by competition from suburban shopping centers and by the loss of its department stores. To the south, the traditional shopping district ends at City Hall Street, where the business district starts. To the north, at the upper end of the mainstream shopping district, a discount shopping district has come into being, anchored by a large sporting goods store and containing pawnshops and discount furniture businesses that have d veloped their own loyal clienteles. A relatively small upscale shopping node has developed on side streets off Granby Street. New restaurants and designer shops are bringing some vibrancy to this area, and its high-quality restaurants are serving customers from the business precinct.

Norfolk's waterfront visitor district centers around the 80,000-square-foot Waterside Festival Market, opened in 1983 and expanding this year to 120,000 square feet. The market connects to a 437-room hotel. Waterside's food court is patronized by a lunchtime crowd of office workers, who help to ensure the success of the festival market. But the tourists and regional visitors who come to Waterside provide little support to Granby Street shops because Waterside is cut off from Granby Street by a wide traffic artery, a parking garage, and the business district.

Norfolk is trying to turn Granby Street around, with most of its efforts focused on strengthening the business district as a customer base for the traditional retail on Granby Street. Thus, the city is encouraging office development in the business district and also supporting development of a hotel there to serve tourists, business travelers, and conference attendees. In other words, Norfolk has decided not to embark on a total redevelopment program, but to seek instead to enhance the success of the mainstream shopping district through a series of smaller programs building on the potential for synergy among the downtown's various districts.

Dealing with Reality

Careful planning and organization around the realities of a downtown's nodes—with the aim of building upon strong nodes, nurturing weak nodes, or minimizing barriers between nodes and maximizing synergy between them — is the most appropriate framework for downtown revitalization.

One important practical step is to encourage the formation of individual district business organizations, perhaps under the auspices of an overall downtown business organization. With organizations focusing on single nodes while also operating under a broader downtown mandate, a city can achieve a more active, diversified approach to revitalization. These more focused organizations are more able to deal with specific issues, issues affecting one block or neighborhood instead of all of the downtown. Instead of mixing small shopkeepers and bank CEOs, district organizations will generally be made up of neighbors with similar concerns; thus, they are better enabled to identify the real problems and practical solutions.

A planning and action framework based on downtown's districts helps a city take the distinctive character of its districts into account in its infrastructure and other programs. For example, focusing marketing programs on a district's specific customer base is a helpful approach. And business and retail recruitment can also be focused toward slotting retailers into the locations where they are most likely to find their target markets.

Managing the growth and revitalization

of a downtown by proceeding district by district may be a complex undertaking. But this kind of management is the way to deal with the reality of what a downtown is and should be encouraged to remain — a many-faceted marketplace reflecting the diversity of the city's population and activities. The management of downtown revitalization should focus on the varied needs of differing consumer and business segments, whether existing or potential. This is what marketing, development, and urban revitalization are all about.

8. CREATING AND USING SOCIAL CAPITAL

Josh S. Weston

What initiatives simultaneously utilize and enhance the problem-solving capacity of inner-city residents and institutions? What does inner-city revitalization look like from a *community-building* point of view?

Such questions can best be answered through illustrations of community-building activities in five problem-solving areas: expanding employment, revitalizing retailing, upgrading housing, ensuring public safety, and promoting youth development. These efforts can be contrasted with more traditional approaches that largely neglect the role of the community.

Expanding Employment

At the top of virtually every distressed neighborhood's agenda is more and better jobs for residents. Inadequate access to quality employment perpetuates poverty, discourages investment in education, and contributes to the hopelessness that encourages early pregnancy, drug use, crime, and gang involvement. The community-building approach emphasizes restoring the frequently weak connections between neighborhood residents and the world of work.

Often, traditional efforts in this direction involve development of jobs within distressed communities, for example, through tax incentives and other inducements for firms to locate a plant or office in an inner city. Unfortunately, these efforts often attract few employment opportunities to target neighborhoods, require large public expenditures or tax revenue losses for each job, and fuel zero-sum bidding wars for jobs among localities. Moreover, when jobs are produced, they often go to persons who commute into the neighborhood rather than to community residents. Failure to employ local residents usually reflects a combination of factors, including mismatches between job requirements and residents' skills, employers' distrust of neighborhood residents, and residents' lack of access to job contacts and information.[1]

Originally published as Chapter 3 of Rebuilding Inner-City Communities: A New Approach to the Nation's Urban Crisis, *1995. Published by the Committee for Economic Development, New York, New York. Reprinted with permission of the publisher.*

Well-designed initiatives to help inner-city residents find employment address these issues of skills, trust, and information and often connect residents to a broader range of jobs than those within their own communities. The majority of job opportunities for inner-city residents are located outside their neighborhoods. Inner-city job seekers, like the majority of American workers, should expect to commute to work. Moreover, jobs outside the inner city promote a mutual flow of information between distressed neighborhoods and mainstream society and create important social and interpersonal networks.

Whether targeting employment within inner cities or elsewhere, the community-building approach focuses on supplying the missing links between job seekers and opportunities. For example, some inner-city community development corporations (CDCs) have become owners or sponsors of businesses within their communities, such as fast-food outlets, health care providers, and housing rehabilitation contractors, that hire local residents. Other community-based organizations act as placement agencies, connecting residents to employers within the neighborhood or across the metropolitan area; by pre-screening job applicants, community intermediaries can often obtain the cooperation of employers too skeptical of the employability of community residents to interview them on their own initiative. An example of one effective effort by a community-based organization to link residents to jobs is Project QUEST in San Antonio.[2]

Revitalizing Retailing

Access to grocery, pharmacy, banking, and other retail and commercial services is taken for granted in most communities. In many inner-city areas, however, the nearest shopping center is miles away, and the retailing that is available offers only a minimal selection of poor-quality products at high prices.

Changes in retail practices make it unrealistic to expect that even in revitalized communities, all eyesore vacant storefronts will be refilled by new retail activity.[3] However, community rebuilding typically involves developing certain kinds of retail activity, particularly *convenience shopping*, the daily purchases of food, pharmaceuticals, and sundries in which easy access is paramount. A common unmet need is for supermarkets offering a variety of quality foods, prices lower than those charged by small groceries, and the convenience of one-stop shopping. In turn, supermarkets generate customer traffic that can anchor adjacent pharmacies, variety stores, restaurants, and other businesses.

Many inner-city communities have experienced decades of virtual retail redlining. In part, this reflects legitimate concerns about limited customer incomes, workforce instability, and neighborhood crime. However, it may also reflect a failure by investors to recognize attractive opportunities. The operational problems of many inner-city areas are often much less daunting than assumed, and many inner-city areas encompass substantial purchasing power.

When false perceptions have been overcome and retail initiatives undertaken in inner-city locations, the results have often been surprisingly profitable. One example is provided by the Winn-Dixie supermarket in Miami's Liberty City. About 250 supermarkets nationwide now operate successfully in low-income areas of large cities.[4]

Development of these supermarkets is often triggered by a community-based organization that identifies a need, conducts feasibility studies, and spearheads the project. In some cases, the subsequent development involves an equity partnership between a supermarket chain and that organization. For example, in Newark, New Jersey, the New Community Corporation, a community development corporation, owns two-thirds of a Pathmark supermarket in the city's Central Ward. In other cases, including Liberty City, a community group may develop the space for a market and lease it to a retail chain.

No matter what the formal structure is, community involvement in supermarket development illustrates the benefits of the community-building approach for both the neighborhood and investors. According to O'Connor and Abell, "Sensitivity towards the community is a characteristic that supermarkets which do well in inner cities have, whether the relationship is formalized in a municipal agreement, a joint venture, or held together as are secure friendships between certain families."[5] Such linkages legitimize a store in a community, increase patronage, and deter crime and vandalism. At the same time, the retail development strengthens the community, generating employment and stimulating economic life. Local retail establishments also become resources for further community building. For instance, a supermarket might collaborate with a local health clinic to promote proper nutrition among mothers and children.

Upgrading Housing

The run-down condition of public and private housing in inner-city areas is sometimes attributable to property managers' outright neglect of maintenance duties. This neglect encourages indifference among residents and discourages all but the most desperate from living there. Sustaining housing quality requires a commitment to maintain buildings properly and consistently.

However, simply administering and repairing properties conscientiously does not ensure quality housing in distressed communities. Even concerted efforts to fix leaky roofs, eliminate graffiti, and control vermin eventually lose ground if social issues remain unaddressed. Sustaining housing quality requires helping residents with individual and family problems, fostering pride and responsibility among residents, and reinforcing norms and relationships that support positive behavior. Residents are in the buildings on a daily basis, choosing to keep common areas pleasant or to allow them to deteriorate and deciding whether to report vandalism, crime, and drug activities. The community-building approach recognizes that physical rehabilitation, however well done, will not lead to lasting improvements in low-income housing unless residents form a functioning community.

Regenerating that crucial sense of community often requires an explicit process of resident organizing. In the past, such organizing has often been confrontational, fighting absentee owners over repairs, security, and similar issues. Although confrontation is still necessary at times, resident organizers now more frequently emphasize stimulating sustained resident involvement. In some cases, tenants have assumed cooperative ownership of their buildings. For example, several groups of residents bought and still successfully "co-op" their buildings under New York City's former Community Management Program.[6] In other cases, tenants, either as volunteers or as paid employees, become building managers, screening residents, establishing and enforcing rules, collecting rents, inspecting units, evicting tenants, and performing maintenance. One widely cited example of tenant management is the Kenilworth-Parkside public housing project in Washington, D.C., where tenants, led by resident Kimi Grey, assumed control in 1982. Subsequently, maintenance and rent collection in the project increased, and crime, teen pregnancy, and welfare dependency decreased. The decline in welfare dependency was largely due to increased employment as tenants replaced nonresidents as employees of social programs and small businesses within the project.[7]

The form of resident involvement is often less important than the involvement itself. A majority of tenants in a particular building may not want to own or manage it. They may prefer a regular forum with management or formal or informal organizations that represent tenant interests. Whatever its form, however, resident involvement promotes safe, orderly, and decent housing. Residents who help to set and enforce rules are more likely to comply with these rules and to pressure their neighbors to comply.[8]

An additional benefit of resident involvement in housing management is that residents develop problem-solving skills and support networks applicable to other challenges in their lives. In meeting these other challenges, however, additional support is often necessary. Another activity common in community-based housing management is facilitating residents' access to programs and services to improve their lives, including remedial or advanced educational activities, child care, medical care, and recreational services.

When such services are available in a neighborhood, the housing management role may only be informational. For example, Manhattan Valley, a CDC in New York City, publishes a handbook describing services in the area and provides residents with referrals. In other cases, a community-based housing manager may sponsor services that the neighborhood lacks. For example, in the West Garfield Park neighborhood in Chicago, the Bethel New Life CDC operates a health clinic and family counseling, employment training, and prenatal and neonatal care programs.[9] Another example is provided by the activities of the St. Nicholas Neighborhood Preservation Corporation in Brooklyn.[10]

Ensuring Public Safety

Two crime problems plague America's cities: crime itself and the fear of crime. The two are only partly related, in that fear may reflect an atmosphere of decline and indifference as much as the risk of victimization. However, both devastate community life.

The approach to policing practiced in most of urban America — vehicle patrols for crime suppression, rapid response to emergency calls, and retrospective investigation — has only limited success at either reducing crime or allaying residents' fears. "Officers flying to answer 911 calls usually arrive, sirens and flashing lights notwithstanding, to find the TV already stolen, the shots already fired, the dope already sold."[11] Most crimes occur out of the view of patrolling police officers, it is rarely possible to prosecute offenders without witness cooperation, and policing methods that minimize interaction with residents do little to address community distrust and fear.

In recent years, growing awareness of these facts has led law enforcement agencies in a number of cities to move toward a *community-policing* approach. The first step in this process is to address fear and distrust by fostering personal contact with residents and making police resources seem accessible. In concrete terms, these goals are promoted by replacing cruising patrol cars with bicycle and foot patrols and making individual officers responsible for personal beats. These beat officers are encouraged to be responsive to a range of community needs. Residents commonly use police as more than crime fighters, for example, for settling minor disputes or providing directions. Under "professional" policing, these requests are viewed as a distraction from "real" police work; under community policing, they are viewed as opportunities to foster community relations and to obtain clues to more serious problems. In addition, officers may distribute information on services such as domestic violence shelters and drug rehabilitation programs. Community outreach also may be emphasized through activities such as officer visits to schools and assistance in organizing neighborhood crime watches.

Community policing works if it engages the collaboration of community residents. Although only a small percentage of inner-city residents participate in criminal activity, many more are passive bystanders. Under a community-policing approach, residents serve as the eyes and ears of the police, and they and their community-based institutions become active partners in enhancing public safety. Residents can be particularly helpful in dealing with problems that erode the quality of community life, such as those associated with vagrants and prostitutes, drug activity, trash, and graffiti.

In some communities, residents take an even more active role in crime eradication, as they do in Marshall Heights, a distressed neighborhood in Washington, D.C. In cooperation with the District of Columbia police, the Marshall Heights Community Development Corporation has organized and trained residents, identifiable by their orange hats, to conduct nightly neighborhood patrols. Among other activities, these patrollers record the license plates of drug purchasers, effectively closing down open-air drug markets in their area.[12]

The Codman Square community in Boston illustrates another dimension of the community policing approach. Although the changes involved in that experience, such as redrawing precinct boundaries, sound simple, they reflect a major overhaul of policing philosophy and methodology.[13]

Promoting Youth Development

Even in affluent suburban communities, young people face serious obstacles on the path to productive adulthood: drugs, violence, and broken families. Most make it through their teenage years intact. However, of those living in distressed neighborhoods with few social supports, jobs, or recreational opportunities, many do not. In despair, these youths often gravitate to the few opportunities for support, affirmation, and recreation that are available: gangs, premature childbearing, and illegal drugs.

Traditional youth service programs are often short term and narrowly focused, providing services designed by professionals to address the "deficiencies" of inner-city youths. However, a number of community-based organizations are seeking to break the cycle of distress among inner-city youths by working under a different set of assumptions.[14] They describe themselves not as social service providers but simply as organizations *for youth* and view their members as resources to be developed, not problems to be fixed. A fundamental premise of their work is that inner-city youths, like young people elsewhere, have the capacity to solve their own problems but need opportunities and support.

An example of such an organization is the Logan Square YMCA in Chicago. The organization's experimental gang-intervention program uses recreational activities to attract gang members and then expands its contact with them to encompass education and employment. The program trains former gang members as outreach workers and mediators to avert violence among rival gangs. It brings rivals together in the neutral territories of classrooms, jobs, and gyms to build personal relationships that make them less willing to attack each other on the street.[15]

Given the range of problems that youths face growing up in the inner city, efforts to overcome negative influences must be substantial in scale and comprehensive in style.[16] A frequent role of community organizations is creative integration of the fragmentary supports available from multiple government programs and other sources to create this comprehensiveness. Another key role is to make programs readily accessible. For example, the Boys and Girls Clubs across the country are mobilizing local and national resources to provide comprehensive programs for youths in public housing.

Initiatives Must Be Sustained Through Community Institutions

A theme common to the examples presented in the previous section is that they involve *sustained and organized* efforts that occur primarily through *ongoing institutions*. Although temporary problem-solving efforts and informal associations are part of the fabric of life in healthy communities, they are not likely to thrive over extended periods or promote evolution of one initiative into additional efforts. Within neighborhoods in turmoil, *community-based institutions* serve as major repositories of the community's social capital.

The following are examples of promising inner-city institutions around which community-building efforts rally.

Community Development Corporations

One of the fastest-growing forms of community-based institutions in inner-city America is the *community development corporation*. CDCs are nonprofit organizations usually governed by boards that include local residents, business representatives, and other community leaders. Their typical goal is longterm, comprehensive community development in a limited geographic area.[17]

The roots of CDCs go back at least to the late nineteenth century, when settlement houses helped immigrants assimilate to life in America. The concept proliferated during the 1960s with federal Great Society programs to empower low-income people economically and socially; in those days, CDCs often shunned or fought city hall in their efforts. Their present shape, however, only faintly echoes these adversarial predecessors. In the 1990s, CDCs emphasize the power of collaboration with governments, business, and others.

The number of CDCs has mushroomed over the past 25 years, from about 100 nationwide in 1970 to an estimated 2,000 to 2,500 today. CDCs now operate in every state in the nation and in both rural and urban areas, although many are concentrated in older industrial cities in the Northeast and Midwest.[18]

CDCs vary considerably in size and strength. A few are massive, for example, the New Community Corporation in Newark, New Jersey, with $200 million in assets and more than 1,200 employees. More typical, however, are organizations with a staff of about seven and an annual budget of $700,000.[19]

Their most common core activity, engaged in by more than 80 percent of CDCs, is housing development, with the typical CDC constructing or rehabilitating about 21 housing units annually. By 1990, CDCs had developed more than 320,000 units of affordable housing, including nearly 23,000 in that year alone.[20] A CDC's role in a housing development project can range from passive cosponsor or limited partner to builder-owner.

Reflecting the need for comprehensive services in their multiproblem neighborhoods, CDCs in the 1990s are increasingly involved in a variety of activities beyond housing development. A survey of CDCs in 1991 found that.[21]

• To supplement their activities in housing development, 75 percent provide *housing services* such as homeowner and tenant counseling, home repair, and weatherization.

• To encourage residents to take responsibility for their neighborhoods and to provide a voice to outside institutions, 70 percent engage in *community advocacy and organizing*.

• To address the social needs in their communities, 60 percent provide *social services* such as job training and placement, child care, teen pregnancy counseling, antidrug efforts, and youth programs.

• To bring capital and jobs into their neighborhoods, 25 percent are *lenders*, *equity investors*, or *business operators*, most often in support of neighborhood small businesses or microenterprises.

• To support businesses and jobs, 25 percent develop *commercial real estate*, constructing, rehabilitating, and managing office and retail buildings and industrial sites.

This diversity reflects in part the fact that with the active involvement of residents, CDCs adapt to meet the needs of their individual neighborhoods. However, underlying all these activities is a fundamental commitment to developing social capital in their communities. This contribution is more difficult to measure than the number of housing units produced or residents served, but it is fundamental to the long-term impact of any CDC activity. CDCs serve as permanent institutions in otherwise-unstable neighborhoods, entry points for the poor and isolated into social networks, and vehicles by which residents can address both neighborhood and individual needs.

Public Schools

Among the most visible, enduring, and potentially powerful community institutions in almost any urban neighborhood are its public schools. Schools are a central thread in the fabric of everyday life, an institution with which nearly everyone comes into contact, and a source of continuity and purpose for area residents and their children. At the same time, most school buildings are underutilized outside of school hours and could offer valuable recreational, educational, and meeting space. Schools also provide ready access to students and their parents as program participants. Schools depend on social, medical, income support, and other services in the community to assist families in delivering students to them ready to learn. In turn, in many communities, schools are attractive locations for the delivery of services and other community-building endeavors.

Utilization of schools as the location of, and access point for, services is not the same as making the schools *responsible* for these activities. The primary mission of schools and the most important contribution schools can make to rebuilding inner-city areas is to *put learning first*: to ensure that children develop the academic knowledge and personal skills that will enable them to function as effective adults in the workforce and the community.[22] This imperative dictates that school budgets should not be regarded as a funding source for health care, recreational activities, family support services, community policing, or other services needed by inner-city communities and their residents. However, as long as they do not interfere with the educational process, many or all of these activities can be provided *at school sites with school cooperation.*

A partnership between a New York City public middle school and a private social service agency, the Children's Aid Society, exemplifies the cooperative role schools can play in community building.[23]

Neighborhood Churches

Churches and other religious establishments are often stable institutions in the frequently transient world of the inner city. Years of impartiality and community involvement have earned churches the trust of residents who are otherwise disillusioned with the police, social service agencies, and private businesses. Regular contacts between church leaders and residents present opportunities for disseminating information and for informal organizing. Congregations provide a traditional context for leadership development, and church members often provide role models of intact families and working parents rare in some neighborhoods. Churches and other religious institutions have a value base — for example, the emphasis on service and justice within the Judeo-Christian and other religious traditions—compatible with community building. Finally, like other inner-city organizations, religious institutions are concerned about the stability and security of the area in which they operate and thus have a self-interest in community improvement.[24]

Churches often also have access to economic assets. Many Americans exercise their volunteerism and charity through their religious institutions; nationwide, African-Americans alone contribute an estimated \$2 billion to churches annually.[25] Church buildings often provide office and meeting space for community events and service activities. Many religious organizations, often Protestant churches in African-American communities and Roman Catholic churches in Hispanic neighborhoods, have recognized their special role and are leading efforts to rebuild their communities.

Part of this activism has involved building relationships and establishing a sense of community responsibility among congregants and residents. For example, the Nehemiah Project in Brooklyn, New York, widely cited for providing housing for low-income families, was the product of a long process of relationship building and training. Ministers and lay leaders from the East Brooklyn Churches Association spent time talking to congregants and holding block and congregation meetings to build a spirit of accountability that was prerequisite to undertaking housing redevelopment.

Other congregations actively provide social services to residents in their community. For example, for nearly two decades, the Bethel African Methodist Episcopal Church in Baltimore has fed the hungry, assisted the unemployed, taught parenting skills, and supported neighborhood anticrime groups.

Community-Based Financial Institutions

Adequate access to capital for housing, commercial real estate, and small-business development is vital to any community. Like other neighborhoods, distressed inner-city areas depend on commercial banks, thrift institutions, mortgage companies, venture capitalists, and similar sources for these financial resources. However, many of these traditional institutions have failed to seize opportunities in inner-city areas and to adapt financial products to this market.

To address this gap, a number of distressed urban communities across the nation have developed special financial institutions, including community credit unions, loan funds targeted to minority borrowers, and development banks. These institutions typically provide not only capital but also business development advice and services to help the money to be used well. The most complex embodiment of this concept is the *community development bank*, of which the South Shore Bank in Chicago is the best-known example.[26] The concept of development banking is that community revitalization requires not only conventional credit but also nonconventional lending and complementary community-building activities. Unlike CDCs, development banks are incorporated as for-profit entities (although often with not-for-profit subsidiaries) and aim to maintain sufficient profitability to be self-sustaining and to instill business discipline in all decisions. However, they sometimes accept lower financial returns than is normal for conventional lending institutions. Their primary goal is to achieve positive interactions among the development projects in which they are involved, eventually creating an environment in their neighborhoods attractive to private investors and conventional lenders.

As financial institutions, development banks and community loan funds try to fill capital gaps in a community, especially by making loans smaller than conventional sources wish to handle and by using their familiarity with the community to provide credit to borrowers that conventional lenders consider too risky. They often successfully lend to borrowers with little credit history or collateral but good standing in the community, relying on a combination of lender monitoring, government guarantees, and knowledge of the neighborhood.

Large Public and Nonprofit Institutions

Many distressed inner-city neighborhoods are the home of large public or nonprofit institutions such as hospitals and universities. Often, these institutions and their surrounding communities remain at arms' length or are adversaries. In better circumstances, however, the institutions serve as major anchors for the community, providing jobs, purchasing power, community identity, health and social services, leadership training, and expertise in neighborhoods where alternative resources are limited. The motivation for such involvement is only partially philanthropic. The future of these institutions is integrally related to that of their neighborhoods. Their clients may choose other hospitals or schools if they do not believe they can go there safely, and local residents themselves will be difficult neighbors if their problems remain unresolved.

Several joint efforts between large urban institutions and their surrounding communities exemplify this form of partnership. For example, the Peninsula Hospital Center and St. John's Episcopal Hospital in Queens, New York, and Misericordia Hospital in southwest Philadelphia are working with local community development organizations to identify health concerns in their neighborhoods and to address both the causes and the symptoms of these problems. In New Orleans, Xavier University of Louisiana has joined with the Xavier Triangle Development Corporation (XTDC) and the local police to develop a neighborhood watch. In addition, XTDC, with help from faculty and students from Xavier and Tulane Universities, completed a needs assessment for its neighborhood and a plan to increase home ownership and promote local businesses.[27]

The Defining Elements of Community Building

As these examples demonstrate, community-building activities are as diverse as the neighborhoods in which they occur and the problems they address. The agenda can be narrow or broad, the effort short term or long term, and the institutional arrangements formal or informal. Through all this diversity, however, runs the common thread of *the centrality of the community's own problem-solving abilities.* Reflecting this centrality, the essential defining characteristic of the community-building approach is that *inner-city residents and institutions can and must be primary actors in efforts to solve the problems of their neighborhoods.*

That common thread is always "two-ply": Community involvement both *utilizes* and *builds* social capital. The power of involvement of community residents and local institutions extends beyond the promotion of any specific effort. Local action builds social capital—community and individual capacity—that can then be applied in future problem solving. A successful community-building activity is, by definition, not an isolated event but an ongoing process. Only in that way are efforts sustained, and only in that way do they advance a broad agenda addressing the multiple problems simultaneously burdening distressed communities.

The author urges that both public and private actors consistently adopt a community-based style of problem solving in addressing the problems of distressed neighborhoods. Residents and **local institutions should be central participants in identifying neighborhood problems and constructing solutions.** Such efforts apply to the realm of social problem solving the approach of many business efforts to reengineer their operations and empower their workers.

Another defining characteristic of community building is that efforts are *comprehensive* and *interrelated*, acknowledging and confronting the multiple problems of distressed neighborhoods. The interrelated nature of problems, discussed in Chapter 3, prevents efforts focusing on single problems from succeeding, as they are quickly overwhelmed by other forces in the community. Similarly, the problems of individuals and families living in the inner city do not arise in isolation from neighborhood conditions. Therefore, addressing their problems requires strengthening the norms, supports, and problem-solving resources of their community.

Creating the Social and Physical Prerequisites

Social capital is most easily generated when communities have some social resources on which to build. This principle implies that local problem solving will be difficult to stimulate and sustain in neighborhoods so distressed that few social resources remain.

Carried to its extreme, this consideration would imply that severely distressed inner-city areas should be abandoned rather than rehabilitated. Such a position is generally not appropriate because, despite their distress, most inner-city areas still possess some social capital. Contrary to the presumptions often held by outsiders, there are remarkable quantities of underutilized resources even in terribly distressed neighborhoods. Among these resources are the majority of inner-city residents who, despite their low incomes, have the same aspirations as middle-class persons: a safe place to live, a steady income, opportunities for their children. When given the chance to pursue these aspirations, most inner-city residents work hard to achieve them. Against tremendous odds, many are already trying to do just that. Even in many high-poverty areas, the majority of residents are not poor, at least as defined by federal poverty standards,[28] and many distressed neighborhoods have indigenous institutions that are potential resources for community building.

In some instances, however, neighborhoods may have too few resources on which to build. For example, some cities have suffered such large population losses over many years that insufficient population remains to support rehabilitation of all their distressed neighborhoods. Detroit, for example, lost 44 percent of its population between 1950 and 1990.[29] In such circumstances, the appropriate approach may be selectively to clear and recycle some areas of the city to other uses, such as in-city industrial or office parks, while targeting community-building resources to a limited number of neighborhoods with the greatest potential.[30]

Another variation on the same theme arises in neighborhoods where social conditions are so severe that sustained change through local problem solving is all but impossible without more radical alternations in the neighborhood environment. The level of distress among inner-city communities is a continuum. Some neighborhoods, although suffering many symptoms of distress, nevertheless retain many hardworking residents and stable community institutions from which community building can emerge. Many of these are *threatened neighborhoods*, areas adjacent to distressed neighborhoods that may fall into further distress if current processes are left unchecked. Because they mix some strengths with some aspects of decay, threatened neighborhoods are often excellent candidates for community building.

At the other extreme, certain neighborhoods, such as the Robert Taylor public housing projects in Chicago, offer far more limited resources to build upon. In such cases, it would be naive to assume that community-building efforts, however well crafted, can make extensive progress unless accompanied by major changes in the physical and social circumstances in which they operate. For example, one precursor of distress in public housing is the physical density of projects; another is the absence of two-parent, employed families. Community building is not likely to thrive where large numbers of distressed families are concentrated and isolated within a badly designed physical environment.

Just a few miles from the Robert Taylor Homes is another Chicago Housing Authority property, Lake Parc Place, that illustrates how environmental transformation can set the stage for effective community building. There, under a special demonstration project, a dramatic process of physical de-densification and repopulation with economically and socially mixed residents is under way.

To ensure that community building is effective, it should reflect a realistic understanding of neighborhood circumstances, conditions, and resources. It is often useful to formalize the development of that understanding with an explicit inventory of the assets and challenges within a community. Such a review should, of course, have extensive participation of local residents. To reflect a citywide strategy, it might best be conducted at the city level by a broad representation of resident, business, and government leaders.

In the majority of distressed neighborhoods, such an inventory will confirm the opportunities for community building without major environmental changes. But when the review suggests that more basic social or physical changes in the neighborhood are necessary, these changes should be considered part of the process.

Reducing the concentration of severely distressed families is one example of the sort of prerequisite to effective community building that such a review might identify. Programs such as HUD's Section 8 housing vouchers, scattered-site public housing, and other efforts to move inner-city residents into less distressed neighborhoods can therefore be an important component of inner-city community building.[31] From the point of view of residents moved from distressed neighborhoods into more stable areas, the programs increase their housing and neighborhood options, and the resultant moves are often associated with improvements in educational and economic outcomes.[32] These are worthy goals in their own right. But these same efforts also benefit the communities from which residents are moved. They ease the concentration of distress within inner-city areas, creating more favorable conditions for community building. So long as outward mobility efforts do not leave neighborhoods devoid of their most able and energetic residents, these programs can be a first step toward a more mixed population in inner-city areas. After densification, community building can amplify and sustain the enhanced neighborhood environment.[33]

Notes

1. The cost for each job opportunity created in a targeted area has been estimated to range from $12,000 to $60,000; see Marc Bendick, Jr., "Employment, Training, and Economic Development," in *The Reagan Experiment*, ed. John R. Palmer and Isabel Sawhill (Washington, D.C.: The Urban Institute Press,

1982), p. 265. See also Philip Kasinitz and Jan Rosenberg, "Why Enterprise Zones Will Not Work," *City Journal* (Autumn 1993): 63–69.

2. Joseph Stillman, *Making the Connection: Economic Development, Workforce Development, and Urban Poverty* (New York: The Conservation Company, 1994), pp. 28–30.

3. Marc Bendick, Jr., and Mary Lou Egan, "Linking Business Development and Community Development in Inner Cities," *Journal of Planning Literature* 8 (August 1993): 3–19.

4. James O'Connor and Barbara Abell, *Successful Supermarkets in Low-Income Inner Cities* (Arlington, Va.: O'Connor-Abell, 1992).

5. O'Connor and Abell, *Successful Supermarkets*, p. 21.

6. The Community Management Program turned over tax-foreclosed buildings to community groups and provided funds to rehabilitate buildings and organize residents. The process required 60 percent of residents to agree to cooperative ownership, and tenants participated extensively in planning the rehabilitation.

7. Jerome Cramer, "Turning Public Housing Over to Resident Owners," *Time*, December 12, 1988, p. 15; J. S. Fuerst, "Tenant Management in Low-Rent Public Housing," *Social Service Review* 62 (June 1988): 340.

8. Fuerst, "Tenant Management," pp. 337–345; Mercer Sullivan, *More Than Housing: How Community Development Corporations Go About Changing Lives and Neighborhoods* (New York: New School for Social Research, 1993), pp. 103–121.

9. Sullivan, *More Than Housing*, pp. 77–102.

10. Sullivan, *More Than Housing*, pp. 27–28, 43–75, 83, 95, 97.

11. Malcolm K. Sparrow, Mark H. Moore, and David M. Kennedy, *Beyond 911: A New Era for Policing* (New York: Basic Books, 1990), pp. 5–7 (quotation is from p. 7).

12. Mindy Leiterman and Joseph Stillman, *Building Community: A Report on Social Community Development Initiatives* (New York: Local Initiatives Support Corporation, 1993), p. 44.

13. Other cities incorporating community policing into their departments include Houston; New York; Portland, Oregon; Philadelphia;

and Washington, D.C. See Richard L. Worsnop, "Community Policing: Is It the Answer to the Nation's Crime Problem?" *Congressional Quarterly Researcher* 3 (February 5, 1993): 104–106. Mark H. Moore and Darrel W. Stephens, *Beyond Command and Control: The Strategic Management of Police Departments* (Washington, D.C.: Police Executive Research Forum, 1991).

14. Milbrey W. McLaughlin, Merita A. Irby, and Juliet Langman, *Urban Sanctuaries: Neighborhood Organizations in the Lives and Futures of Inner City Youth* (San Francisco, Calif.: Jossey-Bass Publishers, 1994), p. 114.

15. William Mullen, "Working to Keep the Peace." *The Chicago Tribune*, August 9, 1993, p. C2.

16. *Strengthening Social Infrastructure for Successful Teenage Development and Transition to Adulthood* (Philadelphia, Penn.: Public/Private Ventures, April 1993).

17. Neil Pierce and Carol F. Steinbach, *Corrective Capitalism: The Rise of America's Community Development Corporations* (New York: Ford Foundation, 1987); Avis C. Vidal, *Rebuilding Communities: A National Study of Community Development Corporations* (New York: New School for Social Research, 1992); Renee Berger, *A Place in the Marketplace* (Washington, D.C.: National Congress for Community Economic Development, 1992).

18. Christopher Walker, "Nonprofit Housing Development: Status, Trends, and Prospects," *Housing Policy Debate* 4 (1993): 376–381; Joseph B. McNeeley, *Building for the Future* (Washington, D.C.: Fannie Mae Foundation, November 1993), p. 4.

19. Vidal, *Rebuilding Communities*, p. 43. These numbers are medians from a sample of relatively well-established CDCs and therefore somewhat overstate the size of a "typical" CDC.

20. *Changing the Odds: The Achievement of Community-based Development Corporations* (Washington, D.C.: National Congress for Community Economic Development, December 1991), p. 2; Walker, "Nonprofit Housing Development," p. 373.

21. *Changing the Odds*, pp. 6–7.

22. *Putting Learning First: Governing and Managing the Schools for High Achievement* (1994).

23. Joy G. Dryfoos, *Full-Service Schools: A Revolution in Health and Social Services for Children, Youth, and Families* (San Francisco, Calif.: Jossey-Bass, Inc., 1994), pp. 100–108.

24. Robert A. Clemetson and Roger Coates, *Restoring Broken Places and Rebuilding Communities* (Washington, D.C.: National Congress for Community Economic Development, 1992), p. v; Jeremy Nowak et al., *Religious Institutions and Community Renewal* (Philadelphia, Penn.: The Pew Charitable Trusts, 1989), p. 1–2.

25. Lloyd Gite, "The New Agenda of the Black Church: Economic Development for Black America," *Black Enterprise* 24 (December 1993): 56; Nowalk et al., *Religious Institutions*, pp. 11–15.

26. Richard P. Taub, *Community Capitalism* (Boston, Mass.: Harvard Business School Press, 1988); *Annual Report* (Chicago, Ill.: Shorebank Corporation, 1992).

27. *Annual Report* (Philadelphia: SEEDCO, 1993).

28. For example, within the distressed neighborhoods listed in the Appendix, an average of 54 percent of residents have household incomes greater than the federal poverty threshold. See John D. Kasarda, "Inner City Concentrated Poverty and Neighborhood Distress: 1970–1990," *Housing Policy Debate* 3 (1993): 20–21.

29. David Rusk, *Cities Without Suburbs* (Washington, D.C.: The Woodrow Wilson Center Press, 1993), p. 14.

30. Marc Bendick, Jr., and David W. Rasmussen, "Enterprise Zones and Inner City Economic Revitalization," in *Reagan and the Cities*, ed. George Peterson and Carol Lewis (Washington, D.C.: The Urban Institute Press, 1986), pp. 247–269.

31. These efforts may be accompanied by controversy about the capacity of the receiving neighborhood to absorb these new arrivals. Without bowing to pressures to maintain racial segregation or to the NIMBY syndrome (see Chapter 2), such programs should be administered with sensitivity to residents' concerns.

32. James E. Rosenbaum, "Black Pioneers— Do Their Moves to the Suburbs Increase Economic Opportunity for Mothers and Children?" *Housing Policy Debate* 2 (1991): 1179–1213.

33. Another effort in Chicago, also a result of the Gautreaux litigation, involves *scattered-site public housing*, which consists of developing public housing units not in large projects but either singly or in small buildings. For many years, this initiative was stalled because it was politically unpopular and because of the complexity of managing numerous small projects. In 1987, the federal court hearing the Gautreaux case selected a private developer, the Habitat Company, to take over the effort, and the program began to move forward with rehabilitation of several buildings and construction of additional town houses. More such developments are planned to utilize the more than $100 million that had accumulated over the years of inaction.

9. STRENGTHENING DOWNTOWN BUSINESSES

Dolores P. Palma

Each community must tailor its business retention and expansion strategy to the identified needs— and the identified potentials— of its local business community. With this in mind, it is helpful to consider the initiatives which are most often included in downtown business retention and expansion strategies today. Those initiatives are shown below.

One-on-One Business Counseling

Business district professionals and leaders all across the country have found that technical assistance and professional assistance can often make the difference between small business success and failure. In addition, it has also been found that small business owners are not very likely or able to attend seminars in order to obtain this information. Therefore, personal contact is essential to get the attention of small business owners and to make sure they get the information they need to survive and thrive. One-on-one business counseling usually involves assistance on business matters considered to be private, such as business planning, business financing, record keeping, computerization, etc. For this initiative to be a success, follow-up with business owners— to make sure they got the information they needed and were able to use that information — is essential.

Business Visitation Teams

Long used in programs aimed at industrial retention and expansion, visitation teams are a technique that has been borrowed by downtowns. The visitation team usually involves two to three people who call on the owner of a local business. The purpose of the visit is to first, determine the needs of the business owner and, second, to meet these needs by linking the business owner with information sources. As with one-on-one business counseling, follow-up is essential for this initiative to be effective.

Originally published as "Retaining and Strengthening Existing Downtown Businesses," Municipal Maryland, *Vol. 25, No. 3, October, 1995. Published by the Maryland Municipal League, Annapolis, Maryland. Reprinted with permission of the publisher.*

Referrals to Service Providers

Many downtown organizations provide assistance to existing businesses by referring them to appropriate local service providers such as a Small Business Development Center, a SCORE chapter, municipal government agencies, etc. The rationale here is that the downtown organization cannot be all things to all people and should not try to reinvent the wheel. Instead, business owners and local service providers both benefit if the downtown organization acts as a liaison between the two. Again, follow-up is essential for this initiative to be effective.

Seminars, Workshops, Forums and Conferences

Often offered to business owners on a quarterly basis, these sessions have long been used to convey information that is of interest to business owners as a group. Topics usually covered in such sessions include coordinated marketing, building rehab, effective window displays, interior design and merchandising, etc. Many downtown organizations are holding fewer sessions of this type, since it is often difficult for the independent, small business owner — for whom the sessions are usually held — to attend. The trend that is emerging is to hold one or two sessions a year, with well-known speakers or "experts" who act as a "draw," instead of regular, quarterly sessions with low-profile speakers.

Employee Training

A popular business retention tool in many communities are seminars and workshops for employees of existing businesses. Such programs can focus on the orientation of new employees, training of new employees, and the re-training of existing employees. Often, these programs will focus on topics such as providing excellent customer service, referring customers among businesses located in downtown, and providing information about downtown goods, services, and activities to downtown users. The key to the success of such programs is threefold. First, to determine the seminar topics in conjunction with business owners. Second, to present them to employees as a tremendous opportunity rather than as a chore. And, third, pay employees for the time they spend attending the sessions.

Secret Shopper Programs

Long used by shopping centers and department stores, secret shopper programs have come into use in downtowns. Such programs involve individuals who are asked to, first, anonymously shop at a particular downtown store and then to evaluate the quality of that shopping experience. For these programs to be effective it is essential to hold a training session with each secret shopper, to direct the shopper to shop at a particular store and/or department within that store, to have a standardized method for the shoppers to rate and evaluate the shopping experience, and to maintain strict confidentiality of the results.

Retail and Office Market Analysis

A retail and office market analysis is a critical element of business retention and expansion programs because it reveals the potential of the business district. In addition, the analysis is critical because it provides information which small business owners must have to succeed — but which they commonly do without because they lack the time or money to acquire this information. When the downtown retail and office market analysis is completed, its findings should be widely distributed to downtown's business owners. Ideally, business owners would use the market information to:

• Learn the characteristics and buying habits of customers and office users in their trade area;
• Determine the most appropriate customer groups or office users for their business to target;
• Learn who their competition is and what their competition is offering in the trade area;
• Make decisions regarding changes in the type of merchandise they sell, services they offer or space they rent;
• Test additional merchandise lines or services; and
• Expand their business and its offerings.

Guidelines and Assistance

Many business retention and expansion programs provide guidelines to assist business owners who want to make physical improvements to their facilities. Such guidelines often cover topics such as appropriate exterior rehab, effective window displays, effective interior layout and design, appropriate business signs, etc. Where time and money allow, many business retention and expansion programs provide technical and professional assistance that is related to the guidelines.

Financial Incentives

Local efforts aimed at the retention and expansion of small businesses often focus on providing technical assistance,

professional assistance, and financial counseling prior to— or along with — providing financial assistance. The reason for this is that while financial incentives can provide businesses with a competitive edge, they do not normally help businesses develop the human and technological skills needed for long-term gains in competitiveness.

Financial incentives that have long been used as part of business retention efforts include revolving loan funds, grants for facade rehab and signs, tax abatements, interest subsidies, and supply give-aways (such as paint programs). Today, financial incentives are also likely to be provided through programs such as the Community Reinvestment Act initiatives of the local lending community, through energy audits and subsidies provided through the local government and utility systems, and through design services that help businesses make smart renovation investment decisions.

One-Stop Shops

Realizing that the saying "time is money" is a truism for business owners, many local governments have created one-stop shops— an office where business owners can obtain all required permits, licenses, and approvals. The aim of these shops is to cut both the cost and time business owners spend going through government review and approval processes.

Marketing Campaign

As was said earlier, the findings of the market analysis should be used by a downtown's individual business owners to guide their marketing decisions. In addition, the findings of the market analysis should be used to define a marketing campaign for the downtown. This will allow the business district to be marketed as a single economic entity — much as a shopping center is — and to be positioned in the mind of the consumer as a "special" commercial district. The marketing campaign should be used to strengthen the business district as a whole and, therefore, to strengthen each of the district's businesses.

A comprehensive marketing campaign should include:

• Print pieces which can be used to promote downtown and its businesses;
• A public relations strategy which creates and reinforces downtown's desired image; and
• Collective and coordinated advertising which portrays downtown as a varied and convenient shopping district.

Awards Programs

Often, business retention and expansion strategies will include awards programs for two reasons—first, awards reinforce the positive actions taken by the award recipients and, second, awards market the fact that improvements are being made in downtown.

Award programs are most typically used to recognize outstanding physical improvements, business improvements, volunteer efforts, and employees.

Owner-Match Programs

An emerging downtown business retention initiative is one that involves linking soon-to-retire business owners with entrepreneurial individuals who are interested in becoming business owners. This is a particularly important business retention issue since many downtowns lose their most successful businesses when their independent owners retire without heirs who are interested in taking over the business.

The key to this match effort is to identify future retirees *early* so that prospective successors can be found and nurtured *before* the business is closed. Ideally, prospective buyers are found early enough so that they can join the current owners in running the business for a year or two, and, thereby, be groomed by the successful owners before they retire.

The ten steps necessary to start a downtown business retention and expansion program are highlighted below. These simple steps will help public officials, merchants, and citizens alike begin the journey leading to a successful business retention and expansion program for the downtown in their community.

Step 1: Form a Partnership Between Downtown and City Hall. If they are to succeed, business retention and recruitment efforts cannot — and should not — be the purview of either the private sector or the public sector alone. Instead, both sectors have an investment in downtown and both have a responsibility to protect and enhance that investment. Therefore, successful business retention and expansion efforts require a partnership between the private and public sectors. The role of the partnership should be to assess the area's needs and potential, define an appropriate strategy, and see that the strategy is aggressively implemented.

Step 2: Identify Sponsoring Organization and Staff. For best results, the business retention and expansion effort should be sponsored by a local organization that is actively involved in downtown and well-respected by both the private and public sector leadership of the community. The role of the sponsoring group is to lend credibility and champion the effort.

It should be noted early on that the effort will require the attention of at least one professional staff person who is experienced in downtown business development.

Step 3: Define and Implement a Public Relations Strategy. The business retention effort — and its successes— must be regularly publicized. Doing so will result in businesses, resource providers, investors, etc., seeking out the sponsoring organization and staff so that they do not always have to be the initiator of actions. When this occurs, it is a true sign of success. Therefore, a thorough, on-going public relations strategy should be defined early in the effort and relentlessly implemented throughout.

Step 4: Complete Business Needs Assessment and Market Analysis. A business needs assessment should be completed to determine the needs of the downtown's business owners and their perception of the business district. In addition, a market analysis should be completed which details downtown's potential for retail and office businesses.

Step 5: Analyze and Interpret Results of Assessment and Market Analysis. The needs assessment and market analysis are data collection methods that will involve compiling a great deal of information about downtown and its businesses. However, this information will be useless unless it is analyzed and interpreted to *make decisions about specific business retention activities to carry out.* Remember, data collection alone is a futile exercise. Data collection must be taken to the next step of analysis and interpretation of data so that these findings can be used to drive the business retention effort.

Step 6: Respond to "Red Flags" Uncovered. The needs assessment and the market analysis might reveal issues or situations that require *immediate* attention. These so called "red flags" often mean that action must be taken at once to avoid losing a business. For example, during the process it might be determined that a sig-

nificant downtown business must find space to expand into or it will have to relocate outside of downtown in order to continue operation. This would be a project which requires immediate attention — thus a "red flag" project. Staff and volunteers should be detailed to quickly respond to red flags before moving on to the next step of the program.

Step 7: Select Appropriate Initiatives. Based on the needs assessment and analysis conducted, a business retention strategy must be defined. The strategy should be composed of specific initiatives selected because they allow the effort to address business needs and capture the market potentials identified.

Step 8: Define an Implementation Schedule. Once the appropriate initiatives have been selected, an implementation schedule must be defined. This is a management tool that details when each initiative will be started and completed; who will take the lead in implementing each initiative; how much each initiative is expected to cost; and the source of funds for each initiative.

Step 9: Monitor Progress of Effort. The sponsoring organization and staff should establish a method for continually monitoring the progress and success of the business retention and expansion effort. This will ensure that implementation runs smoothly and stays on course.

Step 10: Update Business Needs Assessment and Market Analysis. Approximately every two years the needs assessment and market analysis should be updated. This is necessary since the characteristics of downtowns and their businesses— as well as their users— are constantly changing. Therefore, the needs and the potentials of the downtown and its businesses will similarly change over time. To stay abreast of these changes— and to ensure that the retention effort is appropriately designed to address needs and potentials— the data on which the effort is based must be updated.

10. WHEN TO USE INCENTIVES

Kurt Hahn

Increasingly, municipal governments are being asked to join states and utilities to provide incentives to attract business or to retain existing business. The incentive may take a variety of forms, but among the most common forms of incentive are the following.

1. **Expedited or preferential processing.** Commonly known as fast-track processing, this technique typically involves prioritizing a desired job and/or revenue-producing project's review ahead of others, as well as coordinating regulatory approvals between departments or agencies so as to speed the processing.

2. **Loan of public assets such as land, building or equipment to business for private purposes.** Sometimes an industrial development authority, redevelopment agency, or even a municipal electric utility will provide bridge financing to attract a job- or revenue-producing project. More common, however, is the provision of conduit private activity bond or industrial development bond financing to the enterprise.

3. **Grant of public funds to business for private purposes.** Direct gift of taxpayer funds is prohibited in most states; however, provision of tax rebates and advance payment of some leases for parking facilities or grants for historic preservation or aesthetic improvements, such as building facades or landscaping, often are permitted.

4. **Loan of public funds to business for public purposes.** Too often ignored is the provision of loans to finance a development's required infrastructure or fees. This technique, when not adversely affecting the municipality's cash flow, can frequently be realized with an interest rate exceeding both investment earnings and bond financing. This can provide a win-win situation for the developer and municipality.

5. **Grant of public funds to business for public purposes.** Many redevelopment agencies or municipalities will provide grants for required infrastructure when a project achieves a positive utility outcome or positive municipal revenue impact.

6. **Lease or sale of public land at**

Originally published as "When and When Not to Use Incentives to Attract Business or to Retain Existing Businesses," Government Finance Review, *Vol. 12, No. 3, June, 1996. Published by the Government Finance Officers Association, 180 N. Michigan Avenue, Suite 800, Chicago, Illinois 60601 (312-977-9700, fax 312-977-4806, e-mail GFR@gfoa.org). Annual subscription $30. Reprinted with permission of the publisher.*

below-market rates. A typical redevelopment strategy is to acquire and/or assemble land using tax increment financing and then sell or lease it at a price that will allow the desired development to be successful.

7. **Legally permissible waiver or deferral of fees.** This technique is always fraught with political problems. Many developers planning a project which they know the city wants will ask for the waiver or deferral of city fees. Some cities have adopted policies to provide partial or whole city-fee waivers or deferral, if a development meets specific criteria, and then substitute redevelopment agency or utility money in the city's treasury to offset the waiver. In many states, performance-based deferrals designed to provide the developer time to build up the business are legal.

8. **Provision of services at public expense (e.g., architectural planning or expediting).** A new incentive that frequently is also a win-win for developer and the city is to provide the developer, at the city's expense, an outside expeditor who knows the city's processes as well as the developer's needs.

9. **Special utility rates.** In an atmosphere of increasing utility deregulation, new businesses will seek or be offered special rates based on incremental added cost to the utility or through discounting the rates for an initial two- or three-year period.

Legal Constraints

The Internal Revenue Code regulates the use of tax-exempt bond proceeds for private purposes, while federal statutes govern the use of federal funds or the reuse of Urban Development Action Grant (UDAG) or Community Development Block Grant (CDBG) monies. Many states impose a variety of legal constraints on incentives, the most typical of which are "gift of public funds" statutes which preclude fee waivers or cash gifts to a private business under a variety of circumstances. Additionally, many states in their redevelopment laws limit public acquisition of real estate and subsequent price write-downs in resale. Many state development fee statutes have equity provisions between business and residential development which indirectly limit fee waivers in either area unless fully funded from a third source, such as an industrial development authority, a redevelopment agency, or the state.

Locally adopted investment policies or state statutes adopted since the Orange County bankruptcy may further limit the use of public funds for incentives. Finance directors and city attorneys need to be involved in incentive negotiations to assure their legality.

What Is a Desirable Incentive?

In the broadest possible terms, a desirable incentive is one that is financially profitable to the city and its redevelopment or industrial development agency and produces jobs. Profit can be defined in this case as net revenues from the project exceeding the cost of incentives plus recurring costs of providing municipal services. Another criterion for a desirable incentive is that it does not immediately create a charge of unequal treatment of businesses in similar circumstances. Lastly, a desirable incentive should be one that causes an investment or relocation that would not have otherwise happened.

In determining whether an incentive is a positive one or not, a finance director should be prepared to produce a discounted proforma indicating the public investments and tax or utility revenues generated to determine the payback period and compare current values of each. The public investments should include not only incentives but recurring costs to provide services including, if applicable, utility services.

Sound incentives can be secured loans to developers in which the city is assured of full repayment with interest equal to or above the rate of the city's investment pool. Many cities will finance utility-related infrastructure or developer/capacity fees and add loan payments to utility bills. Another example is a grant/loan that positions the city as an equity partner in the development and provides for loan repayment with interest and/or participation in the income flow of the development. Typically used in many UDAG projects, this approach is increasingly employed when local incentives are sought by the developer. Similarly, a positive incentive can be a land sale or lease that gives to the city a downstream share of a project income flow and recovers the city's investment in the site. Others are those in which the city or redevelopment agency recovers in new revenues the cost of the incentive plus a significant net gain for the community in jobs and revenues.

There is nothing wrong with a city making a good investment. The challenge often is to have the courage to ask for something in return for an incentive. Most entrepreneurs do not react unkindly to an entrepreneurial approach by the city.

What Is an Undesirable Incentive?

First, undesirable incentives are those that look bad to the public. They can create the appearance of unequal treatment of similar businesses under similar circumstances. Secondly, they also can be activities that cause or offer the potential for litigation, such as a developer fee rebate or sales tax exemption. Thirdly, an incentive is unwarranted when the recipient would have come to the community regardless of the incentive. Lastly, an incentive is not a positive one if it is likely to cause a future budget or cash-flow problem for the city.

No finance director should be bashful when it comes to preparing a confidential report for the city manager or legislative body 1) indemnifying specific cases or prospective cases where there could be the charge that unequal treatment was provided, 2) analyzing the financial ramifications if similar incentives were provided generally, and 3) pointing out potentials for litigation based on gifts of public funds. If, in the view of the finance officer, a business will come to the city absent incentives or if future budgets will be adversely affected, the finance officer should so advise the city manager loudly and clearly.

Undesirable incentives take many forms, but the most typical is one in which virtually all new revenues generated by a project are returned to the developer, which has been the case in a variety of "big box" transactions. Another case is the use of incentives in bidding wars to relocate an existing business, in some cases from a nearby municipality. Still other examples are a grant or loan to business which would have come to the town without an incentive, a retroactive incentive, or a tax rebate incentive to every business in town just to create the image of a business-friendly locality.

If cities should eventually be denied the option to use tax-exempt private activity bonds as a tool for economic development, it will be because of abuses, typically involving assistance to developments that would have happened without the incentive. Not only the federal government but many state legislatures as well as reacting negatively and in some cases punitively in response to the perception that many incentive transactions are a waste of tax resources and do not achieve a public purpose. The role of finance officials is to make sure every incentive can be defended.

Conclusion

The pressures associated with economic development are substantial. Frequently the elected official is invited to the negotiating table before the finance director is. Jobs sometimes can take priority over balancing the city budget. The challenge to the finance director is to pre-educate the city council, then ensure that he/she is at the table. This calls for horse sense and close consultation with the city attorney. The approach to incentives should be entrepreneurial: the city is seeking to make money. While portraying a pro-business attitude, dollars on the table for the city is by far the most important approach to successful incentive negotiations.

11. CALCULATING THE COSTS AND BENEFITS OF INCENTIVES

Wim Wiewel, Joseph Persky, and Daniel Felsenstein

Governments rarely have good information about the actual costs or benefits of a business incentive package. When negotiating incentives for a firm expansion or new location, it is difficult to assess the long-term effects on the local economy as a whole or to the government's own fiscal condition, and government officials admittedly often do not know the real cost of what they are putting on the table or the value of what the firm is offering. This may result in offering firms more than the ultimate benefits are worth or offering too little. In the summer of 1992, the catalog clothing company Spiegel rejected the City of Chicago's final offer of incentives to keep the national warehousing and distribution center in Chicago and decided to leave for Columbus, Ohio, taking more than one thousand jobs with it. Public criticism was swift and strong — why did the city not offer more? Was its package too little, too late? This reaction was quite a contrast with the public outcry a few years earlier, when the State of Illinois managed to retain the headquarters of Sears' merchandising group through several hundred million dollars worth of free land, infrastructure improvements, and job-training dollars — generally characterized as a "corporate giveaway."

Spurred on by the criticism, the Chicago Department of Planning and Development (DPD) asked the Center for Urban Economic Development at the University of Illinois at Chicago (UICUED) to develop a methodology that would allow the department to assess in advance the costs and benefits of any particular subsidy package. This chapter presents the methodology, which is now being used by the department in a computerized spreadsheet format. It first discusses the experience of other cities and then focuses on how the key theoretical issues in assessing costs and benefits are resolved. Finally, it describes how the spreadsheet works and what would be required to make it applicable in other cities.

Chicago is not alone in how it negotiates subsidy packages. A survey conducted by the UICUED turned up no cities that used a comprehensive cost-benefit analysis to determine the level of business subsidies to be given. Of course, all cities

Originally published as "Are Subsidies Worth It?: How to Calculate the Costs and Benefits of Business Incentives," Commentary, *Vol. 18, No. 3, Fall, 1994. Published by the Urban Economic Development Council, Washington, D.C. Reprinted with permission of the publisher.*

require companies to provide estimates of jobs created and retained or produce their own estimates. Several cities, such as Phoenix, Milwaukee, and Columbus, also require targeted hiring to increase the economic benefits to low- and moderate-income persons or city residents. Most cities do not analyze secondary benefits. San Jose and Philadelphia sometimes examine increased tax revenues, as does Jacksonville, which also looks at other categories of benefits, such as the increase in services to poverty areas. Columbus tries to estimate jobs created indirectly by a project but does not use this in determining the amount of subsidy to be given. Thus, the state of the art in evaluating possible costs and benefits of subsidies, especially in advance of the investment, is quite limited.

Cost-Benefit Analysis

At its most basic level, cost-benefit analysis compares two situations: the city with the project and the city without the project. Economic models, whether formal ones or consisting of educated hunches of program administrators, must be used to forecast the most important economic variables both with and without the project. For Chicago, the authors decided to build cost-benefit analyses around simulations from the model developed by Regional Economic Modeling, Inc. (REMI). This is an econometric model, available for many counties and states, of the regional economy, based on an input-output model and a larger set of equations about the local economy. Other cities could use their own local versions of the REMI model or a different model. Even starting with a sophisticated regional model, there was a series of technical and conceptual hurdles.

The first question to be answered in developing a methodology is to define the population for whom costs and benefits are

to be calculated. To a certain extent, this is a policy question rather than a theoretical one, and DPD decided to count benefits to any current resident or potential residents who migrate to the city to take a job created by a subsidy. This also implies that benefits to suburban residents are excluded. It also means that subsidies that merely improve firm efficiency, without thereby increasing payroll or without saving jobs that otherwise would be lost, do not create relevant benefits.

In addition to general economic costs and benefits, DPD also wanted to know the distribution of the benefits over different income categories and a separate analysis of the fiscal effects on city government.

Finally, many economic development projects produce important benefits other than jobs or taxes. These benefits—and possible costs—often relate directly to the location of the project. Putting these neighborhood spillover effects, such as increased neighborhood confidence, improved appearance, or increased congestion, in dollar terms is often misleading and limits the analysis to easily quantifiable effects. Therefore, a separate index of neighborhood spillover effects was designed. Because of its experimental nature and space constraints, the authors do not discuss this index in this article; the technical references contain a complete discussion of their approach.

Thus, the final product of this approach consists of four major parts: 1) an overall cost-benefit analysis, 2) a fiscal impact statement, 3) a distributional analysis of project benefits, and 4) a neighborhood spillover index.

Employment Effects

New or retained jobs are at the heart of the economic effects of business incentives. The first question is whether the investment or activity would be undertaken by the proposing firm or developer in the absence of public subsidy — the "but for" question. In the case of a request for a loan, direct evidence of a firm's inability to do the project without assistance is the refusal of a bank to make a loan. In that case, public support clearly provides gap financing. If private credit is available but the firm is being offered incentives by other places, a subsidy may similarly be needed to keep or attract the firm. Finally, a firm may be able to show that its costs would be much lower elsewhere and thus needs a subsidy to cover the difference. The spreadsheet model used here contains simple questions to ascertain whether any of the above conditions pertain.

Just answering the "but for" question is not enough, though. It may well be that the firm requesting assistance might not go ahead without subsidy, but another firm in the industry might well take its place. In many industries, especially those serving local markets, such substitutions are to be expected.

The model deals with this issue primarily by looking at the industrial sector (standard industrial classification) of the firm. If most of the output of firms in the sector is exported outside of the city, the firm is much less likely to be competing with other local firms. Thus, it is assumed that the new or expanding firm divides its output between local and out-of-city customers in the same proportion as the industry as a whole, as indicated in the REMI model. (If firm-specific information is available, it can be used in the spreadsheet.) The export share of any expansion or new facility is then counted as new employment to the area. The only exception to this is if the industry already is growing very rapidly locally compared to the nation. In that case, it is assumed that investment in the sector already is recognized as profitable by the private sector and does not need additional subsidy.

Much of the business of new or expanding firms will be oriented toward local markets. New jobs for Chicago residents should not count those that would otherwise appear in other Chicago firms in the same industry. Thus, even if a firm meets the "but for" standard, the spreadsheet model should not give full credit for jobs oriented to local production, since other local firms are likely to fill the hole in the market. Since firms on the periphery of the city are competing in part with suburban firms, however, the model considers 30 percent of locally oriented economic activity on the periphery as export to the rest of the metropolitan area; in the central district, only 10 percent is counted as exports, and the model gives credit for the associated jobs.

Estimating the number of jobs retained by a project is more difficult than estimating the new jobs. Research on relocating firms points to space constraints and ownership of existing facilities as the most important determinants of moving. In most cases, expanding firms are constrained from staying in the city by the difficulties of assembling land, environmental problems, or other externalities. In the spreadsheet, information on space constraints and ownership is entered to determine the likelihood that a firm would actually move. If the firm is export-oriented, the analysis also takes into account projected growth rates to determine the likely extent of a substitution effect by other producers in this industry. This information is then used to determine whether credit should be given for job retention.

Jobs, Personal Income, Fiscal Gains

To calculate the effect of new or retained jobs on personal disposable income, one first has to estimate the multiplier effect generated by the expansion of direct employment. For this, the REMI model is used. Its output, already included in the spreadsheet model, provides a predicted figure for the change in total employment (direct plus indirect), the total change in wage bill, and the occupational structure of both the direct and indirect jobs.

While all the direct jobs are located in Chicago itself, not all people holding them will be Chicago residents. In addition, some of the indirect jobs, and many of the workers holding those, will be in the suburbs. The model has the ability to specify the share of direct jobs held by Chicagoans. For example, this would be 100 percent if the company has promised to hire only Chicago residents. Lacking such specific information, the model assumes that for each occupation, the place of residence of direct workers is distributed between the city and the suburbs in the same way that all Chicago workers in that occupation are distributed, according to the U.S. Census. For indirect jobs, it is assumed the workers are distributed in the same way that all workers in the county are distributed.

With these residence distributions, the total change in the wage bill for Chicago residents can be estimated; however, a few more adjustments must be made before the number is meaningful. First, the transfer payments that will be lost because of the increase in employment must be subtracted. Second, there needs to be adjustments for the fact that many of the workers could have done equally well in some other job, in Chicago or elsewhere. Recent studies show that as many as one-half to two-thirds of new or retained jobs are held by potential outmigrants or new immigrants from outside of the city. Higher-skilled workers are especially likely to have access to jobs elsewhere. Thus, the model discounts income gains by the top two occupational quintiles by 75 percent and for

the middle quintile by 50 percent. For the bottom quintiles, the opportunity cost is equal to the transfer payments that are given up when employment expands. All of this information is obtained from the REMI data on the relation between occupational structure and income distribution.

While general economic benefits are important, city government also has to be concerned about its solvency as a fiscal entity. Thus, the model also calculates the specific fiscal gains attributable to the project in order to compare it to the costs. In Chicago, property taxes and local sales taxes vary quite directly with disposable income even though they are not, of course, levied against income. As this ratio remained fairly stable at 5.7 percent during the 1980s, this historical ratio was used in the model. Non-tax local revenues, such as fees for services, are assumed to be offset by corresponding increases in expenditures and were not included as either a cost or a benefit.

Measuring Costs

Originally, the model builders anticipated that DPD staff might estimate the opportunity cost of different funding sources, such as Community Development Block Grant funds or local funds, at different rates. Occasionally this is indeed the case, especially toward the end of the fiscal year when funds may be lost altogether if left unspent. On the whole, however, staff felt that there were no grounds to value one possible use over another. The exception is the State of Illinois' Community Services Block Grant, which can only be used to create jobs for very low-income individuals and has been difficult to spend down. Therefore, the model gives this program an opportunity cost of zero and counts all other programs at full value.

The actual cost of making loans then is the difference between the interest rate the city would have to pay to borrow funds and the rate received, adjusted for expected losses due to default. Additional costs are the income foregone through tax credits or in the form of tax increment financing payments and the administrative costs for city government in processing and monitoring the project. On the other hand, if some infrastructure spending merely reflects expenditures that the city would have had to make in a few years anyway, they should be counted as costs foregone in the year in which they would otherwise have taken place.

A seven-year time horizon was chosen for measuring costs and benefits. Given the uncertainties of the marketplace, it seems reasonable to require projects to show positive benefits within seven years. The discount rate used for private funds was the real long-term mortgage rate and for public funds, the long-term municipal bond rate.

Although this discussion may seem complex, even though it is only a summary of the full technical description of the model, to run the spreadsheet a project analyst only has to answer 12 questions and enter basic numbers about the financing terms and the sources of funds. Everything else is contained in the model. The accompanying case study (an amalgam of several city-sponsored projects) shows the output of the spreadsheet, which runs on Quattro-Pro 4.0. The key numbers are the summation of the total benefits minus costs and the total fiscal benefits minus costs.

This methodology for determining the costs and benefits of a proposed new development is illustrated in the following case study of Associated Paper Forms, Inc. (APFI), in the City of Chicago, using the REMI formula. Basic input data for this project is summarized in Figure 1. The various costs and benefits of this proposed development are shown in Figure 2. From the analysis of the APFI project using the REMI formula, it is clear that this project makes good sense from a number of different economic perspectives determined from using this formula, and that this project would be in the best interest of the City of Chicago and its taxpayers in many ways. The final section of this chapter describes the applicability of using this formula for major projects in other communities throughout the United States.

Case Study: Associated Paper Forms, Inc.

This business forms manufacturing company applied for a loan to purchase new equipment and build a warehouse addition to its current plant. The total package looked as follows:

- $450,000, commercial lender;
- $375,000, city loan; and
- $75,000, company equity.

The city used Community Development Block Grant funds for the loan at 75 percent of prime for seven years. Collateral and personal guarantees were adequate.

The first three questions on the spreadsheet (Figure 1) ascertain whether the "but for" condition holds: Is there evidence that the financing is gap financing? Are there competing incentives from other locations? Does Chicago have a demonstrable cost disadvantage? Only one of these has to receive a "yes" answer for the model to assume that indeed the firm would not go ahead with the project without public assistance; in this case, the bank indicated gap financing was essential due to the company's liquidity position.

The next set of questions pertains to job retention. In this case, no claim is being made that jobs would be lost if the deal fell through. The company owns its building and has room on site for expansion, making it less likely to move. There are no pressing problems in the neighborhood. The company is locally based and has no alternative production locations. There is no evidence that the firm will necessarily lose market share in the near future if it does not invest in new technology, and the firm does not meet the very strict federal guidelines related to job retention. Thus, the model will give no credit for job retention.

The two-digit standard industrial classification (SIC) code and information about the location of the firm are entered next. The model uses this to calculate how many of the new jobs would be likely to be created by other local firms in the industry, even if this particular firm did not. Finally, the analyst enters information on the number and expected occupational and residential distribution of employees (not shown in Figure 1). The firm has said low- and moderate-income individuals will be hired but not necessarily only Chicago residents. All other information to be entered relates directly to the financing itself: the terms of the loan and the amounts and sources of funds.

Based on REMI data and other information contained in the model, the spreadsheet now calculates all the other numbers shown. (See Figure 2. The exhibit only shows present values and first-year data; the model actually presents data for all seven years). For instance, based on the projection of 32 project-related jobs, the model counts 29 genuinely new jobs — based on the fact that about 10 percent of the output in this industry is oriented towards the local market. The output also shows that 32.5 indirect jobs will be created by these direct jobs and that 37.7 of all the jobs will be held by Chicago residents. This yields $963,000 in new income per year (measured in 1994 dollars), which after adjustments for taxes and workers' opportunity cost is reduced to $683,000. The distribution across income categories is shown as well.

In addition, the expansion generates $55,000 in new taxes per year and $50,000 in loan repayments. The only costs are the $375,000 loan and $10,000 in administrative costs. Subtracting these from the benefits leaves a net present value of fiscal benefits of $244,000, for a 7.3 percent rate of return, as shown in the summary section of Figures 2. The net present value of all benefits over the seven-year-period is $4.2 million, for an internal rate of return of 42.5 percent.

In summary, it is clear that the Associated Paper Forms project makes good sense. It generates considerable Chicago employment, wages, and tax receipts. Their distribution favors those who need it most. A modest interest subsidy is the only cost to the city. Given that the project was not likely to obtain financing from the private sector, it represents a good investment for Chicago.

Applicability to Other Cities

As it now exists, the model is valid only for Chicago, since it contains Chicago multipliers, tax rates, occupational distributions, industry characteristics, and other data. The basic logic and approach to theoretical issues, however, should be applicable anywhere. Customization for other cities would require the use of parameters from the appropriate local econometric models and other local data.

The model can be improved in many ways. For instance, more research on the extent to which different types of firms and industries export or serve only the local economy would strengthen understanding of whether jobs are really new to the econ-

```
┌─────────────────────────────────────────────────────────────┐
│                FIGURE 1— COST-BENEFIT                         │
│                EVALUATION SPREADSHEET                         │
│   The UIC Center for Urban Economic Development Cost-benefit  │
│      Evaluation Spreadsheet                                   │
│   NAME: Associated Paper Forms              01-Mar-94         │
│                                                               │
│   ═══════════════════════════════════════════════════════    │
│      SECTOR A-1: BASIC INPUT DATA                             │
│   ═══════════════════════════════════════════════════════    │
│                                                               │
│    1. Gap financing? (yes=1, no=0)                    1       │
│    2. Competing incentives? (yes=1, no=0)             0       │
│    3. High Chicago costs? (yes=1, no=0)               0       │
│       Consider: a. Wages                                      │
│                 b. Taxes                                      │
│                 c. Utilities                                  │
│                 d. Input costs                                │
│                 e. Distribution costs                         │
│   ─────────────────────────────────────────────────────      │
│    4. Demonstrable space constraint? (yes=1, no=0)    0       │
│    5. High neighborhood costs? (yes=1, no=0)          0       │
│       Consider: a. Local service deficiencies                │
│                 b. Security                                   │
│                 c. Local transport problems                   │
│    6. Firm leases building or building fully depreciated      │
│       or residential encroachment? (yes=1, no=0)      0       │
│    7. Duplicate capacity? (yes=1, no=0)               0       │
│    8. Potential technological gap (yes=1, no=0)       0       │
│    9. Meets federal retention guideline (yes−1, no−0) 0       │
│   ─────────────────────────────────────────────────────      │
│   10. SIC code    26                                          │
│   11. Peripheral location (yes=1, no=0)               0       │
└─────────────────────────────────────────────────────────────┘
```

which it requires answers, force analysts to clarify their assumptions and have indeed brought out different perspectives among key decision makers.

Thus, the model is an aid in analysis rather than the only tool needed to make decisions about business subsidies. Whether and how much of a subsidy will be given will continue to depend in part on the nature of the negotiation game between firms and governments and, especially for large projects, on political considerations. Use of the model, however, will clarify the assumptions of the analyst and give guidance about costs and benefits.

The usefulness of the model also depends on the political and organizational context. If decision making about business incentives is highly po-

omy or not. Also, there may be other questions that need to be asked to determine whether a firm really needs the subsidy or is truly likely to move and take jobs with it if no subsidy is given.

As long as theories of local economic development and firm location remain relatively tentative, any model built on those theories necessarily rests on assumptions that can be debated and improved. The authors, however, already have found that the use of the model, and the questions to

liticized, use of the model may be seen as a threat. Similarly, if the model is used by a research or evaluation unit to check on the work of business finance specialists, the latter may perceive it as an attack on their autonomy and therefore seek to attack the model's accuracy. To avoid such problems to the extent possible, the Chicago model was developed in close collaboration and consultation with all staffs who were likely to use it.

FIGURE 2 — COST-BENEFIT RESULTS

The UIC Center for Urban Economic Development Cost-benefit Methodology Spreadsheet

NAME: ASSOCIATED PAPER FORMS   01-Mar-94

SECTOR A-4: BASIC SPREADSHEET

You now must enter data on projected job expansion and current employment (lines 1–2) for each year. Then enter all cost data (lines 3–13). To run spreadsheet enter ALT-S.
To run neighborhood spillover index enter ALT-N.
All $ values in 000s of 1994 $s

SIC Code:26

BENEFITS	Project Fiscal Impact	Project Present Value	1994 Year 0	1995 Year 1
1. Projected job expansion			—	32.0
2. Current employment			—	96.0
New and/or retained direct employment	29.0		—	29.0
Indirect employment	32.5		—	32.5
Total employment	61.6		—	61.6
Total Chicago resident employment	37.7		—	37.7
Chicago resident disposable income		5,567	—	962
Chicago resident disposable income (Net of resident paid prop. & local taxes)		5,356	—	926
Income group 5		566	—	98
Income group 4		285	—	49
Income group 3 (net of transfers)		1,530	—	264
Income group 2 (net of transfers)		2,609	—	451
Income group 1 (net of transfers)		366	—	63
Opportunity-adjusted Chicago resident disposable income		3,952	—	683
Income group 5 (25%)		141	—	24
Income group 4 (25%)		71	—	12
Income group 3 (50%)		765	—	132
Income group 2 (100%)		2,609	—	451
Income group 1 (100%)		366	—	63
Tax revenue generated				
All Chicago based govts.	342	342	—	55
Property tax	228	228	—	37
Other taxes	114	114	—	18
City govt. budget only	167	167	—	27
Property tax	66	66	—	11
Other taxes	101	101	—	16
Loan repayment (Planned)	359	359	—	63
Loan repayment (Expected)	<u>287</u>	<u>287</u>	<u>=</u>	<u>50</u>
Total all Chicago based govts. benefits	629		—	105
Total city govt. budget only benefits	455		—	77
Total benefits		4,581	—	788

		(Figure 2, continued)			
COSTS		Project Fiscal Cost	Project Present Value	1994 Year 0	1995 Year 1

All $ values in 000s of 1994 $s

Funding sources:
> Note: Do not count as a cost any funding which would not come to Chicago in the absence of the project.

Loan sources:					
3.	Federal CDBG	375	375	375	0
4.	State CSBG (zero opp. cost)	0	0	0	0
5.	Other state sources	0	0	0	0
6.	City of Chicago loans	0	0	0	0
	Grant sources:				
7.	Federal & state grants				
	City of Chicago funds	0	0	0	0
8.	Department funds	0	0	0	0
9.	Bond issue	0	0	0	0
10.	TIF funds	0	0	0	0
11.	Value of all local tax forgiveness	0	0	0	0
	Total project loans (opp. cost)	375	375	375	0
	Total project grants	0	0	0	0
12.	Total city admin. costs	10	10	10	0
13.	Cost foregone (would have been spent even in absence of project)	<u>0</u>	<u>0</u>	<u>0</u>	<u>0</u>
	Total city govt. budget costs	385		385	0
	Total costs		385		

SUMMARY — IMPACT TO CHICAGO

Benefits-Costs (Total)		4,196
Benefits-Costs (All Chicago based govts)	244	
Benefits-Costs (City govt. budget only)	70	
Capital cost per direct job		13.26
Capital cost per total job		6.25
P.V. benefit per direct job		157.75
P.V. benefit per total job		74.38
Internal rate of return		42.49%
Fiscal internal rate of return		7.27%
City govt. only internal rate of return		2.41%

PART III

The Tools for Renewal

12. BUSINESS IMPROVEMENT DISTRICTS

Richard Bradley

Imagine people using words like "clean," "safe," and "friendly" to describe Times Square. Imagine that the program to make this happen would be paid for by business and property owners rather than by local government. Imagine that this is happening not only in midtown Manhattan but also in more than 1,000 communities, large and small, in North America. Business improvement districts are real and are having substantial impacts in renewing and revitalizing downtowns and commercial areas in local governments of all sizes throughout North America. All of this activity is part of a larger process of bottom-up renewal, or, in this case, from the street level up.

Downtown management districts, often known as business improvement districts (BIDs)—or as business improvement zones (BIZs), special improvement districts (SIDs), or special assessment districts (SADs)—take advantage of state and provincial enabling legislation allowing for property owner assessments, which will be used for both capital and operating im-provements in a commercial district. Districts, which have existed for 20 years, continue to increase in number and are excellent mechanisms for supporting community and economic development.

There are two fundamental dimensions to business improvement districts. One is their use to raise money for physical improvements and enhancements in downtowns and commercial districts; the other is their use for management services that make downtowns clean, safe, and friendly. Representatives of Baltimore's downtown district recently announced, for example, that crime had been reduced by 27 percent after the district's first year of operation. Many communities, however, are adding other dimensions to their concepts of what districts can do, including business and economic development, transportation and parking management, management of such social problems as homelessness, and operation of major special events and arts-related activities.

Originally published as "Downtown Renewal: The Role of Business Improvement Districts," Public Management, *Vol. 77, No. 2, February, 1995. Published by the International City/County Management Association, Washington, D.C. Reprinted with permission of the publisher.*

Historic Functions

Improving Public Service. The origins of the 1990s downtown management districts were rooted in a long tradition by which property owners in certain areas either have agreed to assess themselves or have been assessed to fund physical improvements. Historically, these assessments have been used to fund the creation of sewer districts or road improvement districts or even to finance capital facilities like schools and other public-purpose programs. In the middle 1960s, cities established districts to cover the cost of putting together pedestrian and transit malls and/or major streetscape improvements, as in the case of the pedestrian and transit mall in downtown Minneapolis, Nicollet Mall. This tradition continues today, with BID monies used to pay for everything from pavement renewal and benches to newspaper stands and vending carts. The Center City District in Philadelphia is about to launch a $35 million effort to rebuild much of the streetscape in the center of this city. Smaller downtowns may use such resources to pay for new holiday lighting.

Supplementing City Services. A secondary origin of the modern management district was the need to supplement city services so as to provide a high level of maintenance and security, especially for newly redeveloped areas. Once again, the most prominent early example was Minneapolis, where property owners agreed that, in addition to paying off capital costs, they would provide funds to ensure that the pedestrian mall was maintained appropriately. The New Orleans Downtown Development District followed suit in a big way, committing half of its annual funding to physical projects and the other half to increased maintenance and security for the downtown.

By the 1970s, some downtowns simply were raising funds to provide revenue to cover these supplemental services without committing any resources to physical improvements. Today, communities are using BID resources to hire off-duty police officers or full-time private security personnel — sometimes called "hosts" or "community service representatives" — to provide an on-street security presence. Santa Cruz, California, for instance, is adding seven such individuals to help in its downtown. Correspondingly, additional maintenance workers are added to do everything from sweeping streets to shoveling snow. In some areas, such as the garment district of Los Angeles, these maintenance positions are offered to formerly homeless people.

Shopping Center Competitions. A third purpose for districts grew out of models for shopping center management. Once the concept of using monies for public space "management" had been accepted, these funds began to be applied to management functions besides security and maintenance but still related to improving the economic climate of the downtown. Such applications included helping to organize retailers, providing marketing and promotional activities, putting on special events, and funding a variety of activities that improved both the retail and office markets in the districts.

Helping to crystallize the importance of these services to downtown property owners was the realization that suburban shopping centers that were providing these services were competing with downtown retailing. Thus, shopping center competition, together with the application of the common-area maintenance concept, became a model and an impetus for downtowns using the mechanism of a management district. Today, a continuing focus of all BIDs, from 42nd Street in New York to Main Street U.S.A., is making downtown retail work. Some downtowns, like Neenah,

Wisconsin, have evolved a focused approach to improving the downtown marketplace called "centralized retail management"; through this approach, the district enables downtown property owners and merchants to receive the same kind of leasing assistance provided by shopping center management firms.

Long-Term, Equitable Financing. Underlining all the concerns that led to the initiatives described above was the need for long-term, substantial, and equitable financing. Many communities had tried voluntary contributions and assessments to pay for physical projects and/or administrative and operating costs. Given the changing economic conditions for different kinds of businesses or property owners, this strategy never provided a sufficient or reliable stream of funding.

As a consequence, many communities began using districts as a way to achieve this financing assurance. In most cases, the revenues resulted from an assessment on existing property tax, ranging from $.05 to $.15 extra per square foot. A delightful paradox is that most BIDs require that property and business owners agree voluntarily to be assessed mandatorily. This requirement usually translates not only into direct financial commitment but also, equally important, into direct personal involvement and interest. This private sector involvement increases the potential for success.

New Dimensions of BIDs

Economic Development. Most recently, BIDs have launched explicit economic development and business enhancement initiatives. An implicit goal of all BIDs has been economic renewal. At the most basic levels, this effort has been directed toward retaining and attracting retail businesses. Through programs aimed at improving business management or enhancing business opportunities, retailing is improved.

On another level, these activities have been directed toward growth of other commercial enterprises through other, similar retention and recruitment activities. Many districts assign staff to contact many businesses in the district at least annually to learn what their needs are for expansion and development. In Millburn, New Jersey, for example, SID leaders helped establish a bank CDC to provide loans for businesses, after learning that access to capital was a major need.

Social Development. In many communities, the problems of homelessness and panhandling spill over into the downtown. Rather than treat these problems as public nuisances, many BIDs are organizing coordinated programs involving social, health, housing, and police services to address issues related to the homeless and other street people.

In Portland, Oregon, the downtown association, using BID funds, manages an antipanhandling campaign, deploys security workers to intervene when someone is causing a "social disturbance," coordinates support programs for the homeless, and, when necessary, calls upon backup support from the police department. This balanced approach is acclaimed by homeless advocates, merchants, and downtown users.

Transportation and Parking Maintenance. In Kalamazoo, Michigan, the local downtown organization, which also operates a BID, took over the management of the city's parking "ramps" years ago. Asking themselves how Nordstrom's department stores would manage garages, the downtown group proceeded to improve facilities maintenance and customer services by offering valet parking, car cleaning, and repairs, thereby increasing uses and revenues for the facilities and making parking a downtown amenity.

Other BID-supported organizations are establishing transportation management organizations to facilitate transportation improvements. In Indianapolis, efforts are under way to improve management of on-street parking. Transportation, in other words, lends itself well to management by BIDs.

Services. As the use of the management district financing tool to aid in the renewal of downtowns has progressed over the last two-and-a-half decades, the range of services provided by management programs has grown and evolved. The following is a list of service categories (each of which usually encompasses a number of subservice elements) that generally describes what district funds are being used for today.

Physical Improvements
Streetscapes, signage, banners, benches, and lighting

Supplementing Local Government Services
Security
  Providing additional security officers
  Coordinating public and private security
  Supporting mounted patrols
  Increasing activity programming
  Offering design assistance
Maintenance
  Providing additional maintenance workers
  -Sweeping and cleaning of sidewalks
  -Removing snow
  -Maintaining amenities
  Increasing frequency of trash pickups
  Providing more litter receptacles

Improvement of the Downtown Marketplace
  Management/retention/recruitment of retail
    -Organizing retailers
    -Organizing property owners
    -Undertaking market analysis

  Developing a retention/recruitment program
  Developing leasing plans
  Providing leasing funds

Events and Activity Programming
  Sponsoring image events and festivals
  Sponsoring retail promotion events
  Organizing downtown worker events

Vending/Public Markets
  Developing ordinances
  Management street bending
  Organizing "stall" markets
  Establishing and managing farmers' markets
  Planning and organizing public markets

Assistance in Office Leasing
  Undertaking market analyses
  Coordinating leasing assistance
  Developing a retention program

Informing and Promoting
  Marketing and advertising
  Communications and media management

Animating
  Programming events and activities
  Planning and managing arts and entertainment districts

Address Social Needs
  Homelessness
  Daycare
  Employment assistance

Improving Access and Mobility
  Parking management
  Employee/employer transportation management assistance

Smaller communities generally spend their resources on hiring a downtown manager, organizing retailers, running special events, and making small-scale physical enhancements. Larger communities devote a higher proportion of their budgets to supplementing city maintenance and security services.

Benefits of Management Programs

While in each case the benefits of a management program are tailored specifically to the needs for which a community chooses to raise resources, there appear to be a number of generalized benefits, including:

- Providing a cleaner, safer, more attractive downtown.
- Ensuring an adequate resource base on a predictable, certain, and sufficient scale.
- Requiring direct, community-based, ratepayer oversight and direction.
- Compelling entrepreneurial management: nonbureaucratic, flexible, and creative.
- Responding to market and community needs.
- Helping to maintain and improve property sales.
- Helping to maintain and improve retail sales and tenancy.
- Making downtown more competitive with surrounding business and retail centers.

Revenues and Expenditures

The amounts of money raised in communities vary greatly, depending on the size of the area, commitment, and willingness to be assessed. Small communities with populations ranging up to 25,000 have budgets ranging from $25,000 to $100,000. Several medium-sized communities of up to 80,000 people have budgets as high as $300,000 but usually average from $100,000 to $125,000. Big-city budgets, like that for the Center City District in Philadelphia, range as high as $7.5 million annually.

Reasons for Success

Apparently, a major reason for BIDs' success is that, while the districts live and work in partnership with the local government, they usually are led and governed by representatives of the businesses upon which the assessment has been placed. This feature ensures a high level of accountability and entrepreneurship. At the core, however, is the recognition that it is cooperation, not simply between the public and private sectors but also among the business people and residents/users of downtown, that is the fundamental value making for successful downtowns.

Lastly, districts succeed because of their public entrepreneurial styles. They must be responsive and must evolve quickly to stay close to their clients and to the downtown customer. BIDs likely will grow in number and size as new roles and responsibilities emerge. From Main Street to Times Square, they will play increasingly important roles.

13. BUSINESS INCUBATORS

Thomas Ressler

Business incubators, as their name implies, are "mother hen" programs and facilities that help "hatch" new and fledgling companies by providing support services and professional advice the firms might not obtain otherwise.

Business incubation programs usually are housed in facilities which offer start-up companies space at below-market rental rates. In some cases, however, incubation programs provide professional services and advice, but not space, operating as "incubators without walls."

Highly adaptable to meet the needs and goals of their founders, incubators' missions range from bringing jobs to (and increasing the wealth of) inner cities, to diversifying rural economies, to transferring and commercializing technology from universities and major corporations.

Business incubation is a relatively new concept: In 1984, there were only 50 business incubators in the United States; today, there are more than 500 in North America, with new ones opening at a rate of four or five per month.

In California, where business incubation is just beginning to gain momentum, the first incubators opened in the mid-1980s; today, there are more than 25 incubation programs, with another dozen in various stages of development. In addition, California is one of only a handful of states to have a state incubation association, the California Business Incubator Network (CBIN), founded in 1990.

Given California's current economic climate, business incubation makes a lot of sense, says a national authority.

"Business incubators are proven tools for creating jobs, encouraging technology transfer and starting new businesses, all of which can help reverse California's economic downturn," says Dinah Adkins, executive director of the National Business Incubation Association (NBIA), a professional organization of more than 690 incubator developers, managers and industry friends.

Business incubators accelerate the successful development of entrepreneurial companies, Adkins adds, by providing hands-on assistance, a variety of business and technical support services, and milestones for start-up and fledgling firms during their most vulnerable years.

Originally published as "Hatching Incubators," Western City, *Vol. LXIX, No. 7, July, 1993. Published by the League of California Cities, Sacramento, California. Reprinted with permission of the publisher.*

"An incubation program's main goal is to produce successful graduates, businesses that are financially viable and free-standing when they leave the incubator, usually in two to three years," Adkins says, observing that about 30 percent of incubator clients "graduate" each year.

In all, more than 6,000 developing businesses are part of incubation programs, with the latest NBIA research showing that 35 percent of those are service companies; 27 percent, light manufacturing; 22 percent, technology products and research and development; and, 17 percent, other kinds of firms.

"The earliest incubation programs were focused on technology in general or on a combination of light industrial, technology and service firms. Today these programs are referred to as 'mixed use/general purpose' incubators," Adkins says.

"However, in more recent years, new incubators have been developed to target specific industries, such as food processing, medical technologies, space and ceramics technologies, and wood working," she adds.

"Incubators also have been created for arts and crafts people, for retail firms and for software development, as well as for women and minorities, and microenterprise creation."

Incubator sponsors include local governments, economic development agencies, four-year universities, two-year colleges and combinations of these groups, as well as for-profit incubators launched by individuals or corporations. There also is a growing segment of nonprofit and for-profit incubators.

North Carolina First Flight, Inc., operates 12 business incubators scattered around the state. Originally a state agency charged with boosting the state's economy, the organization recently became a nonprofit agency. The agency's offices are located at George Mason University where one of its incubators, focusing on high-tech businesses, is located. Businesses incubated in First Flight have included a software firm, a company which manufacturers a thermal faces identification system which allows business security systems to recognize the faces of individuals who are authorized to enter, a geographic information system company which makes use of NASA technology, and an auto repair firm. One company, which provides a central reservation system for hotels grossed $300,000 last year, but revenues surpassed $3 million in just the first quarter this year. While the incubator located at George Mason focuses on high-tech companies, most of First Flight's incubators are located in more rural areas of the state where the focus is on textiles, consulting services, and crafts. One incubator has helped launch a small city's only travel agency.

Incubated Companies Have High Success Rate

Whatever their mission or location, business incubators share a common bottom line: success in helping new firms.

"Studies show that new businesses are most vulnerable during their first several years of operation, during which time 60 percent fail," Adkins says.

Not so, however, for new businesses affiliated with an incubator.

"Research shows that more than 80 percent of firms that have ever been in an incubation program are still in operation," Adkins says, describing research conducted by state government agencies in Michigan and Pennsylvania. "Furthermore, Coopers & Lybrand, the accounting and business consulting firm, has found that 'graduates' of incubators—firms that have left incubators for their own commercial space—are increasing revenues and creating jobs."

For some incubator graduates, the sky's the limit: at least two of the firms included on *Inc.* magazine's most recent *Inc. 500* are graduates of incubator programs. One, MapINFO Corp., a spinoff of Rensselaer Polytechnic Institute, recorded $15 million in revenues last year on its business mapping services. The other, Restek Corp., is a fast-growing business in State College, Pennsylvania. With $6.5 million in revenues in 1991, it manufactures capillary columns and accessories for analytical labs.

Adkins explains that incubators are achieving success by providing precisely the assistance many start-up businesses need.

"Most start-up companies are launched by an entrepreneur who has a great idea, but no business or management experience," Adkins says. "Incubators—through their own expert staffs and a wide array of outside consultants and advisors—can provide assistance in every aspect of running a business, from developing a sound business plan to marketing the product or service."

Equally important is the financial assistance incubators can provide.

"Through a variety of programs, incubators can help their clients and tenants obtain the financing and capital required to grow their businesses," Adkins observes, noting that, in addition to helping clients qualify for loans from commercial lenders, many incubators also have their own micro-loan and seed capital funds. Further, many incubators help match young firms with venture capitalists and other private investors, and some incubators take equity or royalty positions in their companies.

Business Incubators: A Model for Urban Revitalization

In California, inner-city business incubators are operating, or are being developed, a trend Adkins says can help restore hope in such neighborhoods as those of South Central Los Angeles.

"Business incubation programs have a proven track record of being able to help revitalize inner-city neighborhoods," Adkins says, noting that one of the best examples of this type of facility is Wisconsin's Milwaukee Enterprise Center (MEC), which opened in 1986.

Housed in a six-story, 195,000-square foot former Nunn-Bush shoe factory, MEC was founded and is owned by the Wisconsin Foundation for Vocational, Technical and Adult Education (WFVTAE) and Milwaukee Area Technical College (MATC). The building, donated to WFVTAE by Nunn-Bush, had been vacant 10 years and was in serious disrepair; it has been renovated section by section.

MEC's accomplishments are impressive. According to Julius Morgan, MEC's director for entrepreneurial development, the incubator's 70-some tenants employ some 400 people and generate monthly revenues of $1.6 million. Minority ownership accounts for more than 70 percent of the tenants. (Of the 30 percent "majority"—white—owners, many commute to MEC from the suburbs.)

Almost one-half of the tenants' employees live within a one-mile radius of MEC, where the unemployment rates are the city's highest. In addition, MEC recently opened a second facility, a 120,000-square foot former Square D battery factory.

To meet the needs of inner-city entrepreneurs, MEC provides extensive educational and training programs, including those offered through its Basic Literacy Center, which helps companies and their employees develop literacy, math and computer skills.

Business Incubators: What's New in California

Although business incubator programs in California are fewer in number than those in Northeastern and Midwestern states, they do reflect the diversity common to the industry nationwide. Examples include:

Rural Economic Development. In Winton, located in rural Merced County, Winton Business Adventures occupies a new, 18,000-square foot facility built specifically as an incubator facility and sponsored by the Central Valley Opportunity Center.

"Our objective is to bring jobs to a rural community with a 70-percent minority population," says Thomas Abdul-Salaam, economic development specialist and facility manager.

Open since late 1991, the incubator, which is designed for light manufacturing and office use, is meeting its objectives: it is 90 percent occupied, and its 10 tenants employ 41 people. The incubator has not yet produced any graduates, but it also has not had any failures.

"Our tenants range from a bakery equipment repair company to the publisher of the community's minority newspaper, with others in sales and marketing and service businesses, and we also have one high-technology firm," Abdul-Salaam says.

The incubator also assists external clients by providing them with all the services available to incubator tenants, including counseling and technical assistance.

"Our external programs are an excellent way for us to service entrepreneurs and small firms that basically don't need office space, but rather, office-type support services, as well as the counseling and technical assistance," Abdul-Salaam says.

"The truth is," he adds, "we did not anticipate as many people wanting office space and the associated services, so these programs give us a way to reach these people."

Food Processing Incubator. Among only three such incubators nationwide, the Foodworks Culinary Center in Arcata is flourishing.

"I thought that in a rural, isolated area such as ours, where food is the natural resource, there could be a type of vertical integration, including growers, processors, wholesalers, and retailers," says Cindy Copple, executive director of the Arcata Economic Development Corp., Foodworks' owner and operator.

Growers, wholesalers and retailers, of course, were in place, but local processors were not.

Copple, whose background includes working in the food industry, began to hear about incubators while serving on a national food cooperative and realized an incubator might be a way to help establish local food processors.

She began to plan the incubator with a group of some 30 potential tenants, which over time "self de-selected" to nine committed tenants. After a combination of public and private funding was obtained, Copple oversaw the design and construction of a 20,000-square foot incubator facility.

Foodworks opened in July 1992 and was fully occupied — with the original nine companies plus three more — a month later. In addition to food processors, who produce a wide range of products, tenants include a labeling and packaging firm and an assembler of gift baskets filled with tenants' products.

For-Profit/Technology Transfer. A good example of a for-profit business incubator is the Technology Development Center (TDC), founded in 1991 in Davis by partners Mary Ferguson and Charles Soderquist.

"Our focus is on technology transfer

from the University of California at Davis, where there are many ideas and patents that have not been commercialized," says Ferguson, who serves as the incubator's executive director.

Ferguson and Soderquist bring a winning combination of experience to the incubator: she served 14 years as program manager for two major research grants at UCD; he is a well-known Davis-area entrepreneur with a Ph.D. in agricultural and environmental chemistry who in 1985 helped engineer a complex triple merger that resulted in a national network of laboratories known as Enseco, Inc.

To assist companies with high growth potential, TDC has established a $1 million seed fund, financed by private investors. TDC retains an equity interest in the businesses it helps get started.

TDC has worked with 10 client companies, three of which have graduated. The incubator also is managing a company, which commercializes technology spun off by another incubator firm. Ferguson is president of this company, which is field-testing a naturally extracted product that repels beavers from trees in areas where beaver dams are not appreciated.

An Inner-City Focus. The business incubator, San Francisco Renaissance, focuses on assisting inner-city minorities and women informing new businesses. An outgrowth of an intensive entrepreneurship training program, the incubator offers business consultation, phone answering services, a place for entrepreneurs to network, and other assistance.

Now in its fifth year, San Francisco Renaissance has assisted the start-up of 11 businesses including a general contractor, a firm which assists newcomers to the area in locating rental housing, and a Spanish-language book seller. The companies had gross revenues of more than $1 million in the past year, and the budget for the incubator itself runs between $100,000 and $130,000 annually with funding coming from Community Development Block Grant funds and from contributions from such private-sector sources as Bank of America, the San Francisco Foundation, Pacific Gas & Electric and Pacific Telesis.

Business Incubation: A Brief History

While there have always been shared spaces, services and management in the real estate market, business incubators as we now know them in the United States came into being in the late 1970s.

The industry began in the industrial northeast, where the "rust-belt" economic conditions of the late 1970s and early 1980s prompted not only a renewed entrepreneurial spirit, but an emphasis on economic development and job creation.

This emphasis resulted in three simultaneous movements. The first was the attempt to use old, abandoned factory buildings in distressed areas of the Midwest and Northeast by subdividing them for small firms; the second was begun as an experiment funded by the National Science Foundation to foster entrepreneurship and innovation at major universities.

The third movement arose from the initiatives of several successful individual entrepreneurs or groups of investors who sought to transfer their own new venture experiences to new companies in an environment conducive to successful technological innovation and commercialization.

America's First Business Incubator

The oldest U.S. incubator on record — which, decades ahead of its time, reflects the movement to "recycle" old buildings— was launched in 1959 in Batavia, N.Y.

Known as the Batavia Industrial Center (BIC), this incubator grew out of one family's desire to offset an economic downturn.

"In 1957, Massey-Ferguson, the farm implement manufacturer, closed its 850,000-square foot plant, putting almost 2,000 employees out of work," recalls Joe Mancuso, who with his four sons manages BIC.

"In a town of only 17,000 people, this was a tremendous blow, and my family, who owned a number of retail businesses in town, decided to buy the building in an attempt to attract new industry and create jobs."

During its 30-year history, BIC has had more than 600 tenants, virtually all successful, representing a wide range of business and industry, from traditional manufacturing firms to high-technology companies.

Chickens Help Hatch a Name

Mancuso believes he may have coined the term "incubator."

"In our first year, one of our tenants was a chicken company, which had about 400,000 chickens in 80,000 square feet of space," Mancuso says.

"We were out on the road a lot of the time, trying to interest investors and attract companies to the center, and in a joking way, because of all the chickens, we started called it 'the incubator.'

"The name caught on and we continued to refer to the center as 'the incubator'

throughout the 1960s, long after the chickens were gone."

Mancuso's claim carried some weight: throughout the 1960s, he was extremely active in economic development circles—he was president of New York State's economic development association in 1967 — telling one and all about the success of his new idea, the business "incubator."

Despite the BIC and a couple of other early examples, it wasn't until the mid–1980s that incubators came into their own. The impetus, Adkins recalls, was from the U.S. Small Business Administration (SBA), which promoted incubator development from 1984 until 1987 through its Office of Private Sector Initiatives.

Under the direction of John Cox, now SBA's director of finance and investment, the agency held a series of regional conferences to disseminate the word on incubation; SBA also published a newsletter and several incubation handbooks. As a result of this activity, incubator development grew from just over 20 openings annually in 1984 to more than 70 in 1987.

NBIA, which was formed by industry leaders in 1985 and which initially had but 40 members, today serves 690 members with training programs. It also offers a clearinghouse for information on incubator management and development issues. The association, which by 1987 had become the primary source of incubator information, also publishes a wide range of "how-to" materials to assist incubators and their start-up and fledgling firms.

14. COMMUNITY-BASED DEVELOPMENT ORGANIZATIONS

Herbert J. Rubin

Community-based development organizations (CBDOs) are nonprofit, housing and commercial developers who do "the difficult job of providing service and leadership in communities that need help and that other agencies cannot or will not serve" (Vidal, 1992, p. 111). Within neighborhoods that the mainstream economy has neglected, CBDOs build homes, offices, and commercial centers, manage apartments, and create jobs. For the dispossessed, CBDOs provide a stake in society through home ownership; for the welfare poor, they open the possibility of employment; for impoverished neighborhoods, CBDOs provide a focus for planning and local control. The accomplishments of CBDOs reduce the sense of disempowerment and failure felt by those trapped in poor communities (Rubin, 1992, 1993).

In partnership with local governments, CBDOs have accomplished much. Yet, CBDO directors feel that the public sector has hesitated in fully committing to the nonprofits. Public administrators face regulatory and bureaucratic constraints that restrict their support of nonprofits. Further, public administrators are con-cerned about the limited administrative capacity of many nonprofits and the documented failures in the past. CBDO directors, in turn, argue that regulatory and bureaucratic constraints can be changed through the political process and that the limited administrative capacity of CBDOs would improve if the public sector provided more of the operating expenses of community developers.[1]

Directors of CBDOs suggest that those in the public sector do not understand the CBDO perspective toward community development and fear that public officials have difficulty comprehending what it means for an organization to be simultaneously nonprofit, community based, and a developer. As developers CBDOs build homes and businesses, but as community-based non-profits (and recipients of grant funds) their work is guided by community residents and, in part, is intended to empower the poor. As developers of physical properties, they perform very much like for-profit builders; as organizations responsive to community needs, they behave more like nonprofit service providers. To those in the public sector, CBDOs seem to

From Public Administration Review, *Vol. 53, No. 5, September/October, 1993. Published by the American Society for Public Administration, Washington, D.C. Reprinted with permission of the publisher.*

act both as a nonprofit fish and a commercial fowl, a confusing combination.

Partnering Between CBDOs and Local Government

With local government support, community-based development organizations have shown they can produce. They have constructed shopping centers in burnt out areas of inner cities, established quality housing in place of slums, enabled the poor to own homes, helped start up minority-owned companies with small loans, and sponsored job development programs for minorities and abused women (Peirce and Steinbach, 1987, 1990; Kelly *et al.*, 1988). Physical output has been impressive. For example, CBDOs "have produced almost 320,000 units of housing in total for very poor people, including close to 87,000 in the past three years ... [and] almost 90,000 permanent jobs were created or retained in the past five years" (NCCED, 1991, p. 2).

For success in these projects, local government support is vital. Of the 1,160 CBDOs responding to a study, 413 reported receiving support from local government, in addition to pass-through money from the Community Development Block Grants (NCCED, 1991). Some local governments provide the core administrative expenses that enable CBDOs to maintain themselves while planning development projects. In several cities, CBDOs receive public funding as the delegated representatives of city governments in programs to retain jobs, repair store facades, and facilitate neighborhood fix-up. For instance, under Mayor Washington, Chicago's economic development office funded neighborhood organizations to help keep industries in their communities. More than a hundred CBDOs obtained their core financing through such programs (Clavel and Wiewell, 1991).

Supportive administrators have played catalytic roles in community projects by using city or CDBG funds to take the least-secure position on a mortgage for a CBDO-sponsored housing or commercial development project. By assuming the financial risk, government encourages conventional financiers to participate (Dreier, 1989; Suchman *et al.*, 1990). Government has also supported CBDOs indirectly by focusing portions of the city capital budget on neighborhood needs. Local government funding is especially useful and appropriate when it picks up the added costs of development caused by its location in a declining neighborhood. It costs more to refurbish a building adjacent to an abandoned environmental hazard; likewise, it is more expensive to build in a neighborhood where construction materials might be stolen by those needing money for a drug purchase.

Government support extends beyond financial aid. For example, local officials have provided administrative waivers of building and inspection fees and have donated buildings to CBDOs from those obtained by government because of tax liens. Supportive officials have joined with CBDOs in building inspection programs that pressure slumlords to sell their property for rehabilitation by community groups. Cities help fund training for CBDOs. Cincinnati, for instance, has a line item in its development budget that provides community-based developers with training and expertise.

Some public administrators offer strategic and tactical support to CBDOs. In one city, a progressive administrator described how he worked with community groups to pressure the banks to set aside funding for neighborhood development. While negotiating with the banks on a set-aside for poor neighborhoods, this administrator informed community activists which of the banks were recalcitrant and suggested those that might be responsive to direct action campaigns carried out by the community groups.

Tensions in the Partnership

Although cooperation is often successful, tension can develop between city officials and community developers, a tension aggravated through mutual misunderstanding. Public officials comment on the ephemeral nature of many community groups, and delicately refer to scandals in neighborhood expenditure of public funds. They worry about the capacity of CBDOs to produce to scale.

Community developers, on the other hand, sometimes feel they are treated by the cities as second-rate citizens. The head of a successful, large-scale producer of housing described her feelings that city officials often show "disregard or disrespect for [CBDOs].... It is incredible like feeling that [CBDOs] are not worth all the time and effort." She argued that "a for-profit person does not have to go through the months of work that we put in to prove to them that we were a professional, viable organization." CBDO directors complained about the extensive paperwork and long delays involved in obtaining public money, especially pass-through federal grants. Others questioned the paternalism involved when cities placed large sums into community redevelopment while insisting that CBDOs follow city planning procedures. In a city where that was occurring, a director of a successful neighborhood-based CBDO pondered whether "you can encourage the development of a bottom up system from the top?"

The perspectives of both government officials and CBDO directors are based on their experiences. CBDO directors can legitimately argue that they are not getting enough money to stabilize and develop the

administrative capacity cities would want them to have. Although large numbers of CBDOs report receipt of city money, the total amounts are small, especially in comparison to city development budgets (NCCED, 1991; Vidal, 1992). In comparison to conventional economic development programs, public support of community-based work is limited. A national survey of low-income housing concludes that it is doubtful if cities "are providing the assistance necessary for [CBDOs] to operate effectively" (Goetz, 1992, p. 421). Moreover, support is disproportionately concentrated in a limited number of cities in which public officials already recognize the need to work with the communities (Vidal, 1992, p. 15). Even in cities reputedly most supportive of the neighborhood movement, CBDOs were, at best, relatively invisible to governmental agencies involved in the development business (Vidal, 1992, p. 95). For instance, despite an announced tilt toward the neighborhoods, community groups in Cleveland receive only a small percentage of that city's development funds (Schorr, 1991).

Government officials, in turn, face the realities of past failures of the community movement and fear new funds might also be misspent. They remember the scandals of the Model Cities era in which some community-based agencies did little to alleviate problems of the poor. City officials are aware of stalled production among CBDOs. Two of the organizations I am studying have each worked for over half a decade on projects that have received city money and have yet to break ground. While the downturn in the economy can be blamed, from the city's perspective, little has been accomplished, while much support has been provided.

On a daily basis, administrators who support the community movement witness the contention between CBDOs, and shudder as racial and social class schisms become evident. In recent meetings in one city, CBDOs fought with one another and the city in trying to word the Community Housing Assistance Strategy[2] in ways that favored the particular needs of their neighborhoods while depriving other neighborhoods of city money.

Even when they work to help CBDOs, public administrators still confront limitations created by state and federal regulations. For example, federal community-development block grant regulations are so cumbersome that both officials and CBDOs alike fear using such funds in innovative programs, especially those creating revolving loans. In both Wisconsin and Ohio, public administrators were limited in their involvement in housing projects as housing was not considered by the state constitutions as a public purpose.[3]

In projects in which CBDOs, for-profit investors, and the public sector partner, city officials are caught in a bind. For the CBDO, it is of no great import whether the city or a for-profit partner provides the equity share in a community project, so long as adequate funds are available. The city contribution allows the project to work by providing the for-profit participants a comfort zone for their investments. However, to extend the impact of its limited development funds, the city tries to encourage the maximum investment from for-profit participants. A senior public official described the resulting bargaining over how much public money and how much private money will be invested: "So it is like you are playing a game of financing chicken, you know, where we will give you money if they will give you money. They will give you money if we give you money." The delays created by these negotiations may create resentment and anger by those in the community movement at the apparent dalliance by the public sector.

Toward an Understanding of Community-Based Development Organizations

Directors of community-based development organizations must renew the trust of public administrators who have been disappointed by community groups in the past. Once trust has been earned through the completion of successful projects, those in the community-based movement then can work to educate public officials to understand their ethos toward community renewal. Three areas of dialogue are needed.

First, CBDOs do not define themselves primarily as a delivery system for a public service. Rather, they see themselves as activist, community promoters in which the physical project is a tool for community empowerment and capacity building. Their mission of holistic change is accomplished by linking social welfare or training programs with physical construction. Many CBDO projects are both fish and fowl.

Second, CBDOs feel that the mindset of public administrators toward nonprofits has been shaped by the service-delivery nonprofits—agencies engaged in counselling, aiding the abused and the abandoned, providing special job-training skills, and other similar endeavors.[4] At times, CBDO successes are visible and countable—number of houses built, for instance. These outcomes are similar to those of service-delivery nonprofits whose accomplishments are measured by the number of clients served. But CBDOs are a markedly different form of nonprofit. They are nonprofits that own and manage property and invest capital and whose clients are often a community, not individuals.

Third, to further complicate the picture, the service provided by many CBDOs is to facilitate the efforts of others who deliver the actual product. CBDOs encourage meetings between local entrepreneurs and building owners that create jobs within the community. CBDOs are asked to verify the bonafides of one business person to another. They place start-up businesses in contact with pro-bono law firms and affordable accountants. On one occasion witnessed, the CBDO, through its neighborhood contacts, was able to reassure a local housing investor that a fire in an adjacent building was an accidental occurrence and not part of an arson scam. Such actions are hard to document and to show as "products" to funders in the public sector.

Acting as mediator and facilitator while providing unfunded services to community members—advice on how to pay for a mortgage, referrals to family service agencies, small loans for appliance replacement, backup support for community anti-crime campaigns—places the CBDO on the financial edge. CBDOs try to support their administrative costs and fund these services to the poor through developer fees received from physical development projects. To the public sector, these fees appear as "profits." To the CBDO, they are the way the organization stays alive between projects and the means to handle the unanticipated problems of community members. The very projects in which CBDOs engage almost necessitate the provision of a social service. An apartment building for abused women, for instance, may require a social worker to counsel the tenants.

CBDOs use physical development as a tool toward empowerment, and advocate for community change. They do not fall cleanly into the existing roles that city officials work with, for-profit developers, or not-for-profit service providers. Moreover, CBDOs as advocates for community empowerment, suggest to some city officials the bumbling, perhaps corrupt, community organizations of the past. Because city officials have no positive and accurate pre-existing role for the CBDO, their directors must present their case to those in the public sector. What follows is such a discussion.

The Ideology of Holistic Empowerment

To CBDO leaders, physical development is a tool, the means, toward accomplishing the broader end of economic empowerment and economic transformation for the poor. To aid the CBDOs in these efforts, those in the public sector must first understand the holistic vision for the community held by CBDOs in which physical and social consequences of projects overlap and the equity consequences of development are as important as its profitability.

To remain solvent, CBDOs need to break even in their work, but unlike for-profit companies, CBDOs try to ensure that at least some of the benefits redound to the poor and support a broader community renewal. A CBDO will refurbish an abandoned convent or school to house the elderly poor in the neighborhood who no longer can afford or are able to maintain fully independent living. It might be cheaper to move people away but far less equitable. In addition, maintaining the building preserves a community symbol.

CBDOs encourage community members to share in the self-esteem that occurs as a neighborhood that others have abandoned takes on a new life. In north Chicago, a CBDO converted an abandoned supermarket to a "Mercado," a shared market for small-scale community merchants. In Grand Rapids, a community organization helped transform a derelict block into a minority-owned shopping mall that returned to the community stores that had abandoned it. In South Chicago, the community-development organization refurbished an eyesore building into an art incubator, housing artists whose work reflects local ethnic and cultural pride.

Doing holistic programs involves linking together service and training programs with physical construction projects. In programs found in several cities, the poor are placed in an ownership position in rehabilitated homes through a lease-purchase arrangement. The CBDO buys and refurbishes the home and rents it at affordable rates (made possible by public subsidies) to the working poor. Part of the rent is treated as a down payment and the poor accumulate assets. Meanwhile families who have never owned a home receive ownership training — in making repairs, funding a reserve fund, and making a mortgage payment. The financing is established so that within a few years, title can be passed to the renter and empowerment occurs as community members gain economic and social control. Ownership gives the poor a stake and a willingness to fight back, as a CBDO director argued, "If you own your own house, you are empowered."

Ownership empowers not only those within the community, but also the community-based development organization itself. Having equity on which to borrow allows the community-based organization to take the initiative, create a project, and then persuade others to join in; a reversal of top-down paternalism. The need to follow the changing fashion of granting agencies is reduced, enhancing the capacity for community-directed change.

The combination of goals in holistic development can complicate projects, especially as the goals of material ownership and empowerment of the poor merge. The development of the Mercado in north Chicago incorporated a conscious effort to demonstrate to community members their power, but that effort made the project more difficult. The CBDO director described how it was done:

> Community people have been involved.... We now have a group that includes both businesses, representatives from other [community] groups and churches, some of our tenants, some of our poor people. We have tenants on our board to help make sure that the board doesn't take control away from that steering committee.... This Mercado committee ... is going to select the contractor. [The goal was to] put the knowledge and experience in the hands [of poor people], and make decision.... The whole approach is community controlled development and empowerment through development.

Another approach to empowerment is to assure that those in the neighborhood, rather than outsiders, benefit from the consequences of the projects. In explaining the motivation for undertaking a $2 million building in an economically marginal community, a CBDO director said:

> a lot of stuff is all owned by people from outside.... There are eight bars ... all with, we call them shirts, people who are professionals.... They are all owned by people from outside. And, employees are family or people from the ... suburbs ... all the cash those eight bars generate, none of it ever changes hands in the community even once. It leaves at two and it is gone. We are going to put businesses on the first floor, then do a restaurant, nightclub, and have small businesses ... and maintain ownership [in the community].

The CBDO owns, designs, runs, and manages a project itself and then spins-off ownership to those in the community as part of a holistic social agenda.

Community empowerment can be a source of contention with city administrators. An inexperienced community board may not inspire trust in their judgments. Boards composed of minority group members can evoke negative stereotypes among city officials, even though the board members are highly trained professionals. One director in an African-American community reflected that because his CBDO board was all Black,[5]

> the city ... would demand things of me that had nothing to do with the proficiency of the project. They even went so far as to suggest that I put some Caucasians on my board of directors, [they said] "you need to expand your board." I said, "what do you mean expand your board?" "You know, so you have got a more diverse representation on your board." Now I got school teachers, I got business owners, I got directors of alternative education programs. I got an accountant. You know, all of them African-American. But ... [a]ll he saw was a bunch of black folk down there and "you need to expand your board." So I said, "what do you mean expand my board?" [the city official responded] "Well, you know it is perceived as being a very closed corporation and you know a lot of people won't trust that situation, the way it is, so if you expanded it, you know, a little more expertise, and what not." "So you're talking, put some white people on my board?" "Well that would help, you know, that would help." I gave him their $50,000 back.

From the perspective of CBDO directors, public administrators show distrust of neighborhood people. They put more faith in people from the business community, and are more comfortable when business people tell those in poor communities what is needed. Such a model is problematic to CBDOs, not only because of the top-down decision making, which is disempowering, but also because the business people that city officials trust may be the same ones who have already disinvested from the community. As a Caucasian CBDO director in a small city put it,

the mayor had a mayor's housing forum. Good folks, well-intentioned people. But the people who run the whole damn thing are the same people who discriminated against inner-city neighborhoods, community leaders, bank presidents. They don't give a s_____ about one of these neighborhoods.

Holistic development represents a different approach to development than cities generally use, but for precisely that reason, it can bring jobs, shops, and housing to neighborhoods that have been abandoned by traditional investors. City officials need to realize that they cannot use top-down tools in these circumstances, as they have already failed. The newer tools are community directed, and require a different set of techniques to evaluate competence and the likelihood of success.

Spanning the Developmental Gap

To accomplish their ideological agenda of economic empowerment for those in need, the CBDO must bring together resources from government, charities, and private investors. With their knowledge of neighborhood problems and capabilities and access to outside resources. CBDOs can customize projects for specific neighborhoods and attempt new approaches to community problems. An astute CBDO and neighborhood association director observed:

> I think that is the great value of [CBDOs], you can conceive of an idea and test it. And, the whole world doesn't fall apart if it doesn't succeed because it is a small enough activity that you can adjust it the next time ... and, I don't think cities or government understand or appreciate that. That they want to do something that applies everywhere all at once and that is the only way, it has to be a comprehensive program. You don't have to

make a comprehensive program cause one shoe doesn't fit every foot.

Many cities do understand the value of such tailored projects for distressed neighborhoods, but lack the staff and detailed knowledge of the neighborhoods to create appropriate, targeted projects. Supportive public administrators seek out constructive partnerships with community groups to capitalize on the CBDO's ability to both get outside funding and design projects of appropriate, neighborhood scale.

CBDOs sometimes manage loan funds for micro-enterprises. Such funds provide a few hundred to ten thousand dollars to community businesses, sums too small for the city or banks to bother with, but precisely the amounts needed to handle start-up or cash flow problems of neighborhood businesses. This ability to target programs to the smaller beneficiaries also occurs in employment training and job retention efforts. A CBDO can focus on the employment needs of manufacturers too small for the attention of public agencies. Cities can support such activities financially, without the impossible commitment of staff time for supporting numerous small businesses.

Community-based development organizations bridge the gap between city-wide development goals and those within neighborhoods. In Cleveland, a coalition of community groups was established to prevent industrial flight from a working class neighborhood. The coalition convinced the city to oppose a mall that would have displaced many small industries that employed community members. A Board member of the coalition explained,

the City of Cleveland was approached by [downtown developers] who targeted a piece of land to be the first indoor shopping mall … we would lose 450 jobs and very highly paid unionized jobs … we had to convince the city that the choice was not just rejecting

a mall, but making a commitment to the industry that was there and saying "this is not a good trade off…." The City of Cleveland, when they were approached, had no idea of what was going on in that industry … the manufacturers don't trust the city. [The manufacturers] will not share that type of [financial] information with them directly, where they will share it with us, because they know that we can be trusted.

Community-based development organizations span the gap between large governmental programs and specific needs within their communities.

In addition, they can do something else that governmental agencies find it difficult to do, and that is to combine physical development with social programs in a single project. Government agencies are normally specialized and find it difficult to manage projects that involve multiple agencies with different ideologies, clients, and methods of operations.

CBDO projects combine physical development and social improvement recognizing that within the neighborhoods of the poor, the two are inseparable. People need housing, but cannot be expected to pay the rent unless they have the jobs. Owners will not repair homes when drug-trade is rampant, and small shopping malls provide a base for increased community integration. As a community developer reflected when "you get it down to the community level that is where people will force it to be integrated. Because, their lives are integrated."

When local government partners with a CBDO in restoring a community mall, or supporting a small business, the CBDO, through its knowledge about community members and its permanence within the neighborhood, can assure that community people are hired and trained for the specific needs of local businesses. In a case in which such a project was carried out, the community developer of the $2 million building observed, "We've got an agree-ment with the construction trades who are going to provide journeymen as trainers [for community workers].... The focus is going to be training people and then mov-ing them into apprenticeships and then skilled training."

Both government and CBDOs to-gether and separately can build homes and house the dispossessed. By themselves, or through linkages with community service agencies, CBDOs introduce social service programs to housing programs. The CBDO maintains the trust with community members that allows it to provide the training in family budgeting and home maintenance that poor people require to make the transition from renter to owner. Organizers working for a CBDO have helped tenants form a tenant's organiza-tion to empower the tenants and encour-age them to assert control over unruly el-ements that could damage the property. CBDOs have joined with neighborhood-based anticrime programs to root out the drug trade that discourages community reinvestment. Joining social concerns with physical redevelopment makes projects successful and gives the community more hope.

CBDOs can initiate such projects. In one city, a CBDO that had gained credi-bility with public officials through its pre-vious successes in housing and industrial park development, moved to span the gap in community needs. It combined em-ployment training and a gap in social ser-vices in the community with physical de-velopment by establishing home-based daycare for the children of the working poor. A foundation provided the CBDO the wherewithal to plan the scheme. The CBDO, with city funds, refurbished derelict homes up to the standards required for home daycare. Teenagers from the com-munity were employed on the housing construction to obtain job experience.

Meanwhile, with the support of public welfare officials, women on AFDC received instruction as daycare providers. The day-care would be provided primarily for com-munity members in the newly refurbished homes that they would own. Government support allowed the daycare providers to continue AFDC benefits while starting up their businesses. A gap is spanned by the CBDO between social needs, community objectives, and government programs.

Being the Smallest Guy on the Block

The perception of public officials that community-based development organiza-tions lack administrative capacity is gen-erally correct. Surveys show that CBDOs are administratively fragile, can only fund small staffs, and operate on a marginally adequate administrative budget (Vidal, 1992). Although a handful of CBDOs have a stable income stream from a successful apartment or commercial complex and others are fortunate enough to receive a subsidy from religious organizations, most live from hand-to-mouth, dependent on small grants for their core expenses and hoping to eke out a small surplus from housing or commercial development pro-jects. Community-based development or-ganizations must meet overhead expenses and find subsidies for the social costs as-sociated with their development pro-grams. Foundations provide some of this money, but the lion's share is obtained through governmental sources, especially CDBG funds.

For organizations working with the poorest people, organizations whose need for a social subsidy is greatest, the with-drawal of public funds can lead to the death of a CBDO. After a minor financial scandal, one CBDO temporarily lost its local government support, yet, retained its moral and legal responsibility for hundreds of affordable apartments:

> Oh, it's been hell! The past three years, it's been pure hell, believe me! Because we were 65% dependent upon the City for funding, then all of a sudden the City voted ... to withdraw all funding. Just like that [make a "shoo" sound]! It's like having a welfare check and all of a sudden 65% of it's gone. And they still expected me to run this organization and provide housing for poor and low-income. So, we have not had any City funding. We have been living just by rents. A lot of bills have been unpaid. I went without salary, any kind of money at all for nine months.
>
> Just recently, [name] Bank, [I was] trying to borrow there. And, the banker says to me "Well, we understand you've had your problems in the past. It's only been a couple of years. Why don't you continue to operate for another couple of years and come back and see us in a couple of years. Let's see you build your track record back again." Well, two years from now we'll be out of business. You know, I need financial help now.

To avoid such frightening losses, CBDOs may try to build their own economic base from earned equity in projects or charging management fees. A second approach is to work as members of coalitions to pressure government to set up steady funding sources for CBDOs. Both efforts can be misunderstood by local administrators and complicate the government-nonprofit relationship.

Is a Nonprofit Allowed to Make Money?

Each of a handful of larger, nationally known community-based development organizations has sufficient equity so they can, if necessary, invest their own funds, or borrow on their equity. Other organizations seek this freedom by making a small profit on a development project. CBDO directors, however, indicate that city administrators are puzzled by the idea of a nonprofit increasing its own equity reserve from a development fee on a project to help the poor. In a more extreme case, the CBDO director argued:

> The city has its kind of little ideas about how much developers ought to get and how much overhead, how much the nonprofits ought to get. And, for the most part they think the nonprofits ought not to get very much. And for the most part we are starving because of that idea.

That organization was economically marginal and resentful of the situation. But a similar feeling was expressed by a stable organization, whose director claimed the stability in part was due to not taking losses on projects "[CBDOs] cannot work for free and we are not going to work for free.... You have to pay your people."

To city officials, restricting what a CBDO can take out of a project might be a responsible way of stretching community development funds. To many of the community developers, however, not allowing a CBDO to pull ahead on a project indicates a lack of respect for the nonprofit in comparison to the commercial developer (Rubin, 1992).

In an effort to keep alive, CBDOs take on far more neighborhood tasks than thin administrative resources permit. While negotiating on multimillion dollar housing or commercial development projects, to pay for their fixed costs, CBDOs have to divert their small staffs to run paint-up fix-up programs, or store-facade rehabilitation efforts. These bread-and-butter programs are useful for the neighborhoods and necessary to keep the CBDO alive, but doing them distracts effort from the broader, holistic projects that can lead to community empowerment.

Coalition Building

To stay alive, CBDOs become political advocates for a public agenda that refocuses city efforts on the neighborhoods and provides core funding for community-based development. As Lipsky and Smith (1990, p. 645) point out "nonprofit agencies routinely tried to affect contract requirements or state regulations governing their programs" yet, feared public retribution. To bypass that fear and increase their political power, CBDOs band together and form coalitions to pressure for change in the laws and regulations that make community-based development difficult. For instance, the CBDO trade association, the NCCED, is involved in a major lobbying effort for federal legislation to provide administrative support for community-based economic development organizations.

Once coalitions are formed, they work aggressively to influence public policies in favor of locally based development. The CBDO coalition in Cincinnati was set up in response to the slowness of the city's payments to community groups. One of its first accomplishments was pressuring the city to form a department of neighborhoods, separating community development from the more dominant downtown interests. In Chicago, coalitions convinced city administrators to apply to their neighborhoods laws that had been passed to benefit Chicago's downtown. A tax reactivation program initiated through coalition actions in Cook County enable CBDOs to obtain deteriorating properties on which slumlords were refusing to pay taxes. CANDO, a coalition of community business-development groups in Chicago, pressured the city to adopt the CDFLOAT program that allows community groups to borrow against city CDBG funds that have not yet been expended. Getting this innovation accepted required a pressure campaign in which CANDO acquire data from HUD on Chicago's woefully slow use of CDBG funds and threatened to embarrass public officials with disclosure. A similar tactic was used by a housing coalition that produced a data book showing both the need for inner city housing and the city's lack of responsiveness to this need.

Coalition actions can create a tense environment between supportive city officials and community groups because community groups are biting the hands that feed them. Coalitions are formed because relationships with the local governments are not working well enough, but forming activist coalitions risks making relationships worse.

Conclusions and Implications

With increased understanding between those in the public sector and the community movement, the public-nonprofit partnerships can be strengthened. But why should those in the public sector want to work to bridge the gap and work more intensely with CBDO? Community developers require extensive nurturance, are not fully sympathetic to the regulatory constraints faced by government, and demand large amounts of time for what appear to be modest results.

One reason for support is that CBDOs work in the poor neighborhoods whose redevelopment is not only fair on social grounds, but may be necessary for the survival of the city as a whole. The neighborhoods in which CBDOs work are those from which the private sector has withdrawn and "private entrepreneurs have exhibited relatively little willingness over the past two decades to invest their capital in such communities" (Stephenson, 1991, p. 111). CBDOs provide a viable and customized approach to economic development and job creation in poor communities. And, they do so by promoting many of the broader values of the society — self help, entrepreneurial spirit, home ownership, and other icons of present day America.

There are also programmatic reasons for supporting the movement. The multibillion dollar HOME program, the most recent incarnation of a federal program for low-income housing, requires that at least 15 percent of its money be spent by qualified not-for-profits (Center for Community Change, 1992). Later amendments to the legislation encourage money to be spent to support the operating costs of community-based housing organizations (Development Times, 1992, p. 1).

Cities can partner with CBDOs in ways that encourage neighborhood input into development planning. The city, however, should not insist on standardization of programs within these partnerships (Lipsky and Smith, 1990), as standardization undermines the strength of neighborhood focused, community-based development movement. What might work in the more stable south side of Chicago would fail in the transitional west side. It is not isolated homes that are being built, but homes in distinct neighborhoods with markedly different configurations of social and economic problems.

Such projects need a public subsidy to make up for social costs: they are often built in neighborhoods in which construction is more expensive because of crime or environmental contamination. Furthermore, they are owned by people who have no experience in property maintenance and need be taught.

In part, this social subsidy can be paid if public administrators fund the core operating expenses of credible CBDOs. That way, the time of CBDO directors can be spent in packaging projects, not merely in struggling to keep the organization alive. A social partnership enables CBDOs to develop their capacity to undo the damage of business flight and racial animosity that plague poor communities.

Meaningful partnerships can be accomplished by the creation of city-wide organizations in which city officials, CBDO activists, and funders meet as equals and share with one another their different language and developmental ethos. Or the public sector can employ as developmental administrators those who both understand and are sympathetic to the community movement, as it did in Cleveland by hiring Chris Warren, former CBDO director, later head of a city-wide CBDO network, now the development director for the city. To bring about effective partnering means, as the National Conference of State Legislatures argued, "local organizations cannot continue to be considered agencies that just mobilize public resources. Rather, they must be viewed as able concerns that will manage the entire development process" (National Conference of State Legislatures, 1991, p. v).

Most important, *governmental officials should learn that the partnership with CBDOs involves a process and not just a project.* CBDOs use physical development as a lever for community economic empowerment, to encourage reconstruction in areas that others have abandoned. The particular projects, whether building affordable housing, working with women to extend home-industries to the marketplace, or creating the psychological uplift of a new supermarket in an abandoned lot, differ from place to place and from time to time. To CBDOs, development is a bricks and mortar process, but development is also an ongoing process of building toward economic empowerment and community capacity.

Community-based development organizations are neither effervescent advocacy organizations nor passive, delivery systems for government programs. They understand the importance of fiscal responsibility, and balance it with response to social need. They are willing to experiment with economic projects that others fear to try and are proudest when they become the catalysts for community improvement. They are physical developers that live and die on the economic success of their projects. CBDOs are exposed to the vagaries of the marketplace; but they gain their sense of direction by maintaining their roots in communities of the poor. Small is beautiful, not for any abstract reason, but because only a small organization can find the gaps between social and physical needs and respond to the many demands in communities of the poor.

Community-based development organizations span the development and advocacy models (Rubin and Rubin, 1992) by fighting for the wherewithal to provide community members with economic empowerment. Their strength is in demonstrating the capacity of poor communities to create organizations that can succeed. Government has often been willing to accept CBDOs as delivery systems for services and products, but less often been willing to accept their role as system transformers. The former is easy to measure — homes built, facades improved — and constitutes no threat to the status quo. But community building is far more important. The real impact of CBDOs lies not in the number of housing units produced, but in the community's sense of pride and collective achievement, in the renewal of a sense of possibility. Development organizations with a firm community base are the wedge for entry into the communities of the deprived. Regenerating these communities physically and socially is a goal worth working toward.

The community-based development movement requires an empathetic city administration that recognizes that the movement requires nurturance not dominance. Public administrators should be willing to help CBDOs because their ex-perimentation provides one hope for the renewal of the inner city. Government can help achieve these goals by listening carefully to the voices of those involved in the field.

Notes

1. For example, local officials point out that federal housing funds under HOME could not be used to pay for administrative expenses of community-development agencies. Revisions in the Housing and Community Development Act of 1992 that resulted from lobbying by nonprofit housing agencies and advocates, now allow up to five percent of the HOME funds to be used for CBDO operating support.

2. A planning document required by the Department of Housing and Urban Development (HUD) before housing support is provided under the HOME program.

3. A state-wide referendum initiated by the nonprofit sector eliminated this restriction in Ohio.

4. CBDO directors reinforce this image. Like other nonprofits, CBDOs and local administrators contend over the degree of detailed contract monitoring and uniformity in service provision (Lipsky and Smith, 1990, p. 626). Additionally, CBDOs, like direct service providers, want to be selective in their choice of clientele whereas government is more interested in providing broader service (Lipsky and Smith, 1990, p. 635).

5. I have no way of judging the truth of the director's assertions. His group was successful and the projects a visible boost to the community. Yet, he felt awkward in his continuing negotiations with the city, an awkwardness he claimed grew out of the politics of race.

References

Center for Community Change, 1992. *The HOME Program: A Brief Guide for Community Organizations.* Washington, D.C.: Center for Community Change.

Clavel, Pierre, and Wim Wiewell, eds., 1991. *Harold Washington and the Neighborhoods: Progressive City Government in Chicago, 1983–1987.* New Brunswick, NJ: Rutgers University Press.

Dreier, Peter, 1989. "Economic Growth and Economic Justice in Boston: Populist Housing and Job Policies." In Gregory D. Squires, ed., *Unequal Partnership: The Political Economy of Urban Redevelopment in Postwar America.* New Brunswick, NJ: Rutgers University Press, pp. 35–38.

Emerson, Robert M., ed., 1983. *Contemporary Field Research: A Collection of Readings.* Prospect Heights, IL: Waveland.

Goetz, Edward G., 1992. "Local Government Support for Nonprofit Housing: A Survey of U.S. Cities." *Urban Affairs Quarterly*, vol. 27 (March), pp. 420–435.

Kelly, Christine K., Donald C. Kelly, and Edward Marciniak, 1988. *Non-profits with Hard Hats: Building Affordable Housing.* Washington, DC: National Center for Urban Ethnic Affairs.

"Key changes to HOME will benefit CDCS." 1992. *Development Times*, vol. 1 (5), p. 1.

Lipsky, Michael and Steven Smith, 1990. "Nonprofit Organizations, Government and the Welfare State." *Social Science Quarterly*, vol. 104, pp. 625–648.

National Conference of State Legislatures, 1991. *Breaking New Ground: Community-based Development Organizations.* Denver: National Conference of State Legislatures.

National Congress for Community Economic Development (NCCED), 1991. *Changing the Odds: The Achievements of Community-based Development Corporations.* Washington, D.C.: National Congress for Community Economic Development.

Pierce, Neil R., and Carol F. Steinbach, 1987. *Corrective Capitalism: The Rise of America's Community Development Corporations.* New York: Ford Foundation.

_____, 1990. *Enterprising Communities: Community-based Development in America.* Washington, D.C.: Council for Community Based Development.

Rubin, Herbert J., 1983. *Applied Social Research.* Columbus, OH: Merrill.

_____, 1993. "Community Empowerment Within an Alternative Economy." In Dennis Peck and John Murphy, eds., *Open Institutions: The Hope for Democracy.* New York: Praeger, pp. 99–121.

_____, 1992. "Renewing Hope in the Inner City: Conversations with Community Based Development Practitioners." Paper presented at the 22d Annual Meeting of the Urban Affairs Association. Cleveland, April/May.

Rubin, Herbert J., and Irene S. Rubin, 1992. *Community Organizing and Development*, 2d ed. Columbus, OH: MacMillan (Merrill).

Schorr, Alvin L., ed., 1991. *Cleveland Development: A Dissenting View.* Cleveland: David XPress.

Spradley, James P., 1979. *The Ethnographic Interview.* New York: Holt.

Stephenson, Max O., 1991. "Whither the Public-Private Partnership: A Critical Overview." *Urban Affairs Quarterly*, vol. 27, pp. 109–127.

Suchman, Diane R., D. Scott Middleton, and Susan Giles, 1990. *Public/Private Housing Partnerships.* Washington, DC: Urban Land Institute.

Vidal, Avis C., 1992. *Rebuilding Communities: A National Study of Urban Community Development Corporations.* New York: Community Development Research Center, Graduate School of Management and Urban Policy, New School for Social Research.

15. COMMUNITY-BUILDING RESOURCES

Josh S. Weston

The community-building efforts described in Chapter 8 are, by their nature, decentralized and adapted to local circumstances. Moreover, these examples represent some of the best community-building practices rather than typical ones. How can these *local* and *pioneering* initiatives be systematized into a *national* response to inner-city distress?

In discussions of community building, this question is referred to as *the challenge of going to scale*. This challenge encompasses five dimensions:[1]

• The first dimension is *geographic*. Resident-participatory approaches and community-based institutions flourish to a much greater extent in some urban areas than in others. For example, community development corporations (CDCs) are more numerous and successful in certain cities in the industrial Northeast and Midwest and on the West Coast than in much of the West and South.[2] For other types of community-based organizations, the localities in which progress is most pronounced may be different, but the geographic unevenness is similar.

A variety of factors contributes to this pattern, among them local past experience, individual leadership, and cultural considerations. While accommodating such considerations, **a national inner-city community-building agenda must expand throughout the nation's urban areas initiatives and institutions that currently are common in only some communities.**

• The second dimension involves the *issues* to which the community-building approach is applied. To date, the construction, rehabilitation, and operation of low-income housing are the primary areas in which institutional infrastructure is well developed and the local-initiative approach has a substantial record of production. Because housing development involves a relatively well-known process and the results are immediately visible, it is often a sensible initial activity through which a community-based organization can build its skills and reputation. However, the challenge in inner-city revitalization is not just in housing but also in employment, education, health, youth

Originally published as Chapter 4 of Rebuilding Inner-City Communities: A New Approach to the Nation's Urban Crisis, *1995. Published by the Committee for Economic Development, New York, New York. Reprinted with permission of the publisher.*

development, public safety, and other aspects of life. **A national agenda for inner-city community building must ensure that the style of problem solving that has achieved notable success in housing is routinely applied to other aspects of community development.**

• The third dimension involves the *managerial strength and efficiency* of community-based institutions. To emphasize the potential of the community-building approach, this chapter discusses some of the most impressive programs and best-run institutions in the country. Examination of more typical community-based initiatives reveals a widespread need for strengthening leadership and management.

Many community-based institutions are young and their staffs relatively inexperienced. For example, across the nation, an estimated 39 percent of CDCs are less than ten years old, and as many as 64 percent have annual budgets of less than $250,000.[3] In addition, staff turnover in CDCs is often high.[4] **A national agenda to rebuild inner-city communities must include enhancement of the leadership, managerial, and organizational capacity of community-based organizations. It should help promising organizations to achieve the strength and performance exemplified by the best of their peers.**

• The fourth dimension reflects the sometimes bewildering *number of public and private organizations* involved in community building at the local, state, and national levels. This diversity promotes flexibility and innovation, and it reflects the multiple problems being addressed. However, the multiple initiatives address interrelated problems and ultimately involve the same residents and institutions. Unnecessary duplication of organizations can increase complexity, costs, and delays. Therefore, **a national agenda for inner-city community building must enhance coordination among the many participants in the community-building system.**

• The fifth dimension involves the need to bring the numbers and achievements of community-based initiatives more in line with the *magnitude of the problems* being addressed. Consider, for example, low-income housing. In 1990, CDCs throughout the country produced almost 23,000 units of badly needed housing, approximately two-thirds of them in urban areas.[5] Yet, an estimated 600,000 to 2.2 million persons nationwide are homeless, and 2.4 million low-income central-city households pay half or more of their income for rent.[6] The disparity between need and achievement is even more pronounced in problem areas other than housing. **A national agenda to rebuild inner-city communities must bring substantially more resources to bear on the problems of these communities. To do so, it must redirect public and philanthropic funds and creatively mobilize market forces and incentives.**

The common element among these five dimensions of going to scale is the relative newness of the community-building approach. This newness is reflected in its limited inclusion in current public policies and in the modest scale of many local initiatives. It is appropriate to treat this approach as the *infant industry* that it is, a promising direction that should be brought to fruition through conscious policies of support and development.

The author believes that the resources invested in community building should be expanded in an incremental fashion. Several of the recommendations in this chapter call for additional public, corporate, and philanthropic support through grants, tax credits, contracts, and other mechanisms. Although we recommend no specific levels of expenditure, our vision is one of *modest but constantly growing* investments. In the early stages of this process, the majority of additional resources should represent reallocations toward community-building initiatives from other, less community-based efforts. The freshness of the community-building approach, the breath of hope it brings to a problem over which many have despaired, provides an attractive rationale for this reallocation. As the effectiveness of community building becomes more widely recognized, political support for additional expenditures—particularly from public programs—should follow. By pursuing this incremental approach, the nation can appropriately balance its concerns about the unmet needs in its distressed urban communities and fiscal responsibility in the public sector.[7]

An Agenda for America's Inner Cities

The author believes that the nation should adopt the community-building approach as the core of its agenda for the inner cities. Many important institutions in American society already support the community-building philosophy, and a number of institutions, collaborations, and alliances already exist. One approach to the future growth of such activities would be to centralize them, for example, in a more powerful U.S. Department of Housing and Urban Development. The author does not endorse such an approach. To attempt to bring administrative or managerial coherence to his national effort would make organizational engineering the focus, not inner-city problem solving. A centralized effort would also concentrate responsibility in a few hands and reduce the sense of obligation felt by the rest of society. And centralization would dampen the innovation that is the hallmark of this approach. Accordingly, the author believes that **national efforts should continue to**

manifest themselves as they have to date: pluralistically, as a movement rather than a single organization. The heart of the effort should be parallel institutions working in support of a common vision.

The core of that vision is how organizations addressing inner-city problems should relate to each other. Community building requires that **whenever possible, residents and community-based institutions should be the frontline implementers of community-targeted initiatives. Supporters from the business, government, and philanthropic sectors who share the goals and concerns of these local programs should align themselves not as separate efforts but as support systems for these initiatives.** The role of these support systems is to sustain, bolster, and expand, rather than to parallel or supplant, locally based efforts.

Although this approach may reduce the role of government agencies, major corporations, and philanthropies in direct service delivery, it does not lessen their responsibilities. **Commitment to this national agenda should manifest itself in specific actions and provision of substantial resources. Institutions should redirect their current efforts in major ways.**

The national commitment must also be *long term*. The growth of distressed areas has been under way at least since World War II. Stabilizing and revitalizing these neighborhoods will be the work of a generation. An aggressive national effort must be sustained by long-term vision and commitment.

It is also essential that support be *broadbased*. No single institution or coalition can provide all the insights or resources needed to relieve multifaceted inner-city distress. Adherents to the approach must include those focused at the citywide, state, and national levels, with interests in a range of social problems, and those from the public, private, and philanthropic sectors.

The Importance of Support Systems

As an example of the institutional relationships involved in implementing this approach, consider the Washington-Columbia Apartments in the Codman Square neighborhood of Boston.

By the early 1970s, Codman Square had become typical of many distressed inner-city areas in its lack of investment, substandard housing, high concentration of poor residents, and negative interaction of problems. Many of the residential buildings in the area were dilapidated, among them the 326-unit Washington-Columbia Apartments.

Since 1981, the area has been served by a community development corporation, the Codman Square Neighborhood Development Corporation (CSNDC). Through its work in the neighborhood on public safety and through participation of community residents on its board and in its programs, by the mid–1980s, CSNDC had become a focal point for grassroots initiatives in Codman Square.

In 1987, CSNDC decided to renovate the Washington-Columbia Apartments. This was a major undertaking for the organization, which even in 1994 had a total staff of only nine and an annual budget of only $550,000. This initiative required more than $21 million in project financing, all from outside the Codman Square community:

• Predevelopment funds for project planning came from the City of Boston's Public Facilities Department, allocating money from HUD.
• A mortgage for more than $18 million was obtained from the Massachusetts Housing Finance Agency, a state agency with bonding authority to underwrite development of affordable housing.

• An additional $2.6 million was raised through syndication to private investors of federal Low-Income Housing Tax Credits.
• A loan of $500,000 came from the Boston Neighborhood Housing Trust, a capital pool funded by "linkage" payments from downtown developers.

In assembling this complex package of financing, CSNDC relied on technical assistance and political support from the Metropolitan Boston Housing Partnership (MBHP). This was a typical role for MBHP, which is a public-private partnership organized in 1983 to enhance the quality and availability of low-cost housing throughout the Boston area and to strengthen nonprofit housing developers working in distressed neighborhoods. CSNDC also received support from Boston's Neighborhood Development Support Collaborative (NDSC), a non-profit organization created in 1987 to improve the fiscal, organizational, and program capacity of Boston's CDCs. NDSC, in turn, is supported by seven Boston-area funders, including the United Way and five foundations.

Working with these Boston-area organizations was the Local Initiatives Support Corporation (LISC), which has supported both MBHP and NDSC, as well as CSNDC. LISC is a leading national intermediary founded by the Ford Foundation in 1979 to support community development nationwide.[8]

By 1990, brick-and-mortar rehabilitation had been completed on the first 151 units of the Washington-Columbia property. However, crime, drug dealing, vandalism, and quality-of-life problems quickly threatened to overwhelm the newly improved buildings and the nascent sense of community among the residents. Using a grant and technical assistance from MBHP, CSNDC hired a community organizer to kindle resident action. With the organizer's help, residents evicted drug dealers, created a crime watch, and designed and built a playground on the building grounds. The organizer also helped young unemployed residents of the building to form a business to repair apartments and clean graffiti in their own building and at other properties.

The relationships in this project among CSNDC and its supporting institutions exemplify the approach to problem solving advocated in this statement: extensive involvement of the community and its organizations in service delivery (in this case, rehabilitating and managing low-income housing), with powerful public and private organizations providing expertise and financial resources. In fact, the Washington-Columbia project illustrates how support systems contribute to each of the five dimensions of scaling up.

Geographical Coverage

CSNDC did not exist in 1980, and MBHP was created only in 1983. Yet, Boston is considered a national leader in community-building efforts. There are now about 120 public-private housing partnerships that support housing development across the nation.[9] That leaves many communities with neither strong community-based groups nor systems of supporting intermediaries. These gaps have been recognized, and several activities have been undertaken in recent years to increase the geographic coverage of CDCs and other community-based institutions. For example, LISC has supported community-organizing campaigns in such cities as New Orleans and Little Rock.[10]

Diversifying Beyond Housing

It is no coincidence that the Codman Square example involves housing rehabil-

itation. Housing is the problem area in which community-based activities and support systems are most extensive. As is typical of many CDCs, the mission of CSNDC has gradually expanded beyond housing rehabilitation to housing management and social services involving its own tenants and to a broader community development agenda for the Codman Square neighborhood.

Such expansion to additional problem areas is difficult without support systems comparable to that in housing. Fortunately, in recent years, nonhousing support systems have begun to emerge. One example is the Robert Wood Johnson Foundation's community-based efforts to reduce substance abuse."[11]

Increasing Organizational Capacity

With appropriate assistance, many community-based organizations could become more stable, well-managed entities operating at a substantial scale. Consulting and staff training in technical aspects of community development (in the Codman Square case, packaging the financing for housing development) are typical examples. As community-based institutions proliferate, the need for technical assistance and consulting continues to grow.

However, training and good advice alone are not sufficient to strengthen community-based organizations. A common problem is that funds are available for specific projects, such as rehabilitation of the Washington-Columbia Apartments, but are difficult to obtain for development and maintenance of the core managerial competence of organizations. Little support is available, for example, for long-range planning, exploring new opportunities, or retaining staff between projects.

Many of these organizations also need assistance in basic managerial systems, such as accounting, data processing, and personnel. Without investments in their institutional strength, they cannot undertake projects efficiently. At various times, LISC, MBHP, and NDSC have all provided operating support and technical assistance to strengthen CSNDC.[12]

A final but critical need for expanding the scale of community-building activities is leadership. At times, community leaders simply emerge when an opportunity arises. More frequently, however, leadership must be developed.

Across the nation, a number of specialized training institutions and programs at colleges and universities have come into being within recent years. The Fannie Mae Foundation has suggested a number of alternatives for expanding such resources to foster community development leaders: a community leader education and internship program to assist in the transition of community residents from volunteer to paid positions, undergraduate programs to place talented students in internships with community organizations, a graduate school initiative to develop curriculum and promote community development as a career, and a career transition program for experienced men and women from other fields.[13] Such developments make sense as part of a long-term commitment.

Businesses often have unique leadership, technical, and management experience that can be used to strengthen the capacity of community organizations through internships, mentoring, technical support, or other programs. For example, the charitable contributions program of the St. Paul Companies provides operating support and resources for human capital development in community institutions, including a leadership development grant program.

Coordination and Collaboration

Because inner-city problems are interrelated, and because the residents and local institutions involved with each problem overlap, community initiatives need to work in close harmony. In some cases, effective integration may occur within one institution, where community organizations combine assistance from several support systems to address interrelated problems. In more cases, however, this harmony is achieved by independent institutions consulting and coordinating with each other.

One level at which such collaboration is essential is the neighborhood. There it can serve as an antidote to the categorical, crisis-driven nature of most public and private programs, allowing creation of comprehensive programs to address interrelated problems. For example, a resident-centered housing management group receiving most of its support from a housing-oriented system might also receive funding from a human service system to provide counseling to families living in their properties. Or a housing group might encourage a local day-care provider or job-training program to locate within a rehabilitated building. Some federal grants require collaboration among neighborhood service organizations; for others, many neighborhood groups and local public agencies voluntarily pursue this end.

A demonstration program in the South Bronx section of New York City illustrates such collaboration on an ambitious scale. The Comprehensive Community Revitalization Program (CCFP) is a seven-year project, supported by Surdna and 11 other foundations, that will invest more than $5.7 million in six South Bronx CDCs. All six organizations have track records in housing production and therefore have a base of experience and institutional credibility from which to pursue a broader agenda. CCRP's support has enabled the CDCs to engage in long-range planning and to identify new opportunities. They have initiated health care clinics, begun development of a child care service, and secured commitments for a $21 million shopping center and a state-of-the-art paper-recycling plant.

Collaboration among six CDCs, in combination with support from prominent foundations, has enhanced the credibility of the individual organizations and made private and public investors more willing to become partners with them. New York State, for example, has given the CDCs special planning grants, regulatory waivers, and priority access to 26 state agencies through the state's Neighborhood-Based Alliance program. The partners in the recycling venture are the Natural Resources Defense Council, a national environmental organization; the S. D. Warren Company, a Boston paper firm; and the Modo Paper Company of Sweden, a recycling firm.

Collaboration is also important in support systems. These systems generally are not linked at their upper end to one central source. Rather, they are affiliates of sources with different program interests, such as housing, health, or public safety. However, these systems need not function like narrow categorical programs. At their best, all see their efforts as part of a broad community-building agenda and actively communicate with and promote the goals of others working in the same communities.

Effective partnerships at the city level almost always derive their impetus from close cooperation with the mayor, the city council, and key municipal agencies. Most mayors welcome collaboration among a city's business, philanthropic, and community leaders,[14] in part because these partners can provide support for taking what are sometimes politically difficult po-

sitions. Mayors may also elect to undertake inner-city revitalization through flexible public-private partnerships rather than through cumbersome or overly restrictive government agencies. Moreover, these public-private organizations can sustain activities beyond the terms of individual elected officials.

The Indianapolis Neighborhood Housing Partnership (INHP) illustrates how these dynamics can create a strong force for inner-city revitalization. Since its inception, INHP has had strong support from the city's mayor and city agencies. The organization was founded in 1988 to implement the recommendations of the city's Housing Strategy Task Force, which had included representatives of several city agencies, private developers, lenders, social service agencies, and neighborhood and religious leaders. To launch the partnership, the city committed $1.5 million from federal funds under its control. The partnership has created new financing mechanisms for housing development, helped strengthen neighborhood housing developers, and provided counseling for needy families seeking housing.

Like other strong citywide intermediaries, INHP receives support from a broad cross section of the city and commands significant resources. A major Indianapolis-based foundation, the Lilly Endowment, has provided loans and grants totaling $8.9 million, which INHP has used to leverage more than $10 million from a consortium of 12 Indianapolis banks and savings institutions. Thus, collaboration among business, foundation, and government leaders has led to a sustained program of assistance to the city's resident-centered initiatives.

Another ambitious metropolitan initiative to mobilize and coordinate support for local initiatives is The Atlanta Project in Atlanta, Georgia.[15]

Expanding Resources

Community-based organizations such as CSNDC do not possess substantial internal financial resources, nor do other entities in their inner-city communities. When neighborhood organizations seek resources from outside the neighborhood through conventional channels, they often encounter skepticism and disinterest, even for bankable propositions. Accordingly, institutions that support community-based initiatives first and foremost play the role of *unconventional* channels of finance. They raise and/or leverage funds in the form of grants, below-market loans, market-rate loans, and equity investments.

If the community-building approach is to continue to grow, the resources available through support systems must be sustained and expanded. Three examples point the way:

• The *National Community Development Initiative (NCDI)* is a joint venture of seven major foundations, three national businesses, LISC, the Enterprise Foundation, and HUD to advance urban and rural community development. During its first round of funding, from 1991 through 1993, it raised nearly $63 million for community building in 20 cities. Its second round, begun in 1994, will deliver more than $87 million to CDCs in 23 cities. This initial investment is expected to leverage an additional $660 million from other sources.

• Since authorization of the *Low-Income Housing Tax Credit (LIHTC)* in 1986, an estimated $500 million has been channeled into the community-building system[16] through sale of the credits to corporations and affluent individuals. These instruments offer attractive financial returns and risk protection and thereby can attract investors motivated by financial rather than exclusively social objectives. In this way, thousands of individuals and corporations across the nation have invested in and have a financial stake in neighborhoods into which they are ordinarily reluctant to venture.

• The Federal National Mortgage Association (Fannie Mae) was chartered by Congress in 1938 as a publicly traded, privately managed corporation. Its mission is to promote home ownership by expanding the supply of capital available to mortgage lenders through its secondary mortgage market, and its contributions are visible in every suburban neighborhood across America. Now, as part of its *Showing America the Way Home* program, Fannie Mae has committed an additional $150 billion to reach moderate-income but creditworthy potential homeowners in inner cities. It will open 25 local offices to work with governments, lenders, and community groups.

These initiatives signal a growing national movement in support of inner-city community building. To date, however, neither their number nor their scale is sufficient to match the distress in the nation's urban areas. The author urges business, foundation, and civic leaders working on all aspects of inner-city problems to strengthen and expand such support systems to sustain and amplify local community-building initiatives.

Roles for the Business Sector

All executives, including those working far away from America's central cities, should respond to the injustice, threat to social order, and economic waste of the nation's inner-cities. Senior executives from America's major corporations have a key role to play within a national community-building agenda, and the skills of top executives are uniquely suited to provide needed leadership. Business leaders are results-oriented, understand the importance of strategic planning, and control substantial financial and political resources. Moreover, they oversee organizations with leadership, managerial, and operational resources that can be utilized to strengthen community-based institutions.

Most business leaders have yet to fully embrace this role. This is in part because they fail to see a direct link between their company's health and the health of central cities, even the cities of their own metropolitan region. Yet, even companies that have a relatively limited connection to individual cities have a stake in the nation's broader economic and social health.

Other firms choose to do nothing because they feel there is little they *can* do to address seemingly intractable inner-city problems. Yet, the examples cited throughout this statement suggest a multitude of ways for businesses to make a positive impact in inner-city communities. Emerging community-based institutions and programs, metropolitanwide partnerships, and national intermediaries offer numerous entry points for supporting a national community-building agenda.

Because of the diversity in circumstances among companies, their level and form of support for inner-city community building are likely to vary widely. However, no matter what a company's resources, knowledge, location, or business situation, all firms have strengths that they can and should utilize to help revitalize inner-city communities. **The author urges corporate leaders to support the national community-building agenda in four ways** (see Figure 1, "Recommendations for Business Support of Inner-City Community Building"). **Corporate executives should evaluate their company's strengths and market position to determine which ways best fit their own circumstances.**

First, **executives should reconsider the potential of inner-city communities in their firm's business activities.** Although opportunities will vary widely across industries, nearly all firms could utilize inner-city resources in some way. Inner-city neighborhoods may offer attractive locations for plants or offices. For example, Pfizer Inc.'s pharmaceutical manufacturing plant in Brooklyn combines proximity to downtown areas and transportation facilities with low real estate costs. They may offer customers that are underserved despite the profit potential that they represent, as in the case of supermarkets in Liberty City and Newark. Or they may offer employees, suppliers, and other valuable production resources, as in the case of Martin Greenfield Clothiers in Brooklyn. As community-building efforts take hold and improve the business environment in inner cities, executives must lend their firms to give these areas a second look. Otherwise, many firms will continue to assume that such opportunities do not exist.

Second, the support systems whose proliferation was described earlier in this chapter offer another opportunity for business executives and their companies. **Executives and their firms should join local and national systems of support for inner-city community building.** Multisector partnerships at the city and national levels, such as the Metropolitan Boston Housing Partnership and the Local Initiatives Support Corporation, are central to inner-city community building.[17] They not only control resources and develop community-building strategies but also function as social enterprises, bringing together business, foundation, government, and community leaders who form personal relationships and coalesce into an influential constituency for inner-city renewal. **Corporate executives should exercise the same leadership in community-building partnerships and intermediary organizations as they have historically played in civic partnerships to boost downtown** development, attract sports franchises, and support cultural institutions.

Third, many of America's top executives wield wide influence outside their corporations, for example, as board members of civic, educational, and human services organizations. Business leaders also serve as political opinion leaders. When thoughtful and committed business leaders speak for inner-city communities, public officials, both executive and legislative, are less likely to treat inner-city constituencies as politically weak or marginal. **Business leaders should encourage both private and public organizations to target additional resources to distressed inner-city communities, to involve residents and community institutions in service delivery, to identify and train community leaders, and to remove impediments to community building.**

Corporate philanthropic efforts offer a final avenue for business leadership. Philanthropic efforts within most major corporations take many forms, from cash grants to employee involvement, and support a range of worthy causes. Inner-city distress is among our nation's most pressing problems. **Executives should encourage their companies to devote an increasing proportion of their philanthropic resources to these communities, and they should ensure that these resources support community-building activities.** Through investment in Low-Income Housing Tax Credits, internship opportunities for inner-city community leaders, philanthropic contributions, loaned executives, technical advice, and other means, the nation's business leaders can strengthen community-based institutions and support resident-centered initiatives.

FIGURE 1— RECOMMENDATIONS FOR BUSINESS SUPPORT OF INNER-CITY COMMUNITY BUILDING

- **Encourage utilization of emerging inner-city resources in business activities.**

  Particularly where community-building efforts have begun to create a more stable and hospitable environment, executives should encourage their firms to reconsider the potential of urban neighborhoods as locations for plants and officers, minority-owned firms as subcontractors or suppliers, inner-city residents as employees, and inner-city communities as commercial and consumer markets.

- Join local and national systems of support for inner-city community building.

  Executives and their firms should joint multisector local and national partnerships to support community building. They should exercise the same leadership in relation to inner-city community building as they have in the past to boost downtown development or attract sports franchises.

- **Advocate reshaping public and nonprofit programs to reflect the community-building approach.**

  As members of the boards of civic, human service, and educational organizations and as political opinion leaders, business leaders should influence public and nonprofit institutions to allocate increased resources to distressed and threatened urban neighborhoods, to involve local residents and community institutions in service delivery, to train and identify community leaders, and to remove impediments to community building.

- **Guide corporate charitable activities and community involvement toward inner-city community building.**

  Executives should encourage their firms to focus more of their corporate community-involvement efforts on distressed and threatened inner-city neighborhoods and ensure that the community-building style shapes their involvement. For example, corporations might invest in Low-Income Housing Tax Credits, provide financial support to strengthen community-based institutions, provide internships to community leaders, or offer loaned executives to strengthen community-based organizations.

Through these multiple channels of influence, committed business leadership can increase the effectiveness of community-building initiatives and help elevate inner-city issues to prominence on the national agenda.[18]

Making the Public Sector a Community Development Partner

No agenda for the inner cities will succeed without the participation of federal, state, and local governments.

One level at which the public sector affects inner-city communities is through economic and social policies that affect these areas in common with all communities across the nation. Appropriate macroeconomic policies to generate employment growth, initiatives to reform the public assistance system, efforts to improve the performance of the nation's schools, and similar initiatives all significantly affect inner-city communities. Failures in the nation's public assistance and educational systems in particular adversely affect the life chances of residents of distressed urban areas. Inner-city community building cannot substitute for national action to improve these inadequate systems.

Yet, in the absence of strong support for resident-centered initiatives, government action on any of these fronts will have only a marginal impact on inner-city distress. Federal, state, and local government policies and programs can directly promote community building in inner cities in ten specific ways (see Figure 2, "Recommendations for Government Support of Inner-City Community Building").

FIGURE 2 — RECOMMENDATIONS FOR GOVERNMENT SUPPORT OF INNER-CITY COMMUNITY BUILDING

- **Control the weapons that disrupt community life.**

  Violence and fear can fatally disrupt efforts to build community in distressed inner-city neighborhoods. Federal, state, and local jurisdictions must restore a basic level of safety in these areas. Their efforts should include vigorous enforcement of existing laws to eliminate the national plague of cheap handguns and assault weapons and to take firearms out of the hands of juveniles and criminals. Additional legislation should impose substantially broader restrictions on weapons and ammunition.

- **Reduce the impact of illegal drugs on community life.**

  Drugs represent another major disruptive force in inner-city communities. Federal, state, and local governments should reduce the adverse impact of illegal drugs on community life, particularly by shifting the emphasis in drug policy from incarceration of drug abusers to prevention of drug abuse and rehabilitation of addicted individuals.

- **Review and modify policies that further concentrate social and economic problems in distressed communities.**

  Across many issues—housing, criminal justice, environmental management, and others—the public sector has often promoted the concentration of distressed populations and undesirable facilities in small geographic areas. Decision makers need to reconsider such policies in light of their impact on communities and reverse those that overstress the ability of communities to respond resiliently to problems.

- **Work to eliminate racial, ethnic, and other forms of discrimination in access to jobs, credit, and housing.**

  Discrimination continues to undermine the economic and social bases of inner-city communities. Public agencies should vigorously enforce antidiscrimination statutes aimed at redlining in lending and discrimination in employment, housing, and public accommodations. Additional legislation to gather data on financial services not covered under the Community Reinvestment Act is also desirable.

(Figure 2, continued)

- Encourage partnerships that unite inner-city residents and their community-based organizations with the philanthropic sector, local government, and the business community.

  Public agencies are essential partners in community-rebuilding efforts. Public leaders and agencies should routinely consult community-based organizations on decisions affecting their neighborhoods, join ad hoc coalitions with community groups to implement specific projects, participate in ongoing multisector partnership institutions, and require collaborative planning and matching grants for publicly funded initiatives.

- Expand the use of community-based organizations in implementing programs and delivering services in inner-city communities.

  Federal, state, and local governments should routinely contract with community-based organizations for delivery of publicly funded services. Community-based organizations can be effective delivery vehicles for services in inner cities because of their existing relationships within a community, understanding of community needs, ability to coordinate multiple programs into comprehensive packages, and employment of local residents. Moreover, these organizations can gain experience that strengthens them as resources for addressing other problems.

- Operate government services and programs in a community-building style.

  Direct government delivery of services should be implemented in a more community-based style. For example, public agencies should aggressively seek opportunities to integrate and coordinate services and design administrative boundaries and service areas (such as police precincts) to match neighborhoods.

- Invest public funds in strengthening the capacity of community-based organizations.

  Sustained community building occurs primarily through ongoing institutions. Public funds from sources such as Community Development Block Grants should be used to enhance the leadership, managerial, and organizational strength of CDCs and other community-based institutions.

- Expand the Low-Income Housing Tax Credit and create a similar tax credit to support the development of commercial properties in inner-city areas.

  Inner cities need the resources of, and connections to, investors outside their neighborhood. The federal government should expand the Low-Income Housing Tax Credit program, which connects investors to housing initiatives in distressed communities, and should develop a parallel mechanism to support commercial and industrial development.

- Support research on inner-city problems and community-building programs.

  Evaluation of community-building initiatives and dissemination of information on best practices in these efforts are currently inadequate. Government (as well as foundations) should support such activities, as well as monitor conditions in urban areas.

• Public officials and agencies should begin by **controlling the violence and weapons that disrupt community life.** Daily life in some inner-city neighborhoods is so violent and out of control that terms such as *community building* and *shared civic values* are meaningless. No community organization can thrive on streets where children murder each other without remorse and where gangs, drugs, and violence have replaced family, work, and the rule of law. No social capital can be created in neighborhoods where residents are afraid to leave their homes to go to the grocery store, to recreation programs, or to community meetings. No enhanced connections between inner-city neighborhoods and mainstream society are realistic when outsiders refuse to enter the neighborhoods and many Americans fear their residents. Where civil order has broken down, local, state, and national governments must work to restore a basic level of safety and sense of security in these neighborhoods and across urban America.[19]

The proliferation of firearms, especially among juveniles, significantly contributes to civil instability within inner-city neighborhoods and the fear-based separation between these communities and the broader society. The number of gun homicides by juveniles increased nearly threefold between 1984 and 1991 while nongun homicides remained constant.[20] **Federal, state, and local governments can support community building by eliminating the national plague of cheap handguns and assault weapons and taking firearms out of the hands of juveniles and criminals. Such efforts have been advanced by recent federal legislation mandating waiting periods for the purchase of guns, banning selected assault weapons, and enhancing data systems to track weapon purchases. At the federal, state, and local levels, these approaches should be continued through vigorous enforcement of existing laws[21] and expanded through legislation imposing substantially broader restrictions on weapons and ammunition.**

• The traffic in illegal drugs that is rampant in many inner-city neighborhoods is another major disrupter of community life. This pernicious trade leaves shocking numbers of inner-city young people dead or scarred with criminal records. It leaves addicts (and often their children) unable to function as learners, earners, parents, or community members. It leaves communities disabled by violence among rival drug-selling gangs and from drug-addicted individuals and may influence those not involved in the drug industry to arm themselves.[22]

Current drug-fighting efforts rely too heavily on interdiction and not enough on education to reduce drug use. Incarceration of drug abusers only scars them with criminal records without addressing their fundamental problem of drug addiction. **Federal, state, and local governments should reduce the adverse impact of illegal drugs on community life. In particular, they should shift resources from the current incarceration-oriented approach to preventing drug abuse through education and to rehabilitating addicted individuals.**

CED's proposed approach is more consistent with community building in giving individuals the opportunities and support to make the right choices about drug use instead of merely punishing them and removing them from the community. It is also the approach most frequently advocated by inner-city community leaders. For example, in one recent survey, community leaders favored allocating 73 percent of antidrug efforts to prevention and treatment. This proportion contrasts sharply with the current pattern of federal spending, in which less than 30 percent is allocated to prevention and treatment.[23]

• A fundamental characteristic of distressed inner-city areas is the concentration of distressed individuals and undesirable facilities. Through a range of explicit and implicit decisions, the public sector has often promoted this concentration, and the resultant load and negative interaction of problems have overwhelmed the problem-solving resiliency of many inner-city communities. Therefore, across all programs and policies that affect inner cities, including housing, criminal justice, environmental management, and social services, **the public sector should review and modify policies that concentrate social and economic problems in distressed communities.** For example, in public housing, the criteria for locating housing sites and selecting tenants have tended to collocate large numbers of troubled families in already-distressed neighborhoods. In other cases, undesirable facilities such as waste treatment plants and halfway houses for ex-offenders are concentrated in poor neighborhoods. Instead, **federal, state, and local housing programs should promote a more disbursed distribution of low-income residents through scattered-site public housing and housing mobility programs, as well as recruit intact, working families as public housing tenants; and federal, state, and local governments should avoid concentrating undesirable facilities in distressed communities beyond their capacity to absorb them.**

• **The public sector should continue to work to eliminate racial, ethnic, and other forms of discrimination in access to jobs, credit, and housing.** Discrimination in many aspects of daily life continues to deny many inner-city residents opportunities to improve their lives. It perpetuates and concentrates poverty inner-city communities and thwarts connections between those communities and the rest of American society. Public agencies should vigorously enforce antidiscrimination laws aimed at redlining in lending and discrimination in employment, housing, and public accommodations. At the federal level, the most important of these laws are the Civil Rights Act of 1965, the Community Reinvestment Act, the Fair Housing Act, and the Equal Credit Opportunity Act. Additional legislation should extend data collection to credit practices of financial services not covered under the Community Reinvestment Act.

• **The public sector should encourage partnerships that unite inner-city residents and their community-based organizations with the philanthropic sector, local government, and the business community.** Community-based initiatives within distressed neighborhoods cannot proceed far or fast without the participation of powerful public and private actors from outside their communities to provide financial, technical, and political support.

The public sector should routinely consult community-based organizations on decisions affecting their neighborhoods; join ad hoc coalitions with community groups to implement specific projects; participate in ongoing institutions that convene the public, business, philanthropic, and community sectors; and require collaborative planning and matching grants for publicly funded initiatives. Through such means, local, state, and federal governments can make these partnerships important institutions and establish the partnership approach as the standard in addressing inner-city problems.

The Federal Empowerment Zone and Enterprise Communities programs are, in one aspect at least, good examples of public efforts designed to implement this principle. We do not endorse such programs' efforts to relocate businesses to distressed areas, a central aim of these initiatives, because they are likely to fuel unproductive bidding wars among localities. However, we endorse the *planning process* required of cities applying for the grants. Each applicant had to create a strategic plan through a bottom-up process that involved a city's government, business, community, and philanthropic sectors. The programs also require private resources and support that can be leveraged with public resources.

This principle of partnership can also be applied to government policies addressing the needs of inner-city communities for financial services. As useful as community-based initiatives (such as community-based credit unions and development banks) may be, public policy must not consider them a substitute for connecting underserved areas to financial markets and institutions outside inner-city neighborhoods. We therefore favor efforts that increase access to mainstream banking and investment services for inner-city customers as well as efforts to create separate community-based financial institutions.

An exclusive focus on the latter might leave inner-city areas reliant on financial institutions with only narrow constituencies and limited capital bases and fail to integrate inner cities into national capital markets and networks.

State and local governments can often reshape existing programs to support community-based initiatives. The federal government gives state and local governments wide discretion in administering a number of national programs, such as the HOME housing program and the Low-Income Housing Tax Credit program. States and localities also run their own programs for housing, community development, education, and public health and can target them to support a community-building agenda.

• **The public sector should expand its use of community-based organizations in implementing programs and delivering services in inner-city communities.** Community-based organizations are often particularly effective at delivering services because of their existing relationships and reputation within their communities, understanding of community needs, ability to coordinate multiple programs into comprehensive packages, and employment of local residents. They may also be willing to work in neighborhoods in which other organizations are reluctant to operate. At the same time, the revenues and experience these organizations gain can strengthen them to serve as resources for addressing other community problems.

The federal, state, and local governments should aggressively seek opportunities to employ community-based organizations as frontline implementers of public initiatives. Federal, state, and local legislation should encourage contracting with community-based organizations for the delivery of publicly funded services.

The HOME program of the U.S. Department of Housing and Urban Development has been among the first to recognize that community-based organizations constitute an important infrastructure for program implementation, in this case, the 2,000 CDCs in distressed communities across the nation that are developing decent, low-cost housing. HOME is designed to strengthen city- and state-level partnerships and gives state and local government agencies the discretion and incentives to put community-based organizations at the center of their efforts. All jurisdictions receiving HOME grants must set aside at least 15 percent of their funds for community-based organizations and may grant all of their funds to them.

Other federal, state, and local programs should increasingly adopt the same structure, funding community-based organizations as frontline service deliverers.[24] This approach can be implemented in many law enforcement, education, youth development, social service, health service, family planning, housing management, and employment training programs.

• **When implementing programs directly rather than through community groups, public agencies should operate in a community-building style.** Currently, public agencies tend to operate in isolation from each other, frustrating community attempts to provide comprehensive services to residents. One hallmark of the community-building style is aggressively to seek opportunities to integrate previously uncoordinated services and deliver them comprehensively, for example, by collocation of services administered by different agencies, case management to integrate multiple forms of assistance to an individual or family facing multiple problems, and "passport" eligibility for persons who qualify for one program to participate in other programs without filing repetitive eligibility applications.[25] A second hallmark is establishment of administrative boundaries and service areas (such as police precincts) to match neighborhoods.

• **The public sector should invest in strengthening the organizational capacity of community-based institutions.** Sustained community building occurs primarily through ongoing institutions. Some distressed inner-city communities have few local leadership institutions. In others, such organizations exist, but make only limited contributions because they must constantly struggle for survival. Public funds, from such sources as Community Development Block Grants and the HOME program, should be used to enhance the organizational strength of community institutions so that they are able to deliver services and join partnerships.[26] Typical needs are staff development, more efficient management systems, and enhancement of organizational stability through multiyear funding and funding not tied to specific projects.

• **The federal government should expand tax credits that create connections between outside investors and inner-city communities.** The new national agenda for the inner city advocated in this statement relies on redirecting the support of resource-rich, influential, established outside institutions toward inner-city initiatives. Investment in inner-city projects by those outside the neighborhoods brings capital into distressed areas and builds linkages of information and concern between inner-city communities and mainstream society. Each year, the federal government's Low-Income Housing Tax Credit (see page 49) connects thousands of corporate, individual, and institutional investors and billions of dollars to projects in distressed urban neighborhoods. Nationwide, it supports development of an average of 110,000 units of low-rent housing per year.

Low-income housing might alternatively be built through direct government expenditures: Some cost-benefit studies have indicated that such direct approaches produce housing at a lower cost per unit.[27] However, tax credits have the important advantage of creating new networks of stakeholders in inner-city areas. The thousands of individual and institutional investors who participate in the LIHTC suddenly have a *connection* to the inner city. Instead of marginalizing the construction of affordable housing as an activity of a few government agencies, the LIHTC system creates a powerful link between housing-deprived areas and national capital markets. In addition, the LIHTC supports a type of housing production that produces more than shelter. The community-based organizations that often utilize tax credits to develop housing are leaders in community-building efforts that produce a range of improvements. **We recommend an expansion of the total pool of Low-Income Housing Tax Credits available nationwide and an increased allocation of these funds for work in inner-city communities. Because the economic development agendas of distressed inner cities extend beyond housing, we also support creation of a parallel tax credit to support commercial and industrial development in distressed communities.**[28]

• There is a key role for publicly supported research and development. Although community building has many successes to its credit, it is only beginning to undergo the systematic experimentation, evaluation, assessment, and dissemination of information needed to support a broad national commitment to the approach. **We applaud the past efforts of those foundations that have taken the lead in funding and evaluating innovative community-building pilot programs and urge them to continue to do so. We urge others in a position to sponsor research, in academia, government, and philanthropy, also to support the systematic study of**

community-building activities. Carefully designed, controlled evaluations are needed to develop a knowledge base to support further development of community-building policies and practices. Dissemination of information about best practices can help strengthen the performance of community-based initiatives. Finally, there is a need to monitor the condition of urban areas and to publicize trends so that the nation can gauge the urgency of urban problems and measure the impact of the community-building approach.

On a subject where a constant din of negative news too often leads the nation to despair, CED's message is one of hope. We are excited by local efforts that are solving complex inner-city problems and rebuilding distressed communities. These examples teach that where social capital is insufficient, it can be developed; that leadership and commitment can make it grow; and that distressed communities can flourish once again.

Business, government, and the philanthropic sector should recognize the new opportunities demonstrated by these impressive examples. Through a *new partnership* between community-based initiatives and resources from outside the inner city, that recognition can be translated into action. Together, we can rebuild an urban environment that contributes to, rather than detracts from, a humane and healthy American society.

Notes

1. Christopher Walker, "Nonprofit Housing Development: Status, Trends, and Prospects," *Housing Policy Debate* 4 (1993): 369–414.

2. This pattern is particularly pronounced for the limited number of CDCs with long histories and programs of substantial scale, such as Newark's New Community Corpora-

tion (see page 29). See also Walker, "Nonprofit Housing Development," pp. 376–381.

3. *Changing the Odds: The Achievement of Community-based Development Corporations* (Washington, D.C.: National Congress for Community Economic Development, 1991), p. 4; Avis C. Vidal, *Rebuilding Communities: A National Study of Community Development Corporations* (New York: New School for Social Research, 1992), p. 30.

4. Joseph B. McNeely, *Building for the Future* (Washington, D.C.: Fannie Mae Foundation, November 1993), pp. 5–6.

5. Walker, "Nonprofit Housing Development," pp. 373, 379.

6. Carol Steinbach, *A Decent Place to Live, Revisited* (Columbia, Md.: The Enterprise Foundation), p. 19.

7. CED's concerns about fiscal responsibility and reduction of budget deficits are presented in *Restoring Prosperity: Budget Choices for Economic Growth* (1992).

8. While LISC has been at work in certain cities, another major national intermediary, the Enterprise Foundation, has been providing a similar portfolio of services to community development organizations in other localities. Enterprise was created in 1982 under the leadership of developer James Rouse. In the Sandtown-Winchester neighborhood of Baltimore, for example, Enterprise is testing an ambitious model of neighborhood transformation that attempts to improve almost every aspect of inner-city life, from education and health care to housing and sanitation, during a five-year demonstration.

9. Robert Whittlesey, National Association of Housing Partnerships, personal communication, 1994.

10. *Concept and Background: Consensus Organizing Institute* (Boston, Mass.: Consensus Organizing Institute, 1994).

11. LISC *Annual Report* (New York: Local Initiatives Support Corporation, 1993); Karen E. Klein, "Empowering the People," *Los Angeles Times*, March 15, 1993; Benson Roberts, Local Initiatives Support Corporation, personal communication; "LISC Launches National Investment Fund to Develop Retail Centers in Poor Areas," *Economic Opportunity Report* 29 (October 17, 1994): 327–328.

12. W. Anderson Spickard, Gregory L. Dixon, and Frankie W. Sarver, *Fighting Back Against America's Health Enemy Number One* (Nashville, Tenn.: Vanderbilt University Medical Center, 1993).

13. McNeely, *Building for the Future*, p. 13.

14. In some localities, political or community leaders may attempt to gain political advantage by hindering cooperative efforts. To minimize such problems, supporters of community building, especially at the metropolitan-area level, should ensure that their public-sector and community partners are legitimate leaders who enjoy broad community support and political credibility.

15. Carole Ashkinaze, *Because There Is Hope: Gearing Up to Renew Urban America* (Atlanta, Ga.: The Atlanta Project, 1993), p. 8; Jimmy Carter, *Turning Point: A Candidate, a State, and a Nation Come of Age* (New York: Random House, 1992), pp. 205–211.

16. Benson Roberts, Local Initiatives Support Corporation, personal communication, 1994.

17. CED previously urged business participation in these partnerships in *Public-Private Partnerships: An Opportunity for Urban Communities* (1982). See also Scott Fosler and Renee Berger, eds., *Public-Private Partnership in American Cities: Seven Case Studies* (New York: Committee for Economic Development, 1982).

18. *Pfizer in Brooklyn — A Redevelopment Story* (New York: Pfizer Inc., n.d.).

19. Thomas J. Klutznick, "The Peril of Our Inner Cities," *Aspen Quarterly* (Summer 1994): 82–90.

20. Alfred Blumstein, *Youth Violence, Guns, and the Illicit-Drug Industry* (Pittsburgh, Penn.: Carnegie Mellon University, 1994), Figure 7.

21. For example, local authorities may disrupt illegal gun markets and possession of guns by juveniles by tracing weapons used in crimes, conducting "reverse stings" in which police pose as gun dealers to arrest buyers, and targeting enforcement efforts against drug and fencing organizations known to sell guns to youths. See David M. Kennedy, *Can We Keep Guns Away from Kids?* (Cambridge, Mass.: Harvard University Press, 1993).

22. Blumstein, *Youth Violence*, pp. 14, 18–20; Elijah Anderson, "The Code of the Streets," *Atlantic Monthly*, May 1994, pp. 80–94.

23. *Community Leaders Speak Out Against Drug Abuse* (Princeton, N.J.: Join Together, 1993), p. 34.

24. Atelia I. Melaville, Martin J. Blank, and Gelareh Asayesh, *Together We Can: A Guide for Creating a Pro-Family System of Education and Human Services* (Washington, D.C.: U.S. Department of Education and U.S. Department of Health and Human Services, 1993).

25. Melaville, Blank, and Asayesh, *Together We Can*.

26. In support of these same goals, the proposed National Community Economic Partnership Act of 1993, introduced in the 103d Congress by Senator Edward Kennedy, called for $40 million in fiscal 1995 to "enable [community development] corporations to support an administrative capacity for the planning, development, and management of low-income community economic development projects."

27. *The Cost-Effectiveness of the Low-Income Housing Tax Credit Compared with Housing Vouchers* (Washington, D.C.: Congressional Budget Office, April 1992); Michael A. Stegman, "The Excessive Cost of Creative Finance: Growing Inefficiencies in the Production of Low-Income Housing," *Housing Policy Debate* 2 (1991): 357–373.

28. A limited demonstration of a broader credit was enacted by Congress in 1993, but it does not connect inner cities to private markets as the LIHTC does. Under the 1993 CDC Contributions Tax Credit program, donors to 20 CDCs designated by the Secretary of HUD qualify for an additional tax credit equal to five percent of their tax-deductible contributions annually for up to ten years.

16. CURBING URBAN SPRAWL

Brian Robinson

Many of the nation's cities are enjoying the fruits of the best economy in decades, with the indicators of civic health — tax receipts, economic investment levels and employment rates— all pointing up.

Yet the good times have brought some negatives: an insatiable appetite on the part of consumers and developers for more space, choking transportation systems and service infrastructures. In short, urban sprawl.

These problems, which come with fairly toxic environmental side effects, have become so severe that the nation's mayors consider the containment of urban sprawl a top priority. The National League of Cities reported recently that nearly half of the 393 mayors surveyed believed development in their communities was poorly planned or "sprawling."

To sort through such problems, communities are rallying around "smart growth" policies that attempt to balance community life and economic development. Increasingly, those plans involve information technologies— including geographic information systems (GIS), graphic modeling software and land-use systems— that use population and demographic databases to project growth scenarios.

End users of those systems include elected officials, urban planners and citizens. "I think GIS — now that it has been used as a tool for many, many years— is past the early adoption stage and is viewed as an essential tool for helping make decisions in these areas," said Preetha Pulusani, executive vice president for mapping and GIS at Intergraph Corp., a large GIS developer.

The rise of the Internet also is enhancing the role of technology in urban planning and decision-making. "We are seeing more and more citizens, along with a growing number of departments within a local government, taking an interest in planning," Pulusani said. "That means they need access to information almost in a real-time manner. The convergence of the Internet and GIS technology is especially crucial in situations where a government wants to keep citizens involved and apprised of the progress they are making."

The Sierra Club — which has declared sprawl its No. 1 issue for the year — also has become a proponent of GIS after realizing

From civic.com, *Vol. 3, No. 5, May, 1999. Published by FCW Government Technology Group, Falls Church, Virginia. Reprinted with permission of the publisher.*

that a map can be worth a thousand words. The group is making Environmental Systems Research Institute Inc.'s ArcView products available to citizens in several communities to encourage them to get involved in anti-sprawl campaigns. "We are trying to make available tools that visually show the effects of urban sprawl so that citizens can help stop sprawl in their areas," said Brett Hulsey, director of the environmental group's "Challenge to Sprawl" campaign.

Environmental lobbyists are urging state and local governments to map future urban growth electronically, emphasizing the need to model highway expansion. "There is massive highway building going on, and we are urging governments to use modeling technology to find the most efficient ways to move people from one place to another," Hulsey said.

But each community has a different urban sprawl crisis and, therefore, a different approach to reining in out-of-control development. To examine these approaches, *civic.com* looked at how three communities harnessed technology to curb sprawl.

The first city was Portland, Ore., which often has been held up as the epitome of smart urban planning since the 1970s, when the city set limits on development by establishing urban growth boundaries. Austin, Texas, is at the other end of the planning spectrum. There, city officials have to sell smart growth to a constituency that does not take kindly to growth management ideas of any sort. Finally, we looked Fairfax County, Va., a suburb of Washington, D.C., where the politics of development — like the politics of everything else — is notched way up.

Ultimately, technology will help find the course, but final decisions on sprawl will be political. "Technology helps you track things [and] assess things, but what it doesn't do is tell you what to do about those things. It takes initiative on the part

of state and local governments to ask questions like, 'Do we have enough land, and is the land being used at the right intensity level?'" said Stuart Meck, senior researcher with the American Planning Association.

Portland: Pillar of Planning Prowess

Portland is a pioneer in the smart growth movement, as the city 20 years ago visualized an integrated approach to urban development. In the 1970s, all Oregon cities established urban growth boundaries, cordoning off acres that will remain rural. New development within the urban boundaries is strictly apportioned.

Those early decisions have produced remarkable statistics: From 1970 to 1990, the Portland metropolitan population grew by 50 percent but used just two percent more land. To put that in context, the population of metropolitan Los Angeles grew 45 percent in the same period and gobbled up 200 percent more land. Chicago's population grew by only four percent, but developed land increased 46 percent.

Technology is entrenched in Portland officials' effort to manage the city's urban growth policies. For example, Portland uses an array of GIS tools. "We've relied very heavily on GIS. The GIS data allows us to be better managers because we have a lot more information available to us. We can measure more accurately just where the urban growth boundary is," said Mark Turpel, manager of long-range planning for Portland Metro, the elected body responsible for management of the metropolitan region.

GIS use in Portland replaced a laborious manual mapping effort that dates to 1980, when Portland Metro went to put the previous decade's land-use laws into action. The city had settled on urban growth boundaries by doing a vacant land inventory so that it could tell how much extra land it had and where that land was.

"We drew paper maps of land use by visiting the various jurisdictions, looking at their maps and coloring them in by hand," said Alan Holstead, Portland Metro's GIS supervisor.

The GIS department today has swelled to about 40 developers and users who work with ESRI's Arc/Info, ArcView and Map-Objects software running on a mix of Hewlett-Packard 730 Unix workstations and 233 MHz Intel Corp. Pentium II PCs with Microsoft Corp.'s Windows NT.

Technology allows planners to model situations and try development approaches before any construction begins. The result is a coup in terms of the accuracy that planners can achieve, but it is an even bigger boost in terms of development options that they can contemplate — ideas such as infilling and redevelopment — all of which can equate to smart land use.

Because GIS is no longer an arcane science, policymakers on the Portland Metro council are often handed electronic mapping products that give better technical assessments of growth. Invaluable to those officials is the ability to tell regional authorities in a simple, visual manner how actions at the local level will affect the whole region's growth, Turpel said.

This kind of communication is crucial because Portland Metro only oversees planning on a regional level; the final say on planning and development rests with each city and county. Soon Portland Metro will delegate not only development decision-making but also the maintenance of the region's GIS assets. Metro is giving back to the local jurisdictions the responsibility of pulling together and maintaining the digital data for their own areas.

"Our job will be to aggregate all of that information and stitch it together in a regional layer," Holstead said. "For that we'll need to standardize some of the data

structure formats so they will work better with each other." The GIS data resides on a two-CPU Compaq Computer Corp. AlphaServer with a Network Appliance Inc. file server supplying files to the Unix and Windows NT desktop systems as well as for World Wide Web pages that provide mapping information over the Internet.

The Freedom to Sprawl

Austin, Texas, is like many communities that are just starting to struggle with urban sprawl. But even if Austin officials admire Portland's uniform approach to planning, they lack the wherewithal and the political mindset to use it.

"That's a challenge," said George Adams, senior planner for Austin. "This is Texas, and the whole idea of growth management, let alone urban growth boundaries, is not looked on kindly here."

The city is confronting the Texas-size resistance using basic technology to convince citizens of the need for management, particularly in the downtown areas. For instance, city planners have scanned photographs of buildings and streets in Austin and manipulated the photos with Adobe Systems Inc.'s Photoshop to show what the scenes would look like when the buildings and streets are remodeled. City planners have taken the refashioned pictures on a citywide "roadshow."

"The city has a bad history of development initiatives," said Leslie Oberholtzer, an urban designer and senior planner with Austin's Planning, Environmental and Conservation Services Department. "So we need to show the neighborhoods what they will look like after the redevelopment.

"Growth in Austin really started after World War II, so we don't have examples of some of the traditional styles of buildings," Oberholtzer added. "Most of the downtown now has wide roads with set-back sidewalks and lots of parking lots. We want to show people what it will look like if we move buildings closer to the edge of the road, put a median in a five-lane highway that now uses the center lane as a turn lane, and so on."

The next few months will decide the eventual shape of Austin's smart growth initiative, Adams said. The city council seems to be supportive of smart growth, he said, but the trick will be in selling the idea to a suspicious community.

The city is a recent convert to smart growth, having launched in 1998 a full-blown initiative to take on sprawling development. The city council first appointed a group of civic leaders three years ago to look into the problem. Recommendations pointed to a two-pronged mission: Tackle urban sprawl and traffic congestion, and bring life back into a dilapidated downtown.

Like the effort to surmount sprawl, the technology tools the city will use also are new. But it helps that the city has enjoyed an enterprisewide GIS system since 1991— far ahead of most local governments, which still are deploying GIS to the desktop. Austin uses ESRI's software, including Arc/Info running on Unix for "heavy duty" creators and maintainers of the GIS data and ArcView running on Windows NT for casual users of the data. Both groups use Pentium II or Pentium III PCs with a standard 64M of RAM, 8M of video RAM and 21-inch monitors.

About 90 percent of the GIS data is housed on a server that acts as a central data repository, said Dean LaBonte, the city's GIS administrator. So workers in different city departments can take any data they need from the repository for their own applications. Each department also has a say in the kind of data it wants to be digitized and put into the repository. With this main server almost full, LaBonte said

other city department servers are being linked with it to form a "virtual" data repository that will be the basis for expanding the GIS system.

GIS has proven itself in planning projects, but if the technology is to be used effectively in the smart growth initiative, it needs to be more widespread in government. "We have 10,000 city employees, and just 500 are using GIS now," LaBonte said. "We could easily have half the people in the government using GIS in one way or another."

> **FIGURE 1— THE 10 CITIES MOST THREATENED BY SPRAWL**
>
> 1. Atlanta
> 2. St. Louis
> 3. Washington, D.C.
> 4. Cincinnati
> 5. Kansas City, Mo.
> 6. Denver
> 7. Seattle
> 8. Minneapolis-St. Paul
> 9. Fort Lauderdale, Fla.
> 10. Chicago
>
> *Source: The Sierra Club*

America's Sprawling Capital

This spring, headlines in Washington, D.C.-area newspapers shrieked about congestion and the sprawl of the suburbs. Particularly hammered was the Tysons Corner area of Fairfax County, Va., where new office buildings are going up in a small area already bursting at the seams.

For James Zook, director of planning and zoning for the county, these are some realities that planners along the Capital Beltway have learned to live with. Zook knows that Fairfax County will continue to grow. For him, it is not so much a question of how much but where that growth will occur. For political and other reasons, the idea is to encourage growth in urban areas and discourage it in environmentally sensitive ones.

"My take on smart growth is that it's not that different from what's been happening in Fairfax and other jurisdictions in Virginia anyway," he said. "We call it comprehensive planning, and that has been going on ever since we made a major revision to the county plan in 1975. We revisit the plan frequently, but its basic nature remains the same."

Zook's office uses a mix of GIS and computer-aided design to churn out options for each planning move, which, Zook said, "makes it much easier to put recommendations together for our policy-makers." Fairfax planners also rely on demographic and economic development estimates and population data produced by the county's Office of Management and Budget.

Larry Bizette, a demographer and computer analyst for Fairfax County, said his staff often works with the county's GIS division to build maps used in planning and executive decision-making. The staff produces information that is used by most county agencies, including the Department of Planning and Zoning, and the Depart-

ment of Public Works and Environmental Services, which uses the numbers to forecast sewage requirements.

Bizette also passes demographic and other information to the Washington Council of Governments, the area's regional agency for transportation planning. "They collect the forecasts of jurisdictions and model the numbers to decide which roadways are more problematic than others and what some of the solutions to some of those problems would be," Bizette said.

Resolved to booming population and urban development, Fairfax officials are counting on technology to help them make the best decisions. "I would suggest that a great deal of the development that has occurred has taken place in as orderly a fashion as any human being can make it," Bizette said. "Certainly there is congestion in some areas. But we are producing a lot of information and evolving our methods as technology changes to produce the best projections we can.... No one has a crystal ball, and no one can say for sure the best course development should take."

17. DEVELOPMENT AND PUBLIC SERVICES

David Salvesen and Craig Richardson

One of the traditional responsibility of government is to provide public facilities to meet the needs of the community — a tradition that dates back at least 2,000 years to the construction of roads and aqueducts by the Greek and Roman governments. Most local governments quietly fulfill this responsibility — providing drinking water, treating wastewater, and building and maintaining schools, roads, and parks without much strife. In rapidly growing areas, however, local governments struggle to keep pace with the demands created by new development and risk being choked by their own success, as rampant growth threatens to destroy the very attributes that attracted people there in the first place.

Faced with the prospect of clogged roads, overcrowded schools, dwindling open space, and overburdened water and sewer systems, a growing number of communities have adopted programs that link development approvals to the capacity of their public facilities. Such adequate public facility (APF) requirements are emerging as one of the most common techniques for managing growth in the United States.

"The APF issue is hot right now," observes Eric Kelly, a planning consultant and professor of planning at Ball State University. "Fast-growing communities are looking for ways to keep up."

Birthplace of APF Ordinances

The concept of linking development approval to the capacity of public facilities was first tested in the small town of Ramapo, New York. In 1969, the town adopted an ordinance stating, in essence, that new residential development could not take place if the capacity of the town's public facilities was not adequate to serve it. Developers were given points based on the available capacity of roads, water and sewer service, drainage facilities, fire and police protection, schools, and parks and recreation facilities. Those who failed to earn enough points could provide the necessary facilities themselves or wait for the town to add sufficient capacity. The town, however, was in no hurry — its capital improvement plan called for infrastructure investments to be carried out over an 18-year period.

Originally published as "Keeping Up with Growth," Urban Land, Vol. 58, No. 9, September, 1999. Published by the Urban Land Institute, Washington, D.C. Reprinted with permission of the publisher.

Following adoption of the ordinance, housing construction dropped dramatically. Builders sued, but New York's highest court upheld Ramapo's system (*Golden v. Planning Board of the Town of Ramapo*, 324 N.Y.S. 2d 178 N.Y. 1971). The decision legitimized the use of APF requirements and spawned similar ordinances elsewhere. Montgomery County, Maryland, adopted an APF ordinance in 1973. And in the mid–1980s, Florida required all local governments to ensure that sufficient public facility capacity was in place concurrent with new development—a requirement known as concurrency.

Today, programs linking development approvals to the capacity of public facilities can be found in a growing number of communities, particularly those in California, Colorado, Washington, Florida, and Maryland. According to *Managing Growth in America's Communities*, by Douglas Porter, president of the Growth Management Institute in Chevy Chase, Maryland, about one-third of California cities have adopted APF provisions. In Maryland, 13 counties and four cities are administering APF regulations. Most programs focus on the adequacy of road capacity.

In Florida, the state's 400-plus local governments are required to implement APF standards for six public facilities (roads, potable water, wastewater treatment, parks and recreation, solid wastes, and drainage). And in Washington State, local governments around Puget Sound and the state's other fast-growing counties and cities are required to implement an APF program for roads and are strongly encouraged to adopt APF programs for other public facilities as well.

Ironically, Ramapo eventually scrapped its APF ordinance, primarily because the town had discovered that it lacked direct control over certain public facilities, such as water and sewer service. More recently, Chapel Hill, North Carolina, decided against adopting an adequate public facility ordinance since key facilities—water and sewer, roads, and schools—are not controlled by the town.

Different Strokes: A Sample of APF Programs

Montgomery County, Maryland, administers the longest-running APF program in the country. Subdivision approval is linked to the capacity of schools, roads, public transit, water and sewer facilities, police stations, firehouses, and health clinics, although roads are the primary focus of the program. Exemptions are provided for affordable housing, for small projects generating fewer than five peak-hour automobile trips, and for development near transit stations. To encourage transit-oriented development, the county permits greater congestion in "policy areas" with transit accessibility. Thus, development can occur near transit stations even if the capacity of roads is inadequate.

In analyzing the adequacy of road capacity, the county assesses the impact of a proposed development on traffic congestion at nearby intersections as well as over a wider geographic area called a policy area. The county is split into 25 policy areas, plus the cities of Rockville and Gaithersburg. For each policy area, the county calculates the capacity of the transportation network to accommodate new development and determines the maximum amount of development, called the staging ceiling, that can be approved each year. The staging ceilings are published in the county's annual growth policy. In short, developers must pass two tests for roads—one demonstrating that their projects will not exceed the capacity of nearby intersections and another showing that their projects will not result in clogged roads throughout the policy area.

If development exceeds the staging ceiling in a policy area, the county imposes a development moratorium on that area. In 1999, this occurred in six policy areas. A moratorium does not preclude development, however. Developers can proceed with their projects if they provide the needed transportation facilities, mitigate the traffic impacts, or pay a fee in lieu of making improvements.

The program is supported by strong analysis backed up by maps and policies in the comprehensive plan. "It's very sophisticated stuff," says Kelly. Still, the program is not without its problems. The in-lieu fee amounts to an additional impact fee. Says Porter, "The local area review is a device to generate exactions." Also, notes Kelly, "The program is so complex that it's essentially untransferable."

At the other extreme is Cabarrus County, a fast-growing suburb of Charlotte, North Carolina. In response to several years of rapid growth, which threatened to overwhelm its schools, the county adopted an adequate public facility ordinance in 1998. The ordinance — which consists simply of a two-paragraph insert to the county's subdivision regulations — applies to all facilities but is used mainly for schools. According to county planner Roger Lentz, "The ordinance was meant as a stopgap measure to prevent school overcrowding." Yet, the ordinance lacks standards for adequacy. For this and other reasons, it is vulnerable to legal challenge.

Since the ordinance was adopted, every subdivision application has been rejected by the county planning board. On appeal to the county commission, however, each of the subdivision developers obtained approval in exchange for paying a fee of $500 per lot. Unfortunately, the ordinance has not solved the county's school overcrowding problem and has not raised enough money for new schools. "It operates like a cheap impact fee," observes Lentz.

Calvert County, Maryland, also adopted an adequate public facility ordinance to combat school overcrowding. Adopted in 1988, the ordinance has helped the county keep pace with development by holding down the number of new subdivisions until the county can build new schools. The school board, however, has not always redistricted students to the new schools. As a result, some schools remain overcrowded while others have seats to spare.

Florida was the first state to require all local governments to link development approvals to the capacity of public facilities. Its 1985 Growth Management Act required that adequate facility capacity be in place before new development could be approved. Public facilities needed to serve the expected population at the locally set level of service (LOS) standards must be incorporated into the comprehensive plan's capital improvement element, which, in turn, must meet standards for financial feasibility.

Carlsbad, California, set performance standards for 11 types of public facilities, including water and sewer, schools, parks, libraries, open space, and traffic circulation. For example, its standard for libraries is 800 square feet of library space for each 1,000 residents, while its standard for parks is three acres per 1,000 residents. Carlsbad is split into 25 zones (much like Montgomery County's policy areas), which are used in calculating facility capacity. Developers must prepare a zone plan that determines whether a proposed project will exceed the performance standards for any of the 11 facilities. If the standards cannot be met, developers must pay their fair share of necessary improvements.

Unintended Consequences

In the early 1990s, urban jurisdictions in Florida became concerned that concurrency was encouraging sprawl and discouraging urban redevelopment. While roads in urban areas were at or near capacity, those in the suburbs enjoyed excess capacity. "Concurrency was working against one of the main objectives of Florida's growth management laws—compact development," says Dale Eacker, administrator of transportation planning at the Florida Department of Community Affairs in Tallahassee.

In response, the Florida legislature amended the concurrency program in 1993 and created two programs designed to give local governments greater flexibility in meeting the concurrency requirements for roads: long-term transportation concurrency management (LTTCM) and transportation concurrency exception areas (TCEA).

Before the amendments were passed, local governments could approve a development proposal even if road capacity was unavailable, as long as the necessary road improvements were included in the capital improvements plan (CIP) and were scheduled for completion within three years. The LTTCM extended the period from three years to as long as 15 years. In addition, TCEAs allow a community to exempt congested areas from the concurrency requirements altogether, as long as the community meets certain conditions, such as adopting a comprehensive plan that meets state standards, ensuring that future development is consistent with the plan, adopting a CIP that will address deficiencies in capacity, and requiring developers to pay a fair share of the costs of proposed facilities. Thus far, only one community has implemented a long-term transportation concurrency management system and 20 have adopted transportation concurrency exception areas. "The programs haven't been widely used," observed Eacker. Orlando exempted most of its downtown from the concurrency requirement. "We couldn't have achieved the

LOS standards downtown without destroying neighborhoods," explains Dan Gallagher, chief planner for the city of Orlando. "The concurrency requirements were too rigid." Instead, the city has focused on improving the bus system. "We invested a big chunk of our gas tax money in regional transit," says Gallagher.

Despite the amendments to Florida's concurrency program, a 1999 report by the Florida Transportation and Land Use Study Committee, commissioned by the state legislature, suggested that concurrency may encourage sprawl and discourage redevelopment and infill of urban areas. If roads are congested in urban areas, developers simply go where capacity exists, usually rural areas. The resulting sprawl funnels increased congestion onto the very roads where development is limited by concurrency.

"Concurrency has tended to lower densities and spread development out," states committee member Richard Bernhardt, former director of planning for the city of Orlando and now a planner with EDAW, a consulting firm in Orlando. Bill Spikowski, a planning consultant in Fort Myers, Florida, agrees. "To the extent it works, concurrency tends to push development into the boondocks."

Others disagree. "The idea that APF ordinances cause sprawl is absurd," counters Mark White, a partner with Frielich, Leitner & Carlisle, a land use planning and law firm in Kansas City, Missouri. "Houston doesn't have an APF ordinance. Neither does Phoenix. Yet both are sprawling metropolises. Sprawl was probably going to happen anyway."

Thus far, there is no empirical evidence that APF programs, by themselves, lead to sprawl. "The evidence is 100 percent anecdotal," asserts Carl Moritz, planner with the Maryland National Capital Park and Planning Commission.

Interestingly, Carlsbad's program

may actually encourage infill, since most of the available infrastructure already is downtown. "If you build in outlying areas, you have to build the infrastructure too," says Don Rideout, a planner with the county. "It's too expensive."

Do APF Programs Work?

At a minimum, adequate public facility programs have forced local governments to think about the connection between development and infrastructure and to prioritize their capital improvements. "Concurrency serves as an early warning system," notes Bruce McClendon, planning director of Orange County Florida. "It tells you where you should focus your investments." But as a tool for helping local governments keep pace with development, the results of concurrency are mixed.

Some critics assert that, at least in Florida, concurrency has largely failed. "It hardly works at all," asserts Spikowski. "Small communities [in Florida] just don't do it. That's the dirty little secret. The proposals come in and the permits go out."

Spikowski suggests that the remedy for inadequate capacity — a moratorium — is too severe. Local governments are not going to shut down development, he says. If infrastructure capacity is stretched to the limits, jurisdictions can simply lower their standards or measure concurrency in a different way to avoid a moratorium. Another strategy is to count planned improvements, whether funded or not, as current capacity. "There are all sorts of tricks communities play to avoid moratoriums," asserts Porter.

For facilities other than roads, however, some argue that concurrency is working. "Concurrency is working for water and sewer," says Wayne Daltry, director of the Southwest Florida Regional Planning Council in North Fort Myers, Florida. According to Daltry, water and sewer moratoriums have been imposed when capacity is lacking. "They're not forbidden fruit." Similarly, Calvert County has clamped down on new development when school capacity was inadequate. "We've closed the county to new subdivisions on numerous occasions," remarks planning director Frank Jaklitsch. "It's the most effective ordinance in the state."

Where APF programs have been used to manage growth rather than to stop growth, they seem to work best. In many cases, local governments have been able to anticipate infrastructure demands and plan accordingly. In other cases, however, local jurisdictions have failed to keep pace with growth and have resorted to lowering their standards for adequacy to avoid imposing a moratorium on development. "APF ordinances can work for or against you," cautions Porter. "That's the rub."

18. FEDERAL
EMPOWERMENT ZONES

Renee Berger

For the armies of anti-poverty activities battered into near oblivion during the Reagan and Bush administrations, 1993 was an unexpectedly good year. Buried in the federal budget was a mammoth new program — known as the Empowerment — that promised to resuscitate impoverished neighborhoods by providing new housing and decent jobs for the unemployed.

There was some initial skepticism. Urban commentator Nicholas Lemann wrote in the *New York Times Magazine* in January 1994 that the EZ/EC program was politically wired and programmatically flawed.

Nevertheless, local officials greeted President Clinton's December 1994 announcement of the first designations with enthusiasm. Six empowerment zones were created — in Atlanta, Baltimore, Chicago, Detroit, New York City, and jointly in Philadelphia and Camden. Two "supplemental empowerment zones" were created in Los Angeles and Cleveland, while four cities — Boston, Houston, Oakland, and Kansas City, Missouri — were designated "enhanced enterprise communities." Three rural empowerment zones and 105 enterprise communities were designated as well. (See "Power to the Zones," February 1995.)

Even before the winners were chosen, grassroots activists in the chosen cities had begun caucusing, foundation executives had organized brainstorming sessions with officials of the U.S. Department of Housing and Urban Development, which runs the urban part of the EZ/EC program, and mayors and their planning staffs had begun dreaming about how to kindle hope and, perhaps, provide real opportunity.

The EZ/EC program offers tax breaks whose estimated value is $2.5 billion over five years. It also provides $1.3 billion in flexible grant assistance from Title XX of the Health and Human Services block grant. Total cost to taxpayers: $3.8 billion over 10 years.

The six urban empowerment zones will each receive $100 million in grant money and a variety of financing tools, including loan guarantees, tax-exempt bond financing, accelerated property depreciation, and wage tax credits. The three rural zones will receive $40 million each plus the same financing tools.

As for the 105 enterprise communities,

Originally published as "People, Power, Politics," Planning, Vol. 63, No. 2, February, 1997. Published by the American Planning Association. Reprinted with permission of the publisher.

each will get $3 million in grant funds, and some of the same tools. All the designated communities will get preference for certain federal programs—community development banks, for example.

So how are they doing? Have the zones lived up to their promise? Most of all, have they generated jobs? Those are the questions that concern us here.

Slow Timetable

It should be noted first of all that it took far longer to set up the empowerment zones than anyone had anticipated. For the better part of 1995 and, in some places, part of 1996, empowerment and enterprise zone cities were consumed with creating organizational structures and formulating the performance benchmarks required for federal grants. During that time, there were many complaints—from neighborhood activists and the media — that "nothing is happening."

"Business groups often spend years working on a new product, all behind closed doors," says Diane Bell, the head of Baltimore's empowerment zone. "But here we don't have that luxury."

Producing organizational plans for the zones also turned out to be more difficult than expected. Those involved had to deal with all sorts of power plays by mayors and city councils, government agencies, and community groups.

"You're dealing with people from different worlds," says Bell. "Some knew the complexities of the process, others didn't." Even more problematic were the debates in Chicago, Atlanta, and New York City about whether the plans outlined in the city's application had to be followed to the letter — or not at all.

Hurdles

The focus here is on two of the EZ cities, Baltimore and Detroit. Both are battlescarred from years of disinvestment and the loss of their manufacturing base, which in turn has meant the loss of thousands of jobs.

Detroit's zone is a large one, covering 18 square miles and three neighborhoods, where half the residents are below the poverty line and almost a third are unemployed. Fewer than half the zone residents are likely to graduate from high school.

That makes the hurdles high — even with $100 million per city. "We are not going to obliterate poverty," says Detroit's empowerment zone transition chief, Kate Levin. Levin was hired by the city to establish the management structure to run the zone program.

Detroit ran into snags in the very beginning. A coordinating council composed of local activists, members of the religious community, government and business representatives, and others, was formed to write the zone application. If the zone was designated, the council hoped to establish an independent nonprofit corporation to implement the plan.

After receiving designation, coordinating council members met privately with lawyers to draft state and local legislation that would enable them to establish the new Empowerment Zone Development Corporation. But several city council members argued that an autonomous development corporation would conflict with the city charter by undermining the council's contract oversight responsibility. The six-month battle that ensued between the coordinating council and the city council brought things to a halt.

Eventually, the nonprofit corporation was established, but it's not autonomous. The city council reviews all contracts—and the city manages them.

The other battle waged in Detroit was over the coordinating council's resistance to using Title XX money to fund the operations of the development corporation. Years of cynicism, bred during the administration of former mayor Coleman Young, had led to fears that the city would siphon off the funds. Instead, the coordinating council wanted the private sector to foot the bill for administration.

Levin and Mayor Dennis Archer contended that this stricture was unrealistic and that the private sector would not pay 100 percent of the operating costs. After months of debate, the council and the city agreed that the zone grant funds would pay for part of the operating costs. Reluctant to de-designate a city, appreciating that progress can be slow in a new program. The contrast with the more prescriptive, hands-on programs of the 1960s and 1970s, the years of the Great Society, could not be greater.

New Jobs?

According to HUD's EZ/EC FLASH website (www.ezec.gov), the empowerment zones would appear to be generating thousands of jobs. Again, Detroit serves as a microcosm. In recent speeches, both Vice President Gore and Secretary Cisneros agreed.

More of the Same

Chicago, Atlanta, and Camden (half of the Philadelphia/Camden empowerment zone) had similar tales. In each, strong mayors weighed in after receiving empowerment zone designation, rekindling wars with community groups that had been partners during the initial planning.

Baltimore's empowerment zone covers seven square miles, ranging from barren industrial areas to densely populated neighborhoods dominated by public housing projects. The poverty rate in the zone is 41 percent, the unemployment rate 17 percent. Roughly 72,000 people, 10 percent of the city's population, live within the zone.

Yet Baltimore's experience, though not friction-free, was more positive than Detroit's. The initial board was formed almost immediately after the zone designation, and last year representatives were added from the six newly formed "village centers"— nonprofit organizations established to provide a meeting place and neighborhood voice in the empowerment zone.

The Rouse Corporation provided free office space in a downtown building and Mayor Kurt Schmoke dug into city coffers (later reimbursed by Title XX money) to staff the new Empower Baltimore Management Corporation. Substantial additional support came from the Baltimore-based Annie E. Casey Foundation.

The management corporation, a local observer explains, "is remarkably autonomous, despite the mayor controlling a significant portion of the board positions and its executive director having been a mayoral appointee." A 50-member advisory council provides community input. The board is responsible for approving and overseeing contracts. It has its own procurement procedures, a fact that has "frustrated some city agencies," Bell says.

Assessing Progress

After organizing their empowerment zones, cities next had to produce performance benchmarks— not an easy task, according to those involved. "There was a changing cast of staff and requirements, as the federal government itself was figuring out what it wanted," says Bell. Gloria Robinson, Detroit's planning director, says delays occurred when HUD changed the forms needed to report on performance benchmarks. With the change, the entire process took six to nine months.

Even when HUD signed off on the benchmarks, the money didn't arrive immediately. First the zone cities had to develop financial procedures for drawing down Title XX grant funds, which are administered by the states. Some states were reportedly concerned that the cities involved would be unable to meet fiduciary requirements. Other states used this argument as an excuse for governors to torment mayors they didn't like.

In Georgia, for instance, according to a senior HUD official, "state officials have, for over 18 months, systematically stymied Atlanta's efforts to use their Title XX allocation." In other states, Title XX money is only now beginning to flow.

HUD has played an active role in the benchmarking but is keeping hands off in matters of state and local governance. The agency views itself as a facilitator in the early stages of the EZ/EC program, says the official cited above. Vice President Al Gore and outgoing HUD Secretary Henry Cisneros claimed that the city's empowerment zone has attracted $1.8 billion in private money. Part of that money, they say, comes from Chrysler's $750 million investment in a new engine plant.

But Rosa Sims, a veteran community activist who currently heads the Detroit office of the Local Initiatives Support Corporation, a prominent national intermediary organization that fosters community development, explains that the $1.8 billion private-sector investment was actually a *pledge* by area financial institutions.

Moreover, says Sims, planning for the Chrysler plant had been under way for over three years before Detroit won empowerment zone designation. Meanwhile, Robinson, the city's planning director, estimates that 700 to 750 jobs have been generated in the zone since designation.

In Baltimore, the Empower Baltimore Management Corporation, working through a city job placement effort called the Employ Baltimore Initiative, reports that 400 zone residents have found positions. The city recently received a HUD grant for its reverse commuting program, which will help bring enterprise zone residents to unfilled jobs in the outer suburbs.

As for finding jobs for zone residents, the obstacles are profound. Michael Seipp, director of the Historic East Baltimore village center, estimates that more than half of the people he sees have substance abuse problems and many have criminal records that will prohibit them from working in certain kinds of jobs. Title XX funds are earmarked for job training and counseling services for such residents.

Baltimore's performance report, submitted to HUD last July, identifies roughly 30 businesses as having newly located or expanded in the empowerment zone. Most are mom and pop outfits, with two larger concerns, the Sandtown-Winchester Nursing and Rehabilitation Center and the Parrot Island Restaurant, accounting for nearly half of the reported 500 jobs created. Many of these jobs existed before the zone was created.

One of the zone's small businesses is Dynatech Integrated Systems, a four-year-old, computer-testing firm based in Columbia, Maryland. It employs 15 people in a new, 13,000-square-foot plant in the East Harbor neighborhood. Marsha Parham, Dynatech's director of operations, says Baltimore's empowerment zone management corporation helped the firm obtain financing for its new building.

But according to Pamela Trickey, Dynatech's director of technology, only two or three workers there this fall were EZ residents. Moreover, they were not regular employees. They were temporary contract workers, earning about $6.50 an hour with no fringe benefits. Co-owner Earl Scott, who grew up in the neighborhood, reportedly has ambitions to hire more local residents. But the fact remains that small businesses, while crucial to the regeneration and economic balance of empowerment zones, typically pay less and offer less security than large firms do.

This shouldn't come as a surprise. During the 1980s, while federal legislation to create what were referred to as "enterprise zones" languished, 36 states took the initiative to form their own. Studies of the zones, which chiefly rely on tax incentives, conclude that few if any net new jobs have been created. Mostly, the studies note, "new" jobs are actually existing jobs that have shifted from one location to another in the same region.

On the other hand, the empowerment zones use tax incentives, wage credits, and grant support—a combination that promises greater inducements to businesses. In addition, state and local economic development financing tools, which can supplement those offered by the empowerment zone program, are more sophisticated today than they were even a few years ago. These are factors that bode well for the future.

In addition, business development and potential "new" jobs are a less important measure than whether more zone residents are job holders earning a living wage—regardless of whether the jobs are in the zone or are in new or existing businesses. And even if it turns out that much of the business development and job activity actually comes from regional shifting, one must welcome any new employment efforts that focus on needy residents in these long-abandoned areas.

Defining Empowerment

The real test of the empowerment zone program, says one analyst, will be its ability to build capacity in the neighborhoods. But capacity building is a more exciting concept to academics and foundation executives than it is to the residents of the empowerment zone communities. For them, "empowerment" means a job and the power to manage their environment.

The strategic planning process that led to empowerment zone and enterprise community designation got lots of people fired up, and 300 communities submitted applications. Representatives of community groups sat down to work with city officials, and corporate moguls met with neighborhood merchants—often for the first time.

To be sure, there were fights. As in the 1960s, voices were raised over community participation versus community control. A HUD official confides that the agency worried about whether city planning departments, the likely agencies to coordinate the citizen outreach, would get past their "land-use approach." Many did. In Detroit, says Rosa Sims, the grassroot strategic planning process "got people who had been disconnected reconnected." Hundreds of people participated in meetings.

The next step, organizing, produced enormous pressures as boards were created, staff hired, and financial systems put into place. Baltimore's efforts in this respect are exemplary. A retreat organized by the board of the Empower Baltimore Management Corporation was attended even by the high-level corporate representatives.

The board also recommends half the members of the 50-member advisory council; the rest are recommended by the village centers. The council has become a significant force. As a result of its input, a third of the 19 positions on the board that are appointed by the mayor must come from empowerment zone representatives.

The progress of the six village centers

has been uneven. In general, the communities that were better organized, such as Sandtown-Winchester and Historic East Baltimore, got off the ground more quickly. Other places such as Poppleton, which is dominated by public housing projects, have had far more difficulty.

The empowerment zone plan calls for the management corporation to provide $200,000 to $300,000 the first year to each center to support job-readiness programs in literacy, substance abuse, and other areas. Future support will be contingent on performance. But so far, only three have submitted acceptable plans to the management corporation, and programs are still not under way.

A Little Luck

"We'd be dead in the water, if we looked at the $100 million as the end," says Baltimore's Diane Bell. The key is to use the funds strategically and to come up with financing tools to leverage other monies. Judging from Detroit and Baltimore, hardly any of the treasury has been tapped.

On the other hand, Detroit bankers now carry maps and brochures and make sales pitches for empowerment neighborhoods, says Kate Levin, and she — along with Rosa Sims and Gloria Robinson — praises the involvement of local residents. Moreover, some of the $1.8 billion that the city has attracted with the designation is already committed to real projects, which have provided jobs for at least some Detroiters.

In some respects, it seems that serendipity is as much a factor in the success of an empowerment zone as strategy. Chrysler would not be building a state-of-the-art plant in Detroit if the auto industry weren't on an upswing. And Baltimore has been encouraged to start a reverse commuting program because suburban businesses happen to be desperate for workers.

Another vital factor is political leadership. Mayors are key. Detroit's Dennis Archer was viewed as the city's savior by the businesses that supported him in his 1994 election. The empowerment zone gave the business community a focus for its good will, says Levin. And, though the state role is small, Baltimore's Diane Bell says that Gov. Parris Glendening made it clear that his staff should do everything possible to assist the zone. Undoubtedly, a future challenge for empowerment zones will be sustaining support as political leadership changes.

There is no doubt that the initial planning phase of the zone program was extremely valuable. The plans themselves provided clear directions, minimizing post-designation debates over program initiatives and priorities. As to whether the toolbox of waivers, preferences, and financing incentives — including Title XX funds — will make a real difference in empowerment zones, the jury is still out.

One problem for any urban program is unrealistic expectations. Baltimore's empowerment zone application included a goal of developing 5,100 housing units, but the zone has only the barest outline of a housing program. One empowerment zone staffer calls the goal "dreaming."

The problem with unrealistic expectations is that they breed skepticism when they fail. Think about how presidents Reagan and Bush used the alleged failures of the War on Poverty to justify draconian cuts in inner-city resources. The legacy is the defeatist belief that no government effort can make a difference.

The empowerment zone program could, in fact, lead to meaningful change — but it won't happen overnight.

19. HISTORICAL PRESERVATION INCENTIVES

Donovan D. Rypkema

Advocates for historic preservation usually argue their case by citing the aesthetic, cultural, educational, social, and environmental benefits the rehabilitation of historic structures provides to a community. But over the past few years, public sector economic benefits and private sector investment opportunities have emerged as important arguments for preservation as well.

Over time, historic preservation has moved from being an end in itself—saving old buildings to save old buildings—to being an effective vehicle for larger goals. Downtown revitalization, tourism development, neighborhood stabilization, reattraction of residents to center cities—all are examples of public policy initiatives that have used preservation pragmatically to achieve their objectives.

As a rule of thumb, the cost of new construction in the United States is divided equally between the cost of labor and of materials. In rehabilitation, on the other hand, labor may account for 60 to 70 percent of the cost, with the balance in materials. A rehabilitation project thus can have a substantially larger local economic impact than would a new construction project with an equivalent total cost. While a project might require timber from Oregon, sheetrock from Texas, and an HVAC system from Ohio, the services of the carpenter, the electrician, the plumber, and the laborer usually are bought across the street. Because their wages largely are spent locally, the impact on the local economy is significantly greater. While the numbers vary from state to state, $1 million in building rehabilitation typically will create four to eight more jobs and add in excess of $100,000 more to local household incomes than will the same amount in new construction. City leaders looking for ways to stretch the public benefit of economic development activities are recognizing that since more jobs and more local income are generated by rehabilitation, historic preservation should be among the alternatives carefully considered.

Any community's core of historic buildings is going to be in areas where taxpayer-funded infrastructure already is in place and paid for. On the commercial side, that means downtown and neighborhood business centers. Much of that

Originally published as "Preserving for Profit," Urban Land, Vol. 57, No. 12, December, 1998. Published by the Urban Land Institute, Washington, D.C. Reprinted with permission of the publisher.

infrastructure, however, is being used at only 40 or 50 percent of its capacity, effectively wasting taxpayers' dollars daily. The public sector response has been to develop downtown and neighborhood revitalization programs, usually directed by a public/private entity charged with creating a strategy and overseeing its implementation. The most successful downtown revitalization efforts in both the United States and Canada have had historic preservation as a central element. Contrary to the claims of some critics, this is not a "never tear anything down" strategy; rather, it emphasizes maintaining and effectively reusing the best of the character-defining buildings in a city's center. Further, those places where preservation awareness is the strongest are also the places attracting construction of the best-designed, highest-quality new buildings.

Heritage-based tourism has become a central component of many cities' overall economic development plan, and the preservation and reuse of historic buildings is essential to that plan. Heritage- and culture-based tourism are among the fastest-growing segments of the hospitality industry. Not only are historic resources in many locations a major tourist draw, but heritage visitors stay longer, visit more places, and spend up to two and one-half times more per trip than do other visitors.

For the first time in a generation, places as different as Philadelphia, Atlanta, Phoenix, New York, Dallas, Cleveland, Denver, and New Orleans are seeing new housing in and near the downtown area. But as diverse as those cities are, there is a common denominator — most of the new housing is in old buildings. Today, 1920s office buildings on Wall Street, former industrial buildings in Philadelphia, over-the-store apartments in Atlanta, and unused warehouses in New Orleans are finding profitable new life as residential units. What Roberta Gratz, author of *Cities Back from the Edge*, calls the "SoHo Syndrome" is rejuvenating central cities throughout the country. In a recent analysis by the Brookings Institution, all but one of the downtowns of 21 U.S. cities anticipated further center city population growth in the next decade, which can mean increased tax revenues, reduced vacancies, and vibrant downtowns.

Many mayors, city managers, economic development directors, and tourism advocates have begun to recognize that historic preservation can advance their broader goals. But many also have come to two related conclusions: redeveloping historic properties entails challenges not present in greenfield development, and not all of the public benefits are reflected in a property's net income by the time the first mortgage payment is due. Many states and municipalities therefore offer additional incentives to those willing to tackle a preservation project. In addition to the federal rehabilitation tax credits, several states have enacted an equivalent credit against state tax liability. In some locales there are tax freezes, assessment freezes, low-interest loans, design assistance, special taxing districts, tax increment financing funds, property writedowns, and other tools to encourage private sector investment in historic buildings.

These local incentives have aided preservation projects in two ways. First, the incentives themselves add to the net return from the property after completion. Second, the sheer existence of the incentives and their promotion by preservation advocates have attracted the attention of developers who in the past would not have considered anything but new construction projects.

Debunking the Myths

The redevelopment of historic properties can generate a significant profit. The first step is to sort the myths of conventional wisdom from the realities of historic property redevelopment. Three myths are particularly widespread. Myth number one is that historic preservation costs more than new construction. As with any real estate project, costs will vary widely from one project to the next. In fact, many tax-certified rehabilitation projects are completed for 60 percent or less than the cost of comparable new construction. When a historic preservation project requires a complete rehabilitation, however, including exterior repairs and replacement of all systems and the roof, it is likely that something could be built less expensively. But when quality is part of the equation, preservation can be a competitive alternative. While there are exceptions on both ends, most historic rehabilitation projects will end up costing between 85 and 120 percent of the cost of a new building of equivalent quality.

Myth number two is that a structure designed and built for one use cannot be converted to a totally different use. While the most cost-effective reuse of a building is a use that is the same or highly similar to the original, totally new uses can be made of old buildings. Today, high-end residential units as well as luxury hotels are being created in older office buildings. In Philadelphia, for example, five downtown hotel projects— Loews PSFS, Philadelphia Marriott, and Hawthorne Suites, among others—currently are underway, every one of them in a historic building.

Myth number three is that the market demands a 20,000-square-foot floor plate. Developers often will argue against historic preservation, contending that historic buildings, usually built on a smaller scale and often irregular in shape, do not have sufficient contiguous space. While it certainly is true that some firms do need, or think they need, one very large floor, the vast majority of downtown tenants do

not. In most cities, 75 percent to 90 percent of the tenants have fewer than 20 employees. While historic buildings are not necessarily adaptable for every use, both the floor size and layout of the vast majority of historic buildings are appropriate for the vast majority of downtown tenants.

Adhering to Principles

For those developers who can get beyond the myths of historic preservation, economic opportunity can await. The following principles may be useful:

• Use architects who have successfully completed a tax-certified historic rehabilitation project. Compliance with U.S. Department of the Interior standards for rehabilitation is necessary to receive the federal tax credit. Do not assume that an architect who has not previously worked through the standards will understand them; although the standards seem simple, they may not be. Use an experienced architect. The same precaution applies to the general contractor, subcontractors, and other members of the development team. If they have not done historic preservation work before, do not let them use your project for on-the-job training; it could be expensive.

• More historic preservation projects get in trouble because they run out of time than because they run out of money. More time will elapse between the issuing of the building permit and the issuing of the occupancy certificate than for a similarly sized project in a suburban office park. Have a time contingency allowance as well as a cost contingency allowance.

• Contact regulators at the outset. Before the option agreement is signed, go through the building with the architect, a representative of the state's historic preservation office, and local building officials.

This first tour will clarify many of the "must's" and cannot's" that can determine project feasibility. In many states the section of the building code devoted to historic buildings allows greater flexibility than in new construction. The state's historic preservation office can be a significant ally in encouraging local building inspectors to be as flexible as the law allows.

• Make use of the "funky peculiarity" of the building. Tenants who opt for historic buildings see their architectural character — even some features that might otherwise seem to create functional obsolescence — as attractive elements. To homogenize the interior of a historic building with standard office cubicles sacrifices the building's competitive advantage.

• Physical and environmental analysis and estimates of the cost to cure structural problems, remove lead paint, or abate asbestos should precede property acquisition. The costs of remedying those problems should be part of negotiations with city preservation advocates. Remember, however, that even those costs are eligible for federal rehabilitation tax credits.

• Look for allies. Unlike an office building or a retail mall, a historic building likely will have an advocate in an existing group of local preservationists. Around the country, these groups are becoming both more sophisticated and more politically influential. A developer who wants to undertake appropriate redevelopment of a historic building will have vocal supporters. Early contact with these groups can provide valuable information about the building's history and also may provide access to financial resources and political support not otherwise available. It is far better to have a citizens' group at the city council meeting cheering on your project than one actively opposing it.

• Be prepared to secure multiple layers of financing. It is not uncommon for historic rehabilitation projects to require public subordinate financing, particularly early in a cycle of reinvestment when there has been a long-term pattern of disinvestment. The good news is that cities that have made historic preservation a key component of their revitalization strategy are likely to have a package of incentives available.

Nearly every city in the United States provides an opportunity for developers to specialize in historic properties. Because of the great variety of sizes of historic buildings, opportunities exist not only for the large institutional investor converting an office building into a 500-room hotel but also for the small developer redeveloping a 5,000-square-foot, two-story commercial building. Developers of historic properties often are surprised to find themselves hailed as heroes for restoring the historic fabric of a city. The reason is simple — saving a historic structure is not just about saving a building, it is about building community.

20. MUSEUMS AND REVITALIZATION

Patrick Gallagher

Among the cards for trendy clothing and drinks on the postcard advertising rack at Manhattan's Chelsea Piers Sports and Entertainment Complex is an advertisement for a current museum exhibit: Love It. Hate It. Don't Miss It. The Whitney Biennial.

While arguments can be made that the Whitney show will never be part of the mainstream, even among museum events, the card indicates the emerging role of museums in the entertainment scene. According to the American Association of Museums (AAM), America's 8,200 museums attract more than 600 million visitors every year. More specifically, the *New York Times* (April 24, 1997) reported that economic impact studies show that cultural activities in the New York metropolitan area generated $9.8 billion in 1992 with roughly one quarter of those revenues attributable to tourism. One exhibit alone, the 1996 Cezanne exhibition, brought 550,000 visitors to the Philadelphia Museum of Art, breaking that museum's attendance records for a single exhibit and generating $87 million for the city. If not exactly trendy, it is certainly a trend worth tracking.

The current popularity of museums on the American tourist's list of favorite destinations is the result of the convergence of developments on two fronts. First, faced with eroding industrial bases and the continuing residential flight to the suburbs or "edge cities," urban centers across the country are competing for a burgeoning group of mobile tourists with a desire for culture and the disposable income to pursue it. According to the *Tourism Works for America Report: Travel Scope 1996*, cultural tourism that combines museums, cultural events, and arts and music festivals attracts more visitors than all amateur and professional sports events, movies, and performing arts events.

As the original anchors for downtown cultural centers, museum buildings of architectural merit have been the last outpost of fading cosmopolitan areas. Today, they are more frequently catalysts for metropolitan renewal. Their iconic presence and growing popularity provide a base for new development activity and encourage communities to create economic development strategies that leverage their potent draw. Remarkably, this renaissance is not

Originally published as "Captivate and Educate," Urban Land, *Vol. 57, No. 2, February, 1998. Published by the Urban Land Institute, Washington, D.C. Reprinted with permission of the publisher.*

limited to acknowledged cultural centers like New York and Chicago.

In second-tier cities across the country, museums are playing an important role in urban revival. Consider Baltimore, where tourism is the city's second-largest industry, after health care. Success has encouraged that city's leaders to support unprecedented new museum development including the Columbus Center, a marine biotechnology research and exhibition center; the American Visionary Museum; the National Museum of Dentistry; Morton K. Blaustein's City Life Exhibition at the Baltimore City Life Museum; the Baltimore Civil War Museum; the Babe Ruth Museum; and Baseball Center and Port Discovery, a children's museum. Other cities like Kansas City, Atlanta, and Orlando have embarked on aggressive cultural tourism programs that will increase the numbers of new museums dramatically. Kansas City recently opened the co-located Jazz Museum and National Negro Leagues Hall of Fame, the Rock 'n' Roll Hall of Fame regularly draws crowds to Cleveland, and the Orlando Museum showed its clout last May when it opened a blockbuster exhibition — the Imperial Tombs of China.

Few cities can afford to ignore the potential in statistics published by the Travel Industry of America that report that in 1996, 54 million Americans took at least one trip of 100 miles or more from home that included a visit to a museum or historic site and 33 million took a trip specifically to visit a cultural event or festival.

Rethinking the Museum Experience

Are museums ready to play a key role in local economic development scenarios? Not too long ago the combination of cutbacks in city budgets and the waning of philanthropic spirit put the 8,000 or so existing museums on the endangered species list. Further handicapped by an out-of-date image of dusty collections and dry programming, museums came face to face with an identity crisis. Struggling for survival, museum professionals began to address the problem of losing their audiences to theme parks and the Internet and looked to revitalizing their image.

Now, many museums are working to redefine themselves as lively learning environments. As they study their audiences and would-be competitors carefully, a number are preparing to meet the dual challenges of increased demand and decreased funding. New science and technology centers, more than 50 of which were established during the 1990s, and children's museums, 36 of which were established in the last five years, are examples of institutions that have benefited from the analysis.

Working closely with a new generation of museum consultants and designers many of whom have done similar work with theme parks, museums are exploring new concepts for presentation and programming, while searching for answers to questions about their consumers.

• What do visitors want?
• How do they learn?
• Where do they come from?
• How much time will they spend?
• How much money will they spend? On what?
• What will create value in their estimation?

To date, audience answers reveal a sophisticated profile. Forty percent of the museum-going market have computers, a large percentage have experienced an IMAX theater presentation, and a very large percentage have been to a Disney theme park. They will not accept the same experience they found at a theme park. When they venture out to a museum, they want to discover something unique and inviting.

Entertaining Education

The showy attraction of artifacts like King Tut's tomb, the Russian crown jewels, or Fabergé eggs notwithstanding, modern museum goers indicate that they want to learn. In a media-drenched society where facts are plentiful, these visitors want real content. To create an experience that will make that content accessible yet challenging, museum planners are adapting story-based development techniques that have been perfected in other entertainment venues. Videos of rock stars at the Rock 'n' Roll Hall of Fame appeal to both MTVers and their slightly senior fellow visitors, Steven Spielberg's videotapes of Holocaust survivors at the Museum of Jewish Heritage in New York City affect everyone, and interactive learning games in science museums everywhere capture the attention of arcade-trained young hands and minds. Museum planners are finding that capitalizing on the collections that have long been the heart of museum exhibits and presenting compelling stories about them has the potential to capture the attention of the audience and encourage repeat visits.

More conversation than lecture, this new educational approach to exhibit design recognizes the shift from textual to visual literacy among the young. Museum planners are pushing the limits of both hardware and software to enhance visitors' experience of multisensory exhibits. For example, advanced audiotechnologies allow for the transmission of multiple soundtracks so that visitors of different ages, interests, and language groups can enjoy audio programs customized for them, even outside the theater setting.

Technology is only part of the picture. The new frontier in museum experiences is moving beyond the high-tech sound and motion hardware that has defined "interactive" until now. Innovative museums are pioneering learning environments designed to engage the audience more completely than any of the current approaches. Interpretive immersion re-creates real-life settings in which visitors can participate in real-life adventures facilitated by a story line. Total immersion environments combine the mission and collections of the museum, the educational interactivity typical of science and technology centers, the customer-centered service of theme attractions, the emotional engagement created by the actors, the special effects of true theater, and the market focus of retail. "Sailors" tying knots at the Mystic Seaport Museum and other performers making exhibits come to life at the Smithsonian are educational as well as entertaining. Plans for a new generation of museums like "Science City" in Kansas City call for using actor/facilitators as part of the audience experience.

What Price Success?

Perhaps the more difficult issue for museums and their civic partners is the question of financial support. Economic feasibility studies are the first step for the planners of new facilities, and time after time the comparables show that even successful small museums in hot markets are not self-sufficient. With the help of public funding at one-third and public support at one-third, museums are able to finance new construction by borrowing the final third — a luxury most private companies would like to have. The building program, however, is just the first round of funding anxiety.

Under intense pressure to bring in revenue, creative museum directors are asking yet another tough question. How many functions can be added to the mix without diluting the mission of the institution? Contrary to the "build it and they will come" approach of an earlier generation, today's professionals are willing to explore the full range of potential revenue sources. For example, how long will the audience stay and how does the length of stay translate to food and beverage sales? To date, few museums have offered much more than fast food, but that is changing: new museums and even established museums, such as Washington's Smithsonian Institution, are upgrading the dining options for their guests.

Industry studies by Economics Research Associates that suggest visitors will spend, on average, a dollar an hour, in addition to the cost of meals, have encouraged museums of all kinds to enter the retail business. Careful merchandising of museum-related goods protects the nonprofit status of the institutions but does not prevent them from being aggressive retailers. Without losing sight of their educational missions, museums are creating exciting new merchandise based on objects and images in their collections and are taking healthy advantage of the ongoing popularity of catalogs. Increasingly, museum retail stores are becoming big money-makers for museums, selling everything from pasta shaped like Rodin's *The Thinker* to emblazoned baseball caps and mouse pads. With the AAM reporting that profits from stores contribute 18 to 26 of a museum's earned income, museums from the Smithsonian Institution, the Museum of Modern Art (MOMA), and New York's Metropolitan Museum (where one in five visitors leaves with a shopping bag) to the smallest historical societies are developing branded products to meet the desires of their visitor/shoppers.

Like other, essentially daytime venues, museums are extending their programming to generate after-hours revenue. Large-format theaters bring crowds, but their programs date quickly, creating a need for new films. In fact, a number of science museums have banded together to finance and produce films that they share among themselves and sell to other museums. This entrepreneurial approach helps ensure the quality and quantity of appropriate films and returns royalties to the bottom line of the partnering institutions.

Creative programming is not limited to high-tech features. The Smithsonian's Air and Space Museum's kite flying event on the mall in Washington, D.C., is an example of the high-touch, people-centered programs that create excitement and interest in the museum itself. Lectures, educational workshops, performing arts events, and family outings are so much a part of the program mix that institutions are creating special venues, like the North Carolina Museum of Art's new Museum Park in Raleigh with its 500-seat amphitheater, outdoor cinema, picnic areas, and miniforest of native trees and plants. In addition, museum-sponsored trips and tours have drawn positive reviews from museum members who seek an educational component for their travel.

Finally, when the museum succeeds in creating a new focal point, a nucleus of activity in the community, what is the extent of its influence in terms of surrounding area? Studies by Economics Research Associates have shown that a museum's draw can be broad and diverse — from school kids and groups to couples on dates.

Leveraging Opportunity

Competition among American cities for cultural tourists has led to cooperation among museums. Collaboration is the watchword as museums explore coventuring opportunities with once-rival, neighboring museums and as they work with other national institutions to cosponsor major exhibitions. In Connecticut, for example, 12 museums and sites historically connected with the development of American Impressionism have joined forces to create the Connecticut Impressionist Art Trail. Along the Mississippi River, St. Louis, Memphis, and New Orleans forged an alliance to attract visitors to "America's Music Corridor," 700 miles of live performances, heritage sites, and museums.

Corporations have long supported culture and the arts with quiet philanthropy; today, however, they are just as likely to lend their names along with their dollars to sponsor attention-getting exhibits. On the back of that hip postcard, the Whitney credits the Biennial's sponsor, Beck's Beer. For sponsorship of major shows, corporations from Bell Atlantic, sponsor of the recent Picasso exhibit at the National Gallery in Washington, to Orkin, which sponsored the Insect Zoo exhibition at the Smithsonian's National Museum of Natural Science, reap multiple benefits, including onsite recognition, promotional use of the "proud sponsor" tag line, and the ability to organize client or employee incentives around the exhibit.

At new museums, market-oriented thinking begins in the planning stages. Everything is part of the programming effort, including selecting a site that lends itself to itinerary planning in a cultural corridor, researching the state of the art in applicable technology, and understanding the learning styles of the intended audience. New planning teams include traditional consultants—urban planners, architects, exhibit designers, and landscape architects—and a new set of specialists and consultants—set and scenic designers; special effects technicians; and ride and show, special events, and attraction production.

Meanwhile, established museums seek to leverage their reputations and serve a broader audience both at home and on the road. Large-scale, permanent exhibitions are making way for more timely and topical exhibits that address current audience concerns or are linked to other cultural events in the city or region. Traveling exhibits maximize the exposure of significant permanent collections by reaching culture-hungry audiences across the country.

Museums' move to marketing is not without controversy among professionals who understand the value of their role as guardians of public trust. The integrity of the institution and its collections must be enhanced and not cheapened by the effort to increase revenues. One critical difference between the museum experience and that of the theme park is authenticity. While the current generation of demanding visitors is responding enthusiastically to magical new museum environments, it does not confuse them with other entertainment-related attractions.

Fluid Integration

Among industry consultants, like market strategist Peter Spurney, one of the rules of thumb for market penetration is the perceived four-to-one value ratio (i.e., if the visitor drives an hour, the average length of stay is four hours). This extended time commitment on the part of the audience suggests that there is enormous capacity for expanded programming and partnering with related facilities. As newly transformed museums bring visitors to town, cities have an opportunity to develop libraries, retail establishments, hotels, and entertainment venues at or near the museum. This increasingly fluid approach to integration ultimately will create a new museum form—a hybrid project that has the ability to captivate, educate, and entertain a diverse and discerning audience.

21. PARKING FACILITY MANAGEMENT

John W. Dorsett

Parking is not just a convenience, it is a necessity — one that many customers and tenants take for granted. There are real costs associated with providing parking, and they can significantly affect real estate projects and even block their development. When shopping centers, office buildings, and hotels do not charge for parking, there is the popular misconception that it is free; however, someone must pay for the parking facility — as well as for the land under it and the lighting, insurance, security, and maintenance needed to keep it functioning — and that money must be recouped. There also are design, testing, and contracting fees, as well as financing costs, developer's costs, and surveying costs. On top of all that, owners of parking facilities often pay property, sales, and parking taxes.

If these costs are not covered by parking fees, they are passed on to the facility owner and ultimately to the facility users. For example, to cover parking costs at a shopping center, the owner charges tenants higher rents and common area maintenance fees. In turn, the tenants charge consumers higher prices for their services and merchandise. Hotels indirectly bill the cost of parking to their guests as part of the cost of overhead. In short, just as there is no such thing as a free lunch, there is no free parking.

Identifying Need and Clients

Many owners do not worry about parking facility finances until they think they need a new facility. Before exploring financing options for new development, however, owners should make sure that existing parking spaces are not going unused because of poor management. Is a new lot or garage really needed? If it is, then the owners should be able to pass on all or part of the project's capital costs and operating expenses to parking patrons, or financing may be difficult to secure.

Owners also must determine what type of parking facility will be most efficient. The cost of construction of a parking garage runs five to ten times higher than the cost of surface parking; however, if a proposed structure is in an urban location where land is at a premium, a multilevel

Originally published as "The Price Tag of Parking," Urban Land, Vol. 57, No. 5, May, 1998. Published by the Urban Land Institute, Washington, D.C. Reprinted with permission of the publisher.

parking facility, which requires less land, should be considered. Other options that could be considered before constructing a garage include the following:

• If it is cost effective, provide shuttle-bus service to transport parking patrons from a remote surface parking lot to their destination.

• Restripe existing parking facilities to increase the number of parking spaces, and implement additional parking management strategies (such as shared parking, which minimizes the number of reserved spaces) that allow existing parking resources to be used more efficiently.

• If a loss of green space is acceptable, build a surface lot on existing vacant property.

After choosing either a structure or a surface lot, the question remains: Can the project generate sufficient revenues to offset operating expenses and potential debt service? If not, how can the operation be subsidized? Structured parking facilities that are not profitable often are subsidized by companion office buildings, hotels, or retail shops.

When projecting revenues for a prospective parking facility, it is important to identify user characteristics. Who will use the garage? Considerations that will help identify likely patrons include:

Cost. What are the customary parking rates within the immediate area? What rates could be supported at the proposed parking facility?

Traffic and Pedestrian Circulation. Is the parking facility easy to get to? If it is located on a one-way street that makes access awkward, fewer motorists will use the facility than would if it were located in a more convenient spot.

Ease of Use. Can patrons enter and exit quickly? Can they find their way around the facility easily? Can they easily locate their vehicles?

Cleanliness. Is the parking facility clean? If it is dirty and the one across the street is clean, patrons could be lost to the tidier facility.

Ancillary Services. Does the parking facility operator provide services within the garage such as car washing and/or detailing, vehicle repairs, oil changes, or a dry cleaning pick-up/drop-off facility? Such benefits often can sway patrons toward a facility.

Safety and Security. Is the parking facility perceived by patrons to be safe and secure? Is it well lighted? Is the facility equipped with security features appropriate for its environment?

FIGURE 1— EXAMPLES OF PARKING SPACE SOLUTIONS

Shopping Centers: Instead of employees occupying spaces closest to the stores, create remote parking facilities for employees and establish protocol that discourages employees from parking in "shopper designated" parking areas.

Mixed-Use Parking: Hotels and office buildings can experience a shortage of parking spaces. Hotels have shortages during evening hours, while office buildings have shortages during business hours. Instead of each having exclusive parking privileges, they can negotiate an agreement to share their parking with each other, thereby circumventing the need to develop additional parking.

Remote Parking: To increase the use of remote parking, develop a tiered-pricing scheme that requires higher parking rates for convenient spaces and lower parking rates for spaces in remote locations.

Site and Market Area Characteristics

The parking facility's site and market area determine, to some extent, its ultimate success or failure. Factors that need to be considered when projecting revenues include:

Parking Space Supply and Demand. How many parking spaces exist in the market area of the proposed parking facility? Are they now being used? Are there a lot of inexpensive, unused spaces?

Nearby Land Uses. What land uses exist within a block or two of the proposed site? Will those uses generate significant numbers of patrons?

Building Occupancy. What is the building occupancy rate in the market area? Is it expected to increase significantly in the future, thereby creating additional demand for parking?

Future Developments. Are any proposed developments slated for construction in the near future? How will they affect future parking demand?

Competition. Who provides parking in the market area? What rates are charged? Are those rates subsidized? If so, how does that affect the feasibility of a new parking facility?

Measuring demand for a garage involves identifying the number of patrons who will use the garage by hour of day, day of week, and month of year. This includes an estimate of how long patrons will park, how many times each space will be used during a 24-hour period, and when demand will occur. Does the surrounding environment consist primarily of offices in which most employees work 8:00 a.m. to 5:00 p.m. on weekdays? Are there other uses such as retail stores, restaurants, hotels, or entertainment venues that create evening and weekend demand?

FIGURE 2 — DISTRIBUTION OF PARKING GARAGE OPERATING EXPENSES	
Maintenance	13.5%
Utilities	14.5%
Miscellaneous	19.4%
Cashiering and Management	53.0%

Development and Operating Costs

Development and operating costs of parking projects differ widely. Construction costs vary depending on geographic area because of differences in labor rates, materials, and construction methods. Typically, developers can count on construction costs ranging from $6,000 to more than $15,000 per parking space for a garage built below grade. Land costs affect development costs; for that reason, structured parking facilities instead of surface parking lots often are built. Soft costs such as design and testing fees and financing costs also must be considered during the project planning stage.

Since few parking projects are paid for in cash, the cost of financing becomes an important factor. Most parking projects are financed at fixed interest rates with no equity. The interest rate is determined by the debtor's credit history, the amount of collateral, and possibly the amount of insurance purchased to secure the loan. Currently, parking projects are being financed as both tax-exempt and taxable facilities at rates ranging from six percent to more than 10 percent. The customary term for most loans is 20 years.

Operating expenses of parking facilities also vary dramatically. Variations are due to geographical location, size of facility, staffing patterns, method of operation, and local legal requirements. These expenses include the cost of utilities, supplies, daily maintenance, cashiering, management and

FIGURE 3—MONTHLY REVENUE NEEDED TO ACHIEVE BREAKEVEN*

Construction Cost/Space	Annual Operating Expense per Space					
	$200	$300	$400	$500	$600	$700
$1,500	$ 42	$ 50	$ 58	$ 67	$ 75	$ 83
5,000	74	82	91	99	107	116
6,000	85	94	102	110	130	139
7,000	97	105	114	122	130	139
8,000	108	117	125	133	142	150
9,000	120	128	136	145	153	161
10,000	131	140	148	156	165	173
11,000	143	151	159	168	176	184
12,000	154	163	171	179	188	196

*Construction cost inflated by 35 percent to include contingency, design, testing, and financing cost; bond financing terms assumed on eight percent annual interest for 20 years (ten years for surface lot).

accounting services, on-site security, structural maintenance, and insurance. Types of insurance coverage include comprehensive liability, garagekeeper's legal liability, fire and extended coverage, workers' compensation, equipment coverage, money and security coverage (theft occurring on the premises), blanket honesty coverage (employee theft), and rent and business interruption coverage (structural damage resulting from natural phenomena). Annual operating expenses for structured parking facilities typically range from $200 to more than $700 per space.

Development and operating costs together determine the revenue necessary for the project to generate a positive or break-even cash flow. The monthly revenue needed to reach the break-even point usually ranges from $42 to $196 per parking space, excluding land costs.

Parking facilities frequently are not profitable ventures and therefore must be subsidized. For that reason, parking authorities or city parking departments often become active in their ownership and operation. Public sector involvement typically is motivated by a desire to encourage economic development by keeping parking rates artificially low rather than charging market rates. Parking authorities and city parking departments sometimes have the advantage of not having to pay debt service on older parking facilities. In addition, public entities often supplement off-street parking operations with revenues generated by on-street spaces and through parking violation fines.

While many people believe that parking should be provided free of charge, parking is expensive and the costs must be recouped by the owner, whether by direct or indirect means. Owners should explore less costly options before deciding to build a new parking structure. If a new structure is necessary, the next question is whether or not it is affordable. Determining project affordability can be difficult due to problems in projecting operating revenues and costs. Care should be taken to budget for realistic operating costs and debt service. Because of variations in these factors, some parking facilities provide lucrative investment opportunities while many others must be subsidized.

22. PUBLIC SAFETY STRATEGIES

Dolores P. Palma

Safety is becoming a prominent issue in downtowns all across the country today. When dealing with this issue, downtown leaders frequently find that downtown safety concerns are more often rooted in perception than reality. However in terms of downtown safety, perception is reality — meaning that the issue must be addressed and resolved if our downtowns are to thrive economically.

A downtown that is unsafe — or that is perceived to be unsafe — will not be able to attract the customers, users, and investors needed for that downtown's economy to flourish. Therefore, the issue of safety must be addressed as part of an economically-driven downtown enhancement effort.

Contributing Factors. Research has shown that a variety of factors contribute to the perception that a downtown is unsafe. These tend to fall into the following three categories:

• *Physical and Environmental*— These items involve the condition of property, the presence of litter and graffiti, the phys-ical layout of public spaces, and downtown lighting levels. A downtown that is in poor physical condition gives the impression of being abandoned, and therefore, unsafe.

• *Social*— These items involve the presence of homeless individuals, people "hanging out" on the street, the public use or sale of drugs and alcohol, and the presence of panhandlers. These situations tend to be intimidating to customers who, therefore, try to avoid the areas of downtown where social issues exist.

• *Image Related*— These items involve the frequency of media reports and the message conveyed in these reports concerning safety issue in and related to downtown. Media reports about downtown tend to heighten the potential downtown customer's awareness of what is— and what is not — occurring in downtown.

It is ironic that the physical, environmental, social, and image-related items discussed above often carry greater weight — in terms of a downtown being viewed as unsafe — than incidents of real downtown crime. This is because the items above are extremely visible in a declining

Originally published as "Effective Strategies for a Safe Downtown," Municipal Maryland, *Vol. 24, No. 7, February, 1995. Published by the Maryland Municipal League, Annapolis, Maryland. Reprinted with permission of the publisher.*

downtown. Downtown's customers, clients, employees, and visitors see these items on a daily basis and, therefore, constantly have their perceptions reinforced of downtown as abandoned, scary, or intimidating. On the other hand, real downtown crime (muggings, robberies, bad checks, etc.) is comparatively invisible — it occurs in a very finite time period and all visible evidence of the occurrence is often gone immediately.

Effective Safety Strategies. According to recent national research, strategies to effectively deal with downtown safety issues primarily fall into the seven categories discussed below. It must be noted that, first, these safety strategies are most effective when they are implemented as part of a comprehensive downtown enhancement effort. And, second, safety strategies must be tailored to the specific needs of each downtown.

• *Community Policing.* A discussion of safety cannot take place today without mention of community policing — the "hot" law enforcement "buzz word" of the 1990s.

Community policing, in its simplest form, is getting back to the basics — to local police personnel and citizens working together to address and resolve the problems facing their community. Community policing is a "user-friendly" form of policing that is based on the philosophy that the community, as well as the local police force, have a responsibility and a role in preventing crime. This partnership between community and police force creates a strong community which is the best weapon against crime.

Community policing typically involves establishing and maintaining a highly visible and personal police presence. Common ways of accomplishing this often include making a shift from car patrols to foot and bicycle patrols; police substations; and crime "watch" programs.

Developing a personal relationship between police officers and area residents and business owners is an integral part of community policing. This approach has been embraced based on the belief that an individual's feeling of safety is enhanced by knowing police officers personally. Community policing is being used in business districts to afford business owners and employees an active role in both controlling criminal activity and addressing the public's fear of crime.

• *Communication and Networking.* Most efforts being implemented to address downtown safety issues include communication and networking. The goal of such efforts is to open lines of communication — between the downtown organization, downtown business owners, community residents, and the local police force — in order to identify, address, and resolve safety issues. One example of this safety strategy is the Downtown Security Fax Network in Phoenix, AZ. Operated as a collaboration between the downtown Phoenix Partnership and downtown business people, the fax network allows immediate dissemination of information about crimes reported in downtown Phoenix.

• *Education and Training Programs.* Several downtown organizations have developed programs that go a step beyond networking and improved communications. These organizations provide educational programs for downtown business owners and employees regarding how to deal with safety issues. An example of safety education and training can be seen in Baltimore. The Downtown Partnership of Baltimore employs a retired police officer to conduct crime prevention seminars and training programs for merchants. The training sessions are aimed at providing a variety of business-related security tips — such as how to improve security through store layout.

• *Physical Improvements.* Physical

eyesores—such as dilapidated vacant buildings, uncontrolled litter, and graffiti—are often viewed by the public as indications that downtown is unsafe. Therefore, many downtown organizations have instituted aggressive maintenance, clean-up, and beautification programs in the belief that a clean, well-maintained, and inviting physical environment is one of the best deterrents to crime and fear of crime.

Examples of communities making physical improvements to address safety follow:

• The Trenton Downtown Association implements a highly visible maintenance program. Four full-time personnel work six days a week cleaning, sweeping, picking up litter, etc., in downtown. The Association has found that these efforts persuade people not to litter by setting a good example and make downtown's users feel more comfortable and secure.

• The Downtown Berkeley Business Association has a program specifically aimed at graffiti removal. The "Graffiti Kit" was developed in cooperation with a local paint company. The cardboard kit—which is shaped like a building and is part of the Association's "Grime Stoppers" campaign—includes a can of color-matched paint, a paint brush, a mixing stick, rags, wet paint signs, and a throw-away plastic tarp—everything needed to "get it clean and keep it clean."

Addressing Social Issues. Today, the social issues that exist in downtowns are being addressed not only as social concerns but as economic concerns. Social issues often associated with downtowns include homelessness, panhandling, public drinking, public urination and defecation, public solicitation and use of illegal drugs, disorderly conduct, and lewd behavior. Those downtown organizations seasoned in addressing social issues seem to unanimously advocate taking a "tough love" approach and working directly with social service agencies. Examples include the following:

• Launched by the Center City District as part of the Mayor's comprehensive policy on homelessness, downtown Philadelphia's Campaign for Real Change has proven to be a highly visible and successful initiative with over 800 downtown retailers participating. The campaign seeks to educate the public so that any donations which might be made to panhandlers are redirected to non-profit and charitable organizations in the business of helping people move from the streets to more productive lives.

• The Security Task force of the Downtown Phoenix Partnership implements a program in which downtown guides distribute cards to panhandlers and homeless people. The cards contain information about social service agencies and programs that provide relevant assistance.

Enhancing Police Presence. While downtown organizations are becoming more involved in downtown safety issues, it is important to note that their efforts are not meant to supplant the local police force. Instead, the safety efforts of downtown organizations are usually implemented through close and continued cooperation with the local police force. In addition, the safety efforts of downtown organizations are often aimed at increasing "user-friendly" police presence in downtown.

An outstanding example of this is the Escondido, CA, bike patrol which is administered by the local police department and supported by the Downtown Escondido Business Association—through financial contributions toward equipment, helmets, and winterization. Escondido's police officers regard the bike patrol as the "foot beat of the 20th century" and cite mobility as the biggest asset of bike patrols. Being able to travel where cars cannot, the downtown Escondido bike patrols have an average response time of under 40 seconds.

Augmenting Police Presence. The safety strategy most commonly used today to augment police presence in downtowns is the downtown "guide" or "ambassador" program. Downtown guide programs are generally implemented to supplement the efforts of local police officers by serving as additional "eyes and ears on the street" or by serving as downtown ambassadors— thereby relieving police of this "hospitality" function.

Examples of downtown guide and ambassador programs follows:

• The downtown Trenton guide program is operated through an agreement between the local community college and the Trenton Downtown Association, so that college students have the opportunity to be downtown guides. Each guide is assigned a specific section of downtown to patrol and is expected to observe any safety-related behavior or incidents, report suspicious behavior, and serve a hospitality role by providing information to visitors and other downtown users. In addition to being paid an hourly wage, downtown Trenton's guides are reimbursed for 100% of their tuition, up to $600 per semester, if they carry at least 12 credit hours per semester and maintain a 2.0 grade point average.

• Three years ago, CITYCENTER Danbury — the private sector organization that represents downtown Danbury, CT — began a downtown guide program. While the program was successful in addressing safety issues and perceptions, it ran into financial difficulties. To remedy this, the Danbury Police Department gave CITYCENTER Danbury a grant to finance 40% of the guide program cost.

• The downtown guide program in Long Beach, CA, is operated by the downtown organization. The distinguishing feature of this guide program is that the Downtown Long Beach Association obtains guides through a contract with an arm of Wells Fargo security. Downtown guides work closely with local police in fulfilling their primary mission, which is to address disorderly street behavior and provide hospitality services.

23. RESIDENTIAL OPEN SPACES

Christopher Leinberger and Gayle Berens

It is easy to forget that each generation has different open-space needs. Like fashion and music, parks and park design become outdated. Recreational preferences also change: 30 years ago, no one used in-line roller skates, and few Americans played soccer. City, state, and federal funding priorities shift. The public sector often forgets what successful private sector entrepreneurs never do: responding to market preferences is critical to success.

How individual Americans value their parks and open space changes from generation to generation and does not always reflect public sector budgeting priorities. The nation's parks have never had as many visitors as they have now, and many suffer from overuse and insufficient public funding. Many large city parks have been allowed to deteriorate, in large part because they came to be regarded as unsafe environments and city budgets were inadequate to counteract real or perceived security issues. Usable open space, however, is an invaluable amenity that most people instinctively desire. The emotional attachment that people have to open space(and the idea of it) is often the catalyst for revitalizing parks over and over again.

For urban residential neighborhoods to survive and prosper, parks and open space have to work with and unify the built environment. Walking access to parks and community gathering places is one of the few reasons that urban neighborhoods continue to be meaningful alternatives to the suburbs for middle-class households that have the option of moving. To maintain their middle-class tax base—a necessity for remaining fiscally viable—cities must focus on the things that they can do better than the suburbs, and one of the most important is to provide parks and open space within walking distance of every household, reinforcing the urban neighborhood's viability in the automobile age.

While each city, each piece of land, and each parks department is unique and each effort must be started anew, lessons can be learned from other cities' efforts.

Lesson 1: Involve the neighborhood. Encourage—do not bureaucratically resist—the active participation of neighborhood groups in planning, funding, and maintaining parks. In virtually every case

Originally published as "Designing for Urban Parks," Urban Land, Vol. 56, No. 12, December, 1997. Published by the Urban Land Institute, Washington, D.C. Reprinted with permission of the publisher.

study, residents provided input (and often resistance) that ultimately made the park a better place.

Lesson 2: Design with a vision. Do not underestimate the power of imaginative design. Park design is more than a matter of recreating the soft, pastoral, "Olmstedian" spaces beloved in many American cities. Visionary design can affect a park's safety, viability, and usability — and it most certainly affects its long-term success.

Whether the dangers are perceived or real, safety concerns are among the biggest contributors to the downfall of urban parks. But even in neighborhoods where safety has been a long-standing concern, changes in design, landscaping, and use patterns can make parks viable once again.

Using art as a fundamental feature of a park can give it a special quality that will endure over time. Incorporating old uses and structures into the design of a park also can add character and create an inexpensive link to the past. The history of a site may suggest an unusual and visually interesting theme, and building on it may be less expensive than clearing the site and developing a theme from scratch.

Lesson 3: Revive underused or unused space. Underused, unused, or unusual space — such as underground parking garages, piers, air space, and floodplains — can be successfully transformed into viable parks and open space. In Harlem, the state of New York provided much-needed recreational facilities by building Riverbank State Park atop a wastewater treatment plant. Careful planning of load capacities and the use of lightweight materials did not compromise the integrity of the park's design. In Boston, the Park at Post Office Square rests on top of a seven-level underground parking garage. Park users relax in peace, barely aware of entrance and exit ramps for the many vehicles that use the garage daily, and the revenues from the garage support upkeep of the park.

Formerly underused or abandoned floodplains — particularly when they are adjacent to expensive downtown real estate — can be transformed into parks and open space that recover easily after flooding. Instead of fighting Mother Nature, it is wise to consider accommodating the low-cost, flood-prone land that may be adjacent to some of the highest-priced land in the region. Mill Race Park, for example, was successfully reclaimed through a design that allows all elements to withstand annual flooding. Among other features, the park has an automatic shutoff for electric power that goes into effect when the water reaches a certain height and restroom walls begin eight inches above the ground to allow easy drainage. While a park that is not in a floodplain would not incur the costs associated with the process of flood cleanup, the cost of cleaning or rehabilitating flood-damaged open space is almost too small to measure when compared with the cost of rebuilding flood-damaged residential or commercial neighborhoods.

Lesson 4: Program park activities. Make a concerted effort to program activities in the park, insofar as programming is manageable and appropriate for the type of park and open space. Steady use has been shown to enhance revenues, and, as Page Gifford in the Mill Race Park case study puts it, "A high level of activity is the cheapest security."

Lesson 5: Remember that cleanliness equals respect. Keep public open spaces clean and well maintained. Several factors can influence the cost and relative ease of maintaining a park: first, the availability of adequate operating funds, whether from public, private, or civic sources; second, strategic use of maintenance staff; and third, a design that is not only attractive but also inherently low maintenance. Users tend to respond to a pleasant, well-designed space by exhibiting orderly behavior.

Lesson 6: Be creative in funding

parks. By "pushing the envelope" of possibilities, resourceful public and private sector groups have been successful in finding money to develop and maintain parks. They have, for example, taken advantage of federal programs that may not be intended for parkland per se. For example, the Intermodal Surface Transportation Efficiency Act (ISTEA), due for reauthorization and probably modification in 1997, has been an important source of funds for rail-to-trail conversions. Linear park development can be a particular boon to a region because it not only adds recreational space but also adds to the transportation network of a region or community. While obtaining such funds may involve cumbersome bureaucratic procedures, a certain percentage of ISTEA money spent in every metropolitan area must be spent on nonhighway, transportation-related projects.

In addition, groups like the National Endowment for the Arts have various public arts program funds that can be applied to parks and open space. The sale of shares at the Park at Post Office Square was an innovative entrepreneurial approach to funding that jump-started that project and provided purchasers with a real benefit: access to parking in a dense city center. Private sector donations for a successful first phase may spark increased public support for subsequent phases.

Lesson 7: Consider using parks as organizing elements. An urban park can create a sense of place, a landmark, and a community focal point, which may in turn increase property values and create incentives for new development. Since few great downtowns have evolved without some connection to nature, an urban park should be an important component of any successful city redevelopment.

Lesson 8: Parks departments must play a leadership role. Most parks departments in the country have the capability, but for many reasons may lack the motivation and leadership, to play a strong role. Sometimes leadership must come first from elected officials. But regardless of whether the impetus comes from an elected official or a city department, the public sector needs to reclaim its leadership role in protecting parks, which are among the most valuable assets of the nation's cities.

Riverbank State Park

The 28-acre Riverbank State Park, located in West Harlem, Manhattan, is built atop the North River Water Pollution Treatment Facility. Paid for with public funds, this park and recreational facility represents the transformation of an unwanted but necessary facility — a sewage treatment plant — into a heavily used community resource. Like most public projects of this scale, this project had a percentage of total costs set aside for beautification. Although the community, which was actively opposed to the plant, was not won over by promises of beautification, the state moved forward to secure an easement for the air rights above the plant to develop a park.

The initial project proposal, commissioned from Philip Johnson in 1968, involved flooding the roof and building a series of fountains that would spring from the resulting pool. When community residents discovered that the pool was going to use clean New York City water, they were outraged. Then-Governor Nelson Rockefeller subsequently committed the state to constructing a state park on the roof instead.

Numerous alternatives were evaluated; ultimately, in 1980, a committee of state officials and community representatives chose architect Richard Dattner to spearhead the design and development of a rooftop state park and recreational facility. Between 1980 and 1993, when the park finally opened, the project was designed and redesigned and shown to every community group imaginable. According to Dattner, "The decision to locate in Harlem resulted in 25 years of community protest, political struggle, and a variety of efforts to assuage the community by balancing the pain of locating a sewage treatment plant in its front yard with the benefits possible from its construction."

"We met with the steering committee every two weeks," noted Dattner. "We started with six schemes and a list of design criteria to use in evaluating and ranking the schemes. The design criteria included things like protection from north winds, orientation to the sun, energy conservation, proximity to access points, flexibility of use, views of the river, preservation of views from surrounding buildings, and so on. The steering committee and design team then ranked the six schemes against the design goals and assigned numerical scores. Based on their scores, two schemes were chosen for further development."

Most design problems were related to the limited amount of weight that the building below the park could support. Concerns included the loan-bearing capacity of the plant's caissons, columns, and roof spans. Load equations also had to take into account expected live loads (people, vehicles, and snow). Adding to the project's complexities was the fact that much of the construction had to take place without interrupting the sewage treatment plant's operations.

To comply with load-bearing criteria, the park's buildings had to be made of lightweight steel with metal- or tile-faced panels. The 28-acre roof, which is almost a half-mile long, consists of 14 separate sections that move independently as the roof expands and contracts with changes in temperature. To avoid damage from movement at expansion joints, each of the park's buildings is completely contained within one roof plate. Every column in a park building is located directly over a corresponding sewage plant column. Original plans called for the roof to carry 400 pounds per square foot throughout, but the design team was able to shave $10 million off the project's cost by identifying those roof plates that had to support that much weight and designing other areas for lighter loads.

Weight limitations also made it necessary to limit the depth of the pool to four feet, to use wood instead of concrete for the walls of the handball court, and to clad the facade of the buildings in prefabricated brick tiles (five-eighths of an inch thick) instead of whole bricks. Because pipes, drains, and electrical conduits had to run over the plant's roof, utilities required special attention. Stormwater collected by the park's sophisticated drainage system is channeled through the sewage plant for treatment.

Riverbank State Park includes five major structures: a 50-meter pool with two movable bulkheads that allow it to be divided into three areas; a covered skating rink for ice skating in the winter and roller skating in the summer; a cultural center; a multiuse athletic building designed for basketball, volleyball, gymnastics, and martial arts; and a 150-seat restaurant with a 100-seat outdoor terrace.

Outdoor facilities include a 25-yard lap pool; a wading pool 18 feet in diameter; four basketball courts; four handball/paddleball courts; four tennis courts; a waterfront amphitheater; a running track surrounding a football/soccer field; a community garden and greenhouse; picnic areas; and a children's playground.

Because of the treatment plant's location on the riverbank, decisions on how to site the park's buildings had to take into account a number of factors, including wind exposure and the potential for flooding. For protection against winter winds blowing off the Hudson, four major park buildings are clustered inward around a south-facing courtyard. In addition, the buildings needed to offer views of the river without blocking river views from nearby buildings.

"We designed the project to be as flexible as possible," explained Dattner. "Everything is multipurpose, to adapt to different sports trends." The park is ringed by a promenade high above the Hudson. A knee-high, striated concrete barrier along the promenade discourages graffiti. To shield neighbors from noisy concerts and events, a boat landing and an outdoor amphitheater are located 50 feet below the athletic building, at the river's edge. From there, the sewage treatment plant is highly visible, but its design is inconspicuous. Clad in concrete, the plant has arched openings that reflect the form of a nearby bridge.

Operated and managed by the state, Riverbank State Park has become the second most heavily used state park in New York: over 3.7 million users visited it in 1995.

Mill Race Park

Mill Race Park is a park of high ambitions. Its planners and designers intended to reclaim a floodplain and toxic waste site for community use, to provide support for downtown revitalization efforts, and to leave a legacy to the community on the 500th anniversary of Christopher Columbus's voyage to America. If that were not enough, they were determined to match the world-class level of design for which Columbus, Indiana, is nationally known — and to accomplish all of those goals without major capital funding from the city.

The resulting 85-acre park, located at the west end of downtown Columbus, substantially succeeds in realizing its ambitions. Dedicated in 1992, the park is now a focal point for concerts and community activities and a source of civic pride. The park's design has attracted national attention, and the once swampy, sleepy bottomlands have been recalled to life with minimal public investment.

Located "at the meeting of city and river," a project landscape architect Michael Van Valkenburgh described it, the park's built forms and landscapes range from urban to wild, its uses from communal to solitary. Along the park's urban edge, the landscape and hardscape tend to be rectilinear — parking lots framed by the remnants of old concrete floodwalls, rows of Kentucky coffee and hackberry trees, and an 80-foot observation tower, axially sited in line with the primary park entrance and the downtown area. The urban edge soon gives way, however, to softer forms, terminating in the natural vegetation of the meandering riverbank, which borders the park on three sides. Taking advantage of the site's proximity to water and the abandoned gravel pits from its industrial past, the landscape also includes two lakes: 450-foot-diameter Round Lake and the previously existing North Lake.

Interspersed throughout the park is a series of red-painted structures designed by architect Stanley Saitowitz — an amphitheater stage, an arbor, picnic shelters, fishing piers, a boathouse, and restrooms. Park facilities also include a playground, a basketball court, a horseshoe pit, a wetlands interpretive area with a raised boardwalk, a wildflower area, and the scenic Riverwalk, which connects to the city's People Trail outside the park borders.

According to Van Valkenburgh, designing Mill Race Park was a matter of editing the landscape. "It was both additive and subtractive, like putting paint down on a canvas and taking it up," he said. The design process included a four-month master-planning period, during which Van Valkenburgh met with community leaders, interested citizens, groups such as the River Rats, and even elementary-school children. The very public consultations and design presentations "allowed people to feel an involvement in the process," he said, and aided him in creating a vision for the park.

With the site's riverfront location and long history, there were a variety of positive elements and memories to draw upon, as well as "found objects" that had been brought to the site over time. To maintain a sense of continuity with the past, old tannery floodwalls were retained, as was an old gravel-pit lake. Similarly, four old bridges representative of early wood and steel bridge technology, which had been brought to the site, were incorporated into the design.

Despite its rich history, Mill Race Park was "like the Tin Man looking for a heart," commented Van Valkenburgh. To remedy this, he designed a new lake in the shape of a grand circle, formally ringed by old-fashioned lampposts and ornamental trees. The "civically scaled" and "democratic" Round Lake, as it has come to be known, stands in deliberate contrast to the nearby river and North Lake.

Several landscape mounds also were added to the site. One crescent-shaped mound forms the amphitheater, with concrete-and-grass benches carved out of the slope. A second grassy mound flanks a basketball court, giving the court a strong presence in the otherwise flat and open plain. The mounds echo those built by Native American tribes indigenous to the Midwest. They also served as disposal sites for earth excavated in the construction of the lake.

The principle of "editing" was applied to the landscaping as it was to other park features. More than 700 trees were planted at Mill Race Park, and some 200 were removed. Of those removed, some were dead or diseased; others were removed or pruned to open up vistas and create connections to the water. New trees were added strategically to complement the existing landscape, to protect park structures from flood-borne logs and debris, and to create the formal landscapes desired for Round Lake and the "city" edge of the park.

The flood-prone character of the site was accommodated in other ways as well. Drainage was planned carefully to minimize ponding and retention of floodwaters; pathways were made strong enough to resist flood scouring and wide enough to accommodate standard cleaning machines; and off-the-shelf playground equipment was selected because it could be easily replaced in the event of flood damage.

The park's structures also had to accommodate the annual flood cycle. The structures, which serve a variety of purposes, contain many of the same materials, including steel tubing, wire mesh, perforated metal, concrete, and glass blocks. The design intention, according to Saitowitz, was to "establish a family." Though each structure is specific in function, "all share the same genetic structure." The "family" includes three picnic shelters, the Custer-Nugent Amphitheater structure, an arbor, a boat pavilion, two fishing piers, restrooms, and the lookout tower near the park entry.

All of the picnic shelters are circular in form, though each varies in detail from the others. "The marking out of a circle," explained Saitowitz, "is the most primitive and universal way of claiming territory." Within the circle, the picnic tables, benches, barbecue pit, and trash receptacle are poured-in-place concrete. Roof coverings over the shelters are designed as warped planes supported on red metal tubing.

The amphitheater has both architectural and landscape components and resulted from a collaboration between Saitowitz and Van Valkenburgh. The open-stage structure, which is topped by a red steel canopy shaped like an inverted curve, plays on one side to the concrete and grass terraces, which seat approximately 600. On the opposite side, the stage plays to an open lawn capable of supporting 10,000 or more concert patrons.

The design of the restrooms addresses not only the threat of flooding, but also the more routine problem of bringing light and air into typically damp and dark spaces. The restroom walls are made entirely of translucent glass blocks and are raised approximately eight inches off the ground to allow floodwaters to drain more easily. The walls also stop short of the roof, maximizing natural ventilation within the restrooms. In a bit of whimsy, the steel-tube and corrugated-metal roof structure is bent into the shape of a "W" on the women's side and an "M" on the men's.

According to the master plan objectives, the design of Mill Race Park provides multiple recreational environments and opportunities for a broad range of experiences, from solitary walks along the river to rock concerts for 10,000. Facilities are provided that appeal to children (playground), teens (basketball court), and families (picnic shelters). Several facilities, such as the amphitheater, the boat rental, the fishing pier, the lakes, and the trails, attract a wide range of users.

The highly popular amphitheater and programmed events attract the largest number of park visitors. From June through September, nearly every weekend is programmed. The amphitheater is the site of the Mill Race Park Live Concert series, which includes rock concerts, country-and-western concerts, and performances by the Columbus Philharmonic as well as Count Basie. The amphitheater also is the site of a noon concert series for kids and the Family Film series.

In addition to the concerts, films, and major events, the park hosts several other smaller programs and camps. Responsibility for planning and staging the myriad events and programs resides jointly with the Columbus Arts Council, a nonprofit organization, and the Columbus Parks and Recreation Department.

Park at Post Office Square

Boston, the city that in 1634 presented America with its very first urban civic space — the Boston Common — has broken new ground again, this time with an innovative park that has the potential to change public thinking about creating new greenspace among downtown skyscrapers.

At 1.7 acres, the Park at Post Office Square is barely large enough to hold all the awards it has won. Its conception and design have led it to be called "the perfect park," and it has become the focal point for the city's dense, serpentine financial district. Because the park has the feel of a comfortable living room, most visitors — and many Bostonians — have trouble believing that it has not always been there.

The park's centerpiece is a walk-through sculptural fountain. A couple of yards away is a 143-foot-long formal garden trellis, supported by granite columns, draped with seven species of vine and lit internally by computer-driven minibulbs that perform a subtle nighttime show. The Great Lawn, raised above the walkways by a granite curb, provides a relaxed retreat, even furnishing a grassy entrance ramp for wheelchairs. Post Office Square includes an airy, copper-and-glass garden pavilion that houses a year-round café. It features wrought-iron fencing and specially monogrammed drainage gates. Seating styles range from stately teak benches, curving steel settees, and movable cast-iron café chairs with tables to hundreds of linear feet of inviting polished granite wall and half an acre of lawn. Under it all are seven floors of parking spaces for 1,400 cars. In an unusual twist, the Park at Post Office Square is supported — both physically and financially — by a 500,000-square-foot parking garage, the largest in Boston.

"The garage functions like a gusher," wrote *Boston Globe* architecture critic Robert Campbell, "spuming people and activity continually upward." More than 2,000 people enter and leave the garage's gazebo-covered escalators daily. The garage also generates about $8.6 million a year — enough to make a sizable payment on the $76 million cost of developing the park and parking lot, manage a $2.9 million annual operating budget, pay a $1 million local tax bill, and, if things go well, contribute to a maintenance fund for neighborhood parks all over Boston.

Two matching, gazebo-type structures rest on the surface of the garage; one houses the Milk Street Café, and the other serves as the escalator entrance to the garage. Constructed of copper and glass, the café building is airy, yet movable doorways and glass panels make it flexible enough to handle the extremes of Boston's weather. These structures and the garage were designed by Ellenzweig Associates of Cambridge, Massachusetts.

The garage includes a complete car wash, repair services for minor automobile problems, numerous security cameras, and backlit walls for better visibility and security. It also houses a marble lobby that features amenities such as fresh flowers, music in the elevators, a shoeshine, telephones and restrooms, 24-hour attendants, a free phone connection to a traffic hotline, and free downtown maps for tourists. "You can even give someone a gift certificate to park here," Harry Ellenzweig noted. "We have a couple of suburban-based repair companies that rent spaces for their service vans, use our phones, eat in the park, and don't even need an office in the city — they're just based at Post Office Square, a couple of minutes from everywhere."

Ironically, the only reason there is a park at Post Office Square is that parking in Boston is so expensive. The reason parking is so costly — more than $25 a day — is that Boston, responding to a U.S. Environmental Protection Agency mandate to control air pollution, instituted a freeze on the number of parking spaces allowed in the central business district. The final tab for constructing each parking space at Post Office Square was $34,000.

Leverage in Value Gained

The character and civility of cities can be vastly improved through the development and adequate maintenance and operation of parks — and for relatively little money, compared with the amount of other public and private urban investments. Moreover, parks and open space can significantly increase the private capital base. The leverage in value gained through properly developed and maintained parks is one of the great unexploited opportunities in cities today, yet it takes effort to create a space that works and provides value. Most often, that effort is best made by taking advantage of the skills and initiative of the public, private, and civic sectors. Relying on the public sector alone risks limiting the resources and creativity that can be brought to bear on development of urban parks and open space and diminishing the sense of ownership and interest that communities can feel in their greenspace.

24. SELF-EVALUATION AND BENCHMARKING

Al Gobar

The key to a successful economic development program is to generate early winners, while keeping an eye on clear, quantifiable long-term goals. But, many economic development efforts have reflected effort more than achievement and style more than substance. Such programs suffer from a lack of clearly defined goals, strategies to achieve these goals, and implementation processes which build on existing resources to achieve the most effective outcome.

Crucial to an action plan for community development is the simple Biblical admonition, "Know thyself." Here's a story to illustrate how important this is: A highly placed policymaker in one California county with an enviable record of economic growth was concerned about the county's job base being composed primarily of "hamburger flippers," when, in fact, the county has more manufacturing jobs per thousand jobs than any other area in Southern California. An economic development strategy based on the erroneous assumption that the area's population was composed of fast food service personnel would have been fruitless.

Therefore, a precondition to an efficient and successful economic development effort is an audit and evaluation of current conditions and the establishment of very specific goals.

The initial self-study process should define a specific reason for an economic development effort that is carefully and objectively articulated. In an over-simplified form, the problem can be reduced to the following simple queries:

1. Why do we want economic growth?
2. What resources do we have that other communities do not have that would be especially appealing to specific engines of economic growth?
3. Would these elements of potential economic growth contribute to the basic reasons we want to expand the local economy in the first place?
4. Who are these elements, how do we reach them, and what is our most appealing message?

Economic development goals should

Originally published as "How to Evaluate and Build on Your City's Assets," Western City, *Vol. LXIX, No. 8, August, 1993. Published by the League of California Cities, Sacramento, California. Reprinted with permission of the publisher.*

be quantified in specific terms such as a target increase in property tax base per capita population, a defined increase in sales tax revenue, increases in local employment opportunities, and removal or mitigation of community limitations.

The first step in this process is a community appraisal of a wide range of objective measures of the community's advantages and limitations. For instance, many communities have consumer support bases well in excess of the level of retail sales activity within their boundaries. That means residents are shopping elsewhere, and their communities are losing retail sales tax revenues, *ad valorem* property tax revenues, and business license revenues to surrounding communities. More successful exploitation of existing and future consumer support increases city revenues from local taxes and provides a source of local jobs.

The City of Apple Valley's retail sector, for example, captures only about 40 percent of the retail expenditure potential of the community, but the scale of the town's population would permit a maximum effective capture rate of approximately 80 percent. Achieving this level of efficiency in the retail sector would double sales tax collections, create more local jobs, and enhance *ad valorem* taxes and business license revenues.

Similarly Tustin and Fountain Valley identified underexploited retail opportunities not only in their own cities' populations but the surrounding population, resulting in a substantial increase in sales tax revenues from the development of such new retail facilities as the Tustin Marketplace, the Price Club, etc.

Another important element is understanding where local employed residents actually work. Antelope Valley's economy, for example, is largely supported by commuters to jobs located in the more urban portions of Los Angeles County. The city loses the *ad valorem* tax base associated with work places and long commutes impose a burden on local residents.

Availability of land is also an important factor. Evanston, Illinois, for example, is bounded by other cities and Lake Michigan. So there is no land available for expansion. As a result, the city's economic development strategy involved reuse of previously developed land to achieve the city's specific economic goals of enhanced property tax base, expansion of local government opportunities based on the skills of local residents, and higher convenience for the people of Evanston.

Public service facilities and infrastructure capacity also represent a community advantage in some instances but a limitation in others. Adelanto has capitalized on abundant land by installing infrastructure to accommodate industrial development, giving the city a significant competitive advantage over communities without adequate and similarly priced inventories of immediately developable industrial land. Irwindale is another example of a community in which economic development has been facilitated by the installation of infrastructure.

Communities that provide an attractive residential environment attract high-energy decision-makers who like to live close to their jobs, which generates more local business, increases tax revenues and raises the level of local job opportunities.

Specific elements to be considered in this category include general neighborhood characteristics including household income profiles, educational levels of local residents, and other factors. Executives work hard and play hard, so recreational opportunities are important to such movers and shakers. They also are concerned about the availability of superior schools and a broad-based cultural program, including church, Lions, Kiwanis, etc.

Such executive amenities have been important to Orange County as a whole, which has a higher ratio of manufacturing employment per 1,000 jobs than any other part of Southern California as well as a higher ratio of employment to population than any other part of California — despite the area's high housing prices and traffic congestion. Its success in attracting manufacturing jobs can be traced to one factor: Corporate executives like to live there. They don't like to commute, and manufacturing jobs grew in this area because decision-makers were attracted to the community as a place to live. This resource is not typically identified in the establishment of a data base for long-range economic development plans.

The Temecula-Murrietta area experienced a mini-boom in industrial development in large measure because of the area's ability to market itself to upper-income, entrepreneurial households as a place to live and eventually to establish businesses. Irvine is another example, as is Newport Beach.

A user-friendly, cooperative local political climate — while difficult to quantify — is another advantage associated with economic growth. A commercial developer we know, whose entitlement process in one California city has now endured for more than four years, has stated that he would "never, ever attempt to develop another project in that city." Executive "flight" is especially problematic when a nearby city is not only passive with regard to new and desirable development, but also active in providing subsidies through sales tax rebates or other techniques which have become increasingly common.

Effective economic development also takes advantage of the city's natural resources. Big Bear Lake — home to two major ski resorts and one of the few major recreation lakes in Southern California— enjoys a substantial advantage in generat-ing economic growth. Modesto experienced a boom in the mid–1980s by promoting its central location to attract distribution and warehouse facilities to serve much of urban California. Ontario has capitalized on the confluence of four major freeways and the existence of a major airport by spurring massive development of distribution facilities.

Barstow, Lake Elsinore, and the unincorporated Imperial Valley community of Cabazon have capitalized on their locations adjacent to major freeways but removed from urban areas to support the development of factory outlet centers. The Oxnard–Port Hueneme area has benefitted from its proximity to port facilities by encouraging distribution activities.

Many of the limitations to economic development are simply the flip-side of the advantages described above. Limited infrastructure or lack of available land implies a redevelopment strategy as distinct from an economic development strategy. Inadequate availability of low-cost housing either within the community or nearby has an indirect, adverse effect on the availability of a suitable labor force. Remote locations with no nearby, easily accessible market imply a strategy aimed at generating businesses which produce products and services with a high value-to-weight ratio to overcome this limitation. Lack of executive housing has also been a contributing factor to the slow economic development of some areas which otherwise have substantial advantages and resources.

Many of the elements described here can be defined objectively and with sufficient accuracy to facilitate decision making on the basis of relatively inexpensive research methodologies. Some of these are as follows:

• Standard retail site analysis techniques are useful in defining underpopulated consumer markets which represent an immediate potential for economic development. The process models retail sales expected within the community in light of its structure, population base, surrounding area population base, etc., in relationship to sales tax patterns and the existing inventory of retail facilities. Retail development in Fountain Valley, for example, was inhibited by the city's proximity to two regional shopping centers and a major auto plaza. Almost by default, the most effective retail development except for some minor fine-tuning was the attraction of a major "big box" retailer. Through a focused effort, Fountain Valley was able to attract a Price Club which, in turn, stimulated an influx of other hyper-efficient retailers. National City had the potential to support regional shopping center facilities. Community support surrounding Murrietta was more than adequate to justify consideration of a conventional regional shopping center there. The High Desert region of San Bernardino County has an inadequate number of new car dealerships in relationship to its market, so targeting such high ticket retailers could be a productive strategy there.

• The 1990 Census data provides a rich source of information from which to define the study area's affluence, its labor force characteristics, commute patterns, employment by industry, and a variety of other elements related to skills, education, and age. This information provides the data base that is a prerequisite to effective economic development. The socio-demographic analysis potential inherent in the data is also useful in evaluating the compatibility of the community with high-income, executive-type residents.

• Analysis of published data regarding land sales, prices, etc., is a reasonable method for identifying the limitations and advantages of a community's land and infrastructure resources.

Evaluation

An audit of local community resources and limitations can be compared with other communities or with averages for the larger area in which it is located. These comparisons define the special advantages and limitations of the local community against potentially competitive local economies. A simple financial analysis of city revenues and costs in the context of a peer group of cities is another useful indicator in defining limitations, resources, and the political climate. Cities with a high per capita cost of development services in relationship to historical development levels typically are communities in which development is difficult. A simple history of building permit activity at the city level as compared with peer group cities in similar locations is also often a useful diagnostic tool.

The results of the audit process can be integrated with input from local community leaders to define and prioritize specific goals of an economic development effort. Examples of goals that can be defined by this process are:

Expanding the Community's Retail Section. This captures sales tax dollars escaping the community by attracting specific types of retailers for which there is a viable market opportunity. The experiences of Tustin, Fountain Valley, National City, and Evanston illustrate this example.

Attracting Industrial Employers. This achieves a better job-to-population balance and minimizes long commutes for local residents. Adelanto has made substantial progress through a program of infrastructure development specifically oriented to industrial users, a process preceded by the establishment of a strong and financially efficient redevelopment agency. Identification of local residents working in the finance sector in Antelope

Valley contributed to the attraction of a major national financial printing organization.

Increasing the Area's Value-to-Weight Ratios in Products and Services. The thinking of many planners involved in community development continues to focus on the outmoded, over-estimation of the economic value of local manufacturing jobs. Although they are a source of job-to-population balance, they are not the solution for all communities. Manufacturing jobs provide little in the way of fiscal benefit to the communities in which they are located, and frequently, the cost of securing a manufacturing job (dictated by the large number of communities competing for these jobs) exceeds their value to the community not only in a quantitative sense but probably also on a subjective basis.

The process of defining resources and limitations would, for example, highlight the limitations of some communities that are located at some distance from major markets. Ideal export industries for such communities would include the types of products that are "shipped" electronically and services and specialized goods which exhibit a high value-to-weight relationship, etc. Credit card processing organizations, for example, have selected such remote locations as the Dakotas, Phoenix and Las Vegas, based on those areas' tax structures and labor force availability because their product is essentially information.

Conceiving a practical implementation program is a relatively simply matter once the community's advantage, limitations, and goals are defined. The most effective implementation programs are highly focused. The process also should result in specific goal prioritization and implementation processes that build on one another. The achievement of an early goal provides a platform for the achievement of

more difficult goals ahead through focused marketing efforts targeted at industries that have a special affinity for the specific attributes of the community.

The entire process should be reviewed on at least a five-year cycle, if not more frequently, to measure progress toward achieving specific goals, to provide a basis for reevaluating the practicality of achieving certain goals, and to redefine the goals in light of the achievement of intermediate goals. This regular review and updating is not often a part of a long-range economic development strategy.

Pre-conditions for an efficient and successful economic development effort include the following:

Goals should be specific and carefully articulated. Such goals could include a target increase in property tax base per capita population, specified increases in sales tax capture, defined ratios of local jobs to local labor force, and defined new development by type — 70 percent residential, 22 percent commercial, eight percent industrial, etc.

An effective development plan also includes an objective definition of the community's resources and limitations.

The next step is a realistic appraisal of how available resources can be mobilized to exploit special opportunities defined by the pattern of resources and limitations. One community with which we are familiar, for example, has a strongly established medical industry economic base which can be built upon to attract retirees and to fill in gaps in the representation of specific types of medical service capability.

Another has ample excess capacity in resort facilities during the third quarter of each year, which would accommodate an increase in visitor population. A small investment in new facilities would contribute to the overall economic efficiency of the facilities themselves as well as the entire community.

Another community, located on the western edge of a population base, is not now served by adequate retail facilities, causing this hinterland population to pass through the community to other, more established retail sectors located to the west of the city in question. Targeting retail business would improve the city's economy.

A commuter city's population base includes a substantial number of residents employed in the finance sector who travel long distances to work. That implies the city has a skilled available labor force which could help attract backroom financial service activities.

Too often communities engage in promotional activities without having a clear-cut definition of their message or their specific target audience, let alone of the appropriate media to reach this target. This means that a valuable community resource for economic development is an objective, comprehensive, and continuously updated data base available to all agencies and private sector elements interested in promoting the local community. Once that information has been gathered and evaluated, then a community can begin to effectively market itself to the business sector.

25. SMALL BUSINESS DEVELOPMENT TOOLS

Edward M. Marshall

An effective small business partnership focuses on the critical needs of small firms and uses tools appropriate to meeting their needs at each stage of their development. The partnership's goals need to be clear, and the strategy must be tailored to achieve those goals. The partnership now turns to address the practical questions of strategy implementation. How do you know what type of small business development to encourage or which tools and resources to use? In this chapter, the following elements will be considered:

• The factors that need to be considered in deciding what type of small business to encourage,
• Specific tools a city can use to encourage small business development,
• Six types of programs cities can adopt to promote new small business growth, and
• The types of federal and state resources available to a city to pay for the development and implementation of the strategy and eight ways to access them.

What Type of Small Business Development Should We Have?

Not all small businesses are created equal. Small high technology companies will not generate the same effect on a local economy as "mom and pop" stores, and a small manufacturing company does not use the same type or amount of labor as a wholesale distribution warehouse. It is critical, therefore, that cities clearly determine what types of small business development are best suited to their local economic needs and resources. To do so requires market research, which allows the city to determine its small business competitive advantage.

The first step in determining this advantage is a survey of the small business community. Until the city understands the needs of its own small businesses, it cannot effectively develop a growth strategy. This survey should ask questions in at least twelve areas:

In addition, the survey should determine what each business plans to do in the next one to two years—for example, hire

Originally published as "Tools for Small Business Development," Chapter 4 of Small Businesses Partnerships, *1989. Published by National League of Cities, Washington, D.C. Reprinted with permission of the publisher.*

**FIGURE 1—KEY ELEMENTS
OF A SMALL BUSINESS SURVEY**

- Perceptions of City Hall
- City small business policies or plans
- Organization and management of small business programs
- Access to capital — working and venture
- Access to public markets
- Employee training needs
- Access to land and new sites
- Regulations
- City's quality of life
- Quality of public services
- Public physical infrastructure
- Business assistance programs

---

new employees, expand its facility, branch out into international markets, scale back/close down, or relocate.

A second type of research should include a survey of the largest employers in the city's economic market, which may extend up to a 100-mile radius around the city. This survey should focus on the supplies or services those businesses need and where they now get them. In Lima, Ohio, for example, market research found that the city's largest employers purchased more than 70 percent of their goods and services from outside the Lima economic market. Information on the supply and service needs of local businesses, the prices being paid and quality control needs, made it possible to open up a major new market for entrepreneurs.

A third type of research should focus on industry growth and decline trends. Several years ago, surveys showed that health-related industries were a high growth part of Philadelphia's economy, and that San Francisco's economy was becoming a service-based economy. Knowing which major industries will grow in your economy allows you to encourage

those small businesses that will serve as producers and suppliers.

Armed with this data, the city and the small business partnership should be able to quickly identify existing small businesses that need assistance, new private market opportunities, and new directions for small business investment.

In making the decision to promote certain types of small business development, the partnership may wish to consider giving priority for assistance by using the following guidelines:

1. Small businesses that can be profitable within the existing market area.

2. Small businesses that increase exports outside the local market.

3. Small businesses that supply goods and services to local, large employers.

4. Small businesses that diversify the local economic base.

5. Small businesses that use local labor.

6. Small businesses that meet the community's needs for a safe and clean environment.

Using these guidelines, the partnership can begin to formulate a strategy which is truly based on the sensitivities of the local market and local needs and resources.

Small Business Development Tools

Once the city has completed its initial research and adopted its plan, the next step is to determine what tools are needed to address the city's liabilities and enhance its assets. There are twelve types of non-financial tools that cities can use to generate new small business investment. Not every city will need to use all of these tools, but may wish to consider them when adopting a comprehensive plan.

1. To Improve Perceptions of City Hall

• Provide high-level leadership and support for efforts.
• Involve small business in a task force or commission.
• Mount a public relations campaign to build city image.
• Sponsor small business fairs.
• Demonstrate a positive attitude toward business.
• Form a small business partnership.
• Appoint an ombudsman for small business in city hall.

2. To Improve Planning and Policy Making

• Establish a comprehensive policy with goals and objectives.
• Conduct a survey of small business needs.
• Involve small businesses in planning.
• Undertake economic research, analysis, and forecasting.
• Target selected types of small business for development.
• Target certain areas of the city.

3. To Improve Organization and Management of Small Business Programs

• Establish a small business development authority.
• Ensure that all city resources are coordinated to emphasize small business development.
• Link state and federal programs with local efforts.
• Develop networks with financial institutions, business leaders, labor, and others.
• Employ skilled staff who have small business experience.
• Monitor and evaluate program efforts.
• Provide continual training for staff.
• Contract with an outside small business adviser to provide perspective and expertise to your strategy.

4. To Improve Access to Affordable Capital

• Establish bank consortium and loan pooling agreements.
• Establish partnerships with financial institutions.
• Deposit city funds at banks that invest in small businesses.
• Target community reinvestment programs for small business interests.
• Access state and federal resources.
• Encourage organization of bank community development corporations.

5. To Improve Access to Public Markets

• Establish a public procurement information/bidding system. Use regional and national systems.
• Eliminate or reduce bid-bonds.
• Establish a bond guarantee and liability insurance program.
• Create local purchasing preferences from firms whose owners live in the community.
• Establish and enforce prompt payment legislation.
• Provide technical assistance to small business on the city bid and procurement process.

6. To Improve Human Capital

• Harness the Job Training Partnership Act program to meet small business employment needs.
• Develop entrepreneurial training programs at local universities and secondary schools.

7. To Improve Availability of Land/ Sites

• Land banking; use city land to leverage private investment and generate a public sector equity stake in small business development.
• Survey available sites and maintain a data bank.

• Assemble parcels.

• Provide incubator space — old public/private buildings that are rehabilitated and opened up to new businesses at substantially reduced lease or sale prices.

• Establish small business parks.

8. To Improve Regulatory Climate

• Create a one-stop permitting center.

• Reduce paperwork.

• Expedite processing.

• Eliminate nuisance regulations.

• Modify zoning to promote small business development.

• Identify an ombudsman.

9. To Improve the Quality of Life

• Upgrade educational institutions.

• Expand recreational opportunities.

• Encourage sports franchises.

• Upgrade cultural opportunities.

• Improve health care.

• Provide day care.

10. To Improve Public Service

• Upgrade visible services like police and fire protection and combat crime.

• Contract with small businesses to provide city services.

• Target services to small business areas or commercial strips.

• Reroute public transit to serve small business areas.

11. To Improve the Infrastructure

• Adopt a long-range capital improvements program.

• Rehabilitate and/or construct roads, bridges, and water lines.

• Upgrade public transportation.

12. To Improve Business Assistance

• Create a management assistance center for small business.

• Provide training for entrepreneurs using local educational institutions.

• Provide ongoing management technical assistance.

• Underwrite management services to small businesses.

New Small Business Growth

The entrepreneurial city is always looking for new ways to increase opportunities for its entrepreneurs and to put people who are not working back to work. The following six tools are new areas of small business development or are potential areas where cities can make a difference: small business incubators, bank consortium/small business partnerships, export trade, youth enterprises, public housing small business development, and welfare self-sufficiency projects. In all six areas, the city can play a critical role as catalyst and partner.

SMALL BUSINESS INCUBATORS

According to the Small Business Administration, incubators are buildings where a number of new or growing firms can locate and conduct business at a much lower cost than in conventional, market rate space. Incubator firms share centralized clerical and administrative services, business assistance, conference rooms, or loading docks. Incubators are most effective for startups where overhead costs are high and markets are not yet fully developed. In some instances, incubators can also serve an economic revitalization purpose by being located in abandoned but rehabilitated factories, or in historic preservation districts where abandoned office or commercial buildings need new life. Cities can identify potential incubator facilities, package the project, underwrite its rehabilitation for small business use, promote its use, and provide management assistance to the firms once they have located in the facility.

BANK CONSORTIUM/SMALL BUSINESS PARTNERSHIPS

Partly in response to the Community Reinvestment Act (CRA) requirements for more community lending, and partly because of the need to reinvest in urban neighborhoods and businesses, banks and savings and loans across the country are forming consortia to promote small and minority business development and low income housing. Since 1982, the Development Credit Fund in Baltimore has been making working capital loans ranging from $5,000 to $750,000 to high risk businesses that normally would not be eligible in the private market. The six largest banks in Maryland, led by Maryland National Bank, pooled over $22.5 million, which is now supported by a Small Business Administration loan guarantee program, to share the risk, reduce transaction costs, and build a bridge to the small and minority business market. Other bank consortia in Oakland, Atlanta, and Pittsburgh are looking to expand access to capital for this underserved population of businesses.

EXPORT TRADE DEVELOPMENT

Greater small business access into the export market is needed. The National League of Cities has suggested a number of ways cities can do this:

• Providing leadership to encourage and assist local businesses to mitigate or expand international business activities.
• Conducting trade missions.
• Encouraging direct foreign investment.
• Forming a foreign trade zone.
• Forming an export trading company.
• Developing an export business assistance center.
• Establishing ties with universities overseas to further develop information on export markets.
• Providing information on trade fairs, exhibits, government-sponsored trade missions.
• Encouraging international tourism.

Any or all of these actions depend upon the city's competitive advantage in exports.

YOUTH ENTERPRISE DEVELOPMENT

To develop the entrepreneurial talents of the next generation, cities can establish young adult community development corporations (CDCs), which can be subsidiaries of an existing CDC or the city's SBA 503/504 corporation. Youth CDCs bring the business world to young adults in a way that generates a sense of ownership and builds business skills. They provide a positive alternative to subminimum wage jobs.

PUBLIC HOUSING SMALL BUSINESS DEVELOPMENT

Public housing projects, particularly larger ones, have an untapped market potential. Hundreds of millions of dollars each year flow from these projects to commercial and retail firms without benefiting the micro-economy of the project. At the same time, the projects often have empty buildings suitable for incubators, people who need work, and services that need to be performed for the project itself or that could be sold outside the project. Cities and their housing and welfare departments could consider converting economically distressed projects into havens for new enterprise development.

WELFARE SELF-SUFFICIENCY PROJECTS

Several cities are experimenting with putting welfare recipients with entrepreneurial talents into business for themselves.

Once a venture idea is identified by a welfare recipient, the city and its small business advisers work with the recipient to start up the new business.

Potential Resources

Mounting a significant, long-term strategy will require upfront investment by the members of the small business partnership. Every member is a potential contributor to underwriting the costs of the strategy, as noted at the end of Chapter Three. The contributions can be either in cash or in kind. Here we will focus primarily on the kinds of assistance federal and state governments can provide, and what cities can do to access and coordinate those resources.

There are eight basic types of federal and state government small business development assistance for cities: legislation, advocacy and research, fiscal aid, expenditures, regulations, financial aid, programmatic assistance, and non-financial aid.

1. Legislative: The power to draft and lobby for specific legislation to support small firms to enhance the capabilities of local governments to aid small firms—for example, home rule.

2. Advocacy and research: It is essential for small business to have a political voice at the top echelons of government at least comparable to the influence of big business or labor. The U.S. Small Business Administration has an Office of Advocacy that identifies, researches, and supports the concerns of the small business community. State economic development agencies and governors either already have the advocacy/research capability to assist cities and small businesses, or they can create it.

3. Fiscal: The tax and revenue sharing powers of the federal and state governments are among the most powerful

tools available for developing a vibrant small business sector. Tax policies should: (a) reduce barriers to the efficient operation of capital markets; (b) be stable and certain; (c) be evaluated regularly to ensure positive impact. Federal and state revenues can be distributed to communities in greater economic need, local governments can be reimbursed for federally and state-mandated programs, while statutes can be passed to enable metropolitan revenue and tax base sharing programs.

4. Expenditure: Federal and state governments are the largest consumers of goods and services in the economy, responsible for over one-third of the GNP. They spend hundreds of billions of dollars annually, only a small percentage of which goes to small business. Procurement policy and programs need to be directed to small and minority firms and targeted to firms in economically distressed communities. Public facility siting can boost local government and small business revenues. Public pension funds can be used as a source of investment or even as a guarantee for a secondary market for small business financing.

5. Regulatory: In the areas of banking, insurance, environment protection, land use, licensing, permitting, and paperwork reduction, federal and state governments can reduce regulatory barriers that impede access to money and markets. For example, these governments can facilitate interstate bank competition, permitting bank equity investments in business ventures, and enforce the Community Reinvestment Act bank investments in small businesses located in distressed areas.

6. Financial assistance: Federal and state governments have available to them a wide range of traditional and non-traditional financial assistance other than tax policies. Table 1 lists several.

7. Programmatic assistance: Specific programs or initiatives, with or without financial assistance, can be developed on

TABLE 1—PUBLIC SECTOR FINANCIAL AID TO SMALL BUSINESS
• Grants
• Loans and loan guarantees; pooling consortia
• Revolving loan funds
• Interest subsidies
• Bonds, taxable and tax-exempt
• Equity and near-equity financing
• Business site development assistance
• Customized job training
• Tax incentives, credits, and abatements
• Venture capital institutions
• Development finance institutions

the premise of supporting the development and growth of small firms. These include: foreign export development, interregional market development and trade, enterprise zones, small business incubators, public physical infrastructure improvements, fostering neighborhood and community development corporations, or other forms of targeted assistance to specific types of small business or to particular places.

8. Nonfinancial assistance: Here again, federal and state governments can provide the management and technical assistance so essential to small firms. They can act as information and referral clearinghouses, and provide public relations or marketing assistance. They can also act to enhance the coordination and partnership capabilities of local governments. Public sector assistance is available, depending upon the state. The two issues cities face are access and coordination with their existing resources.

Access is particularly important. All too often the resources are scattered among agencies, each with different purposes, requirements, and paperwork. Once a small business partnership has decided to develop a plan, the city should be asked to identify and access the key federal and state resources.

Table 2 suggests steps a city can take. The partnership should also spend time regularly (every three months) to brainstorm new ways to bring these resources to bear. The point is to keep federal and state attention focused on your city's small business needs.

Coordination is also critical to a successful small business program, particularly between the state and city governments. The initiative for coordination needs to come from the city and is best located in the

TABLE 2—ACCESSING FEDERAL AND STATE RESOURCES
• Determine the specific types of assistance needed and when they are needed, (for example, planning funds needed immediately, project funds in a year).
• Conduct an agency inventory to find out which agencies have the kinds of funds or assistance needed, their requirements and deadlines.
• Identify key gaps between city needs and federal and state resources, and let the executive and legislative branches know.
• Focus on state department of economic development/commerce financial assistance to small business. Establish relationships with top officials.
• Become aware of state agency allocation formulas and how they can benefit your city; determine if you are getting your "fair share."
• Submit solicited and unsolicited proposals to key state agencies regularly for assistance.
• Increase the number of industrial development bond applications for small business projects that qualify (check per capita limitations).
• Invite federal and state officials and your congressional delegation to tour the city, meet with the partnership, and conduct forums or hearings on small business needs.

mayor's office or the city's office of intergovernmental relations. If the city does not already have an intergovernmental staff member who has expertise in small business, the city may want to consider hiring one. This person should serve as a liaison and communications point, coordinate all grant or program applications, and make sure that all small business gaps identified are filled. Table 3 provides a state-by-state analysis of the typical small business assistance programs provided by each state.

The tools available for small business development are significant, and new approaches to finance, management, and self-help are emerging every year. Public and private sector resources are also substantial and can be carefully crafted into a comprehensive tool kit for small businesses to use at each stage of their development. Paying for these tools, yet another challenge for the partnership, is the focus of a subsequent chapter.

TABLE 3—STATE SMALL BUSINESS ASSISTANCE PROGRAMS

	State 503 Devel. Cos.	Bus. Incubators	Small Bus. Office	Loan Prog.	Procurement Prog.	Gov. Liaison	Advisory Board	Small Bus. Economic Revital. Prog.
Alabama	•	•	•	•	•		•	
Alaska	•		1		•			
Arizona	•	•	•	•		•	•	•
Arkansas	•	•	•	•		•	•	•
California		•	•	•	•	•	•	•
Colorado	•	•	•	•			•	
Connecticut	•		•	•	•	•		•
Delaware			•				•	
Florida	•	•	•		•	•	•	•
Georgia	•	•	•	•	•	•	•	•
Hawaii			•	•	•		•	
Idaho			•	•	•		•	
Illinois	•	•	•	•	•	•	•	•
Indiana	•	•	•	•	•	•		•
Iowa	•	•	•		•	•	•	
Kansas	•	•	•		•	•	•	
Kentucky	•	•	•	•	•		•	
Louisiana	•	•	•		•	•		•
Maine	•	•		•	•	•	•	•
Maryland	•	•	•	•	•	•		•
Massachusetts		•	•	•	•	•	•	•
Michigan	•	•	•	•	•	•		•
Minnesota	•		•	•	•			•
Mississippi	•	2	•	•	•		•	•
Missouri			•	•	•			

(Table 3, continued)

	State 503 Devel. Cos.	Bus. Incubators	Small Bus. Office	Loan Prog.	Procurement Prog.	Gov. Liaison	Advisory Board	Small Bus. Economic Revital. Prog.
Montana		•	•	•				
Nebraska	•	•	•	•	•	•	•	•
Nevada	•		•	•	•		•	
New Hampshire		•	•					•
New Jersey			•	•				•
New Mexico	•	•			•	•	•	•
New York	•	•	•	•	•	•	•	•
North Carolina		•	•		•		•	
North Dakota	•	•	•	•	•	•	•	•
Ohio	•	•	•	•	•		•	•
Oklahoma		•	•					
Oregon	•		•	•			•	•
Pennsylvania		•	•	•	•	•	•	•
Rhode Island	•		•	•	•		•	
South Carolina		•	•	•	•	•	•	
South Dakota		•	•	•	•			
Tennessee		•	•	•	•	•	•	
Texas		•	•					
Utah		•	•				•	
Vermont	•	•	•	•		•		
Virginia		•	•	•	•	•		
Washington	•		•			•	•	
West Virginia	•	•	•	•	•	•	•	•
Wisconsin		•	•	•	•	•		
Wyoming	•		•	•	•			•
Puerto Rico			•		•	•		
District of Columbia			•	•				

1. Incorporated into the Office of Enterprise, Dept. of Commerce and Economic Development

2. 1985 legislation authorizing establishment; funded through state, city, and private sources; it is only in the initial consideration stages at the present time.

Source: *The Guide to State and Federal Resources for Economic Development,* Northeast Midwest Institute, 1988, p. 394.

26. TRAIN STATION REVITALIZATION

Janet Ward

Nothing evokes the American past like a train. That is true despite the fact that Americans, for whom cars are convenient and air travel is inexpensive, have never been on a train.

Still, there is something almost painfully nostalgic about the sound of a distant train whistle. It is no accident that Americans feel a pang when they hear that yet another line has ceased operation, just as it is no accident that Gladys Knight was able to make a hit out of a Midnight Train to Georgia that no one rides anymore. Indeed, it was the 1960s demolition of a train station — New York's Pennsylvania Station — that is credited with launching the historic preservation movement.

That nostalgia explains, at least in part, the reluctance to part with the train stations that dot the American landscape like so many town squares. "Trains are a link with our past," says Gary Wolf, president of Rail Sciences, an Atlanta-based railroad consultant. "Railroad stations anchored every city. Development moved away from the train stations. When I'm working in a city I've never been in, I have no trouble finding the train station. I just go to the center of town."

Because train stations are centrally located, it makes perfect sense for cities seeking to revitalize their downtowns to tap the grand old buildings that once housed the railroad lines. Some, like St. Louis and Scranton, Pa., have turned their stations into prosperous hotels. Some stations, like those in Omaha, Neb., and Cincinnati, have become museums.

Jacksonville, Fla., transformed its old station into a convention center. Stations in Pueblo, Colo., and Collierville, Tenn., now house municipal offices. Still others, like those in Anchorage, Alaska, and Fargo, N.D., have been converted into microbreweries. "That makes perfect sense," Wolf says. "The old stations had big baggage rooms that were perfect for brewing tanks."

Imagination — and Money

In fact, the number of uses for train stations — the massive ones and the little

Originally published as "Cities Engineer Train Station Revivals," American City & County, Vol. 114, No. 6, June, 1999. Published by Intertec Publishing Corp., Atlanta, Georgia. Reprinted with permission of the publisher.

depots—seems limited only by a city's imagination and money. Lack of either can doom the grandest train station to decrepitude. Stations in Detroit and Buffalo, N.Y., as well as countless tiny architecturally interesting depots, have fallen victim to neglect or to ownership battles between railroads and cities.

In Decatur, Ga., for example, a battle between the city and CSX Railroad has meant a slow death for the little building that once was a thriving restaurant. (The railroad wants the city to buy its depot; the city wants the railroad's taxes.) Sacramento, Calif.'s station currently is the focus of a fight between Amtrak, which wants to continue to use it as a train station, and the city, which wants it for virtually anything else.

Because of their size—and the quality of materials used to construct them—aging train stations are outrageously expensive to renovate. For the same reasons, they are nearly as expensive to demolish, according to Rob McGonigal, an associate editor with Waukesha, Wis.-based Trains magazine. "These are massive structures with a lot of heavily built portions to support the tracks," McGonigal says.

However, cities will to do a little legwork can find the financial wherewithal to protect their stations. Federal grants for urban revitalization, state money and local bonds proceeds all have contributed to the renovation of stations nationwide.

Finding the Money Train

In Kansas City, Mo., which is nearly finished with a project that will convert its French Renaissance station into a science museum, voters turned down several referenda that would have jump-started the renovation project. Then, three nonprofit groups—the Kansas City Museum, the Union Station Assistance Corp. (USAC), and Kansas City Consensus—went to work

finding the funding. (All had different interests but the same goal: the museum group wanted to build a world-class science museum; Kansas City Consensus was working on a bi-state cultural district; and USAC just wanted the station restored.)

Two local charitable foundations kicked in upwards of $40 million, and Westwood, Kan.-based telecommunications giant Sprint added another $9 million. "That money made the project real and allowed us to take planning quite far," says Science City Museum Director Dave Ucko.

Meanwhile, USAC worked the federal government for grant money, and Kansas City Consensus began lobbying for a local sales tax. That ⅛ cent sales tax, the first bi-state sales tax ever passed in the area, was approved in November 1996 in three Missouri counties and one Kansas county.

"We had to get identical enabling legislation passed in both states," Ucko says. "Then, each of the counties had to agree to put it on the ballot." Proceeds from that tax eventually will fund half the project's $250 million cost.

Despite their initial reluctance to fund the renovation, Kansas Citians never considered demolishing Union Station. The building was intricately woven into their history and, even when it fell into disuse and underwent unsuccessful attempts at modernization, it retained its caché. (According to an article in Trains, Kansas Citians gathered at Union Station to celebrate the end of World War II.)

Over the years, a number of reuse plans faltered, and a Canadian firm with redevelopment notions bought the station in 1974. When nothing—except construction of an office building that split the station in half—came of the firm's efforts, the city sued for possession of the station. Under a settlement, the company conveyed the station to USAC. With renovation nearly complete, the science museum is scheduled to open in the fall.

All Aboard

Local voters also helped save Cincinnati's Union Terminal, a beautiful Art Deco station that had been unsuccessfully converted into a shopping center. The architecturally significant station was dying when a Save the Terminal campaign resurrected it with the idea that its half-million square feet of space would be ideal for a museum.

In May 1986, Hamilton County voters approved issuance of $33 million worth of general obligation bonds specifically for the renovation of the terminal. State and city grants, individual contributions and money from private companies and foundations filled financing gaps.

In 1990, the Museum Center at Union Terminal opened. Home to the Cincinnati Historical Society Museum and Library, the Cincinnati Museum of Natural History, the Cinergy Children's Museum, and the Robert D. Lindner Family Omnimax Theater, the center was named one of the top 10 new tourist attractions in the United States by the Austin, Texas-based Weissmann Travel Reports in 1991. Currently, it attracts more than one million visitors each year.

It took Cincinnati and their train restoration projects off the ground. However, in Omaha, Neb., there was little question about the rebirth of the city's Union Station.

A classic Art Deco building, the station closed to passenger travel in 1972. Its builder, Union Pacific Railroad, donated the station to the city, and the landmark re-opened in 1975 as the Western Heritage Museum. ("Durham" was added to the name later to honor a locally prominent family that had provided significant financing for the renovation.) The museum features a railroad exhibit that includes everything from rail cars to a 70-foot-long model train layout that portrays the trip from Omaha to Deadwood, S.D.

Pulling in the Private Sector

As in Omaha, private funding was key to the successful restoration of Union Station in Albany, N.Y., which now serves as "the most expensive building per square foot in the Fleet Bank empire," according to Fleet spokesperson Karl Felsen. (It is difficult to transform train stations into commercial space because of the tremendous amount of open area, which in the business world is considered dead space.)

The station, which opened in 1900 and closed 68 years later, was failing fast, according to Felsen. Trees were growing in the roof, which had been stripped of its copper overlay, when local banker Peter Kiernan rescued it.

The Peter D. Kiernan Plaza, as the station is now called, suffered the failure of countless reuse proposals. Despite the best efforts of the late Albany mayor, Erastus Corning, Union Station looked doomed.

Then, in 1984, a plan to convert the facility into a bank was floated. The station reopened in 1986 after a meticulous renovation, during which contractors raised the building's marble floor to install a technology center beneath it. "Technology and history can be wedded together if you're ambitious and clever enough," Felsen notes.

Local and private money also figured significantly in the renovation of St. Louis' Union Station, perhaps one of the best examples of reuse in the country, according to McGonigal. The Romanesque station, which opened in 1894 as the largest single-level passenger rail terminal in the world and closed in 1978, is now a mixed-use development that includes a mall and the Hyatt Regency at Union Station.

Restoration of St. Louis' train station was headed up by The Rouse Co., a Columbia, Md.-based urban renovation specialist. When it was completed in 1985, the $150 million project was the largest adaptive reuse project in the United States.

Building Works of Art

Naturally, the price tag for station renovation dwarfs the original construction costs. However, those were not insignificant. The $6.5 million construction cost for St. Louis' station was considered astronomical for its day. And it was the rule, rather than the exception.

Built largely by the railroads—the most lucrative businesses of the late 1880s—the stations were not designed to be merely functional. They were looked on as the public face of the railroads; thus, the railroad magnates determined that they would be works of art.

"These buildings are magnificent architectural landmarks," says Rail Sciences' Wolf. "They would bring in the best craftsmen from Europe. The railroads commissioned incredible works of art for their stations. It was almost a competition to see who could build the most beautiful train station."

Omaha's Union Station, for instance, features the largest half-dome rotunda in the Western Hemisphere, 105-foot-by-20-foot mosaic murals by German artist Winold Reiss, and beautiful fountains. In St. Louis, the locally based Terminal Railroad Association, which financed the station's original construction, commissioned "Allegorical Window," a stained glass work that is framed by the station's "Whispering Arch." (The arch is so named because of a distinct architectural design that allows a person to stand on one side of the arch, talk into the wall and be heard by someone standing at the arch's other end.)

Most renovators attempt to keep stations' architectural details intact. The St. Louis Hyatt, for example, features not only Allegorical Window and Whispering Arch, but also Union Station's Grand Hall, a 65-foot barrel-vaulted ceiling decorated with gold leaf that spans the building's lobby and lounge. Because of its structural beauty, most of the station's original interior has been carefully preserved. For instance, the hotel's restaurant, the Station Grille, was once a Fred Harvey restaurant.

(A digression: According to the book *The History of the Atchison, Topeka and Santa Fe,* Harvey, a genteel Englishman, made his fortune creating nice restaurants at train stations and alongside depots. Prior to Harvey's efforts, passengers had no choice but to make do with trackside greasy spoons. Those roadside diners, the story goes, would serve the passengers, and moments later, the "All aboard" would sound. The passengers would leave half-eaten meals that the diners then tossed back into pots for the later enjoyment of the passengers on the next train. For their cooperation, engineers would get a nickel a meal from the diners.)

From Sleepers to Hotels

Train stations can be converted to a number of uses, but hotels seem to be particularly popular ones. That is partly because the huge open spaces that are anathema to most commercial owners are favored for hotel lobbies and ballrooms. In fact, the Chattanooga Choo Choo, a hotel in Chattanooga, Tenn., represents one of the nation's first adaptive reuse projects.

The centerpiece of a 1970s revitalization campaign, the Choo Choo features shopping, restaurants and Pullman sleeper cars that guests can rent for the night. It is one of the South's most popular tourist destinations.

Scranton, Pa., also transformed its French Renaissance Lackawanna Station into a hotel. The station, now the Radisson Lackawanna Station Hotel, was the linchpin of Scranton's downtown revitalization program.

Opened in 1908 and closed in 1970, the station was purchased by MetroAction, a Chamber of Commerce corporation that concentrated on downtown development.

Using the financial theories that helped convert Scranton's mining-based economy to a manufacturing-based one, MetroAction began looking into reuse alternatives. Ultimately, the Erie-Lackawanna Restoration Associates, a group of private investors, began the restoration with the support of a financial package involving federal, state and local funds, as well private money donated by businesses and local banks. The station/hotel, renovated for $13 million, reopened on New Year's Eve in 1983.

Like St. Louis' station, the Lackawanna Station was notable for its artwork and its design. The two-and-a-half story waiting room featured a barrel-vaulted, leaded glass ceiling, Sienna marble walls and washboards of Alpine green marble. A series of faience panels modeled after the paintings of American artist Clark Greenwood Voorhees, depicts scenes along the railroad's Hoboken-to-Buffalo route.

Other Uses

Hotels, museums, malls and banks are fine examples of reuse, but train stations also provide some of the nation's most impressive municipal office space. Pueblo, Colo.'s once-derelict station, renowned for its beautiful woodwork, now houses the city administration. So does Collierville, Tenn.'s old station, which still features dining cars that locals can rent for special functions.

Louisville, Ky., won a Design for Transportation award from the U.S. Department of Transportation and the National Endowment for the Arts for the transformation of its station into offices for the Transit Authority of River City. At a cost that was about three-quarters that of a new facility, the authority restored the station, meticulously matching the missing pieces of marble wainscot panels, cleaning stained glass and ceramic tile, and restoring red oak staircases and paneled walls. Most of those aesthetically appealing details would be unaffordable in modern construction.

Renovation and restoration projects involving train stations are as varied as the stations themselves. Cities are capitalizing on the old buildings not just for their intrinsic value but for the boost they provide their communities. "These places are deeply rooted in the American experience," McGonigal says. "That's why there is so much support for saving them."

27. URBAN CULTURAL PARKS

Paul M. Bray

At one time urban parks were in the vanguard of urban planning and often were the rallying point for civic causes. Galen Cranz described the decline in pre-eminence of traditional urban parks as foci for civic pride in her book *The History of Urban Parks*, but she concluded that, "The potentiality of parks to shape and reflect social values is still by no means fully understood. Those with an interest in the character of urban life should seize on parks as one of the vehicles for realization of their particular visions, and the debate about parks should revolve around those visions."[1]

A test of Cranz's challenge has been going on in Lowell, Massachusetts, and in 22 cities, towns and villages in New York State for the last 20 years. These communities have pursued the vision of the urban environment itself as a park, seeking to transform themselves into places where everything is interesting. They have expanded the notion of the park to include inhabited portions of the city.[2]

Cranz described the objective of Lowell: "These urban cultural parks, which were intended to preserve an important part of the nation's industrial and economic history for educational and recreational purposes, were opened on the assumption that all parts of the city — its work spaces, living quarters and connecting streets— have equal aesthetic and recreational potential, that the city was in fact a work of art worthy of appreciation and objectification."[3] Thus, urban cultural parks take measure of the cultural heritage of cities for economic and civic revitalization.

In 1982, New York State enacted a law creating a statewide urban cultural park (UCP) program. It is predicated on three primary objectives: 1) that the urban cultural heritage telling the story of the state should be protected for future generations; 2) that urban cultural parks can be planned and managed for the intersecting goals of preservation, recreation, education, and economic development and revitalization; and 3) that the program supporting UCPs will lead to better intra- and inter-governmental coordination and public-private sector cooperation.

Originally published as "A New Tool for Renewing the Central City: The Urban Cultural Park," National Civic Review, *Vol. 83, No. 2, Spring/Summer, 1994. Published by the National Civic League, Denver, Colorado. Reprinted with permission of the publisher.*

The UCP law places direction of the program in the hands of the state Office of Parks, Recreation and Historic Preservation and creates an advisory council made up of citizens and representatives from state economic development, housing, education, transportation, and environmental agencies. The purpose of the advisory council is to coordinate state actions to achieve objectives of the UCP program.

Each local UCP project represents one or more of the program's themes and is required to have an extensive, state-approved management plan and local historic preservation implementing ordinance to participate. The management plan is a comprehensive scheme addressing each of the three UCP objectives. Economic development concerns are as fully integrated into UCP planning as planning for such traditional park facilities as visitors centers. This assures the features and conditions of traditional parks, including visitor comfort and security in untraditional settings, as well as programming for interpretive and recreational activities. Once the management plan is approved, state agencies are required to meet a "consistency" requirement for their activities within UCP boundaries. Thereafter, state funding is available for programming and capital projects.

UCP planning in New York State generally involves a three-phase process.[4] Initially, a participatory, public planning process promotes the development of a shared community vision with regard to local heritage as it relates to preservation, recreation and education, and economic development. The second, or "revitalization" phase affects communities wishing to use the UCP program as a means to marshal forces to improve and enhance a particular part of town, such as a main shopping street. By concentrating efforts and resources in a specific UCP-designated area, UCP-generated improvements can create an image of uniqueness and importance, reflecting a broader civic vision. Finally, and for the long run, the UCP helps release civic inspiration while providing practical recreational and educational opportunities in urban settings.

Like the management of traditional public parks, the UCP management entity must address a continuing agenda of management, operation and programming tasks, but with a much larger cast of characters.

Fourteen UCP management plans have been completed by local governments and approved by New York State. By the end of 1994 each UCP in the state program will have a well designed and functional visitors center, and more than $60 million in state, local and private funds will have been invested. Importantly, the critical underpinnings of park management currently are in place in each of the 14 UCPs.

Some UCPs have developed innovative educational and recreational programs, taking advantage of urban form and culture in ways that attract and gratify park visitors and residents alike. Urban scavenger hunts, community heritage days (on which city residents are invited to bring family heirlooms to the UCP visitors center for appraisal), and audio-recorded interpretive tours have helped make UCPs "live-in, learn-in parks" for people of all ages.

Several cities and villages have used UCP improvements to catalyze revitalization. The City of Troy leveraged a $640,000 state grant with more than $5 million in private and city funds to renovate a central civic square to serve as the location for its UCP visitors center. Rochester joined forces with local industries like Eastman Kodak to locate its visitors center in a complex of historic industrial buildings overlooking the high falls of the Genesee River. Chris Lindley, former Rochester Deputy Mayor, described the multi-faceted celebration of Rochester's heritage in its UCP visitors center as "a widely acknowledged act of civic affirmation."[5] Today, more than 20 property owners are developing a ten-year plan for further revitalization within the city's UCP.

Other revitalization successes include Kingston's UCP visitors center, which was sited in a previously stalled mixed-use development. It resulted in a fully rented project. Likewise, the Seneca Falls UCP partnered with the private sector to restore a burned-out but historically significant downtown structure.

Yet, the greatest economic success from UCP development may flow from its psychological impact. The UCP approach, by generating a broadly shared community vision for the celebration of urban heritage, produces a climate and attitude conducive to local economic renewal. The process helps change the focus from merely dealing with urban pathology to pursuing urban promise.

The National Park Service has categorized UCPs as "heritage areas" and "partnership parks." These are highly functional descriptions, as encouraging and facilitating partnerships is an essential facet of UCP planning and management. Moreover, the concepts of heritage and culture provide a comfortable common ground from which to attract, link and engage a broad spectrum of civic interests within cities. While traditional historic preservation has been a bit rarefied in its focus on landmarks and historic districts, heritage planning seeks, recognizes and celebrates and full story of human attainments in urban settlements, while finding creative ways to enrich urban life with that history. The partnerships developed through UCP planning, moreover, become the basis and stimulus for forming larger scale partnerships to fully realize the UCP vision.

New York State's UCPs represent a complex and highly developed form of urban heritage initiative, but many other examples exist. In Los Angeles, a nonprofit corporation, the Power of Place, was established in 1982 to address the under-represented aspects of urban heritage.[6] The organization is committed to identifying landmarks of ethnic, women's and labor history for use as cultural resources.

A grass-roots, community empowerment effort in Canada, called the Heritage Project, relies on heritage to forge "linkages and connections ... between community actions today and the heritage we pass on tomorrow."[7] In the U.S., the National Coalition for Heritage Areas has been formed to work for establishing a National Heritage Areas system and program. A number of National Heritage Corridors like the Blackstone River National Heritage Corridor from Worcester, Massachusetts to Providence, Rhode Island, have been established by Congress, and Representative Maurice D. Hinchey (D-N.Y.) has introduced legislation entitled The National Partnerships System of Heritage Areas Act.[8]

The expansion of the idea of a park encompassing all or significant portions of a city to capitalize on "usable history" has progressed encouragingly during the past two decades, but not without frustrations. UCPs have developed in the face of anti-urban attitudes and widely held assumptions that parks must have gates and be separate and apart from the living environment. For too many public officials and others, as Jane Holtz Kay pointed out regarding the early efforts to establish the Lowell Urban Cultural Park, "The view of the city as more pathology that playground does not die."[9]

For people with that viewpoint, treating the city as a park and celebrating the city is a vary daunting challenge. Despite the obstacles, and considering the detailed rules and techniques for establishing these tributes to urban heritage and texture, urban cultural parks have enjoyed substantial success and represent a realistic approach to urban planning.

Notes

1. Galen Cranz, *The Politics of Park Design: A History of Urban Parks in America* (Cambridge, Mass.: MIT Press, 1982), p. 255.

2. Paul M. Bray, "The New Urbanism: Celebrating the City," *Places*, 8:4, Summer 1993.

3. Cranz, p. 141.

4. *A Guide to Developing Urban and Rural Cultural Parks* (Albany, N.Y.: New York Parks and Conservation Association, 1983).

5. Interview conducted by the author.

6. Delores Hayden, "Using Ethnic History to Understand Urban Landscapes," *Places*, 7:1, Fall 1990, p. 11.

7. Marcia Nozick, "Urban Issues Program Underway," *City Magazine*, 14:4, 15:1, Fall 1993 and Winter 1994, p. 47.

8. The bill is styled HR2416. Also, Representative Bruce Vento, Chairman of the National Parks, Forests and Public Lands subcommittee, introduced HR3707, to establish an American Heritage Areas Partnership Program. The National Park Service also has circulated draft legislation to establish a National Heritage Areas System and program.

9. Jane Holtz Kay, "Lowell, Mass.—New Birth for Us All," *The Nation*, 17 September 1977, p. 245.

PART IV

Case Studies

28. BALTIMORE'S EMPOWERMENT ZONE

Charles Mahtesian

On Monument Street in East Baltimore, once a vibrant commercial corridor but now a down-at-the-heels fast-food, liquor-store and check-cashing strip, the whole notion of being an empowerment zone always seemed a little too good to be true.

Community activists in the surrounding neighborhoods thought it highly doubtful that their city would even qualify for one of the massive urban renewal grants the Clinton administration was handing out. That the money might somehow find its way to them sounded many times more improbable still. "When I heard about the process and the application, I thought we had a better chance of winning the lottery," says Vicki Evans, who heads the nearby Ashland Community Association.

So when the news of Baltimore's $100 million grant was made public, Evans and other neighborhood leaders couldn't resist wondering if they had finally hit the jackpot. They didn't expect the whole $100 million — just a small slice of the pie for Ashland and Monument Street. The way they saw it, $100 million citywide could easily cover the tab for all the public safety projects, economic development ventures, human services programs and neighborhood housing renovations that organizations like the tiny Ashland Community Association could never afford on their own. "We had always been excluded from other government programs because we didn't meet some criteria. Either we didn't have enough population or a high enough crime rate or some other thing," says Evans. "This is the first opportunity this community has had in terms of restoration and homeownership."

Just how big an opportunity it may be is an interesting question. Evans' community association is not the only one seeking its fair share of the EZ money. The Madison East End neighborhood has a few ideas of its own for spending the money. So does McElderry Park. And Broadway East and Middle East and a handful of other neighborhoods throughout Vicki Evans' section of the zone. And that is just in East Baltimore. Across town, in West Baltimore,

Originally published as "Showdown on E-Z Street," Governing, Vol. 9, No. 2, October, 1995. Published by Congressional Quarterly, Inc., Washington, D.C. Reprinted with permission of the publisher.

Sandtown-Winchester is also looking for a cut of the action, as are the Penn North, Coppin Heights, Poppleton and Mondawmin neighborhoods. They are all, without exception, badly in need of help.

As in the other five cities that won the urban empowerment jackpot, Baltimore's zone cobbles together a variety of densely packed neighborhoods where disproportionate numbers of the poorest, sickest and youngest reside. Taken as a whole, nearly half the zone's residents live in poverty. The infant mortality rate is higher than in any of the world's 24 largest industrialized nations. Nearly 40 percent of the high school students in the zone drop out before graduating. So it should come as no surprise that within the zone, the federal pot of gold is pitting 33 cash-starved communities against each other. "We're having trouble," says Francis Brown, president of the Broadway East Community Association, "because some people take Empowerment Zone to mean 'power for me.'"

That problem has surfaced not only in Baltimore but in all of the other designated urban empowerment zones—Atlanta, Chicago, Detroit, New York and Philadelphia/Camden. In Atlanta, not long ago, one community activist stood up at a meeting and announced that since 30 neighborhoods were included in Atlanta's zone, the only equitable way to distribute the money was to give $3 million to each to spend at their discretion.

Most activists haven't been so brazen. But that's not to say the promised reward hasn't affected their judgment. "There are a lot of folks who I've never seen in my life or ministers from a church I've never heard of trying to tap into the money," says Vicki Evans. "People get nutty when there is money involved."

It's not hard to understand why, given the dearth of federal urban aid coming out of Washington these days. Urban Development Action Grants disappeared several years ago. Community Development Block Grants continue to shrink, and even in their heftier days, CDBG funds tended to be spread thinly across the urban landscape. Those neighborhoods fortunate enough to garner funding in recent years usually discovered to their dismay that it came with strings attached.

As the first major urban policy initiative in a generation with a neighborhoods-know-best approach, the EZ program is infinitely more appealing to community activists like Vicki Evans. But it is generating a whole array of new tensions, not only neighborhood-to-neighborhood but between the neighborhoods and the central city governments that are nervous about the entire process.

Of course, it's early in the game. Most of the zones are just gearing up to utilize the full force of the $100 million cash grant, the supplementary tax incentives, the assorted federal goodies and leveraged private-sector resources. But even at this juncture, if any conclusion can be drawn, it is this: The competition to win empowerment zone money pales in comparison to the competition to spend it.

"If this was just about handing over a $100 million check to the mayors and saying, 'Live it up,' that would be one thing," says Richard Cowden, executive director of the American Association of Enterprise Zones. "But the Clinton administration wanted to involve communities at the grass roots, and that makes for a much messier issue."

The messiness began well before the winning zones were even designated. It stems from each city's internal zone selection process—that is, the way in which each city chose the areas to be included in the zone. In order to qualify, cities had to design zones that met certain demographic requirements. Population was one. Poverty rates were another. Zone boundaries had to follow census tracts. That, in some places, led to houses and businesses on one side of a street being included within a zone, but those on the other side being left out. One section of Baltimore's Somerset Homes public housing complex, for example, was sited inside the zone, while another section fell just outside the boundaries and is thus technically ineligible for zone benefits.

Since by law only a certain percentage of a city's residents could be included within a zone, and since most cities applying for the funds had large numbers of impoverished residents, it soon became clear that not everyone with a legitimate claim would benefit from the program. In New York, that led to some sharp-elbowed jockeying for inclusion.

Initially, when then–Mayor David N. Dinkins approved New York's boundaries in 1993, the city's zone was anchored in upper Manhattan's Harlem section. But persistent lobbying efforts by Bronx officials — and the ascension of Rudolph Giuliani to the mayoralty in 1994 — led to a reevaluation. Giuliani preferred to expand the zone boundaries beyond Manhattan, not only to assuage the residents of other distressed boroughs that also met the federal qualification criteria but to ensure placement of Bronx-based Yankee Stadium in the zone. That way, any funds committed toward refurbishing the facility and its adjoining areas would count toward the zone's matching requirements for funding.

There was just one problem with that scenario. Since by law the New York zone could not have more than 200,000 residents, any additional Bronx turf had to come at the expense of Harlem. And the Harlem congressman who engineered passage of the empowerment zone legislation in the first place, U.S. Representative Charles B. Rangel, had no intention of seeing the zone he helped create populated with residents he did not represent. In the end, his view prevailed — roughly three-quarters of zone residents are his Harlem constituents. Although the stadium remained within the zone in the final plan, the South Bronx portion ended up consisting mainly of industrial areas.

In many cities, however, it is the role of City Hall that is generating the loudest bickering. In Detroit, neighborhood leaders chafed at Mayor Dennis Archer's broad authority to shape the 50-member governance board for that city's empowerment zone. Besides controlling two direct appointments, Archer also retained veto power over 44 other slots. Chicago Mayor Richard M. Daley was another who moved quickly to consolidate control, creating a centralized governance board that provides him with the authority to appoint 37 of the 39 members.

In Atlanta, Mayor Bill Campbell not only wrested authority to appoint most of his city's executive board but served as board chairman. As if that wasn't troubling enough to the neighborhoods that thought the zone would be theirs to control, Campbell announced his intention to direct $13 million in aid to the Atlanta Housing Authority. Given the AHA's reputation among neighborhood organizers as a pit of spending and fraud, the move came across as a direct and heavy-handed affront to those who were hoping the money would be reserved for community-based, nonprofit housing organizations. The board's six community representatives opposed the proposal, but they were vastly outnumbered on a 17-member board that included two city council members, the county manager, the city school superintendent and, not coincidentally, the executive director of the AHA.

"There was clearly a power struggle over who would drive this thing," says political scientist Michael Rich of Emory University, author of the 1993 book *Federal Policymaking and the Poor*. "The mayor has emerged as that person." As Rich points out,

the Atlanta tug-of-war over its empowerment zone merely continues a struggle
between city hall and the grassroots—in Atlanta as elsewhere—that dates back to the
War on Poverty of the mid–1960s.

The way activists in most of the six
EZ cities see things, the shadow of city hall
is spoiling what began as a bottom-up approach to neighborhood revitalization. In
their view, a strong executive role ensures
an institutional bias in spending the zone
money—that is, an inclination toward
business and city government-backed projects—while diluting the value of neighborhood decision making. Those criti-
cisms are not altogether unreasonable,
given the firm grip most mayors have tried
to retain over the zone purse strings.

But the mayors' reluctance to give free
reign over the federal funds is understandable. The last thing Archer, Daley,
Campbell or Giuliani wants is a rogue
quasi-government charged with doling out
$100 million in projects. All these mayors
are convinced that, whatever the mechanism of distribution might be, they are the
ones who will be held accountable if the
zone dollars are squandered.

So in Detroit, once a project is approved by the board, the money will flow
through the city planning and development department, subject to municipal
contracting requirements. In Chicago, the
city council will sign off on recommendations for spending, after the city planning
and development commissioner reviews
them. Atlanta simply created a new, hybrid
department, in addition to its board, to coordinate EZ spending.

To officials in those cities, such constraints seem logical. Indeed, in Atlanta,
they don't seem to have hurt: The first city
to set certain benchmarks required by the
feds, Atlanta also became the first to receive
a $32 million installment check. Still, at the
street level, the constraints look suspiciously
like the tentacles of old-fashioned power.

For all the rhetoric from Washington
about neighborhood empowerment, only
one mayor so far seems to be following
that directive to the letter: Baltimore's Kurt
Schmoke. With his city's strong tradition
of neighborhood involvement in urban
planning—and its largely successful experience with public-private partnerships—
Schmoke could afford to play the role of
behind-the-scenes convener, less interested in total authority over the dollars
than in taking advantage of the rich network of neighborhood groups and their
expertise. The city council then followed
his lead. "The $100 million in Baltimore
does not go through the mayor or the city
council here," says Michael Seipp, a veteran community organizer who directed
the city's application process. "It goes from
the feds to the state to the Empower Baltimore Management Corporation."

Schmoke had another incentive for
not playing the heavy: a tough reelection
campaign looming in the fall of 1995. The
last thing he wanted was scores of angry
activists motivated by fresh grievances. So
from the earliest stages of the planning
process, Schmoke signaled that the neighborhoods would hold the balance of
power, not city government. It enabled
him to trumpet the mere selection of the
zone as the centerpiece of his reelection
campaign. "The mayor was very clear
about governance and about wanting the
governance to be out of city hall and in a
private corporation," says Tim Armbruster,
president of the Baltimore Community
Foundation.

Yet even Baltimore is discovering that
it is virtually impossible to avoid disputes
when so much is at stake. When the time
came to determine the composition of the
politically crucial "village centers," which
are comprised of clusters of neighborhoods and will recommend projects to the
main governance board, neighborhoods
both big and small came out swinging.

Some of the larger neighborhoods felt they should be village centers all by themselves. Smaller ones objected to inclusion in village centers with larger ones. In East Baltimore, Vicki Evans showed up at one community meeting only to discover a plot to cut the Ashland Community Association out of a proposed village center. In West Baltimore, neighborhoods such as Penn North, Coppin Heights and Mondawmin were wary of being included with Sandtown-Winchester because they feared the larger and well-organized Sandtown-Winchester community would dominate the village center decisions. "In the beginning," concedes Joann Osborne, a West Baltimore resident who is president of the Carrollton Association and a member of the Empower Baltimore Management Corp., "it was every man for himself."

Without the specter of city government hovering over their shoulders, those disagreements proved easier to handle than in some of the other empowerment zone cities. But everyone involved in the program realizes that the neighborhood rivalries are merely under control — they could slip out of control at almost any moment. "When the money comes down, then it really starts as to just what we are going to do," says Broadway East's Francis Brown. "That's when the communities will be bumping heads."

Philadelphia has come the closest to emulating Baltimore's approach. Mayor Ed Rendell has not been as solicitous of the neighborhoods as Schmoke has, but Rendell too has avoided the appearance of heavy-handedness. Like Baltimore, Philadelphia made the conscious decision to address the issues of control and administration at an early stage. There is little centralized authority, just three "community trust boards" set up to govern the three non-contiguous sections of the zone. Just under half of each board's members are appointed by the mayor, with the rest elected by the communities themselves. Although there was some initial grumbling about the number of mayoral appointees, the noise quieted down after Rendell named prominent neighborhood clergymen to chair two of the three panels.

"We don't have a master body, governed by members about whom community activists would always be wondering, 'What does he have against my neighborhood?,'" says Dan Gunderson, the director of economic development for the Philadelphia zone.

Now that the zone boundaries are clear and the various governing boards are essentially in place, the thorniest issue of all still looms: what to spend the money on. Most of the six cities have yet to experience this controversy at full volume, largely because they have been preoccupied putting out other fires. Yet it is the defining question of the entire empowerment zone program.

To a large degree, the perception of whether EZs are successful or yet another squandered federal resource will depend on how much money is actually spent on creating sustainable economic development projects.

Everyone professes loyalty to the notion of job creation, but the means to achieve it are in dispute. Neighborhood-based activists are generally weighing in on the side of funds for human services to prepare people for the work force. The business community and mayors, on the other hand, are lobbying for business incentives that would provide actual jobs. The economic development component is of no small concern in the corporate boardrooms, considering the financial commitments businesses have made to some of the zones. Detroit alone secured commitments from automobile manufacturers totaling nearly $500 million. In return, the auto companies expect sustainable ventures that will last well beyond the five-to-10 year EZ existence.

"The fundamental issue we have to come to grips with is the relative emphasis on economic development, attempts to create jobs, and expanding existing employment opportunities against the understandable desire to do other kinds of community development activities," says the Baltimore Community Foundation's Tim Armbruster. "If at the end of five years the money is gone and it's spent on job training and substance abuse and all those kinds of things—however badly needed—then we will fail."

Mitchell Moss, director of the Center for Urban Research at New York University, argues that by those standards, New York's zone is already doomed. "Current plans for the zone," he wrote recently in the *City Journal*, "look like an enormous safety net for social services, not a launching pad for renewing the economic base of these low-income neighborhoods." He noted such proposals as a "Medicaid Entitlement Zone." Moss warned that "unless steps are taken soon to revise the New York City empowerment zone plan, the Clinton administration's principal initiative in New York City won't make a nickel's worth of lasting difference."

Mayors Archer, Campbell, Giuliani and Daley are keeping the zones on a short leash because of similar concerns. They emphasize that the zones are designed to address the economic factors that have caused poverty, as opposed to helping individuals who are in poverty. Substance abuse centers, literacy training and health and child care services do not exactly fit their economic development definition. And that puts them at odds with activists such as the Carrolton Association's Joann Osborne in Baltimore, who envisions spending dollars on a drug rehabilitation center in Sandtown-Winchester or keeping neighborhood schools open later in the evenings and weekends so children will have a safe place to spend time.

Neighborhood activists contend that those kinds of social services are not only vital to a community's health but to its ability to maintain a stable work force. Job creation and human services support are mutually reinforcing concepts, says Patrick Costigan, vice president of the Enterprise Foundation, a nonprofit that has financed low-income housing efforts in Sandtown-Winchester. "It's fair to say there's been a lot of discussion about the relative emphasis to be put on supportive services that are ostensibly linked to helping people get into the work force and actual job creation activities," he says, "but I think that it's a false division to say that it must be either one or the other."

In Baltimore this past summer, civic leaders spent two days at a retreat to allow various parties to air their differences on that very issue. "It was identified early on as a thing that would cause problems," says Mathias DeVito, chairman of Baltimore's empowerment zone board and the retired CEO of the Rouse Corp., a prominent urban commercial developer. "We came up with an agreement that any money spent on social services had to be tied to job readiness or job creation. Where we're at now is the tough part of taking social programs and deciding on whether the job connections are real."

One sparsely populated area within Baltimore's zone is itself an attempt to address some of those concerns. Based in south Baltimore's Fairfield section, an "ecological" industrial park is planned amidst a forest of refineries and chemical plants. The park would focus on attracting environmentally sound waste recovery industries.

An internodal transit center in West Philadelphia is another close approximation of what business interests and mayors would like to see the money spent on. The Parkside Development would renovate an abandoned railhouse and re-open a commuter rail stop that once serviced the neighborhood. The station would connect local residents with the job-rich suburbs, and the surrounding commercial development project would complement an existing industrial park by offering a new shopping center.

Nearly everybody recognizes that $100 million can cover a wide variety of large and small-scale projects, some pointed toward economic growth, others toward helping the needy. But it can't cover all the projects that people in the chosen neighborhoods will propose. Eventually, each dollar that goes to Ashland and Monument Street on Baltimore's East Side will begin to look like one less dollar for the West Side, and vice versa. And each dollar that goes to the Atlanta Housing Authority will seem to mean one fewer for those who don't live in public housing. "Balancing that act," says Joseph Reid of the Atlanta Empowerment Zone Corp., "is the most difficult thing of all."

29. BOSTON'S RESTORATION RENAISSANCE

Joe Albanese and Scott Martinelli

Boston is a city steeped in tradition. From the Old North Church to the Public Garden, history abounds. Some of Boston's oldest structures are historic commercial buildings that, despite their place in Boston's past, have suffered from years of neglect. A number of factors, including a suburban and office tower building boom in the 1980s and the economic downturn of the early 1990s, dissuaded owners from investing in maintaining or up-grading historic commercial buildings. In extreme cases, buildings stood empty for more than a decade.

In the last five years, however, times have changed. Many of Boston's older commercial buildings are finding new lives as 21st-century office and retail space. After years of inactivity, Boston's original skyscraper — the Custom House — recently was converted into timeshare condominiums. In the city's financial district, a 19th-century granite warehouse located at 163 State Street has been converted into an extended-stay hotel and the art deco Batterymarch Building has been transformed into a mixed-use facility housing retail and food services on the ground floor, a branch of Northeastern University on the podium floors, a mid-priced hotel on the upper floors.

The recent redevelopment of the Liberty Tree Building is one example of the far-reaching effects that renovated buildings can have on their surroundings. Erected in 1850 near the site of the Liberty Tree, a large elm tree that became a symbol of resistance to British rule prior to the Revolutionary War, the Liberty Tree Building has a long history as part of Boston's commercial and cultural landscape.

The Liberty Tree Building is located in what was once known as Boston's Garment District and later nicknamed the Combat Zone for the hordes of armed forces personnel who used to have their uniforms tailored at area shops. The Garment District thrived for most of the 20th century, but 30 years ago, when the city zoned the area for adult entertainment, the garment industry suffered. A few years later, when the local army and navy bases closed down, the Combat Zone hit rock bottom. Buildings such as the Liberty Tree were either converted into adult entertainment outlets or pool halls or left vacant.

Originally published as "Restoration Renaissance," Urban Land, Vol. 57, No. 12, December, 1998. Published by the Urban Land Institute, Washington, D.C. Reprinted with permission of the publisher.

For nearly 20 years the Combat Zone was one of Boston's most downtrodden areas.

In the early 1990s, the economy improved and the Combat Zone started to heal. Plans to close or tear down strip clubs were drafted. Drug use and prostitution began to drop off. And the Liberty Tree Building, vacant since 1988 except for a single adult video store on the first floor, was shopped around Boston by its owner, Kevin Fitzgerald, president of Liberty Tree Associates, as retail and commercial space. In June 1997, the Massachusetts Registry of Motor Vehicles agreed to locate its new Boston branch in the building, and the Liberty Tree reclaimed its lost stature. Reopened this past April after comprehensive renovations by Boston-based Shawmut Design and Construction, the building has renewed economic life in the area as both registry employees and visitors help to revitalize the Combat Zone.

What has sparked this recent trend? And how can a building left partially or completely vacant for years be converted into a modern facility?

The Liberty Tree redevelopment is the result of an ongoing trend in Boston and across the country not only to preserve historic buildings but also to find new uses for them. The force driving this movement is the strong real estate market. In Boston, for example, vacancy rates for commercial space are the lowest in the country and average rental rates for Class A space have soared to more than $40 per square foot.

"The current demand for and cost of renting office and retail space in Boston are very high," says Ira Baline, senior associate at Bergmeyer Associates, a Boston architecture and interior design firm. "Conditions are such that Boston owners are getting an average of $40 per square foot for newer Class A space and $20 to $30 for Class B space. Higher prospective rents help owners convert older, Class C buildings into functioning Class B buildings,"

he points out. "But the conditions that existed in a depressed marketplace made those conversions difficult to do. Today's strong market allows owners to find tenants willing to relocate into historic buildings and sign the long-term leases necessary to finance the extensive renovations they require."

While the strong market has enabled owners to view their historic buildings differently, why would a tenant such as the Massachusetts Registry of Motor Vehicles move into a building that requires thousands of dollars and months of renovation rather than move into or construct a few facility?

Desirability. An obvious advantage of historic buildings is that they already exist. Boston is an old city, and finding available buildable lots within the downtown commercial core is increasingly difficult. Ten years ago, migrating to an office park in the suburbs was an attractive option. Today, the philosophy has changed and the desire to be in downtown Boston has increased.

"In the past, public policy encouraged suburban development, but I think we are in the midst of a real turnaround," comments Stanley Smith, director of Historic Boston, Inc., an organization founded in 1960 to preserve Boston's historic buildings. "The hallmark of civilization has been to get people together, and cities like Boston do that," he says.

Not only are tenants trying to get into the city, they are trying to get into older buildings, whose historic charm they find more attractive than the prospect of redeveloping a site. "People are realizing more and more what historic buildings have to offer," observes Michael Cannizzo, an architect with the Boston Landmarks Commission (BLC). "Because of their unique details and characteristics, people want to work and shop in them."

Location. Boston's newer buildings

have a difficult time duplicating another attribute: location. "The three basic rules of real estate have always been location, location, location," says Fitzgerald. "Older buildings have it. New buildings have to create it."

Most older buildings in Boston are located on or near one of the city's four subway lines, an advantage to both retail and office tenants because customers have easy access to shops and employees have an alternative means of getting to work. Accessibility was one of the main reasons the state found the Liberty Tree Building so attractive — it sits directly above a subway station. Access to public transportation is a real benefit in any city, but especially in a city as congested as Boston, where the country's largest highway construction project is in progress.

Change in Philosophy. The new interest shown by both owners and tenants is accompanied by a recent change in the philosophy of Boston preservationists that has helped create new opportunities for adaptive uses. When the preservation movement first started, the goal was simply to preserve structures for the sake of preservation. That ideal has evolved into "preservation with a purpose": maintaining the building's historical character but finding a reuse option as well. This is a more realistic approach to preservation because there is a greater chance of attracting a tenant and because city governments are more likely to support or fund a project that promises to have a positive impact on the local economy.

Renovation Challenges

Changing the Boston business community's perceptions of historic buildings was a psychological challenge. The physical challenge comes when these often-dormant 19th-century landmarks are converted into functioning 21st-century office and retail spaces. From upgrading a building's internal mechanical and structural systems to preserving its external facade, there are countless issues associated with adapting buildings for new uses.

Interior Renovation versus Leasable Space. To attract a tenant, an owner must provide modern, amenity-filled spaces where small spaces once existed. Significant alterations are required to modernize a building's interior layout, mechanical systems, and exits. Recouping the capital necessary to finance renovations, however, requires that an owner first maximize the building's leasable space. The floor plates of historic buildings, especially of some of the smaller buildings in Boston, were not designed for 21st-century uses. Structural support columns and quirky layouts eat into rentable space. Installing new building systems can further reduce leasable space to the point that renovating no longer is cost effective, forcing the development team to devise plans for installations that maximize space.

In the Liberty Tree Building, a stairway leading from the lobby to the second floor was needed to alleviate the passenger load on the elevator system. The existing monumental stairway, located on top of a subway station entrance, did not meet current structural codes. Locating the stairway in another section of the building was not an option because it would take away too much space. The development team was forced to place a stairway in the existing location, without affecting the hundreds of people who enter the subway station daily. With careful planning, a portion of the subway entrance was removed and the new staircase was installed without compromising structural safety or interfering with foot traffic.

Increasing Space. Historic buildings often have large floor-to-ceiling heights, which can allow building of mezzanines.

"Mezzanines are a common way to add space within the existing footprint of a structure," says Baline. A mezzanine built on the fourth floor of the Liberty Tree Building added five percent, or 2,500 square feet, to the building's 45,000 square feet.

Surprises. While improving exits and upgrading mechanical systems are obvious renovations, there can be "surprises," issues stemming from years of unabated deterioration behind a building's walls. Most surprises are linked to the building's structure and stability, such as load-bearing walls and foundations. These issues cannot be completely determined in a preliminary, noninvasive exploration. Only after the demolition process has begun can the structural system be fully evaluated.

Unseen water damage is a typical surprise. For years, water leaked into the interior of the Liberty Tree Building, severely eroding wood and masonry joints and in many places causing steel to rust and expand, compromising the building's structural integrity.

Hazardous materials—asbestos, lead paint, contaminated soil—are another common surprise. Because records from 100 years ago are not as thorough as they are today, the presence of hazardous materials, such as asbestos, is rarely documented and can be a real obstacle if removal has not been scheduled. In addition, many materials considered toxic today were not known to be harmful when most historic buildings were built. The process is further complicated by new regulations governing the safe removal and disposal of these materials.

Preparing for surprises before a project gets underway is crucial to its success. "Extensive beforehand planning and drawing on the experience of the design/development team as to what to expect are the best ways to anticipate surprises," says Baline. In an empty building with few finishes, such as an old mill, preliminary examinations will reveal most structural problems.

But in urban buildings that have had many uses, the original structure will be more difficult to identify and assess.

To ensure that surprises do not delay the project schedule, the owner should set aside a contingency fund—ideally, a single fund instead of separate funds set aside by subcontractors. This helps keep costs down, since the owner can control disbursements. A thorough building exploration should be able to identify 80 to 90 percent of potential problems.

Exterior Renovations. The interior can have energy-efficient lighting, endless computer stations, and modern elevators, but the exterior must represent the building's past. "Identifying the important features of a building and how to preserve them are the keys to renovating the exterior," notes Cannizzo.

One way to accomplish this is to select a period in the building's history and restore the exterior to reflect that period. Although this is not an "authentic" restoration, it is an acceptable method of office building restoration for organizations such as the BLC. For an adaptive use, the goal is to work the essential historical characteristics into the plan as much as possible. "In an adaptive use, it's not necessary to restore the entire exterior to an exact date," says Cannizzo. "Restoring the quintessential elements of the building's character is what's important."

All of the work on the exterior of the Liberty Tree Building was performed in accordance with the BLC's preservation guidelines and the U.S. Department of the Interior's guidelines for rehabilitating historic buildings. The exterior was restored — using a matching brick that was difficult to obtain — primarily to a period in the late 1800s to early 1900s, when the building was a cornerstone of the Garment District. Essential elements, such as a plaque commemorating the location of the Liberty Tree that reads "Sons of Liberty 1766:

Independence of their Country, 1776," look today as they did 150 years ago.

Some sections of the Liberty Tree Building's exterior were not restored to the early 1900s. The existing roof was completely replaced with new slate and copper because the slate had exceeded its normal useful life of 100 years. The building's wood windows were modernized by replacing the existing single glazing with insulating glass that meets the requirements of the state's energy code.

Community Impact

For the owner, tenant, and team of architects and builders, bringing about the rebirth of a historic building is a great source of pride. But that is nothing compared with what a building can do for its neighborhood, in both economic and social terms. A renovated building can be a catalyst for change. Even in sections as undesirable as the Combat Zone once was, renovated buildings can spark an economic rebirth that in turn can positively affect the area's social makeup. The key is finding an initial tenant or tenants who have the vision to look past an area's present condition to its future potential. "It's a domino effect," explains Fitzgerald. "Getting the first tenants, and it's not easy, will get the ball rolling for the entire neighborhood."

With a foundation in place, it is just a matter of time before the area begins to reshape itself. Socially, buildings become a source of pride for residents and often result in the renovation of neighboring buildings as local owners try to keep pace; economically, the renovated buildings, whether office or retail space, will greatly increase foot traffic in the area. "Once more people start coming into the area, other tenants will want to be there," says Baline. "The market is where the people are."

FIGURE 1— HISTORIC CREDIT: SAMPLE SOURCES AND USES

Sources of Funds

Developer Equity	2,565,000
Tax-credit Investor Equity[1]	2,880,000
Mortgage	30,855,000
Total Sources	36,300,000

Uses of Funds

Acquisition	
Building	15,000,000
Land	5,000,000
Total acquisition	20,000,000
Rehabilitation	
Hard costs	15,000,000
Soft costs	1,000,000
Total rehabilitation[2]	16,000,000
Site Work	300,000
Total Uses	36,300,000

[1](20% historic credit × $16,000,000 rehab costs) × 90% equity investment.

[2]Credit-eligible expenses.

The Liberty Tree is one of the first buildings in the Combat Zone to undergo renovation. Along with the recently renovated China Trade Building and the Hayden Building — designed by renowned architect H. H. Richardson in 1875 and, after renovations by Shawmut Design and Construction in 1995, now home to the Penang Restaurant and a branch of the Liberty Bank — the Liberty Tree Building has had a substantial impact on the community as registry employees dine in local restaurants and registry visitors shop in nearby stores.

The renovation of these initial buildings has greatly increased the entire Combat Zone's viability. In the early 1990s, single-digit rental rates (per square foot) were common in the area. Now, as improvements are being made, average rates are in the high teens, allowing owners the opportunity to renovate many older commercial buildings. Nearby Lafayette Place recently was converted into new office space, and two other buildings were renovated for Emerson College — a dormitory and retail space on Boylston Street and a classroom facility on Tremont Street. Another building on Tremont Street now serves as a residence hall for Suffolk University. New construction also has become prevalent in the area, shown by the massive Millennium Place development, a residential, entertainment, and shopping complex that will open in 2000.

Once Boston's black eye, the Combat Zone is beginning to regain its historical prominence. The Massachusetts Registry of Motor Vehicles keeps the Combat Zone buzzing during the day while the Penang Restaurant has become one of Boston's most popular eateries, bringing in patrons seven nights a week. Emerson College and Suffolk University have ensured that the student consumer will be a permanent part of the area's landscape. And once complete, Millennium Place — which includes a Sony theater complex capable of seating 4,500 people, a 60,000-square-foot Reebok store, and an additional 60,000 square feet of retail space — will have a significant effect on the area.

"For the first time in 40 years, the streets around the Combat Zone will have an overwhelming retail theme that will again be attractive to shoppers," says Fitzgerald. "This is quite a turnaround."

30. CAMBRIDGE'S URBAN CIVIC SPACE

Terry J. Lassar

In 1634, Boston created what would become the nation's first large-scale urban civic space, the Boston Common. Now, 365 years later, another grand civic space, the Common at University Park, has been added to the cityscape. A common ground for neighborhood residents, university scientists, and office workers, the 1.3-acre park is the centerpiece of a new, mixed-use neighborhood developing next to the Massachusetts Institute of Technology (MIT) in Cambridge.

More than 25 years ago, MIT began acquiring land adjacent to its campus for the development of a corporate office research and development (R&D) park that would help accelerate the transfer of technology into the commercial marketplace. In 1983, MIT selected Cleveland-based Forest City Enterprises to develop University Park at MIT. Forest City also owns and operates the development under a long-term lease.

Unlike some suburban-style, corporate research facilities affiliated with universities, such as those at Stanford and Princeton, University Park at MIT is decidedly urban and urbane. The 27-acre corporate campus, located in the heart of Cambridge, is a lively, integrated community of offices, laboratories, restaurants, shops, a hotel, residences, and parks. The first office/R&D space opened in 1987 in a rehabilitated shoe factory. Two office buildings followed in 1989 and 1990, together with 142 loft-style residences in a renovated cookie bakery. Subsequent development was put on hold for nearly a decade until the economy strengthened. In 1998, an additional phase opened, including an office building, hotel, and retail services. A full-service supermarket, which had not been contemplated in the original master plan, also was included in this phase in response to community demand. Located on the second level of the hotel, the supermarket has its own street-level entry as well as direct access from the adjacent parking garage.

The latest development phase — 270,000 square feet of office/R&D space in twin buildings, a parking facility, and the landscaped 1.3-acre University Park Common — opened this past spring. The primary occupant is Millennium Pharmaceuticals Inc., a biotech company that relocated

Originally published as "On Common Ground," Urban Land, Vol. 58, No. 10, October, 1999. Published by the Urban Land Institute, Washington, D.C. Reprinted with permission of the publisher.

its headquarters to the research park. Cereon Genomics, LLC, a collaboration between Millennium and the Monsanto Company, also has established its headquarters there.

The Cambridge market has long been propelled by technology companies that are attracted to the area because of the presence of MIT and Harvard. Forest City's strategy for University Park was to develop buildings that would be sufficiently flexible to address the evolving needs of high-tech companies as they matured, while responding to fundamental shifts in the high-tech industry over time.

The first University Park buildings targeted the high-tech industries that had populated Cambridge for the past 30 years, such as defense, computer, and software firms. In the late 1980s, however, just as the park's buildings were delivered, the region's high-tech market sector, along with New England's overall real estate market, entered an economic tailspin. At the same time, though, a new technology-based industry — biotechnology — was emerging from university research laboratories and beginning to establish itself in the commercial sector. Many early-stage biotech companies require a decade to achieve significant revenues, let alone a profit, and the cost of tenant improvements, which typically ranges between $75 and $100 per square foot, is significantly higher than for traditional office space. Moreover, the city's supply of research laboratory space was severely constrained and unable to meet the needs of emerging biotech firms. Initially, the economic downturn left few developers and lenders favorably disposed to risking their capital to build for the biotech industry. It was in this uncertain environment that Forest City recognized an opportunity to serve a developing market niche.

The flexibility built into the structures at University Park — high floor-to-

ceiling heights, large ventilation shafts, and higher-than-average power capacity — was originally geared for high-tech users but also met the functional needs of the growing biotech sector. MIT scientists were involved in many of the startup companies and were attracted to University Park because of its proximity to the institute. The MIT "halo effect" helped draw other Cambridge-based biotech startup firms. As the number of firms grew over the years, some expanded into additional space at University Park.

By the late 1990s, the industry was beginning to mature, and some larger firms, such as Millennium Pharmaceuticals, which leased space in several buildings throughout the Cambridge area, were looking to consolidate. University Park was the logical choice for two reasons. First, Eric Lander, one of Millennium's founders, runs the genomics center at MIT's Whitehead Institute, and other company scientists also have close ties to MIT. Second, Millennium selected University Park for its new headquarters because no comparable facilities were located nearby. Although other universities in Boston have started developing biotech-related facilities, none is as extensive as University Park and none offers a similar academic campus environment.

Although Forest City did not start out to develop a biotech park, biotech firms now occupy 90 percent of the 700,000 square feet of the park's existing R&D space. "It was a marriage of need and opportunity," explains Peter Calkins, vice president for planning and project development with Forest City. "With an expanding biotech industry competing for a limited supply of suitable space, these value-added buildings generate attractive returns. At full build-out — within the next four to five years, according to Calkins — University Park will encompass 1.3 million square feet of office/R&D space, a 212-room hotel and executive center, 150,000 square feet of retail space and restaurants, 650 housing units, structured parking for more than 3,000 cars, and seven acres of parkland. The development is currently 50 percent completed.

University Park is built largely on blighted, unused industrial land in the Cambridge neighborhood. Located across the Charles River from Boston, Cambridge was once a thriving manufacturing district. As with many other communities in the northeastern United States, Cambridge's economy flagged after World War II when most of the city's blue-collar industrial base moved to the suburbs, leaving behind a jumble of derelict warehouses and neglected parking lots.

The city of Cambridge, after working for several years to spark developer interest in the vacant site, welcomed Forest City's mixed-use concept. In 1988, the city approved the master plan and passed the requisite zoning and design guidelines. In addition to the planned commercial space, the developers agreed to provide a minimum of 400 residential units, including a significant affordable housing component. Some of the affordable residences are located in the renovated F. A. Kennedy Steam Bakery, original home of the Fig Newton cookie. Additional affordable housing is included at Auburn Court, a family-style development on the neighborhood edge of University Park. A community-based nonprofit developer is building this residential phase under rights sublet from Forest City.

In addition to the special zoning district created for the development, the developer, the city of Cambridge, and MIT entered into a series of development agreements governing specific issues—including traffic generation and mitigation, housing obligations, and roadway improvements—that may be changed only by mutual consent of all three parties. University Park represented the first use of development agreements to augment the city's zoning process. The city's community development department views University Park as the new paradigm for large-scale development and will likely employ similar agreements for future projects.

Like many dense neighborhoods in mature urban centers, Cambridge has a scarcity of parks. The public voiced strong concern that large-scale developments such as University Park should provide plenty of green open spaces for the neighborhood. "Because we're in a dense, urban location," says Calkins, "our intent was to create a research park with its own identity that, over time, would knit into the adjacent neighborhood structure." In master plan for University Park, Koetter Kim & Associates, a Boston-based architecture firm, used a framework of street edges and axially related parks and open spaces to integrate the development into the surrounding community. The centerpiece of the interconnecting open-space system — and the heart and soul of the master plan — is the University Park Common. Located alongside Sidney Street, the main north/south thoroughfare, the common will eventually take the form of an outdoor room defined by eight different buildings.

As designated in the master plan, the central open space has always been envisioned as a common ground for both Cambridge residents and University Park office and scientific workers rather than as a corporate enclave, isolated from the neighborhood. The developers hired a Boston landscape architecture firm, the Halvorson Company, Inc., best known for its design of Post Office Square, a park built above a parking garage in Boston's financial district. Halvorson's office worked closely with community representatives on the common design. The community was concerned that the initial concept designs were overly formal, with too much paving and not enough lawn areas to support passive recreational uses. They also felt that the common appeared to be a frontyard to the private office buildings.

In response, the designers reconfigured the plan, minimizing the building entries and making room for a larger green open space at the park's center. To encourage active use of the common as a destination park, the landscape architects integrated attractions—including a ministage area that turns the central green space into an amphitheater—as well as enclosed nodes for picnicking and reading and, most important, an abundance of seating. Its large open spaces make the common an ideal setting for neighborhood festivals. A system of meandering pathways runs diagonally through the common, inviting residents in the adjacent Brookline Street neighborhood to stroll through the park on their way to work at MIT or to pick up groceries at the supermarket.

The Brookline Street community actively participated in developing the art program for the common. The first art phase, Traces of History—a series of plaques and three-dimensional sculptures—depicts the history of the University Park site. Once part of the Charles River, the site was filled to expand Cambridge's land area. A variety of industries operated on and around the area, including Simplex Wire and Cable, shoe factories, a book publishing firm, a bakery, candy makers, audio products, and a telescope manufacturer. The new industry at University Park focuses instead on producing various pharmaceuticals and biotech products such as replacement materials for bone and cartilage.

Also featured in the public art program and placed throughout the park are 18-inch square granite blocks with sandblasted letters and symbols of hydrogen, lithium, and other elements of the periodic table. Some are freestanding on the lawn; others are laid out in a row near the main entryways to the buildings.

As a focus of the second art phase, neighborhood representatives encouraged the landscape architects to design a fountain for the common. Because Boston's frigid winters make it difficult to operate a fountain year round, the team came up with the concept of a fog fountain, designed not to freeze. The system is powered by a compressor pump that boosts water through a hydraulic line under high pressure and forces water out of nozzles to produce fog.

A major challenge for Boston architects Tsoi/Kobus & Associates was to create a building design for the Millennium Pharmaceuticals buildings that was compatible with the adjacent residential neighborhood, located due west of the 45/75 Sidney Street buildings. Since each building is 70 feet high and 200 feet long, scale was an important issue. On the service side facing the residences, the architects articulated the building facade into smaller components to reduce the scale and visually minimize the large plane of the wall. Likewise, the loading bays were buried inside the building and designed to reduce the number of external overhead doors. Residential bay-style windows on the west ends of the buildings—facing the residential neighborhood—frame the courtyard between the two structures that lead into the common. Ornamental street lights, trees, and planters along the west street edge also helped humanize the scale.

Several traffic-calming devices protect the residential neighborhood from the increased flow of cars and trucks to the Millennium buildings. For example, a Woonerf-style road near the exit from the parking garage discourages vehicles from cutting through the Brookline Street neighborhood and instead channels traffic to Sidney Street. This curvilinear road, which resembles an oversized walkway, is large enough to accommodate emergency vehicles in compliance with the city's access requirement.

The skybridge connecting the two Millennium buildings was controversial. Initially, some members of the planning board maintained that the bridge disrupted an important cross axis in the master plan. They were also philosophically opposed to the idea of taking people off the street. The architects responded by designing the bridge as a ceremonial gateway that reinforces rather than disrupts connections to the adjacent residential neighborhood. In addition, the mullions and ornamental curved arch design strengthen the gateway concept.

Unlike the self-conscious presence of many corporate headquarters, the Millennium buildings are deliberately unassuming. "They were intended as background buildings to the common," says Carol Chiles, who headed the design team for Tsoi/Kobus. For this reason, the entry facades facing onto the common were designed asymmetrically with the entryways shifted to the side streets. The entryways—curved glass and metal atriums—project into the park to welcome employees and visitors arriving from the garage or side streets.

"In this business, where change is a constant," says Chiles, "flexibility is critical. Research projects change over time; funding expands and contracts. Labs must be designed with ultimate flexibility to respond to these changes." In particular, modular planning and standardization accommodate changing needs. "You don't want a lab bench that is designed so specifically for one research group that it can't be adapted later for a different group," she adds. The architects created a template for each floor and designated general zones for office or laboratory space. As Millennium's space needs change, "it will be more cost effective to convert office

to lab space, rather than the other way around, to avoid wasting expensive lab infrastructure," notes Chiles. In fact, some completed laboratories were substantially modified even before the first scientists moved into the buildings.

In addition to flexibility, Millennium wanted its new facilities "to encourage communication between the different research groups," comments Janet Bush, Millennium's vice president of finance. So the architects designed a number of informal break-out spaces that permit employees to meet for spontaneous brain-storming sessions. On every floor, 20-foot-long white writing boards are strategically placed near the coffee and snack kitchens. The groundfloor cafeteria, which features large glass windows facing the common, also serves as an off-hours meeting space.

The mixed-use development concept has been an important draw for many anchor tenants, including Millennium. "The central location and proximity of the hotel makes University Park attractive for recruiting purposes," says Bush. In addition, nearby public transit and on-site housing, along with such conveniences as the supermarket, daycare facilities, and restaurants, appeal to prospective employees, she adds.

In the next development phase, a market-rate apartment building rather than the originally planned R&D space will be constructed on the south end of the common. Forest City concluded that a residential building would better enhance the development's open space and encourage greater use of the park after business hours. Furthermore, the area's robust housing market, along with Cambridge's repeal of rent control three years ago, is prompting Forest City to build 246 additional residences beyond its original obligation of 400 units. Besides offering employees nearby living accommodations, a number of University Park companies lease apartments for use by out-of-town employees, consultants, and customers.

"It's rare that designers have the opportunity to work on such a large vacant site in a dense, older city like Cambridge," notes Boston landscape architect Robert Krieg of the Halvorson Company. "University Park, with its mix of residences, offices, laboratories, restaurants, shops, hotels, and parks, challenged us to create a whole new integrated community — a mini-village — within an existing city."

31. CHATTANOOGA'S INNER-CITY MALL

Richard Bailey

The city of Chattanooga's most recent urban revitalization project is not urban at all. After years of successful downtown redevelopment along the city's 200-acre riverfront and more recently in the 640-acre southern end of the central business district, Chattanooga has broadened its focus with a project to revitalize four square miles in the inner suburban ring anchored by the city's oldest suburban mall, long in decline.

When Eastgate Mall opened 35 years ago, it drew shoppers, stores, and economic vitality from downtown Chattanooga to the developing suburbs. Ten years ago, the cycle continued as the larger Hamilton Place mall opened several miles further out, drawing economic vitality away from Eastgate and the surrounding area. But last year, with a new mayor and a new mall owner, the fortunes of Eastgate's declining mall and surrounding suburb began to change. Now "urban" redevelopment is following in the aftermath of suburban sprawl.

Chattanooga's Mayor Jon Kinsey, a real estate developer before his election last March, described Brainerd, the area sur-

rounding the declining Eastgate Mall, as "an older suburb with the same concerns as most downtowns. We need to make sure that we do something about our core city," he stressed, "and Brainerd is clearly part of our core city." After taking office last April, Mayor Kinsey requested that the Chattanooga-Hamilton County Regional Planning Agency develop a plan to revitalize Brainerd. The following summer, the idea acquired reality and momentum when AT&T leased one of the mall's former anchor store sites for a call center and a new owner purchased the southern half of the mall where AT&T would be located.

By fall, a consulting team had been selected for a planning study to be managed by the regional planning agency but funded primarily by the stakeholder group the agency assembled. The winning proposal was submitted by Miami-based Dover, Kohl & Partners Town Planning. The new urbanist firm proposed creating a multidisciplinary team that included Walter Kulash, a principal of Glatting Jackson Kercher Anglin Lopez Reinhart in Orlando, to oversee traffic planning and economic planner Robert Gibbs of the Gibbs Planning Group,

Originally published as "Mall Over," Urban Land, Vol. 57, No. 7, July, 1998. Published by the Urban Land Institute, Washington, D.C. Reprinted with permission of the publisher.

based in Birmingham, Michigan, to handle retail planning. Private sector stakeholders funding 80 percent of the study included 40-percent-leased Eastgate Mall, fully leased Brainerd Village strip center next door, Osborne Office Park adjacent to the mall, and other businesses and banks in the area.

Designing in Public

In January, after preliminary field evaluation and market research, a public design charrette was held by the regional planning agency that drew 300 residents and business owners to help create a new vision for the mall and the surrounding area. The heart of the week-long process was a six-hour "designing in public" event in which 150 community members gathered in an empty storefront inside the mall and broke into groups to create separate plans for the area. Over the next few days, elements of these plans were evaluated and combined to form a composite draft plan that was presented at the end of the week to an audience of about 250. The high level of participation in the charrette and participants' positive emotions surrounding the failed mall surprised planners, local officials, and mall owners. The charrette also was unusual in other ways.

Victor Dover, of Dover, Kohl & Partners, noted that the plans created by 11 groups of "citizen planners" all had a pro-development theme. "They envisioned more development, building their way out of the problem instead of downsizing. That was interesting, because in some communities the reaction to development is much cooler. In many other places, folks have given up on the idea that development can make things better and have adopted a not-in-my-backyard (NIMBY) attitude," he said. "We really didn't see any of that here, which says that folks realize

this place has to be more like a town, rather than less like a town, to be successful."

Even more unusual was that expectations for what could be accomplished rose dramatically during the charrette, particularly for the new mall owner. According to Gibbs, "something very interesting happened at the charrette. The plan kept getting better and better and better in terms of design standards," he said. "I've never seen that before — when the planners started showing sketches, the developer got motivated and said things that made the planners raise the bar. The mayor said some things, and the standard kept rising higher and higher. It ended at a very sophisticated level."

Norie Harrower, who leads Eastgate Mall, LLC, the Hartford, Connecticut-based investment group that purchased half of the mall at the same time that AT&T became a tenant, approached the charrette process with considerable skepticism. "I tend to believe a lot of those things are exercises in futility," he said. "Everybody gets all excited, and the visionaries come into town and spin the wheel and then leave. Nothing happens—and it costs a lot of money."

Owning a mall was not on his mind when, acting as a real estate consultant, Harrower suggested Eastgate as a location for AT&T's new 65,000-square-foot call center. New York Life owned the southern half of the mall, which included the space he recommended to AT&T. But when Harrower proposed that, in return for a ten-year lease, New York Life pay for a $2 million renovation of the empty anchor store in which AT&T would be located, the insurance company would not consider investing in the property. Harrower ultimately assembled a group of investors and bought New York Life's share of the mall, primarily to help AT&T get the space it wanted but also because the price was so low that he could break even without bringing any new tenants other than AT&T to the mall.

When the mayor told the new mall owner that he was integral to the kind of comprehensive revitalization of Eastgate that the city had accomplished earlier downtown, Harrower was not enthusiastic. He had expected only to improve the mall property and sell it for a modest profit. But, at the urging of the mayor and other local officials, Harrower agreed to host the charrette in the mall.

"That was when I got hooked because all of a sudden I saw hundreds of people. I thought 20 or 30 irate citizens would show up and say, 'Tear the damn place down.' I saw some real articulate people coming in who cared. What I picked up on first was the emotion," he recalled. "And the mayor was there. I began to see that the city was really behind this process. It is important to a developer to have a city behind you," adds Harrower. "The citizens were behind it. They didn't want to tear it down. They actually wanted us to revive it. Of course, that was what we wanted to do."

A draft plan was presented in public at the end of the week-long charrette. Harrower had worked extensively with the consultants as they created the composite plan from designs proposed by the citizens. What he asked for in exchange, he says, was that "whatever we came up with had to be doable. It had to be achievable."

Over the next few weeks, the plan was polished and the realities of funding, traffic engineering, and the real estate market were considered. The plan did not change substantially from the January draft, but it gathered so much support from the city, the mall, and prospective tenants that the final public presentation in April — made soon after Harrower's group acquired the rest of the mall in a second transaction — included not only the finalized plan but also announcements of the first projects to implement the plan.

Connecting the Pieces

The new plan calls for creating a town center by turning the mall literally inside out and embedding it in a street grid with new office, retail, and residential construction. The mall's exterior will be refaced with new outward-facing storefronts in one- and two-story urbanistic designs. Much of the 50 acres of parking will be used for new housing, parks, civic buildings, and a town square. The plan also reshapes Brainerd Road, the pedestrian-hostile arterial street on which the mall fronts, which currently has seven lanes and no sidewalks.

One of the plan's most dramatic and symbolic recommendations will be the first to be implemented. Brainerd Town Square is intended to create a signature space for the revitalized district, what planner Dover calls "a center for the town center." The traditional town square will replace the main entrance to the mall — now simply a right turn past a small sign that is difficult to see from the road — with one acre of grass and trees in an unused parking area. Two- and three-story mixed-use retail and commercial buildings will surround the square on three sides.

Before the ink was dry on the new plan — indeed, before the consulting team had provided a final, written plan — construction on Brainerd Town Square was announced. At the final public presentation of the plan in April, Mayor Kinsey announced that the mall owners would donate one acre of parking for the town square and that he would ask the city council to provide $250,000 to build the public park. Mall owners revealed at the same time that construction would begin on three buildings along one side of the square. Retail space in two of the buildings already had been leased by a delicatessen and a dry cleaners.

Urbanism and Economics

Gibbs sees the planned conversion of Eastgate from a mall to part of a mixed-use town center as an example of a new category of shopping center — a hybrid of a main street and a mall — that is beginning to be built in significant numbers. "There is a huge movement right now in retailing to go back to main street. Today all the national chains are looking for space on main street. The shopping centers are learning from the cities."

For now, because these hybrid main streets or village shopping development remain less common, they command trade areas two to two and a half times the norm, said Gibbs. "We're at the very tip of that wave. Tenants are demanding that developers do it, and brokers are saying that it's not doable, that no one will shop there. But tenants and developers are ignoring them and they're being leased out." Under Gibbs's influence, rather than simply defining the highly visible and symbolic Brainerd Town Square as a green space surrounded by mixed-use buildings, the plan calls for five to seven stores totaling 15,000 to 20,000 square feet. This level of detail emerges from Gibbs's "void analysis" of potential retail development in and near the mall. Based on the number of households in the trade area, typical expenditure per household based on demographics, and current spending in stores within the trade area, Gibbs develops an estimate by retail category of spending that can be captured by new stores.

Gibbs notes that preliminary interviews with local brokers and developers were consistently negative about the area's ability to support any new development but that his research strongly contradicted those views. "We found a very viable market area. There is a solid neighborhood, a mature residential community, a lot of office space, excellent visibility, and vehicular access. All the elements you need for a good stew were there. The region had developed a bias against the area that was not true."

Even before redevelopment, there were bright spots. Although the mall had few tenants, some were very successful. A Gap Outlet store that predated the new owners is one of the chain's top performers, and a Goody's discount clothing store has been successful. Both stores face outward. Within several blocks of the mall, Chili's and Bennigan's restaurants, a Lexus dealership, Staples, and other businesses are doing well. According to Gibbs, "The money is here. The potential is here. A lot of businesses are doing well here. It just doesn't look like it."

The plan's overall retail mix recommends a "town center commercial" area around the new Brainerd Town Square and designates most of the northern half of the mall and some new buildings in the eastern parking lots as a "core retail" area, while most of the southern end of the mall is devoted to office, hotel, and recreational uses. Neighborhood retail and services will occupy most of the refaced western edge of the mall, on both north and south ends, as well as an area of new construction between the mall and Brainerd Road.

Connections Within the Town Center

The boldness of building a traditional town square next to a stereo-typical suburban strip-commercial street is matched by another dramatic feature of the plan: a new road that cuts the mall in half and connects it with existing residential and office development on either side and with a proposed greenway.

As it cuts through the mall, the new road will pass new outward-facing, neighborhood-oriented retail stores and a new hotel with an attached conference center built in a former anchor store. At the mall's western edge, the plan envisions a second green square surrounded on three sides by new residential development built in a former mall parking area next to existing postwar single-family housing. Immediately east of the mall building, in what is now parking, the road will pass through new office buildings that will include a proposed transit transfer center, then enter the existing Osborne Office Park. The plan proposes infill office buildings close to the new road to define a boulevard-like passage, encouraging pedestrian and vehicular traffic between the mall and office areas. Similar connections are proposed between the office park and adjacent strip commercial development along Brainerd Road. While the 100 percent-leased Brainerd Village currently turns it back to the Osborne Office Park, the town center plan proposes new pedestrian connections and a new road to pass through the back of the strip center and into the office park.

In addition to humanizing the pedestrian-hostile Brainerd Road arterial street, the plan is notable for what it does not do in terms of transportation planning. The study calls for no new highway access for the mall, despite local conventional wisdom about the necessity for new interstate access from nearby I–75 and I–24. "Eastgate is an example of the departure from allowing infrastructure, in this case a major interstate, to determine how a community grows and regrows," said Ann Coulter, executive director of the regional planning agency. "The community said, and the market and transportation analysis confirmed, that access to I–75 was neither necessary nor desirable for the success of the project."

What Happens Next?

With strong public input, a visionary plan has been created for the future town center that guides its physical design and economic development. Partnerships and working relationships have been established among local government officials, planners, and business owners. The first projects to implement the vision have been announced. If all the pieces fall into place, what happens now and over the next few years?

According to Kulash, "With real success it would look like a true town, no longer auto-dominated. The overriding impression would no longer be that of moving and storing automobiles, which it is now."

In five years "the mall will be a very profitable, highly active center with many strong national and local tenants" and potentially a complementary shopping destination for out-of-town visitors to Warehouse Row, believes Gibbs. This designer label outlet mall built downtown in 1989 in renovated turn-of-the-century warehouses attracts shoppers from as far away as Atlanta.

Harrower envisions "a mall that no one will really recognize here in another 12 months. In five years you'll see a vastly different terrain." He describes a scene with outdoor cafés, streets that have sidewalks and grassy medians, and acres of asphalt broken up with plantings and water features—a place built to human scale, "where people could spend the day and not be in a car."

Dover sees 100 years of sustained economic development and a beautiful, livable community, but he cautions that the vision is just the first step in a long transformation. "We can't predict everything that will happen. The vision should allow you to do anything at any size and know that your piece of it will fit the greater whole that we're attempting to build over time. A single property owner, a mall developer, or a subdivision developer can do that with great confidence because they control all of the land. But here, with a variety of property owners, small and large, the only common manager of the whole process is the community, the city. That's why the city is involved in the planning, because no one else is responsible for the big picture."

The task in this suburban area is the same one Chattanooga is addressing successfully in its downtown: restoring a lost center for the community. The pieces are there — community services, stores, offices, homes, and walking trails. Under the guidance of the new plan and its stakeholders, those pieces will be pulled together to create a vital town center.

32. CHICAGO'S ORGANIZATIONAL RESPONSE

David H. Roeder

In the middle of downtown Chicago, within sight of the city's famous Picasso sculpture, sits a civic embarrassment. It is a square block of vacant space that was to be the centerpiece of the North Loop redevelopment plan. All but one of the buildings on the site — including several that were historically or architecturally significant — were torn down four years ago and a glassy new office and commercial complex promised in their stead. Then the market for office space deflated, and last winter the site known ruefully to local planners as "Block 37" became a makeshift ice-skating rink. During the summer, tents have been erected there for high school students working on art projects.

Block 37 typifies the economic hangover in Chicago's central business district. Almost 40 percent of the downtown office space went up during the wild 1980s, when banks were eager to lend and city officials, dazzled by the promise of added tax revenues, welcomed almost any project. Today, with a 20 percent office vacancy rate in the region, some of the gleaming new towers are more than half-empty and downtown is pockmarked with vacant lots,

legacies of a time when developers received demolition permits before their projects had secured financial backing.

Just west of Block 37 is city hall and the office of Mayor Richard M. Daley. Recent months have been rough on "The Boss's son," who was first elected in 1989, 13 years after his legendary father, Richard J. Daley, died in office. The mayor spent much of his political capital last year seeking approval of two big projects: a new commercial airport at Lake Calumet on the far Southeast Side and a massive casino and entertainment center for an as-yet-undetermined site. Daley repeatedly said his motivation for seeking both projects was simple: "Jobs, jobs, jobs." In both cases, he could not win the necessary assent of state lawmakers.

Fighting Back

Early last year, in an effort to make city government more responsive to business needs, Daley merged his separate departments of planning and economic development and installed a new commissioner,

Originally published as "It's the Economy Stupid," Planning, Vol. 59, No. 4, April, 1993. Published by the American Planning Association, Chicago, Illinois. Reprinted with permission of the publisher.

Valerie Jarrett, to run the superagency. But there was little she could do as companies with a strong Chicago presence — Spiegel, Sears, United, USX, Ameritech, Amoco, American Can, R. R. Donnelly, IBM — one after the other announced plans to reduce or eliminate payrolls in the region.

Jarrett was embarrassed in the case of Spiegel when the catalog retailer, citing a need for more space, said it was pulling out of its inner-city location and moving to Ohio. The new planning and development department hurriedly found a parcel of vacant land on the Southeast Side that it thought would meet Spiegel's needs but, when the company checked it out, it found that some of the acreage was under several feet of water at the edge of Lake Calumet. Jarrett said the city could have drained the property quickly, but Spiegel officials were unconvinced.

In the last year, however, the department has made progress on the development of seven new industrial parks to answer manufacturers' demands for modern, secure space. Jarrett has also instituted a new program called SNAPP — for Strategic Neighborhood Action Pilot Program — that concentrates city resources on selected communities. The $8 million initiative fixes potholes, clears abandoned buildings, constructs housing, plants trees — anything deemed likely to spur private investment in depressed areas.

The consensus among planners and community activists is that Jarrett works hard and is accessible to neighborhood groups, but is hobbled by her boss, the mayor, who remains focused on the megaprojects. They argue that Daley hasn't grasped a reality of the current economy — that the city's economic salvation lies in supporting smaller enterprises in the neighborhoods.

This is, after all, the city that lives by Daniel Burnham's credo — "make no little plans." A century ago, that attitude led engineers to reverse the flow of the Chicago River, ensuring the quality of the Lake Michigan water supply. That spirit survives today in a recent proposal for a 125-story building that would be the world's tallest (and which would arise from a lot so skinny as to make it the world's first anorexic skyscraper).

The big projects are all right, says Ted Wysocki, executive director of the Chicago Association of Neighborhood Development Organizations, but they won't replace the 200,000 or so manufacturing jobs the area has lost in the last 20 years. Wysocki suggests that Chicago should change Burnham's words to "make a lot of little plans."

"The mayor needs to understand that each Chicago community has its own version of a megaproject," say Wysocki, whose organization embraces 65 neighborhood groups with concerns ranging from establishing day-care centers to finding occupants for abandoned factories.

Wim Wiewel, director of the Center for Urban Economic Development at the University of Illinois at Chicago, says he's been impressed by the commitment of Jarrett and her staff. "What seems to be lacking is clear strategic direction and purpose. Her department was out of the loop on the airport and the casino," he says. Indeed, both projects essentially were lobbying campaigns run directly from the mayor's office, although Jarrett insists that was appropriate and that her department would have become involved had either proposal advanced beyond the state legislature.

Both Daley and Jarrett sharply deny that the big projects have consumed planners' attention. "It's an ongoing fight to keep cities alive in America," Daley says. "It's not just one project or two projects." As evidence of his administration's concern for the neighborhoods, Daley points to efforts to clean up graffiti, revoke liquor licenses for nuisance taverns, and install bigger street signs at major intersections.

Such programs "are the nuts and bolts of the city. But, at the same time, you have to have some vision" for the future, Daley says. His motivation for creating an omnibus planning and development department was to improve communications with the neighborhoods, he says. "You can't have planning on the left hand and economic development on the right hand. Government is too divided," Daley says, adding that with the new system, he's "trying to coordinate things and tell people what's going on."

The "Commish"

For her part, Jarrett says the notion that city hall is biased toward megaprojects is "terribly unfair" and that there is no tension between her department and the mayor's office over priorities.

A 36-year-old attorney who has done some real estate work but has no background in planning, Jarrett at first worried neighborhood groups, who feared that the development part of her department would run roughshod over the planning part. It hasn't happened that way and Jarrett now jokes about the concern. "In this economy, we have plenty of time to plan," she says. During her watch, the department has issued long-term guidelines for industrial development on the North and West sides. She also has joined forces with the Chicago Park District and the Cook County Forest Preserve District to begin drafting an open space plan for the city, a program funded by a $400,000 grant from the Chicago Community Trust, a major local foundation.

In February, Jarrett and Daley announced a concentrated attack on blight in Kenwood-Oakland and Woodlawn, two impoverished South Side areas. With $1.2 million in seed money from the Chicago-based MacArthur Foundation, the city will draft a broad framework for redevelopment, including plans for 5,000 new housing units geared to various income levels. The hope is that banks and private investors will provide the capital to carry out the improvements. Jarrett says the project is promising because 70 percent of the land in those communities is vacant, with the city holding title to most of it.

She also hails it as an example of planning done in concert with local residents, including both the Woodlawn Organization and the Kenwood-Oakland Community Organization, whose executive director, Robert Lucas, says he believes Jarrett and Daley are sincere in their stated aim to upgrade the South Side without spawning gentrification.

Still, in Chicago, others invariably disagree. Robert Starks, a veteran activist in black politics, views the development scheme as "top-down planning" with racial overtones. "Daley does not trust African American citizens to make their own decisions," say Starks, who teaches political science and inner-city studies at Northeastern Illinois University.

Since taking over the department, Jarrett has reorganized the chain of command, consolidating sundry functions into eight divisions, including one offering "one-stop shopping" for businesses seeking license and permit information. She has also divided the city into seven planning districts, assigning staff to each. With an annual budget of $39 million, Jarrett asserts that the vast majority of her 240 employees work on neighborhood issues, as opposed to the central business district.

One controversial organizational change merged the commission on Chicago Landmarks, an independent city agency since its creation in 1967, with Jarrett's department. The new landmarks division is headed by deputy commissioner Charles Thurow (a former APA assistant research director). Preservationists criticized the merger, which saves the city about $100,000 a year. But Jarrett says the commission "functioned in a vacuum, without addressing owners' abilities to rehabilitate some of our landmark buildings."

Some outsiders contend that the department's reorganization has caused confusion. "Valerie Jarrett has high ideals but I think she needs at least a couple more years to make that department work," say Willie Lomax, leader of the Chicago Roseland Coalition for Community Control, which serves a neighborhood plagued by crime, joblessness, and abandoned housing. Another source familiar with the department says, "Morale is very poor and you've got people just bumping into each other all the time."

Daley's reshuffling of city hall did not stop with the planning unit. In early 1992, he changed the name of the public works department to transportation, adding some duties and subtracting others. Maintenance of the 90-year-old network of freight tunnels in the downtown area was transferred to another department, a decision Daley may have come to regret.

Last spring, contractors driving a pile into the Chicago River unknowingly breached a section of the mostly unused tunnels. By April, the hole was big enough to admit a torrent of river water, flooding the basements of numerous downtown buildings and prompting concern that the water would spread to the subway system. The ultimate damage was less than feared, although some buildings and businesses were out of commission for days. But in the aftermath, there were indications that, because of bureaucratic confusion, city officials had not responded quickly enough to early warnings of a leak.

Then in September, a span of the Michigan Avenue bridge, gateway to the city's showcase shopping district, snapped open during a reconstruction project and had to stay that way for several weeks while officials gauged the damage and the cause. The bottom line in both incidents was that little harm was done, although liability questions for the flood are unresolved. However, they made the once-vaunted City That Works look more like the City of Snafus.

Such problems aside, North Michigan Avenue exhibits a retail energy that is the envy of other central cities. Meanwhile, State Street is showing renewed vigor as a commercial and cultural nexus, with the city preparing to begin a $30 million "de-malling" project that will reopen the street to car traffic. Unemployment in the city is down to 8.4 percent, a sharp drop from the 10 percent of a year ago. The 1990 census revealed that housing prices in large sections of the city rose 150 percent during the 1980s.

The Bigger Picture

In the region, too, there are many signs that the Chicago area has been spared the worst of the national real estate bust. While housing prices on the East and West coasts have declined, values here consistently rise from year to year. New office parks continue to emerge on former farmland, although the 20 percent commercial vacancy rate in the suburbs is virtually identical to the city's figure. In most parts of the metro area, which now stretches past distant, independent cities such as Waukegan and Aurora, planning agencies are more concerned with managing growth than encouraging it.

On the negative side, each new demographic study confirms that Chicago not only has some of the nation's wealthiest suburbs, most to the north and west, but also some of the poorest, notably Ford Heights and Robbins to the south. For economic salvation, Robbins has seized upon a controversial plan to build an incinerator and collect fees from burning the trash of its more prosperous neighbors.

Throughout the metro area, the overriding issue is the efficient use of land, says Phillip D. Peters, AICP, executive director of the Northeastern Illinois Planning Commission, whose offices are in Chicago. Peters notes that in the last 20 years, the region's population rose only four percent, but the amount of land devoted to residential use increased by 46 percent. During that period, the population of Chicago and its close-in suburbs declined by 770,000, while the outer suburban ring gained a million people.

NIPC's priorities are reflected in the comprehensive plan for the region that it issued last year. It calls for preservation of open space, improved suburb-to-suburb transit, and greater coordination among local governments. This last task is made more difficult by the multiple layers of local government for which Illinois is notorious. In the metropolitan area, there are more than 1,400 agencies empowered to levy property taxes, ranging from cities and school districts to library boards and mosquito abatement districts.

Thus, municipalities fight each other to annex every piece of developable property. Some have had second thoughts about unchecked growth, however, and now are assessing impact fees on home builders within their boundaries. Peters says NIPC wants a state law that will ensure that the fees are shared by jurisdictions affected by a development, not just the host municipalities.

It's widely assumed that the booming suburbs have stolen jobs from the city, but state labor department statistics indicate that most of the manufacturing jobs Chicago lost either vanished or went to another state; the suburbs have had only a negligible increase in manufacturing employment since the 1970s. What is clear is that Chicago has a smaller share of the re-

gional jobs. It had about half the region's workers as late as 1980; today, the figure is under 40 percent.

Reason for Cheer

That trend is likely to continue but it may be deceptive, especially if a rising economic tide lifts everyone, suburb and the city. On this point, economists are sounding almost cheery. "Not having relied on the defense industry, we're not being pulled down by it," says Robert Dedrick, executive vice-president and chief economist for the Northern Trust Company. Dedrick points to recent upticks in the confidence levels of Chicago area purchasing managers.

John Skorburg, chief economist for the Chicagoland Chamber of Commerce, estimates the region gained 50,000 jobs in the last half of 1992, bringing the total of 3.35 million jobs even with the previous year. In contrast, Skorburg estimates that Los Angeles has a jobs deficit of 50,000 from a year ago and New York City 25,000. "It's a tough economy but our good transportation system and our central location has helped. Also, the labor force is good and highly trained," Skorburg says.

Most of the new jobs have been on the service side, and Skorburg acknowledges that the area's 500,000 blue-collar jobs are down about 200,000 from 20 years ago. But, he says, "the manufacturing that is still here is leaner and meaner and more high tech."

Diane Swonk, senior regional economist and vice-president of the First Chicago Corporation, assigns major importance to Chicago's role in the automotive and heavy machinery industries. She notes that when Caterpillar's 12,600 workers in Peoria were on strike last year, the effect on local suppliers was chilling. But now that's over and there is evidence that American car companies are staging a comeback. Ford's Taurus, which has won bragging rights as the best-selling car in the U.S., is built on the city's South Side.

Chicago's City of Big Shoulders reputation was based in part on industries that are severely diminished — meatpacking and steel production. The Union Stockyards closed in 1971. If the old industry has a modern equivalent, it's probably the city's four exchanges — the Board of Trade, the Mercantile Exchange, the Midwest Stock Exchange, and the Chicago Board Options Exchange — which regularly set records in their frenzied trading of stocks, bonds, futures contracts, and agricultural commodities. A 1986 study said the exchanges employ 33,000 people; that number is thought to have risen at least a third since then. To the world, Chicago sets the price of the pork belly even if it no longer slaughters the pig.

According to the U.S. Department of Labor, 187,000 steel-related jobs vanished from Chicago and neighboring Lake County, Indiana, from the late 1950s to the mid–1980s. Last April, the U.S. Steel South Works plant, which employed 20,000 people in its post–World War II heyday, closed for good, leaving unused 585 acres along the lakefront near the city's south end. The parcel would cover downtown if laid on top of it and its future use poses a grave challenge to its neighbors and city planners.

Convention City

In the meantime, industries that Carl Sandburg could not have envisioned when he ennobled his "stormy, husky, brawling city" in verse have taken up some of the slack. The Pullman plant was closed long ago, but Chicago remains a transportation hub, thanks to O'Hare International Airport's status as the world's busiest and to the city's popularity with conventions and

trade shows. While the coastal cities lost some convention business during the last recession, Chicago actually saw an increase of about 13 percent, according to the Chicago Convention and Tourism Bureau, and remains the country's number-one convention city, last year hosting more than 30,000 events. The bureau views the less-than-65-percent hotel occupancy rate as only a blip in the larger picture.

The city has taken steps to protect its flank in this crucial area. The prime exposition center, McCormick Place, is undergoing a nearly $1 billion expansion that will increase its space by about 80 percent. The same board of state and city appointees that controls McCormick Place also is proceeding with a renovation of Navy Pier that will bring shops, cultural attractions, and festivals to the underused space. The projects are being financed largely by taxes on hotel bills, car rentals, restaurant meals, and the like.

At this point, the plan for a new airport at Lake Calumet is going nowhere but Daley has exploited one victory from that imbroglio. In October 1990, he obtained congressional authority to levy a $3 charge on every passenger using O'Hare and Midway airports. The tax was to be a funding mechanism for the new airport; now the money is being applied to improvements at O'Hare and Midway Airport on the Southwest Side. Work at O'Hare includes construction of a new international terminal and a people mover to whisk passengers from one far-flung terminal to another. The work at both airports is under the direction of aviation commissioner David Mosena, AICP, formerly Daley's chief of staff and a onetime APA research director.

As for the likelihood of the mayor's megaprojects being revived, Daley himself sends mixed signals. At one point last year, he declared his Lake Calumet airport "dead, dead, dead." Yet, in interviews, he makes it clear that all he needs is a shift in political winds to start promoting it again. The project, which could cost anywhere from $5 billion to $25 billion, probably would spur about 50,000 new jobs. At 9,400 acres, it would be larger than O'Hare International Airport. However, the city itself counted 28 landfills or toxic waste dumps within the proposed site and about 50 businesses and thousands of residents would have to be relocated.

The mayor stopped lobbying for the Lake Calumet site last June when it failed to pass the Illinois Senate for lack of two Republican votes. The Republicans took control of the senate in last November's election, and their leader, new airport opponent James "Pate" Philip, became the senate president. The mayor says he can't do anything as long as Philip is in charge. Meanwhile, Republican Gov. James Edgar, who had originally sided with Daley on Lake Calumet, has shifted his airport endorsement to a rural site near Peotone, some 35 miles south of the Loop.

Prospects are also dim — but not dead — for the casino, which Daley and his supporters refer to as the "international theme park and casino." The $2 billion complex proposed by Hilton Hotels, Circus Circus, and Caesars World promised to net the city 38,000 jobs. The casino never came to a vote in the legislature, but Daley says, "It's still on the agenda. It's still there." In this case, the opposition comes from Edgar, who contends that a casino would hurt the state's racetrack industry and even its lottery, and would benefit organized crime. In addition, legislators from downstate districts regard a Chicago casino as a threat to their towns' riverboat gambling franchises.

In the last few months, Daley has turned his attention from the megaprojects to issues such as crime prevention (including his proposal to create cul-de-sacs in some neighborhoods). With a new Democratic administration in place and several Daley allies close to President Bill Clinton, the mayor also is looking to the federal government for aid, traveling to Washington with other big city mayors in February.

One area where Daley says help is needed is in environmental cleanup, particularly in connection with the South Works plant, where no one is sure what's left in the soil after more than 100 years of steel making. "We need greater flexibility in EPA rules if you're ever going to bring the land back to where people can go to work," Daley says. A bill pending in Congress would provide $300 million over three years for environmental cleanups. In Daley's view, its passage would signal a new concern with urban needs. "America has treated its cities like foreign governments," he says. "Great countries have to have great cities and America better believe in that."

Neighborhood Power

Greatness in Chicago still means the neighborhoods, from the sturdy bungalow belt to the rows of chic townhouses. On the community level, Chicago, proving ground for Saul Alinsky, is hyperorganized, a result perhaps of the days when city hall was machine-run and people needed to demonstrate strength to get a hearing. "Around Chicago, the joke is that when two people are mad about something, they form a community organization," says Martin Berg, an associate director of the Chicago Association of Neighborhood Development Organizations. Many of those organizations are pursuing their own "mega-projects." Some examples:

• In a North Side Hispanic community, local groups are taking over space in a commercial strip of tawdry liquor stores and starting a day-care center.

• A community group in the impoverished Englewood area on the South Side has convinced one of the city's largest developers to construct a mall along 63rd Street, a moribund commercial artery, and to pay for rebuilding a sorely needed firehouse nearby.

• On the West Side, the Argonne National Laboratory is providing job-training advice to Bethel New Life, an active group with interests ranging from housing development to loan packaging and recycling. Indeed, with a new, privately financed basketball and hockey arena being built and other industrial and residential projects ongoing, there's more happening on the West Side than there has been in years.

Also on the West Side, there are several construction projects on the campus of the University of Illinois at Chicago. Three other city universities—DePaul, Loyola, and the University of Chicago—also have major projects under way even while the overall construction market is taking a breather. Another institution, Northwestern Memorial Hospital, also has mustered the wherewithal for an expansion. Such projects say something about the current Chicago marketplace. Speculation is out, but you can still get something built if the use of the property is assured.

Yet speculation—on a large and small scale—has always played a major part in this city's development. Otherwise, the late novelist Nelson Algren could not have been moved to call Chicago a "city on the make." The phrase implies a robust machismo—building, tearing down, scheming, selling, sweating—all of which have done great things here. That tradition has also saddled the city with Block 37 and other failures of urban planning, such as a horrendous concentration of high-rise public housing.

Today, as Chicago joins other U.S. cities in a competition for global markets, it may be served best by leaders who can identify its core strengths and capitalize upon them. The day for making "many little plans" has dawned.

33. HARTFORD'S RIVERFRONT DEVELOPMENT

Steve Starger

You could talk about a long history of tobacco farming; the major transportation hub of Bradley International Airport in Windsor Locks; the jet engine manufacturing giant Pratt & Whitney in East Hartford; the towering financial, insurance and investment home offices in Hartford; the capital city's rich store of nationally recognized arts and cultural institutions; the suburban communities that have transformed Hartford County's diverse towns into class-driven enclaves; the few working farms that still exist here and there throughout the county.

And, perhaps the most significant feature of all, the Connecticut River, whose 400-plus miles meander through Hartford County on the way to Long Island Sound to the south. The river, a major navigable waterway that nourished the county's history and growth, gives Hartford its most visible symbol of vitality.

Assets ... and Challenges

In recent history, there have been seismic shifts in Hartford County: Steady migrations from the cities to the suburbs have created new, autonomous societies but have left depleted urban areas in their wake, in effect creating two separate and not so equal societies; the wrenching evolution from a manufacturing to a service-oriented economy has cost jobs and businesses but also has held the promise of new opportunities for those equipped to take advantage of them.

Hartford's plate currently is running over with an embarrassment of new development proposals and visions for revitalizing the city. The recent fever to remake and restore the city to a new version of its former glory has put Hartford into the public consciousness in much the same way that revitalized urban centers like Providence, Indianapolis and Baltimore have. Those cities may in fact be models for Hartford visionaries to consider, but Hartford has its own particular range of assets and challenges.

All of this development excitement has come out of an extended period of struggle by Hartford to salvage what many have seen as a dying city. Hartford has

Originally published as "Reinventing Downtown Hartford," CT Business, Vol. 1, No. 4, November/December, 1998. Published by Nolan Media, LLC, Cromwell, Connecticut. Reprinted with permission of the publisher.

absorbed a number of shocks in the wake of the region's socio-economic sea changes. The city has been plagued by financial downturns, a school system seen as racially segregated and bereft of resources, reigns of terror by warring gangs, and a steady drain of its population to the perceived safety of the suburbs.

Major Projects Proposed

For all of its problems, Hartford also has such advantages as a rich, multiethnic core population, a thriving arts and entertainment scene, long-established neighborhoods that feed into the downtown sector, and, of course, the invaluable resource of the Connecticut River.

Tallying the pluses and minuses, Hartford in 1998 — although more than three-and-a-half centuries old — remains a work in progress, which can bode well in terms of creating a high quality of life for its citizenry but can also offer a jolting rollercoaster ride.

Hartford is rebounding from its latest thrill ride, the crashing of the heady financial boom times of the 1980s. The last decade in Hartford, like Connecticut and the country at large, was marked by an almost insatiable lust for acquisition and expansion. Corporate mergers and dizzying deal-making created mega-banks and real estate empires that looked great on the surface but which all too soon collapsed like the proverbial house of cards.

From the stock market crash of 1987 on, the party atmosphere quickly turned noxious in the halls of power. Corporations that had expanded as if pumped with helium began to deflate, expelling assets and personnel. "Downsizing" became the favorite euphemism for job loss. The economic landscape resembled a village ravaged by vandals.

But out of that bleak scenario has sprung a series of development projects that, even if a small percentage reach completion, will have enormous impact on the entire city and will have the potential to restore Hartford to a vibrant center of life, culture and commerce.

Among the major proposals on the boards for Hartford are:

• Adriaen's Landing, a billion-dollar, multifaceted development complex that would encompass a good portion of downtown near to and linking with the river.

• Redevelopment of the old G. Fox and Co. site at 960 Main street as a multi-use facility anchored by the Shaboo Nite Club, a resurrected version of a former eastern Connecticut night club and concert hall that, in its heyday, was one of the East coast's major entertainment venues.

• Purchase and redevelopment of the Hartford Civic Center, a high-profile but problematic downtown mall and arena that has seen more downs then ups in recent times.

• A plan to develop the neighborhood around Trinity College as a cooperative effort between the college and neighborhood organizations, and initiatives to locate Capital Community-Technical College and a University of Connecticut training center in downtown areas.

• A $15 million city bond to renovate and expand the Hartford Public Library.

• A $30 million proposal to build a 950-seat theater addition to the Bushnell, one of Hartford's oldest performing arts centers.

• Six Pillars of Progress, a $300 million plan developed by **Gov. John G. Rowland** to help fund and generate funding for numerous economic, education, and cultural projects over the next decade.

• Various proposals to build new hotels, offices, residences throughout downtown to bring a core population back to the city.

Adriaen's Landing: Massive Plans

Proposed by **Robert W. Fiondella,** president, chairman and chief executive officer of Phoenix Home Life Mutual Insurance Co., Adriaen's Landing is, simply in terms of dollars, the most ambitious plan of the lot.

The plan, unveiled at a meeting of the Hartford City Council last May, includes a convention center and stadium; a 700-room convention hotel; a 14-screen movie complex; a Riverfront Discovery Center with aquarium, space station and history museum; affordable housing; and a network of shops, nightclubs and other recreational amenities.

Also planned is a riverfront pedestrian arcade that would provide walking access to the river, a multiuse sports complex and an intermodal transportation system featuring water, rail, pedestrian, vehicular and air traffic. An underground parking lot with more than 4,000 spaces is also proposed.

Promoters of Adriaen's Landing estimate that the project will generate 7,000 jobs and breathe considerable life to Hartford's economic doldrums. The big consideration, of course, is the price tag.

The current phase of the project involves seeking the needed $500 million in private funding and pursuing some $150 million in federal funding to cover environmental cleanup of the proposed site, housing and transportation costs. A feasibility study also must be done and the city must agree to donate the land, which encompasses the old Hartford Times building, owned by the city's pension committee.

At this point, work is continuing on developing architect's plans, raising the public portion of the funding, and generally drumming up support for the project among business people, community groups and developers, says **Jon Sandberg,** a spokesman for the project. Sandberg says he expects those efforts to continue into early next year.

The city has applied for environmental cleanup funds on behalf of Adriaen's Landing, and the project's leaders will also be talking about funding with the Capital City Economic Development Authority, the group that also controls the $15 million earmarked for the Civic Center makeover, Sandberg says.

Neighborhood organizations throughout the city "have been genuinely supportive" of Adriaen's Landing, Sandberg says, but added that they also have raised such concerns as traffic congestion and the possibilities for jobs and job training connected with the proposal.

For all of its glittering promise, Adriaen's Landing remains at this point a kind of shining vision on a hill, with some major questions and financial challenges yet to be addressed.

But, Sandberg says, "we're as anxious to get working as people are anxious to have us get working. There's a lot of work to do on a project this complex."

Linking the Resources

The short list that includes Adriaen's Landing and the other major development projects begins to boggle the mind. Add to them ongoing projects by Riverfront Recapture Inc. to link the city to its riverfront and to the riverfront of East Hartford, the continued redesigning of the I–84/91 interchange through Hartford to restore links to the city and some neighborhoods, and initiatives by local and regional arts and downtown councils, planning groups, think tanks and the Rowland administration, and Hartford appears to be a kind of giant Lego set looking for the right builders. That's preferable to being compared to a piece of Swiss cheese, as Hartford has in the recent past.

Why this sudden spurt of activity now?

"It was time, says **Rie Poirer,** a spokesperson for the Greater Hartford Growth Council, an economic development agency that serves the Greater Hartford region. The council created the MetroHartford Millennium Project, a coalition of area business leaders led by Pratt & Whitney President **Karl Krapek.**

"Over the past few years, there's been a cry for some kind of cohesive strategy" from business leaders in Hartford and surrounding towns, Poirer says. "We finally had the plan when we put together Millennium. It's really a broad mix of people, and it's the people who can get things done."

The group is charged with overseeing the "action agenda for the region," Poirer says. That means bringing the various downtown development plans into a cooperative situation to reach the resources they need to realize their proposals.

"The myriad activity is a happy problem," Poirer says. "Millennium's role is to provide synergy."

As an example, Poirer pointed to the group's receiving requests from developers who want to build housing downtown that would connect the downtown to the city's neighborhoods. "If the neighborhoods aren't connected, then we've failed," Poirer says.

One proposal to link the neighborhoods to downtown is the so-called "Circuit Line" route that would follow historic and architecturally significant sections of the city and ultimately tie together not only peripheral neighborhoods — such as Asylum Hill, North Meadows, Armory, and South Green — but many of the development proposals for downtown as well.

The Study

That idea was generated by a survey of downtown development activity by **Ken Greenberg,** a consultant with Urban Strategies Inc. of Toronto, Canada, who was hired by the Hartford Downtown Council under its Action Strategy Plan, developed with the Millennium Project.

Greenberg began his study last March and was expected to complete the task by the end of September, according to **Anthony M. Caruso,** executive director of the Hartford Downtown Council. Greenberg interviewed more than 400 organizations, businesses and individuals to "get a feel for what the situation is in Hartford," Caruso said. Greenberg also looked at the Hartford Civic Center and the concept of a new downtown convention center in the context of Adriaen's Landing.

In terms of the Civic Center, Greenberg had worked with LaSalle Partners, a real estate development company that had been given exclusive rights by Hartford city government and Aetna Inc. to propose development plans for the Civic Center mall. Aetna owns the mall. Fifteen million dollars in state funds were earmarked for the mall's renovation.

But uncertainty about how the money would be used resulted in the city and Aetna reopening the search for a developer. The city is rebidding the project, but LaSalle Partners could still be in the picture, Caruso said.

Despite the stalling of that project and the snail's pace on others, Caruso is optimistic about the downtown activity.

"I think we're on the brink of some significant development," he said. "Obviously, these kinds of projects don't happen immediately, but this is the first time in a long time that we're on track to bring a good portion of these projects to fruition over the long term."

The Importance of the River

Perhaps the most visible reclamation project in Hartford — short of the impossible-to-miss construction on the I–84/91 interchange — has been in the works for nearly 20 years: Riverfront Recapture's massive effort to reunite the river with the city. Driving through Hartford on the interstates, one can see real evidence of progress in the form of a walkway down to the riverfront on the Hartford side and continuing construction of a promenade to span the river and connect Hartford to the East Hartford side of the river.

Also planned with the walkway is a landscaped plaza over I–91, which will allow pedestrians to access the walkway to East Hartford. The walkway will be 18 feet wide and will be open to pedestrians, bikers and joggers, says **Joseph Marfuggi,** president and chief executive officer of Riverfront Recapture.

Other plans call for grassy terraces descending to the river from the plaza on the Hartford side, areas that could seat up to 2,000 people for performances and other special events. A bulkhead is also planned to be built along the river's edge to allow excursion boats and water taxis to operate from downtown, Marfuggi says. That construction is scheduled to be completed next summer, he adds.

Since the group was formed in 1981, Riverfront Recapture has raised about $42 million for design and construction, Marfuggi says. The organization was formed out of a public forum held at Hartford's Old State House in 1980 that focused on how the city could take advantage of its waterfront as other cities had done.

The river had been cut off first by flood-control dikes in the downtown area after the floods of 1936 and 1938. A flood-control system was installed in the 1940s that protected the river but also became a barrier between the city and the river,

Marfuggi says. The construction of the I–91/84 interchange "finished off the job and made the river inaccessible."

Since the early '80s, Riverfront Recapture has built a network of public parks and riverwalks in Hartford and East Hartford, "literally taking people by the hand and showing them how to use the river," Marfuggi says. The river has been the site of numerous activities, such as the annual July 4 celebration, which attracts thousands to the riverfront, and such nationally profiled events as a big-money bass tournament held this past summer.

Marfuggi says, "the river is becoming a destination for visitors from outside the region. We're showing that we can use the river as a magnet to attract people. That's a new kind of economic development."

Making Use of Existing Resources

All of these visionary proposals for turning Hartford's economic vitality around are certainly exciting in the abstract, but they're also a bit dizzying. It seems basic that to have any kind of successful urban center, you need to start with an existing population that supports itself and its neighborhood with its own resources.

Hartford evinces vitality through numerous merchants' associations scattered across the disparate sections of the city. Whether in the north, south, west, east or downtown areas, these organizations of local business people share a mission of addressing challenges by adopting a general mission to the specific needs of their communities.

To connect the merchants' organizations and help them take care of business, Hartford's Office of Economic Development contracts with about a dozen different merchants' associations throughout the city, groups that already exist as independent entities usually affiliated with non-profit organizations in their neighborhoods.

The city makes available $30,000 to each association from Community Development Block Grant funds, according to **Hector Torres,** Hartford's acting director of economic development. Typically, the money is used to hire a full- or part-time merchant coordinator who works directly with the associations on a near-daily basis.

How do such associations meld with the big development proposals saturating the city?

"The media are interested in the mega downtown projects," Torres says. "In reality, I've found that the majority of economic development in Hartford — and in most urban areas — with internal, existing businesses and the entrepreneurial activity that comes out of that."

But Torres also feels that the redevelopment picture is a good one for local businesses.

"These projects will certainly provide more life and more economic activity, not only for downtown, but for the neighborhoods," he says. "When you look at the entire picture, if we're able to generate economic activity downtown, that would certainly spill over into the businesses in the neighborhoods."

And, Torres notes, along with those developments come jobs. "If people in the neighborhoods can get jobs, they'll be spending some of their dollars at local businesses."

When all of the dust settles on the development frenzy in Hartford, the city will certainly be transformed. Exactly what the landscape will look like is still unclear. One thing is certain — to be successful, a transformed, economically vital Hartford must be conscious of all of its citizens and users, whether they live in Enfield, Avon, Manchester or within the city limits.

As the comedian Mort Sahl liked to observe: The future lies ahead. In Hartford and Hartford County, the glow seems to be brightening.

34. KANSAS CITY'S HOUSING INITIATIVES

Sharon Colley

The 18th and Vine area of Kansas City, Mo., was once the thriving heart of the city's black community. Over the years, however, the area fell into disrepair, and city officials began studying how best to bring it back. Their efforts led to the creation of the American Jazz Museum, the Hall of Fame for baseball's Negro Leagues and the renovation of the GEM Theater, which currently occupy the center of the revitalized neighborhood.

But Kansas City did not stop there. Reasoning that the city's revitalization efforts would be in vain without re-creating the area as a livable community, officials began focusing on housing. As a result, 204 mixed-rate apartments will be spread through seven buildings to help complete the task.

Nationwide, housing initiatives play an increasing role in urban revitalization. "Housing is an anchor for economic development," says Chandra Western, executive director for the National Community Development Association (NCDA), Washington, D.C. "For any new revitalization strategy, housing is as important as financing and job creation."

According to "Comprehensive Neighborhood Development," a publication of the National Association of Housing and Redevelopment Officials, Washington, D.C., attention to housing is an essential part of a revitalization program that addresses a distressed community as a whole. While some redevelopment programs focus on individual systems, such as jobs or education or crime, a more inclusive program is recommended by organizations such as NCDA and the Department of Housing and Urban Development, Washington, D.C.

Revitalization Combinations

The combinations of housing and other redevelopment components can take many forms, depending on local needs. New York's Storeworks program, a partnership between the city and Neighborhood Housing Services, a local nonprofit organization, renovate downstairs storefronts and between one and four upstairs residential units. "The streets [in the program] are economically viable but have one derelict building bring

Originally published as "Housing Opens Door to Redevelopment," American City & County, Vol. 115, No. 4, March, 2000. Published by Intertec Publishing Corp., Atlanta, Georgia. Reprinted with permission of the publisher.

them down," says Harriet Frank, director of the Homeownership Rehabilitation Program for New York's Department of Housing, Preservation and Development. The properties are sold at market rate to qualified applicants, with the city subsidizing the difference between total development costs and the market price. For example, a property that is worth $250,000 may cost $290,000 once the cost of gut renovations, transfer fees and environmental costs are added in; the city pays the difference. Residential space is ready for move-in at the time of purchase; commercial space is electrically wired and ready for development.

The key to the program's success is a Federal Housing Authority loan that allows participants to pay as little as three to five percent of the purchase price as a down payment, Frank says. (The standard down payment for commercial property would have priced out many potential buyers.) According to Joan Tally, project manager for Neighborhood Housing Services, approximately half of the property owners live in the residential portion of their buildings. Thirty-four properties were sold in the initial project cycle, which ended in 1998; more than 800 people have applied for the 48 properties now available.

Other communities, such as San Francisco, focus on a combination of housing and human services to revitalize distressed communities. "Housing is a prerequisite to neighborhood stabilization, but it is not alone sufficient to stabilize an area," says Pamela David, director of the San Francisco Mayor's Office of Community Development. The city combines support services, funded by both public and private sources and provided by local nonprofit organizations, to help meet the needs of its economically stressed communities.

Ongoing projects in San Francisco's Visitation Valley neighborhood illustrate the value of a diversified plan. A privately-owned housing community, with residents comprised largely of Section 8 certificate holders, had been taken over by HUD because of mismanagement. HUD temporarily relocated the residents, and the city transferred the property to nonprofit developers, who have imploded the two aging high-rises that made up the community.

Those buildings are being replaced with townhouse developments on three separately owned sites. Two of those properties will serve families; the other is a senior community. All three properties have child care facilities and community rooms. The result is that facilities are better equipped to meet the needs of the community they serve.

Affordable Housing

Many federal housing grants, such as tax-exempt bonds, require that a specific percentage of the constructed units be designated for affordable housing. (The definition of "affordable" varies, but Sanjay Jeer, senior research associate for the American Planning Association, Washington, D.C., says that researchers generally regard a family as part of the "affordable" category if its gross income is less than 70 percent of the region's median family income. However, agencies may differ dramatically on their definitions of affordable, depending on a region's economic cycle or the type of relief being offered.)

Urban revitalization programs are not typically driven by affordable housing initiatives, according to John Murphy, executive director of the National Association for County, Community and Economic Development, Washington, D.C. However, in New Jersey, the idea seems to work.

Over the last nine years, the state's capital, Trenton, has worked to change its urban landscape with the help of affordable housing and economic development initiatives. According to Rhonda Coe, director of the Division of Housing Production for Trenton, housing has been a focus of revitalization efforts because of overcrowding and Mayor Douglas Palmer's commitment to the issue.

The ongoing Canal Banks project, located a few miles from downtown, demonstrates how housing can promote economic development. There, the community's population earns less than 50 percent of the county median income.

In 1998, the city and local nonprofits began building or renovating 200 units in a Homeownership Zone within the Canal Banks neighborhood. The project is supported with a "hodge podge of civic, city and state funding," Coe says.

House prices will begin at affordable rates and, as the neighborhood rebounds, the prices will be raised to market value. (A percentage of the properties are being offered at the market rate from the beginning to encourage the creation of a mixed-rate community.)

The city hopes that, as Canal Banks' housing stock improves, so will the economic climate, Coe says. The local Head Start school-readiness program is planning to move its headquarters into the neighborhood; additionally, Trenton is conducting a study to determine the best use of the community's retail/commercial strip.

In other Trenton communities, economic development is preceding rather than following housing initiatives. However, both components eventually are present in the revitalized neighborhoods.

Like Trenton, many cities are using mixed-rate — rather than only affordable — housing to stabilize blighted neighborhoods. That is because local governments have learned painful lessons about how dedicating large areas to nondescript affordable housing can stigmatize neighborhoods.

In Kansas City revitalization projects, such as the one in the Jazz District, include both market rate and affordable housing components. The city's nearby Beacon Hill initiative will create 150 homes and 70 townhouses ranging in price from $90,000 to $200,000 in one of the city's more economically stressed communities. The project is funded by a $10 million Section 108 Loan Guarantee, a $1.25 million Brownfields Economic Development Initiative Grant, Fannie Mae and area banks.

As cities create mixed-rate communities that bring more affluent residents into the neighborhoods, there likely will be a population shift as some low-income residents find themselves less able to afford rents and necessities. That movement over time is a natural progression, according to Jeer; the challenge for cities, he says, is to maintain a stable proportion of affordable housing in comparison to the overall population.

Ensuring Commitment

In the last 10 years, cities have expanded their revitalization efforts to encompass the entire community, which includes housing and all the services that must accompany it. Western notes that cities must plan carefully when considering any plan with a housing component, adding that they must weigh the likely drain on city services such as transportation and police protection.

The support of residents, private investment and all public officials is also essential to the process since, without across-the-board support, the project may not achieve the momentum necessary for success.

Housing projects will continue to be a piece of the urban revitalization puzzle for the foreseeable future. And, while the use of housing will vary by city, combining it with other revitalization strategies seems likely to produce the most bang for the redevelopment buck.

35. LANCASTER'S URBAN STRUCTURES PROGRAM

Gary G. Hill

For years, city governments throughout the United States and Canada, to some extent, have been the mediator between the pro-growth and the no-growth communities, charged with the no-win task of trying to make both sides happy. Opponents of growth argue that it results in a negative change in the quality of life for current residents: new people bring new and costly problems to an established community. Current residents wonder who will pay for new growth. Will increased costs be spread out, thus increasing the cost to current residents? On the other side are newcomers who do not want to provide all of the financing to make up for any deficiencies in current infrastructure. As the government tries to find a balance between these two opposing groups, the conflict usually escalates.

The City of Lancaster, California, has found a solution to this conflict in its urban structure program. The conflict-resolution process for the City of Lancaster required almost two years and hundreds of hours of meetings with citizens, homeowner associations, developers, city staff,

and elected officials. Although reaching a consensus is not always easy, this process was very successful and culminated in a product that has the support of all sides.

The Challenge in Lancaster

The City of Lancaster, incorporated in 1977, is located in the Antelope Valley of Los Angeles County, approximately 60 miles north of metropolitan Los Angeles. In 1980, the city limits comprised approximately 37 square miles with a population of 47,882. During the 1980s, an intense period of building activity extended the urban areas of Lancaster to contain 94 square miles and 125,000 people.

This growth created the need for new and costly infrastructure expansions and increased levels of services. Moreover, several large projects approved for areas formerly restricted to rural use established a pattern of isolated development nodes located several miles from the city's urban core. The farther from the urban core new development locates, the greater the burden it

Originally published as "Paying for New Development: The Urban Structure Program of the City of Lancaster," Government Finance Review, *Vol. 13, No. 3, June, 1997. Published by the Government Finance Officers Association, Chicago, Illinois. Reprinted with permission of the publisher.*

places on the city's financial resources and ability to provide services; however, the fees Lancaster levied on new development were the same no matter where the development was located. Costs to the city for services that increase with distance from the urban core — like street and park maintenance and community safety — were not included in the fee structure at all. Since distance was not a factor in determining fees, developers located their projects away from the urban core where land costs were cheaper.

A secondary impact of this emerging urban sprawl land-use pattern was on city finances. The city imposed four impact fees on new development: streets, signalization, drainage/flood control, and park acquisition. These fees, however, were not sufficient to cover the full impact of new development upon the city budget, and the city faced an ever-widening fiscal deficit. It was therefore necessary for the city to develop a more equitable method of distributing the cost of providing expanded infrastructure and services to those who create the need for them.

Establishing Program Objectives

The city devised the urban structure program (USP) as a means of managing dispersed development and shifting the burden associated with infrastructure and service costs onto those who create the need. The goals, objectives, policies, and action programs that form the foundation of the USP were adopted as an integral part of the city's 20-year general plan in March 1992.

Fiscal Impact Objectives. The fiscal objectives of the USP as expressed in the general plan are presented in Figure 1. These objectives reflect the relationship between urban growth and the cost of capital improvements and public services, establishing the need for development impact

---

FIGURE 1— FISCAL OBJECTIVES OF LANCASTER'S URBAN STRUCTURE PLAN

1) New development shall construct and/or pay for new on-site capital improvements required by the project, consistent with performance criteria identified in the adopted service standards.

2) New development shall ensure all new off-site capital improvements required by the project are available, consistent with the performance criteria identified in the adopted service standards.

3) New development shall provide for public services consistent with the performance criteria identified in the adopted service standards.

4) New development shall not result in any long-term reduction in the level of public services provided to existing development.

5) New development shall not result in any substantial, short-term reduction in the level of public services provided to existing development.

6) New development shall not substantially increase the cost of public services provided to existing development.

7) The system used to recoup the costs of new development shall not be used to influence the rate of growth but shall promote the provision of services in an equitable manner.

---

fees. The estimated consolidated development impact fee was quantified with respect to the type and amount of infrastructure, facilities, and services needed to serve new development.

Service Level Objectives. One of the primary concerns of businesses and residents is the level of service offered by the city: Is water pressure adequate? Do the streets drain quickly? To ensure that infrastructure facilities adequately serve both present and future development, guidelines for urban service levels were established. These adopted service standards were based on local and regional standards and on state and federal statutes.

Urban Spatial Pattern Objectives. The general plan also identified the USP's objectives and policies that define the spatial pattern of new development for Lancaster. One objective is to encourage the location of new urban growth within or adjacent to identified urban nodes so that the provision of services to new development is not a burden to existing residents. Development patterns and growth should contribute to, rather than detract from, the city's net fiscal gains. Urban development not within or contiguous to an existing growth area should be designated as a self-sufficient community in which people live, work, shop, and play. Finally, the city encourages the planning and development of large-scale, mixed-use communities with integrated phasing and financing of infrastructure improvements, public facilities, and municipal services costs.

Establishing Impact Fees

The municipal cost impacts of new development can be divided into capital improvement costs and annual operating costs. The costs of capital improvements, which are composed of infrastructure and facility improvements, cover any physical improvement that requires a one-time, lump-sum expenditure to construct. Infrastructure improvements consist of primarily linear systems of roadways, sewers and storm drains, and related improvements. Facility improvements involve public facilities located at specific sites, including parks, the corporate yard, administrative offices, and related improvements.

Annual operating costs cover municipal budget expenditures for administration, public works, public safety, recreation, and related activities. These operating costs are divided broadly into maintenance costs and service costs. Maintenance costs

are related to the upkeep of capital improvements or facilities, while service costs are all other annual operating costs.

Lancaster directed its attention toward expanding the number of applicable impact fees in order to meet the objectives of the USP in accordance with statutory requirements and local limitations. Officials recognized that the USP would need to integrate both the new and existing impact fees into a unified model that could define, relate, and modify each impact fee in a consistent and comprehensive manner. To meet this objective, it was necessary to develop a model that would satisfy several criteria.

A modular system composed of individual impact fees that can be separately defined, modified, added, or deleted needed to be constructed. This required that each impact fee stand alone with separate nexus documentation and implementing ordinance and/or resolution. In this way, the model could be conceived of as a group of freestanding impact fees that work both individually and collectively to mitigate municipal cost impacts and achieve the desired urban structure.

The model needed to identify the three nexus relationships—burden, type, and cost—for each impact fee, as required by state law. The burden nexus establishes the share of municipal costs to be borne by new development. The type nexus establishes the allocation of qualified municipal costs to land uses. The cost nexus determines how the fees are to be assessed to new development projects.

Coordination among several elements was required. The fee must cover the facility and service standards identified in the city's general plan. Cost estimation factors must be linked to the city budget to ensure fees are based on current operations. Finally, growth trends/forecasts in the general plan must be considered, as they indicate future infrastructure needs and thus allow the new development's share of the costs of providing it to be calculated. This coordination ensures consistent sources of information and enables easy updates.

Finally, the calculated impact fees must reflect the increased cost of providing services and maintaining facilities at greater distances from the urban core. Based on these criteria, the city developed the model for the USP as a major implementation component of the general plan.

Computerized Calculations

The model is composed of many mathematical equations that are used to estimate the impacts of and derive the fees for each development proposal. Once the parameters and the fee-estimating equations were worked out, software was developed so that the model could run on the city's computer system. The model calculates impact fees for new development based upon the size, location, and land-use mix of each project. As detailed in Figure 2, three categories of impact fees are calculated: infrastructure, public facilities, and operations.

Infrastructure fees assess the new development project's need for streets, signalization, and flood/drainage capital improvements. Although sewer and water treatment currently are provided by the county, the model's architecture allows the city to assess fees if it assumes responsibility for these services in the future.

Facility fees pay for public facilities and buildings that will be required as a result of future population growth. These include park land acquisition and development, corporate yard expansion, and expansion of city administrative offices.

The operations impact fee represents the cost of distance-related city services, such as road maintenance, street sweeping, and community safety. A multiyear

multiplier that corresponds with the 20-year horizon of the general plan is applied so that future operating impacts are covered. As Figure 2 shows, the operations impact fee is the net of operating costs, which are based on the city's annual budget, less project-related revenues. Each operating cost element is multiplied by a surcharge for projects located at a greater distance from the municipal facility (service provider). The surcharge, which varies for each service/maintenance, is based upon the distance between the project and the pro-rata service range. The pro-rata service range represents the area surrounding the facility which can be serviced at or below current costs. Projects located beyond the pro-rata service range are assessed the distance surcharge to cover the increased costs for servicing the remote project. The greater the distance outside the pro-rata service range, the greater the amount of the operations impact fee.

Figure 3 provides an example of the results of model runs on two comparable projects, one located adjacent to the urban core and the other located approximately six miles from it. The model run indicates that the total impact fee per single family residential unit for the project located adjacent to the urban core is $6,541.72, while the fee for the project located six miles from the urban core is $10,796.76, approximately 65 percent greater. The higher amount is the result of the increased operations impact fee: the costs of service and maintenance for this project over the 20-year time frame of the model are higher than for the project adjacent to the urban core.

The Results

Although relatively new, the urban structure program is already producing positive results and is achieving the basic objectives for the program. It serves as a

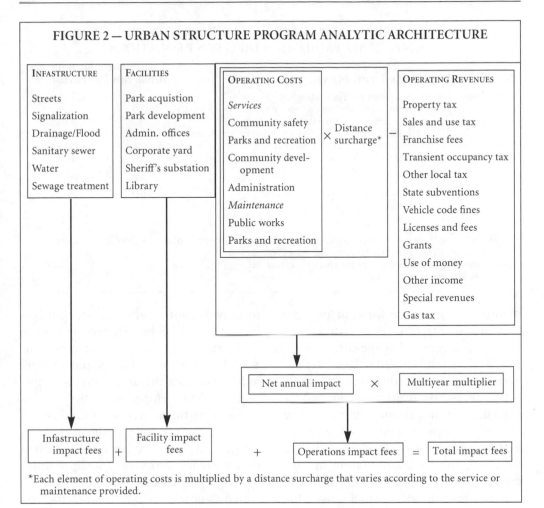

FIGURE 2 — URBAN STRUCTURE PROGRAM ANALYTIC ARCHITECTURE

*Each element of operating costs is multiplied by a distance surcharge that varies according to the service or maintenance provided.

flexible means to shape preferred urban development patterns with economic incentives and disincentives. The link between long-term spatial planning and development impact fees is established by the distance surcharge applied to projects far removed from the city's urban core. The comprehensive set of impact fees to pay for regional infrastructure, public facilities, and fiscal effects covers the 20-year time frame of the city's general plan. Although costs go on in perpetuity, 20 years is a generally accepted time frame in which goals can be achieved, results measured, and performance evaluated. Also, the fees fulfill the burden, type, and cost nexus required by state law.

The easy-to-use computerized fee estimation model includes annual update procedures, which keep fees current, accurate, and fair. The basis for fee estimation is tied to the city's annual budgetary process; this allows the operations fee to be modified to reflect current operations. For developers, the model provides a rapid, one-stop fee estimation process. The developer simply fills out an application and, in a matter of seconds, the model calculates the impact fees from the project. The USP provides developers a means to obtain an independent estimate for extraordinary projects. Developers with projects that include a variety of land use types, including sales tax-producing commercial uses and

**FIGURE 3 — IMPACT FEE COMPARISON BETWEEN
COMPARABLE PROJECTS IN DIFFERENT LOCATIONS**

Project: Single-family Residential Development*	Adjacent to urban core	Six miles east of urban core
Miles between project and nearest sherriff's substation	4.1	10.1
Miles between park operation center and park nearest to project[1]	2.3	8.3
Miles between project and nearest city corporate yard[1]	[4]4.5	10.3
Number of publicity maintained roadway line miles to be added by project[1]	5.94	17.69
Current assessed valuation of acreage within the project[3]	$2,122,416	$165,552
Average daily trip ends (ADTEs) to be generated by project[3]	1,680.8	1,680.8
Total impact fee per single family residential dwelling unit:	$6,541.72	$10,796.76

Notes:
*Projects differ only in terms of location; the number, size, and selling price of the dwelling units is the same.
[1]Affects operating costs and thus the operating impact fee.
[2]Affects operating revenues and thus the operating impact fee.
[3]Affects the infastructure impact fee.

industrial uses, may pay for a full fiscal impact analysis prepared by an independent economist contracted by the city.

The biggest benefit for Lancaster has been the significant reduction in the number of development proposals located far from the city's urban core. Lancaster is one of the fastest growing cities in California. Since the inception of the urban structure program, the city's population has increased by approximately 16 percent, yet minimal growth has occurred outside the urban core.

The USP represents an innovative approach for financing municipal costs induced by new development, for implementing municipal performance standards as identified in the city's general plan, and for integrating the annual budgetary process with the general plan and capital improvement program. Application of the program ensures the coordination of development activity with the provision of public services and facilities, achieves an equitable sharing of the cost of such facilities and services, and promotes the desired long-term spatial pattern for the city and its sphere of influence by discouraging leapfrog development patterns.

Unlike the more traditional approach to growth control of establishing urban limit lines, which restrict development to locations within defined boundaries, the USP does not prevent development from locating outside the urban core. It simply requires the developer to pay the full cost of infrastructure and services necessary to maintain the project over the life span of the general plan. The key is the inclusion of a distance surcharge. Since maintenance/service costs increase dramatically with distance from the urban core, the USP makes it more cost effective for developers to locate their projects closer to existing infrastructure and services.

Keys to Success

A key factor to Lancaster's success in instituting this type of fee structure was to involve the community in the process, obtaining buy-in from the key players. Several impact fee systems were presented to developers and building industry participants to obtain their input on which system would be most fair. In meetings with city officials, homeowner associations expressed their concerns and were assured that the USP would help maintain current infrastructure and service levels. In addition, government districts in the area (e.g., library and cemetery districts) were consulted to determine how new development affects them and how they could benefit from the USP. With the increased demand for citizen input on the operations and financing of city services, involving the citizenry in this way ensured that Lancaster could achieve its goals.

Although the USP was specifically developed for the City of Lancaster, its theory maintains broad applicability to all municipalities. The concepts could work well in a small or large jurisdiction. Integrating an urban structure program with the geographic information system would assist large cities with numerous and complex cost and revenue parameters. Regardless of a city's size, incorporating a distance surcharge into the impact fee structure helps discourage dispersed development patterns and provides a more equitable way of paying for infrastructure and services provided to new development.

36. LOS ANGELES' ENTERPRISE ZONES

Glenda Glover and J. Paul Brownridge

Enterprise zones are depressed areas, specifically designated as such by the state, and involve the application of tax incentives and regulatory relief to encourage private investment, redevelopment and economic well-being in these specific, geographic areas. The purpose of enterprise zones is to revitalize economically distressed areas and to increase employment opportunities, particularly for zone residents. The enterprise zone concept requires less government intervention by removing regulatory barriers which restrict market entry. Ideally, the private sector would be encouraged to locate in the zones, thereby generating income which would be used to revive the existing neighborhoods and create new jobs.

Currently, 35 states and the District of Columbia have enacted enterprise zone legislation and have established 3,172 enterprise zones. Within these zones, 11,658 firms are participating in the various state programs, have invested more than $40 billion and produced 663,885 new jobs.

The eligibility requirements for a geographic area to be selected as an enterprise zone vary from state to state, but an overwhelming number of states require high unemployment, low income levels, pervasive poverty and population decline as major eligibility criteria. Similarly, the states offer a variety of tax incentives to firms that are located in enterprise zones. The most frequently offered incentives include employer tax credit, sales or use tax credit, and property tax credit.

This research presents an analysis of the enterprise zone program in South Central Los Angeles and a determination as to whether enterprise zones, when used as an instrument of urban policy, represent viable incentives to encourage participation from the firms in the South Central Los Angeles area.

California Enterprise Zones

The California enterprise zone program was established in 1984 and amended in 1989. It established two concurrent programs: the Enterprise Zone Act, which was introduced by Assemblyman Pat Nylon,

Originally published as "Enterprise Zones as an Instrument of Urban Policy: A Review of the Zones in South Central Los Angeles," Government Finance Review, *Vol. 9, No. 3, June, 1993. Published by the Government Finance Officers Association, Chicago, Illinois. Reprinted with permission of the publisher.*

and the Employment and Economic Incentive Act, which was introduced by Assemblywoman Maine Waters. Of the 34 areas of the California enterprise zone program, 25 are enterprise zones (Nylon) and nine are incentive areas (Waters). California zones had created 7,041 jobs and $382 million in business investment by the end of 1990.

Both the Nylon and Waters programs offer incentives for companies that locate or expand in the enterprise zones or incentive areas. Some of the incentives included in the Nylon or Waters programs are as follows:

• tax credit for hiring unemployed individuals for at least three months or for hiring individuals enrolled in a job training program,
• tax credit equal to the amount of sales tax on purchases of manufacturing machinery,
• employee tax credit of five percent of wages earned up to $10,500,
• lender income tax deduction of interest income for loans to enterprise zone businesses,
• income deduction of 40 percent of real and personal property in the year purchased of up to $100,000 per year (Waters) or $10,000 per year (Nylon),
• a 15-year carryover of net operating losses applied against taxable income, and
• local fee waivers and other development incentives.

In addition to state tax credits and state assistant services, the City of Los Angeles also offers business assistance when applying for loans, additional support with building permits, job training linkages and management assistance.

Eligibility for enterprise zone or incentive area designation differs between the Nylon and Waters programs. To be eligible as a Nylon enterprise zone, an area must have a population of at least 1,000 and generally must meet the criteria for Urban Development Action Grant program for each census tract in the area. For the Waters incentive area program, the area's population must be at least 4,000 if within a metropolitan statistical area (MA) or 2,500 if non–MA and it must have unemployment and poverty rates of at least 150 percent of the national average.

Registration in Incentive Areas. Firms located in the incentive areas (Waters) must register to participate in the state enterprise zone program, and a determination must be made by the California Department of Commerce as to whether the firm meets the prerequisites for participation. To qualify for certification, a business must meet one of the following criteria:

• at least 50 percent of its employees are residents of high-density unemployment areas; or
• at least 30 percent of its employees are residents of high-density unemployment areas, and the business contributes to an approved community service program; or
• at least 30 percent of its owners are residents of high-density unemployment areas.

Only certified firms in the incentive areas can take advantage of the tax benefits offered by the state enterprise zone program. Another advantage of registering with the program is that a familiarity is developed with the zone managers which often facilitates problem solving aspects of the program.

Studying South Central L.A.

There are five zones in South Central Los Angeles, consisting of two enterprise zones—Central City and Pacioma—and three incentive areas—Eastside, Greater Watts and Wilmington/San Pedro.

The purpose of this study was to identify the factors related to business activity and employment in these zones, as well as the socioeconomic characteristics of businesses located in the enterprise zones.

Zone administrators provided data pertaining to the economic, social and demographic factors of the enterprise zone they administer. This information included the number of firms, designation date of the zone, new business investment, number of new jobs, new business licenses and zone population. Data received from the zone administrators for Central City and Pacioma included all firms located in the enterprise zones; while data received from the three incentive areas—Eastside, Greater Watts and Wilmington/San Pedro—are available only for those firms which have formally enrolled as participants in the incentive area program. Participation from firms in these three zones generally is higher than from the enterprise zones, which do not require registration.

Another set of data was obtained from the business firms. A list of firms within each of the five zones in South Central Los Angeles was obtained from the five zone administrators. A sample of 447 firms was then selected from the population of 4,015. During the months of November and December 1992, each firm was telephoned and questioned regarding the number of employees, revenue of the firm, investment in capital assets, and the types and amounts of credits taken by the firms. Of the firms contacted, 373 supplied data used in this analysis. Of the sample, 31 percent of the responses were from Central City, 10 percent were from Pacioma, 19 percent from Eastside, 22 percent from Greater Watts and 18 percent from Wilmington/San Pedro. Based on the informa-

tion from the zone administrators and the survey of businesses, profiles of the enterprise zones and incentive areas were compiled; these profiles are presented in Figure 1.

Businesses in the Zones

Figure 2 breaks down the data on the 373 firms of the sample by zone, type of firm, number of employees and sales volume. Figure 3 shows how the firms of the five zones took advantage in 1991 of the incentives offered through the Nolan and Waters programs. Thirty-seven percent of the firms surveyed in all five areas were actively participating in the enterprise zone or incentive area programs. It is important to note that, in the incentive areas of Eastside, Greater Watts and Wilmington/San Pedro, all of the firms surveyed are certified and registered with the incentive area program.

Enterprise Zones. Both Central City and Pacioma were designated as enterprise zones in 1986. Most of the firms in the two zones are involved in retail trade, have 10 or fewer employees, and earn between $500,000 and $2 million. Most of these firms were started between 1981 and 1990—59 percent in Central City and 50 percent in Pacioma. More than 85 percent of the firms surveyed in these zones do not take advantage of the credits offered by the enterprise zone program.

Incentive Areas. As in the enterprise zones of Central City and Pacioma, most of the firms in the incentive areas of Eastside, Greater Watts and Wilmington/San Pedro are retail with 10 or less employees. Most of the businesses in all three areas have sales between $100,000 and $500,000; however, while at least one-fifth of the firms in Eastside and Wilmington/San Pedro earn between $500,000 and $2 million, only eight percent of the Greater

FIGURE 1— PROFILES OF LOS ANGELES ENTERPRISE ZONES AND INCENTIVE AREAS

	Central City	Paciloma	Eastside	Greater Watts	Wilmington/ San Pedro
Designation date	1986	1986	1988	1986	1989
Number of firms	2400[1]	1200[1]	148[2]	143[2]	124[2]
Number of new jobs[1] (from 1987–1990)	220	212	157	159	89
New business licenses	863	683	786	756	206
Films using credits	43	19	*	12	*
Credits taken	$326,767	$196,940	*	$80,779	*

*Information not available.

[1]Includes all films located in the enterprise zone.

[2]Includes only films which are registered in the incentive area program.

FIGURE 2 — PROFILES OF 373 FIRMS IN LOS ANGELES ENTERPRISE ZONES AND INCENTIVE AREAS

	Central City	Pacioma	Eastside	Greater Watts	Wilmington/ San Pedro	All Zones and Areas Total
Number of Respondent Firms	116	37	71	82	67	373
Type of Firm						
Retail	49%	42%	46%	52%	41%	47%
Personal/Business	13	17	13	15	14	14
Engineering	8	6	8	11	18	11
Food	15	8	29	22	16	18
Manufacturing	10	8	2		11	7
Other	5	19	2			3
No. of Employees						
1–10	77%	83%	89%	85%	78%	72%
More than 10	23	17	11	15	22	28
Sales volume						
Less than $100,000	20%	27%	19%	31%	25%	20%
100,001–500,000	27	19	38	40	43	27
500,001–2,000,000	32	36	29	8	20	32
2,000,001–10,000,000	18	18	13	18	7	18
More than $10,000,000	3		1	3	5	3

Watts businesses have sales in that range. The majority of the businesses were started between 1981 and 1990.

It is clear that, while some differences exist between the enterprise zones and the incentive areas, businesses in the two pro-grams are fairly homogeneous in terms of type, size and sales. Significant differences, however, occur in terms of utilization of incentives. While barely 10 percent of the firms in the enterprise zones use the tax incentives available to them, between 38

FIGURE 3 — SUMMARY OF CREDITS TAKEN BY 373 FIRMS IN
LOS ANGELES ENTERPRISE ZONES AND INCENTIVE AREAS

	Central City	Pacioma	Eastside	Greater Watts	Wilmington/ San Pedro	All Zones and Areas Total
Number of Respondent Firms	116	37	71	82	67	373
Percent of firms using credits	12%	9%	45%	38%	54%	37%
Amount of credits in 1991	$8,851	$5,358	$13,385	$4,211	$7,895	$39,700
Sales/use tax-%	40%	43%	25%	30%	31%	36%
Sales/use tax-$	$4,166	$2,565	$5,252	$1,561	$2,562	$16,104
Hiring credit-%	38%	34%	38%	55%	47%	42%
Hiring credit-$	$3,885	$2,118	$6,885	$2,650	$3,858	$19,396
Property ded-%	6%	10%	8%	–	18%	12%
Property ded-$	$800	$675	$1,250	–	$1,475	$4,200

and 54 percent of the firms in the three incentive areas take advantage of the credits (see Figure 3).

Conclusion

This study focused on firms operating in designated enterprise zones and incentive areas of South Central Los Angeles and the extent to which they are taking advantage of the incentives available to them through the enterprise zone and incentive area programs. The firms in the three incentive areas showed higher participation rates than those in the areas classified as enterprise zones. This is attributed to the fact that, in the three incentive areas, firms must register before they can participate; therefore, zone administrators work with a smaller number of firms and usually can have more successful marketing efforts. In the two enterprise zone areas, no registration is required. Zone administrators keep track of all firms located in the zone and must extend greater efforts to record the activities of the various firms.

Thirty-seven percent of 373 enterprise zone and incentive area firms responding to the author's survey were participating in the enterprise zone program. Participation rates ranged from nine percent for Pacioma firms to 54 percent in Wilmington/San Pedro. In 1991, 42 percent of the firms took advantage of the employer hiring credits, 36 percent used the sale/use tax deduction and 12 percent used the enterprise zone property tax deduction. These data represent only about 9.3 percent of the 4,015 firms located in the zones.

The authors conclude that enterprise zones and incentive areas have contributed to business development and have created new jobs in South Central Los Angeles; but the areas designated as enterprise zones need continuous attention, increased funding and a complementary federal enterprise zone bill to achieve the level of revitalization needed in South Central Los Angeles.

37. MEMPHIS' RESIDENTIAL REVITALIZATION

Ellen Perlman

From the chrome and vinyl bar stools upstairs at Ernestine & Hazel's, an old brothel-turned-singles bar in downtown Memphis, Phil Woodard can look out across the street and contemplate the Hotel Grand, a red-brick railroad hotel at 508 South Main Street. The building was constructed in 1913 and ruined by fire during the riots that followed the 1968 assassination of Dr. Martin Luther King Jr., which happened just a few blocks away.

The Grand is open again, if anything a little grander than in its working-class hey-day. But it isn't a hotel. Woodard owns it now, and he has turned it into an artist's studio on the ground floor, and two-bedroom apartments above. They rent for as much as $1,400 a month, a pretty steep price for the Bluff City, but all the units are occupied. Woodard kept the sunny top-floor loft for himself.

Across the street, Woodard has just about finished renovating his second building, an old brake-shoe warehouse at 509 South Main. It, too, contains apartments and a street-level artist's studio. Meanwhile, he's purchased a third building, down the block at 505, and he's getting ready to renovate that.

Unlikely as it may seem to many who know the city, South Main in Memphis is a hot residential district. Drab and nearly empty for years after King was killed at the nearby Lorraine Motel, it reverberates every day now with hammering and drilling and the sound of the refurbished trolley cars that run down the middle of the street.

But it's not just South Main. Housing is hot in other parts of downtown Memphis—in the central business district, on the bluff overlooking the Mississippi River, and on Mud Island, which sits in the river just a few minutes away by bridge. "Everything's being worked on," says Woodard. "All of a sudden there's a renaissance." Edmund Armentrout, president of the Center City Commission, a local development group, estimates that downtown Memphis could add 1,000 new residents a year for the foreseeable future.

All of this needs to be put in perspective. There are 1.2 million people in the Memphis metropolitan area, and only about 6,300 live downtown in market-rate housing. Even if the market stays hot for the next decade, it's hard to imagine downtown becoming home to more than a tiny fraction of the residents of the region. But

Originally published as "Downtown: The Live-In Solution," Governing, Vol. 11, No. 9, June, 1998. Published by Congressional Quarterly, Inc., Washington, D.C. Reprinted with permission of the publisher.

that fraction might be sufficient to guarantee downtown Memphis a bright future,
as a safe and lively community with enough
people in residence to attract a diverse
commercial sector interested in serving
them.

Other cities are coming to just the
same conclusion. It has been an article of
faith among urbanists for more than a
decade that a true downtown revival requires a healthy residential component.
But only recently have local governments
begun taking it to heart, and acting on it.
"Downtowns until the last five years were
either housing for the very rich or the very
poor," says Betsy Jackson, president of the
International Downtown Association.
"What's happening now is filling in the
gap. I don't know how it can't be good."

"I've been in the downtown redevelopment business for 15 years," says Jim
Norton, who heads a group called Downtown Tulsa Unlimited. "Unless you have
people living here, the process doesn't
work. When people go home at night,
when downtown closes up at night, it
doesn't create a very viable central business district."

The revival is being stimulated not
only by New Urbanist ideas but also, as in
Memphis, by a surprising demand for almost anything in decent condition. "I have
not run into a constituent involved in
housing that doesn't see more demand
than supply," says Jackson.

The trend does not appear to be regional, and it doesn't seem to be a matter
of size or history. The downtown population is growing in places that have always
had significant central-city housing, such
as Philadelphia, and in places such as Denver, where there is no such tradition, but
where the number of downtown residents
is at 4,000 and growing fast. It is happening in larger cities such as Atlanta, where
there are now 5,000 units of market-rate
housing downtown; in Dallas, which has

10,750; and in smaller communities such
as Richmond, Virginia, which is up to
2,500.

Nor is the phenomenon limited to a
particular style or economic niche. Downtown housing is going up in the affordable
and luxury categories, for rent and for purchase. Developers are working on high-rise
apartment buildings, townhouse developments, loft conversions, units above stores,
condos and restored mansions. "They can
build any housing," says Betsy Jackson,
"and have a waiting list."

And developers are showing interest
in sites that at first glance look rather un-
promising. A generation ago in Milwaukee, three legs of an elevated expressway
loop were built around that city's central
business district. The point was to move
people downtown for work in the morning
and speed them out of town at night toward suburban homes. The last leg, a lakefront expressway proposed in 1958, was
never built.

But the land for that last segment was
cleared of buildings, and after being vacant for many years, it has recently sprouted
new townhouses and apartments. Now the
city is hoping to tear down other portions
of the freeway with the intention of attracting more residential development on
the land underneath, which is currently
used for parking lots. "It would add enormous value to downtown Milwaukee,"
says Mayor John O. Norquist.

More frequently, however, the downtown housing revival does not depend on
new construction, but on finding new uses
for buildings that have lost their traditional
function. Nearly every big city has a large
stock of office buildings, built in the 1920s
or earlier, that no longer can attract commercial tenants. Most companies want large,
square floor spaces where they can put
many employees together. Older buildings
tend to offer funky, oddly shaped smaller
spaces. Perhaps more important, retrofitting

these buildings for present-day office use involves wiring and garage construction whose costs are prohibitive. Remodeling them as apartments—even luxury apartments—is much more practical.

Tulsa has started to take advantage of its abandoned office buildings to create downtown housing for the first time in nearly three decades. One of the first projects is the *Tribune* building, which used to house the offices of the daily newspaper and is listed on the National Register of Historic Places. It will be turned into 33 lofts. The plans await final approval from the state, but there are already 15 names on a waiting list. Meanwhile, developers have broken ground on a 159-unit apartment complex on a vacant downtown site nearby.

In Baltimore's loft district, a stone's throw from the Camden Yards baseball stadium, buildings that once held manufacturers of shoes, sleepwear, straw hats and sailcloth were turned into residences several years ago. Now the city has ambitious plans for a dozen more such projects.

All along Charles Street, one of the major north-south streets running through the center of Baltimore, are venerable buildings whose only practical future appears to be in residential conversion. Last year, the city created a downtown housing council that provides property tax relief, established a loan fund and created the position of downtown housing coordinator, whose job it is to walk developers, investors and lenders through the development process. Meanwhile, the state has increased a tax credit and created new financial incentives to build downtown housing.

After Mayor Kurt L. Schmoke announced the city housing initiative last June, 12 redevelopment projects got under way, even before the downtown partnership could knock on doors to promote it. Developers are about to begin work on the Abell Building, a six-story Victorian Gothic

on South Eutaw Street, built in 1870. Others are attracting similar interest, among them the Women's Industrial Exchange Building and the former YMCA, built in 1890.

Where the downtown housing comeback is strongest, local government is usually involved in a significant way. Memphis, through its Center City Revenue Finance Corp., offers developers tax abatements for 10 to 25 years, depending on the project. Its Center City Development Corp. also offers three percent loans ranging from $10,000 to $60,000 to fix up older buildings.

In addition, the development corporation is using partnerships with developers as a way of pushing the movement along. In one case, the corporation is buying the first floor and basement vacated by an old jewelry store and reserving it for future retail, while providing funding for a developer to turn the top four stories into condominiums. "It's a shot of capital from us," says Edmund Armentrout of the Center City Commission. "We're taking the risk on retail. If they couldn't lease up the first floor, they might be in dire straits."

Baltimore and several other cities have tried a property tax freeze on historic renovation. Until recently in Baltimore, that freeze applied only to projects up to $3.5 million, but under the new housing initiative, the law has been changed so that any size development now can qualify for a graduated freeze.

Tulsa is contributing sales tax money to the downtown housing effort. Residents voted in 1996 to extend a one-penny sales tax for capital improvements that expires automatically every five years. Some $4 million of this money was earmarked for downtown housing development. It wasn't a huge pool of money, but it had the desired effect. "Once the sales tax was approved, developers were crawling all over us," says Jim Norton.

Such local tax incentives can be vital for downtown residential development because federal tax changes in 1986 had the effect of reducing the credits that developers had been using to rehabilitate historic housing. Between 1981 and 1986, more private funds went into restoring historic buildings than during the rest of American history combined. For eight years after the 1986 tax law went into effect — reducing the amount of the credit, barring high-income taxpayers from using it and creating a "passive loss" provision that sharply limited how much of the credit is available to a taxpayer — investment in rehabilitation projects was off by about 80 percent.

For much of the past decade, developers have been largely uninterested in using the federal tax credit provisions that remain. In 1993, Congress made tax law changes that exempted full-time real estate developers from the strict rules that limited how much in tax credits could be used each year. "Now there's probably 10 requests for every credit they've got," says Jay Hollingsworth of Capital Development, a Memphis development company. "They're as good as gold now." The current federal rehabilitation tax credit is equal to 20 percent of the cost of rehabilitating buildings officially designated as historic, or 10 percent of the cost of rehabilitating non-historic buildings that were built before 1936.

Memphis is one of those cities that is benefiting from the rehabilitation tax credit. Such credits have helped renovate crumbling Victorian townhomes and turn the old National Biscuit Co. distribution site, the Gayoso Hotel and the former Memphis Cotton Exchange into luxury apartment units. Some of these projects have been able to use both rehabilitation credits and low-income tax credits by renting a percentage of units to low-income tenants.

In many places, changing the zoning code is equally important. During the 1950s and '60s, cities all over the country wrote segregated-use codes that marked off downtown districts for commercial development and actively discouraged, or even prohibited, market-rate housing downtown. To draw maximum advantage from the renewed interest in central-city living, some cities have rewritten their codes from scratch, codifying the principle of mixed use — stores, offices and apartments coexisting with each other, even in the densest part of the downtown corridor. Others are taking the less cumbersome step of creating special mixed-use overlay districts, or simply making it clear that the city council is prepared to grant variances for downtown residential purposes.

Dayton, Ohio, for example, has massaged its zoning code to create "PUDs" — project unit developments. These are special mini-zones with their own criteria for which uses are allowed and how much parking is required. Two residential projects slated for the edge of downtown in a warehouse district zoned for commercial and industrial development, but not housing, have been designated as PUDs.

Zoning isn't the only factor that can interfere with residential downtown development. Developers in Memphis want the city to condemn buildings more aggressively so they can assemble property and begin their work. Mayor Willie Herenton agrees with them. "They're absolutely right," he says. "If we use our condemnation powers more, we can create more opportunities."

Condemnation proved essential when Memphis began amassing land for a new minor league baseball stadium diagonally across from the Peabody Hotel, one of the city's earliest restoration projects. Memphis condemned more than just the ground that the stadium was to be built on. Additional land surrounding the field now is under contract for the development of high-density market-rate housing.

Memphis lay fallow for so long, due to the wholesale abandonment of downtown in the decades after King's death, that historic buildings were not torn down to make room for shiny new office towers. That provides many opportunities for using the rehabilitation tax credits. "Memphis has everything left," says developer Jay Hollingsworth.

"There wasn't any incentive to build anything. The banks believed downtown was going down the hole and at some point would fall into the Mississippi. We have all the old buildings that can be redone, and are being redone. We've become fortunate because of our previous misfortune."

Hollingsworth himself lives in the old Exchange Building right in the middle of downtown, once the headquarters of the Memphis Cotton Exchange. His two-level loft has mosaic tile floors and 23-foot ceilings in the living and dining area. The building was vacant from 1979 until renovation began in March 1995. Now it has 202 apartments and an occupancy rate of about 93 percent.

Who are the new residents of downtown Memphis? There's no simple answer to that question. Even within the Exchange Building, there are low-income tenants, whose rents start at $425 a month, and wealthier residents such as Hollingsworth, who pay closer to $1,800 for the choicest units.

The best guess, though, is that about three-quarters of those living in downtown Memphis are professionals who either work there or commute outward. Some of them are "empty-nest" gentrifiers, middle-aged married couples who don't want the big house in the suburbs anymore. Phil Woodard, the Hotel Grand developer, is one of those. "I got bored sitting down on the couch and eating pizza on a Friday afternoon," says Woodard, whose youngest child will be out of high school soon.

But there's also a significant "pre-nest" population — students, single adults and young couples with no children, who want the excitement and the buzz of downtown. There are also some elderly people who might have preferred a downtown apartment years ago, if a supply of comfortable ones had existed.

The one group that's not highly represented in most cities' market-rate housing is families with young children. But in Memphis, there are even some of those. Mud Island, the suburban-like enclave in the middle of the river, is home to lots of them. A new city school is planned for Memphis to accommodate all the children living on Mud Island and in some of the other new projects downtown.

38. MINNEAPOLIS REVISES ZONING CODES

Alan Ehrenhalt

On the corner of 19th Street and Nicollet Avenue, a mile south of downtown Minneapolis, there's a massive brick building that stood for decades as the headquarters of the Frenz garage and car dealership. After the business moved elsewhere, the building housed a storage company, and then, as the neighborhood around it declined, it fell vacant for a long time.

Then Steve Frenz, scouting around for a new close-in location for the still-thriving family automotive business, hit on the idea of opening back up at the original site, renovating the empty building, which he owned, and maybe putting some retail on the ground floor.

He found the city zoning ordinance standing in his way. Yes, the building had been a garage for 50 years, but once the garage closed, the property reverted to commercial use. His automotive business is by definition an industrial use. The land wasn't zoned for much except a store — notwithstanding the fact that it wasn't very attractive to stores, or it wouldn't have been empty all those years.

After months of tedious and expensive effort, Frenz managed to get an "ex-ception," and today the renovated building at 1 East 19th has not only a Frenz automotive business but also a flower shop on the Nicollet Avenue side. But he's the first one to admit that he got permission mostly because his family has some clout in Minneapolis and he knows his way around City Hall. "If I had been an immigrant applying for this exception," he says, "it never would have been granted."

There's something wrong with the Minneapolis zoning law. Nobody realizes that better than the city government. Written with the best intentions in 1964, and amended nearly 500 times, to the point of cumulative incoherence, the law now serves more to frustrate creativity and renewal than to encourage them. It arbitrarily places land and buildings in categories that bear no relation to the urban reality of the 1990s. In the words of Bob Miller, head of the city's Neighborhood Revitalization Office, "we've set it up so that zoning codes act against our best interest."

And so Minneapolis has embarked on the daunting job of rewriting the entire 350-page code. It has been working on the project, on and off, since 1989, and it isn't

Originally published as "The Trouble with Zoning," Governing, Vol. 11, No. 5, February, 1998. Published by Congressional Quarterly, Inc., Washington, D.C. Reprinted with permission of the publisher.

finished yet. But with any luck, a year or so from now it will have a whole new law — one that relaxes the rules and encourages new ideas instead of stifling them irrationally.

There's nothing egregious or particularly unusual about Minneapolis. Cities all over the country have discovered that their comprehensive zoning codes, many of them created in the 1920s and updated in the 1950s and '60s, long ago became more of a problem than a solution. Several big cities— New Orleans, Nashville, Cleveland, Toledo, San Diego— are at various stages of what the chairman of the Minneapolis council zoning committee admits is "the agony" of doing it all over from scratch. San Diego's new law won council approval just this fall. New Orleans is hoping to reach that stage this year.

Meanwhile, a whole group of other cities, realizing the need for change but reluctant to return to square one, are writing a new law on top of the old one, in what they call an "overlay" process. The mistakes of the 1950s and '60s aren't being erased, but the ideas of the 1990s are being placed alongside them. Neighborhoods or commercial districts that want to apply the new rules instead of the old ones will have the legal authority to do that.

In all of these efforts there is a bottom line, and the bottom line can be stated simply enough: Zoning has been rigid where it needs to be flexible. In attempting to prescribe the way communities should look, it has mostly made them look worse. It has sought to separate the residential, commercial and industrial lives of American cities, when it ought to have been looking for ways to mix them together.

"So much of what we have on the books today is 1950s zoning based on 1930s and 1940s ideas," says urban historian Laurence Gerckens. "It's about time things were changed. Zoning is one of the most immutable things in the world once it's on the books, but the largest cities are in life-or-death circumstances. They have to look at zoning."

"You have to take a few chances," agrees Minneapolis' planning director, Paul Farmer, who presided over a similar rewrite a few years ago in Pittsburgh. "There are opportunities out there we don't know about. We want to try to allow good things to happen. Zoning can't make things happen. It can allow them to take place."

In seeking to replace the rigidities of the 1960s with an almost diametrically different approach to urban planning, cities are borrowing heavily from Andres Duany, Peter Calthorpe and the other prominent New Urbanists, the dissident architects and planners who preach a gospel of mixed uses, transit-oriented development, pedestrian-friendly streets and sustainable use of resources. In virtually every case, the planners seem at least conversant with the New Urbanist language, and sympathetic to complaints, such as Duany's, that in an effort to save cities, the previous generation of planners mainly served to hasten the process of urban decay.

If you listen hard enough, you can even hear an occasional good word nowadays for Houston, the city that repudiated zoning altogether and served as the 1960s model of what you get when there are no rules: an unappealing urban goulash of expensive homes next to gas stations next to tool-and-die plants. The new zoning writers are not interested in emulating Houston, but they now readily admit that in trying to avoid it, the last set of laws created something that was quite unappealing in an entirely different way. "I don't think anyone here would say we ought to be like Houston," argues Judy Martin of the Minneapolis Planning Commission, "but there's a perception that the hard and fast rules we put in in 1963 just are not the answer."

The history of zoning in America is a series of waves. The first wave broke in the late 19th century, when it became clear that unregulated urban development was creating situations not only unattractive but literally nauseating — tar boiling, fat rendering and carcass cremation right in the middle of a residential block. Keeping these activities out of people's backyards was little more than common sense.

It wasn't until 1916 that New York City codified this common sense into a legal pyramid, with residential uses at the top, commercial in the middle and industrial at the bottom, and most land in the city reservable for one kind of use at the expense of others. This approach is still sometimes called "Euclidean zoning," not for geometrical reasons but because the U.S. Supreme Court approved it in the case of *Village of Euclid vs. Ambler* in 1926.

By the end of the 1920s, most large cities in America had a zoning code modeled after New York's. Sosme went further: Los Angeles invented the distinction between "single-family" and "multi-family" residential zoning, and between "light" and "heavy" industrial uses. But most of these first-wave zoning laws read pretty much alike. In general, they didn't try to dictate what a city ought to look like — they concentrated on giving some stability and order to what was already there and resolving the most serious problems in the least intrusive way possible.

It was after World War II that zoning got more ambitious, and started getting into trouble. In the mid–1950s, most big-city zoning laws were three decades old and clearly in need of updating. That need coincided with the emergence of a generation of planners and local officials who saw themselves making far-reaching decisions about the physical appearance of the city. They assumed that massive urban renewal would be changing the face of older neighborhoods anyway, and thought they could use zoning to determine what these neighborhoods would look like after the bulldozers went away. "Zoning ordinances in the Sixties," says Paul Farmer, "were built on a presumption of massive clearance and renewal." Sometimes they were created expressly to foster renewal: In some cases, the federal government made grant money contingent on a comprehensive zoning rewrite.

The postwar zoning codes discouraged the old pedestrian-scale Main Street corridors that had flourished before World War II, and encouraged their replacement with strip-mall-like businesses that provided large amounts of parking. They took the idea of segregated uses and pressed it much further than the original versions had dared go. The more distance they could create between residential, commercial and industrial uses, planners reasoned, the easier it would be to dissuade residents from escaping to greener pastures. "When cities did zoning codes in the Sixties," says Minneapolis zoning activist Joni Herren, "they assumed what people wanted was something like a suburban experience. They thought if they gave them that, people wouldn't flee to the suburbs. But it wasn't true."

Segregated-use zoning was generally popular with banks and developers, which saw it as protecting their capital from unwanted neighborhood change. It enabled them to establish separate departments for lending to each of the three categories. But it forced planners into making predictions about the future of land that even the brightest of them couldn't make very intelligently. And it saddled communities with the results of those predictions for decades to come. When a parcel of land was zoned for one sort of use, and demographic changes made it more appropriate for a different use, one frequent result was that it ceased to be used at all.

In many cities, the only way to prevent

these zoning codes from stifling renewal altogether has been to amend them on what amounts to a patchwork basis, creating what Stuart Meck of the American Planning Association likes to call "Post-it" zoning. "It becomes like a zoning code with a bunch of Post-it notes attached to it," Meck says. "When there get to be too many Post-it notes, they decide to redo it."

That is a reasonable description of what has happened in Minneapolis. "It's not a code at all in a coherent sense," admits Blake Graham, the planning supervisor who is conducting the current rewrite. "It was established in a rigid, hierarchical era. You add 500 amendments to that rigid hierarchy, and it becomes very difficult to understand and use."

Sometimes it is so difficult to use that it simply isn't used, and the whole renewal process suffers. "Rezoning a parcel of land is not an easy task," complains Bob Miller of the Neighborhood Revitalization Office. "Zoning can take you out of having viable projects. It can be a real problem in terms of getting anything done at all."

Some of the complexities of the Minneapolis zoning law sound like they were written by Abbott and Costello. Let's say you own an apartment building, and you want to know whether you can build an addition to it. You discover that it is zoned R5A — general residential. You go to the codebook and it defines R5A as being the same as R5, but allowing a little more density. So you look up R5, and the basic meaning of that is a little denser than R4. In the end, you are back to R1, and you still can't make any sense of it. About all you can do is consult the planning department. "The only person who understands this is the zoning inspector," concedes Planning Commissioner Dick Little. "You have to rely on his interpretation."

But as confusing as the residential sections of the Minneapolis law may be, the problems are minor compared with those created by the sections on commercial and industrial property. The code sets up more than 20 categories of commercial use, and imposes tight restrictions on most of them. If a piece of land is zoned B-2, for example, that means the 1963 planners meant for it to house small-scale "neighborhood" retail units, such as groceries or bakeries, but not wider-ranging "community" retail, such as pet stores, music stores or photography studios.

To read all the restrictions and qualifications, you might think that Minneapolis was a city with a precious supply of choice locations and a corps of tenants desperate to get one and willing to abide by almost any rules. In the 1950s, this may have been true, but in the 1990s, the exact opposite is close to the truth. Most of the city's old Main Street corridors are struggling to keep a semblance of commerce alive at all. The mom-and-pop bakeries departed years ago; these days, a carpet store is often a far more realistic possibility, but the code frequently discourages that, if it does not prohibit it altogether. Everyone involved with the zoning rewrite agrees this is a problem. "In many of these inner-city neighborhoods," says Blake Graham, "any kind of investment would be welcome."

One of the best examples is the community of Eliot Park, on the outskirts of downtown near the Metrodome sports stadium. Eliot Park was a flourishing commercial neighborhood a generation ago, but the combination of stadium congestion and general inner-city blight all but destroyed it in the 1970s. More than 20 percent of its original buildings have been torn down to make parking lots. Fewer than a dozen active retail businesses are currently operating.

Eliot Park could yet be revived by its proximity to downtown, but ideas for renovation of the buildings run up against the obstacle course of the zoning law. There are five abandoned gas stations zoned in a category that prohibits most other uses. Some of the neighborhood civic activists think there might be an opportunity to combine retail units with second-floor apartments, but the perception is that the code makes this difficult. A larger business willing to take a chance on locating in Eliot Park often encounters parking requirements that it cannot easily meet at reasonable cost.

"Minneapolis is like a lot of cities," says Planning Commissioner Judy Martin, "with a lot that's zoned commercial that can't support it. Why not remove the designation and let something happen?"

A few miles farther out from downtown is the wide, flat expanse of Lake Street, which was once home to the city's gaudiest auto showrooms, but fell into decay as the dealers moved to the more distant suburbs. It's a challenge to find uses for many of these buildings, but there are some. Many of the old auto facilities are convertible to light manufacturing, and there is currently a demand for light industrial property in Minneapolis— a much greater demand than there is for storefronts. Just in the past couple of years, Lake Street has attracted computer assembly, packaging, and metal-plating plants. So far, those new businesses have had to come in as exceptions to the general categories of the 1963 law. One of the goals of the current rewrite is to build in such flexibility by law, not by exception.

As in the case of the Frenz garage, the city may be hampering recovery rather than fostering it. "Minneapolis," says Steve Frenz, "has become very unfriendly to industry."

It doesn't take a degree in planning to see what Minneapolis needs: a new zoning code that pays less attention to the formal uses of land and more attention to the effect those uses have on the community. And that is the sort of law that the city is trying to come up with. "We're moving toward a much wider range of uses," says Planning Commissioner Dick Little, "but based on impact."

Under the proposed new code, virtually all small- and medium-scale commercial property would be in the same category, and the vast majority of business establishments would fit in it — a grocery story and a photo studio would no longer be considered different kinds of uses. Residential apartments above the storefronts would not only be permitted, they would carry incentives for the landlord. Light industrial tenants could be combined with commercial or even residential tenants, provided they produce "little or no noise, odor, dust or vibration." The restrictive industrial category would be reserved for the really heavy-duty uses, such as scrap yards, metal mills, and textile and plastics factories. In the view of Pat Scott, the longtime council zoning chairman, "the potential for combinations of things is going to increase."

In many ways, of course, reaching agreement on the larger issues is the easy part. No one in Minneapolis disagrees that segregated-use zoning deserves to end. The really tricky part of the exercise will be rezoning the city, block-by-block and parcel-by-parcel, in accordance with the new mixed-use principles. That could still take years— which is why so few cities, at this late date in their development, are willing to undertake it.

Nevertheless, early signs in Minneapolis are that the creation of a new zoning law, even in intricate detail, does not inevitably mean organized combat among local interest groups. In the 35 years since the last code was written, the politics of Minneapolis land use law has changed enormously. The banks and development companies that dominated the 1963 effort are no longer intense participants: Minneapolis is an aging, built-out city now, and they don't see many lucrative investment opportunities within its borders. "We don't get lobbied by developers," says Planning Commissioner Judy Martin.

The Minneapolis Community Development Association, the city's primary business recruitment office, obviously does care about development. But it also knows that the mega-projects it is interested in are likely to attract sufficient support from the mayor and city council no matter what the zoning code says. How Minneapolis is zoned on a block-by-block level is not the sort of question the MCDA recruiters spend their time worrying about.

In 1998, unlike in 1963, the real players in the zoning rewrite process are the neighborhoods, the places like Eliot Park that perceive their survival to be on the line. It is the neighborhood activists who have tried to put the entire process in their direction. "Neighborhoods get it," says Planning Director Paul Farmer. "They understand it. I don't think they understood it in the Fifties."

The influence of the neighborhoods is evident in Minneapolis in virtually every aspect of the new zoning law. But the clearest evidence of neighborhood power is the creation of overlay districts— residential areas that will be free to write their own standards for the way streets and buildings ought to look, even if the standards differ from what prevails elsewhere in the city. In a sense, the overlay districts represent a step away from the freedom of combination and experiment and back to rules and requirements— except that instead of the auto-influenced rules of the 1960s, they will reflect the New Urbanist values of the 1990s. The overlay districts will encourage mixed uses, but the mixture of those uses will be very much subject to the dictates of community opinion.

A district has already been established, in Linden Hills, an affluent enclave in the southwest corner of the city. According to the new code, the Linden Hills civic association will be free to restrict car traffic, limit curb cuts and off-street parking, require storefronts to come up to the street, and impose numerous other regulations in the interest of creating a desired aesthetic quality to future neighborhood life.

The overlay concept is proving highly attractive these days, not only to cities such as Minneapolis that are rewriting their entire codes but also to others that are trying to avoid the tedious multi-year ordeal. Overlay districts can simply be grafted on to an existing law, and this is what a number of cities are beginning to do. Austin, Texas, amended its zoning code last year to create what it calls "traditional neighborhood districts," requiring a street grid, increased residential density and substantial open space. Fort Collins, Colorado, chose to keep its basic code but create individually designated neighborhood design standards, drafted with the help of the New Urbanist architect Peter Calthorpe. Fort Collins has banned any future gated communities and decreed that all new subdivisions have at least three separate entry points. Orlando, Florida, which went through a full rewrite of its zoning law in the 1980s, changed it substantially this year to make room for an overlay-style concept.

Overlay zoning is an attractive answer for the Austins and Orlandos of the country, fast-growing cities that have been nimble enough to keep pace with changing demand over the past decade. What is doubtful is whether overlays represent much of a solution for the older Frost Belt cities that have been laboring under the burden of entire codes that are 30 to 40 years out of date. Those cities probably need to do something more like what Minneapolis is doing— start over again from scratch, as tedious and time-consuming as that is. And then they need to keep adjusting their laws to changing conditions, rather than essentially letting them go for 20 years, as most of them normally do.

"You're never done with this," says zoning historian Laurence Gerckens. "By the time you finish it, the conditions that led you to rewrite the law are eight or nine years old. The city is constantly evolving. Zoning has to be constantly changing. We ought to be quietly making changes every year instead of stockpiling them for a generation."

39. NEWARK AND THE PERFORMING ARTS

Marilyn J. Taylor

The much anticipated $180 million New Jersey Performing Arts Center (NJPAC) opened in downtown Newark last October. The red-brick complex is "an ambitious symbol of Newark's pride," proclaimed the *New York Times*, which described its 2,750-seat Prudential Hall as "breathtakingly gorgeous." Other facilities include the 514-seat Victoria Theater, rehearsal space, restaurants and bars, and community rooms.

NJPAC, however, is more than a much-applauded cultural center that hosts opera, symphony orchestras, dance troupes, and jazz performances. Unlike some stand-alone, megalithic cultural centers, NJPAC both merges into and enlivens the surrounding cityscape. The front facade includes a three-story-tall glass wall that allows pedestrians to look into the gleaming lobby and offers concert goers a view out onto historic Military Park (the city's original commons) and the downtown skyline, forging a strong visual connection to the rest of the city.

Of equal importance, NJPAC does not have the subterranean garage typical of many urban performing arts centers, which turns concert going into a drive-in/drive-out experience and does little to support the surrounding neighborhood. Instead, concert goers park their cars in the city-renovated, 1,100-car garage beneath Military Park, take an escalator or elevator to street level, and then cross Centre Street to NJPAC, adding crowds, movement, and energy to the immediate neighborhood.

While NJPAC's design is one factor in downtown Newark's rebirth, its location is another. The center occupies a strategic downtown site at the northern end of Military Park, one block east of once-bustling Broad Street and one block west of the Passaic River waterfront. The city has designated a 20-square-block area along the Broad Street corridor (from NJPAC and Military Park to the Newark Museum and Newark Public Library on Washington Park) as a downtown arts district.

The city also hopes that NJPAC will draw attention and provide a strong link to the redevelopment of the nearby Passaic River waterfront, where a motley collection of warehouses and industrial buildings recently was cleared for a planned riverfront esplanade and hoped-for mixed-use

Originally published as "Newark Turns the Corner," Urban Land, Vol. 57, No. 2, February, 1998. Published by the Urban Land Institute, Washington, D.C. Reprinted with permission of the publisher.

development, including a festival market-place.

Newark civic leaders firmly believe that NJPAC will help lead downtown and the entire city to a more prosperous future. Mayor Sharpe James has called the NJPAC "a proud beginning" that will have a "ripple effect on development." NJPAC president Lawrence P. Goldman declared, "We mean to be the atom that starts the chain reaction."

The Tarnished Crown

Because of its troubles in recent decades, many people have forgotten that Newark was New Jersey's crown jewel from the 18th century into the mid–20th century. At the end of World War II, Newark was a dynamic city of more than 450,000 residents. Its then-thriving economy was solidly based on banking, insurance, ship-building, and particularly manufacturing. The crossroads of Market and Broad streets, the center of the downtown shopping district, reportedly was the third-busiest intersection in the world.

In the 1950s and 1960s, Newark began a several-decade-long decline. Middle-class residents moved to newer homes in nearby suburbs. One by one the downtown department stores, beset by competition from suburban shopping malls, closed their doors forever. Most seriously, the city's employment base was ravaged. Between 1960 and 1995, Newark lost three-quarters of its manufacturing jobs and half its private sector employment.

Poverty, despair, and an often-corrupt municipal government helped fuel the infamous 1967 riots, which left 26 people dead and hundreds of buildings destroyed by fire. Afterward, Newark became a national symbol of the country's urban problems, which only accelerated its decline. In 1977, then-Mayor Kenneth Gibson told a

New York Times reporter: "Wherever America's cities are going, Newark will get there first."

A number of well-intentioned but ill-planned redevelopment programs in the 1970s and 1980s failed to turn downtown Newark around. For example, the four-building, high-rise Gateway Center, which totals more than two million square feet of office space, features a network of pedestrian bridges that connect the buildings to each other and nearby Pennsylvania Station. Designed to offer white-collar workers a sense of security in a supposedly hostile downtown, these bridges perpetuate a harmful separation of office and street life. Thousands of people who commute to downtown Newark every day rarely (if ever) "touch" the streets, thereby diminishing downtown retail activity, movement, and vibrance.

Enviable Assets

Newark also enjoys some important strengths, which are facilitating its turn-around. They include:

Accessibility. Newark is accessible by virtually all modes of travel — airplane, ship, train, bus, trolley, truck, and car. Newark Airport, just one mile from downtown, is the ninth-busiest airport in the United States, having served an estimated 30 million passengers last year. The port of Newark is the second-largest shipping container port in the country and the center of the nation's largest free-trade zone.

Corporate and Institutional Commitment. A number of Newark-based corporations and government agencies — such as Bell Atlantic, Blue Cross and Blue Shield of New Jersey, New Jersey Transit, Prudential Insurance, and Public Service Electric & Gas — have kept the downtown core alive with jobs, economic development initiatives, and generous charitable contributions.

Public Service Electric & Gas (PSE&G) maintains an active economic development office, staffed by relocation specialists who provide information about vacant land and buildings, current commercial lease rates, and incentive programs to companies interested in relocating to or expanding in Newark. Prudential Insurance, which has been headquartered in Newark since its founding in 1875, contributed $6.5 million to NJPAC, its largest charitable gift ever.

College Town. Just north and west of downtown are four rapidly growing institutions of higher learning: Essex Community College, the New Jersey Institute of Technology, the New Jersey School of Medicine and Dentistry, and Rutgers University's Newark campus. The Seton Hall Law School has its own downtown tower. Together, these five institutions serve approximately 40,000 part-time and full-time students, the equivalent of a major state university. To accommodate growing numbers of students and programs, they are building new facilities. Last year, for example, Rutgers University started construction on a $49 million law school in downtown Newark.

Stable, Growing Neighborhoods. The heavily Portuguese Iron-bound district, two blocks east of downtown's busy Pennsylvania Station, is widely known for its restaurants, bakeries, and shops. More significant, this district is a thriving big-city community that is growing in population and expanding in size. Every year, dozens of new homes, ranging in size from one- to four-family units, are built on former industrial land at the neighborhood's edges. The homes, which are privately financed and built, benefit from various government measures, such as partial tax abatements.

A Pedestrian-Scale Downtown Core. Although the big department stores have closed, their massive buildings still stand along Market and Broad streets, waiting for imaginative adaptive use projects that will contribute to Newark's community, commercial, and cultural life; moreover, the downtown streetscape, though frayed and rundown in many places, largely escaped ill-conceived redevelopment initiatives. Gateway Center, with its isolating pedestrian bridges, was not duplicated elsewhere. The blocks around Military Park and Washington Park, which contain some extraordinary pre–World War II buildings and the new NJPAC, have the potential, many believe, to become one of the handsomest and most successful downtown districts on the East Coast.

Rediscovering Newark

In recent years, more and more New Jerseyans, corporations, and real estate investors have recognized Newark's assets and its potential for recovery. Although NJPAC was built as a catalyst for redevelopment, downtown Newark had actually turned the corner *before* the center's opening.

"Newark suffers from a perception that's two years behind the reality," says Arthur R. Stern, chairman and CEO of Cogswell Realty Group LLC of New York, which recently acquired several of Newark's pre–World War II office towers. "If people don't work there, they just don't understand the vitality — and particularly the potential vitality — of Newark's central business district."

Newark boosters point to several encouraging events and trends as solid evidence of the city's turnaround. More than a decade ago, Blue Cross and Blue Shield of New Jersey relocated its corporate headquarters from downtown Newark to suburban Florham Park. In 1993, the insurer left Florham Park and moved into downtown Newark's 18-story Three Penn Plaza, bringing 2,500 jobs back to the city. Other well-known companies that have offices in downtown Newark are increasing their employment in the city. Prudential Insurance has moved several thousand suburban employees to its downtown buildings. By the end of 1997, more than 6,700 Prudential employees worked in downtown Newark, more than double the total a few years ago.

Between 1990 and 1992, three new high-rise office buildings totaling 1.8 million square feet were completed near Pennsylvania Station. Today, the vacancy rate for the cluster of Class A office space around Pennsylvania Station is an extraordinary three percent. In addition, renovation projects have transformed some long-empty or decrepit downtown buildings. Following a $6.25 million renovation, the New Jersey Historical Society moved into the former Essex Club, which was built in 1926 on Park Place, overlooks Military Park, and is one block from NJPAC. The elegant Firemen's Insurance Company building, built in 1922 on Park Place, has been renovated by the Berger Organization into what are now fully leased modern offices. In 1996, the Essex County Improvement Authority helped transform the former Gibraltar Building, built in 1926 on Halsey Street, into the Wilentz Justice Complex, which provides courtroom space and offices for Essex County.

Housing construction has been another key element in Newark's recovery. Hundreds of apartments for low-income residents have been constructed with public assistance. A sizable number of these are townhouse-style units, which have replaced some of Newark's notorious high-rise public housing projects. Privately financed moderate- to middle-income apartments, condominiums, and townhouses make up more than 1,000 additional new residential units.

Newark's largest residential project is the 1,150-unit Society Hill community,

built in the late 1980s and early 1990s on a 45-acre University Heights site that was the epicenter of the 1967 riots. Throughout the 1970s and early 1980s, this neighborhood consisted of trash-strewn vacant lots and run-down or boarded-up buildings blighting the hill between the central business district and University Heights. In the mid–1980s, K. Hovnanian Companies, located in Red Bank, New Jersey, entered into a public/private partnership with the city to build 1,150 townhouse-style units. Approximately 175 units, to be scattered throughout the development, were to be sold to qualified low- and moderate-income buyers.

Offering affordably priced new housing convenient to jobs in downtown Newark and the educational institutions at University Heights, Society Hill sold its first 40 homes from 1986 to 1987 without advertising. In August 1988, the next section of 168 homes opened for sale from plans and sold out within eight hours. As more phases of Society Hill sold out, increasingly affluent buyers, many of whom had abandoned Newark for the suburbs, were attracted to Society Hill. To accommodate these buyers, larger, amenity-filled homes were built in the later phases. Today, all 1,150 units have been completed and sold.

Property values have risen in the area surrounding Society Hill for the first time in decades. The project helped create a "critical consumer mass" that led to the opening nearby of Newark's first full-service supermarket in more than 25 years and a Hovnanian-built 110,000-square-foot shopping center with a second supermarket. Honored by the U.S. Department of Housing and Urban Development, the National Association of Home Builders, Harvard University, and others, Society Hill has become an inner-city laboratory for civic leaders, academics, and real estate developers who want to rejuvenate their older cities.

Turnaround Time

The 1990s may well be remembered as Newark's turnaround decade. At the new 40-acre, $270 million University Heights Science Park just outside downtown, university-based high-tech research and development will be conducted and applied in the Newark business community. One large research lab and the New Jersey Institute of Technology's Enterprise Development Center for start-up companies already are open there, and construction of a third facility will begin shortly. Late last year, the state of New Jersey announced funding for a $78 million International Center for Public Health, which is scheduled to open at Science Park in 2000.

In the heart of downtown Newark, the former Macy's department store, a 1.2 million-square-foot building that anchored the southern end of the Broad and Haley streets retail corridor, is being converted into a mixed-use complex with a small department store, offices, warehouse space, and parking. An investment group headed by Samuel J. Jemal in New York City is putting $1.5 million into the project, while the state and several banks are making $3.3 million in low-interest loans.

At Military Park, the Berger Organizations is renovating the long-empty, 400,000-square-foot Hahnes department store, built in 1901 on Broad Street, which anchored the northern end of the Broad Street retail corridor, only four blocks from Macy's. The first phase, due to be completed in May, includes an 1,100-car garage, first-floor retail, office space, and a restored facade. The second phase of renovation will involve space that has 18- to 22-foot ceilings and will become offices, loft-style apartments, or both. While the building's lower three floors, which formerly contained a piano store, concert hall, and piano factory, are quite large, its fourth to 16th floors are each only 3,000

square feet. "We haven't formulated any specific plans for reuse yet, although the tower floors lend themselves to small-footprint offices or apartments," says chairman Miles Berger.

Of critical importance to Newark's future is the late Harry Helmsley's $5 billion real estate empire, which now is being liquidated. Its four downtown Newark office towers were put up for sale last year. Throughout the 1950s and 1960s, these four buildings, particularly the 34-story National Newark & Essex Building, built in 1930 on Broad Street, were some of Newark's proudest office towers. By last year, the buildings, which are largely vacant, had "fallen into disrepair, victims of age and neglect," reported Newark's *Star-Ledger*. Now, bold investors are buying what the newspaper described as "Helmsley's tattered real estate jewels."

Last October, a trio of investors purchased 24 Commerce Street, which was built in 1926. They plan to invest more than $4 million in upgrading the 21-story tower. "We had an opportunity to buy a building very inexpensively and put a lot of sweat equity into it," partner Christian Benedetto told the *Star-Ledger* shortly after the sale. "The building was neglected for a number of years. Our plan is to modernize."

In December, Cogswell Realty Group purchased 744 Broad Street which was built in 1930 for an estimated $6 million, with the backing of an affiliate of Lehman Brothers, the Wall Street investment banking firm. "We believe that after many false starts, Newark finally has turned the corner," said Peter Marsh, chief operating officer of the investment group, shortly after the sale. Cogswell will spend an additional $45 million to renovate the 34-story, 650,000-square-foot building into B-plus or A-minus space. The renovation program includes all-new electrical and HVAC systems, new elevators, the repointing and refinishing of the facade, new windows, the construction of a new loading dock and freight entrance, the restoration of the lobby to its original art deco appearance, and floodlights. "The building will be a Newark landmark again," says Stern.

Upon completion of the renovation, Cogswell Realty will target three different markets to fill the structure, according to Stern. The ground floor will be retail and restaurant space. The building's third to 13th floors, which have 29,000-square-foot floor plates, and the 14th to 22nd floors, which have 16,000-square-foot floor plates, will be marketed to corporate users. Finally, the 23rd to 34th floors, which have 6,000-square-foot floor plates, will be marketed to law firms that want a full-floor identity and proximity to the courts.

Last month, Cogswell Realty purchased 1180 Raymond Boulevard, built in 1930, from the Helmsley estate. This now-vacant, 35-story, 400,000-square-foot building, which stands diagonally across Broad Street from the 744 Broad Street tower, overlooks Military Park. The city owns the underlying land, and Cogswell intends to negotiate an extension of ground lease. "We don't foresee a renovation into office space, like the nearby 744 Broad Street building, or a market for one million square feet of high-end office product in this area right now," says Stern. "Instead, we foresee a complementary use such as a hotel or some type of residential use, possibly connected with one of the nearby hospitals or universities. We also want a large retail component on the ground floor."

Newark boosters and other downtown property owners are pleased with the quick sale of these important but long-neglected office buildings. "These are buildings that we thought would be written off," says Alfred Faiella, executive director of the Newark Economic Development Corporation. Now, it is believed that these renovated buildings will generate new jobs, tax revenues, and excitement for the city.

A number of proposed developments also are in the works. Last December, a partnership of the city of Newark, Essex County, and the Essex County Improvement Authority announced plans to build a $22 million baseball and multipurpose stadium on a riverfront site just north of NJPAC. Located on an 11-acre parcel, this complex will serve the Newark Bears minor-league baseball team, and it will be accessible by rail, public transit, and highway. In addition, this year work will begin on the $75 million Joseph G. Minish Riverfront Park, which runs along the western side of the Passaic River in Newark. This two-mile-long park, which will include a 40-foot-wide riverfront promenade, will link the new stadium and NJPAC at the northern end of downtown Newark with Pennsylvania Station and the Ironbound District.

Ongoing Challenges

Despite the renewed optimism about Newark's future, the city struggles with some serious liabilities: a declining but still intimidating crime rate, a public school system that had to be taken over by the state, real estate tax assessments that have not been updated in four decades, and a shortage of entry-level jobs for young people, among others.

Equally troubling, the city is not attracting large-scale commercial real estate development, even with the tight occupancy rate in Class A office buildings near Pennsylvania Station. "Nobody is building anything new," reported the December 7, 1997, *Star-Ledger*. "No one builds on spec in Newark." Samuel Crane, head of the Newark-based Regional Business Partnership, concurs: "You are going to see investments in Newark, but they will be specific, not speculative."

Perhaps the greatest impediment to revitalizing Newark is the lack of connection between important but isolated clusters of activity. NJPAC is a step in the right direction because it provides a critical link among Military Park, Broad Street, and the Passaic River waterfront. Other clusters must be connected to create a more unified city, however. The four large colleges at University Heights, for example, must forge stronger physical links (including safe, accessible pedestrian routes and new buildings to fill now-vacant lots) to become a single academic community. At the same time, these colleges must forge stronger physical connections with the nearby downtown. At present, there are several blocks of vacant lots, half-empty buildings, and ill-maintained stores that separate what should be two mutually supporting and enlivening activity centers.

Like most U.S. cities, Newark has experienced dramatic ups and downs throughout the 20th century. Now, like many once-depressed cities across the nation, Newark is on the upswing again. "There are indeed more signs of hope for the future in Newark than there have been for the last 30 years," declared the *Washington Post* last year.

40. NEW YORK PRESERVES OLDER NEIGHBORHOODS

Sandy Hornick

What comes to mind when most people think of New York is the city's famous skyscraper skyline. Few are aware of a very different New York — a city of low-rise neighborhoods where thousands of middle-income families make their home. But, although the lower density areas encompass almost half of the city's land area, they have, in the past, often been ignored by local politicians.

Last year, recognizing the concerns of the lower density neighborhoods, the Board of Estimate adopted a comprehensive amendment to the zoning resolution dealing with many of their needs. The changes were based on a widely (but not universally) praised study by the city planning department. Our study and the report based on it deals with a subject of vital concern throughout the country: how to provide new housing opportunities while preserving the character of older neighborhoods. In addition, the methodology of the study and the zoning solutions we came up with should be useful to planners in other communities.

The Problem

Developed largely between 1900 and 1960, the outlying neighborhoods in the boroughs of Queens, Staten Island, Brooklyn, and the Bronx reflected the new suburban life styles made possible first by the streetcar and then by the automobile. Although low-density by New York standards, at 15 to 60 units per acre, these areas are still high-density in comparison to most suburbs. Nevertheless, they provide an oasis of greenery for families fleeing more crowded parts of the city.

In the last decade, however, the low-density neighborhoods have begun to change. As the city's housing market boomed, developers started buying up the one- and two-family houses, tearing them down and putting up rowhouses in their place. That meant, instead of one house occupying 60 to 80 feet of street frontage, there would be three or four houses, each with two or three apartments, bringing in more families and more cars. Moreover, the new houses were often built in a boxy modern style that seemed out of context in the traditional neighborhoods.

Originally published as "Context Is Everything," Planning, Vol. 56, No. 12, December, 1990. Published by the American Planning Association, Chicago, Illinois. Reprinted with permission of the publisher.

The change was most noticeable on Staten Island and the eastern part of Queens, but was also apparent in other areas. Residents of these communities put pressure on their elected officials and on the city planning department to deal with the issue.

In part, blame for the new type of development can be traced back to 1961, when the city completely revised its zoning map, which varied zoning according to a neighborhood's proximity to mass transit. Areas far from transit were rezoned to permit a floor area ratio of 0.5, which others were rezoned for FARs of 0.75 or 1.25. Some neighborhoods were allowed to build to a higher density than had been allowed in the past.

Subsequent zoning changes allowed development of three-story buildings at an FAR of up to 1.65. As the land became more expensive, developers took increasing advantage of zoning provisions that allowed garages, attics, and recreation rooms to be excluded from FAR calculations. Thus a single building type began to predominate, with an FAR ranging from 0.9 to 1.1.

Objections to this type of development coalesced in 1987 when the city adopted new, contextual zoning for middle- and high-density neighborhoods. The 1987 amendments included a provision allowing new four-to-eight story apartment houses rather than the tall, thin towers encouraged by the 1961 zoning. The new zoning was part of a broader "quality housing program," which also incorporated some of the "defensible space" concepts credited to planner Oscar Newman.

The quality housing program did not, however, address the problems of the lower density areas, as residents of those neighborhoods were quick to point out to their representatives on the Board of Estimate — and to then-mayor Edward Koch, who was gearing up for a difficult reelection campaign. Some elected officials called for a moratorium on new development in lower density areas, but planners noted that such an action could have a disastrous effect on housing production.

Instead, the planning department proposed to take a comprehensive look at the neighborhoods affected and to come up with ways of encouraging new construction that would fit in with the old.

Fast Track

The department's "lower density contextual study" started in early 1988 with the organization of a research group and a commitment to complete its work in a record nine months' time. Forty-six planners and several planning students worked on the project at various times during that period and helped shape the proposal. An additional 25 reviewed parts of the study as they were completed. The quick turnaround time made this effort far more intensive than most such studies. The department even established a small "war room" as the focus of activity.

The study began with an effort to determine the scope of the problem through a neighborhood survey of building characteristics. The survey, designed primarily by Richard Barth and Kim Schmahmann, began with a decision to use as a sample are 10 percent of the census tracts with lower density zoning, randomly selected from the four boroughs outside of Manhattan. The selection of tracts was reviewed to make certain that those chosen included the widest possible variety of building types.

The tracts were aggregated into 77 study areas, and specially trained planning staff and students, armed with field survey sheets, were sent out to identify the elements that contributed significantly to the neighborhood's character. The study areas ranged in size from six to 25 blocks.

The elements included number of stories, number of dwelling units, type of roof, width of side yards and depth of front yards, planting, and parking arrangements. The surveyors were also asked to photograph every housing type — including new construction —characteristics of the neighborhood. Eighteen categories were identified as a result of that exercise. Typical streetscapes were photographed as well, resulting in an archive of some 3,000 views.

Multiplying the various combinations of elements, the surveyors came up with 1,399 different housing types. Surprisingly for a city as dense as New York, almost half were detached houses, most on narrow lots of 25 to 30 feet and separated from their neighbors by driveways just wide enough for one car. Another quarter were semidetached. Most third stories were actually habitable attics under pitched roofs.

Except in Staten Island, which remained largely undeveloped until the completion of the Verrazano–Narrows Bridge in 1964, the researchers found that front and side yards often were smaller than the minimums mandated by the 1960 zoning. That's because most of this housing was built under the liberal standards of the 1916 zoning resolution. The 1961 code, actually developed in the 1950s, followed a more suburban model, requiring wider lots for detached houses, deeper front yards, and wider side yards. Still, this pre–1961 housing had remained stable and highly marketable.

While some of the neighborhoods in the study are surprisingly suburban in character, the new construction is uniformly urban, limited almost exclusively to three-story, boxy buildings. Many of them are rowhouses in neighborhoods where detached or semidetached houses predominated. In effect, the 1980s construction imposed a depressing sameness on heretofore diverse neighborhoods.

Further, many of the new buildings appeared to have illegal ground-floor apartments. It is clear that zoning regulations that permitted additional floor space helped to create them.

To make matters worse, car ownership patterns in these neighborhoods are more typical of suburbs than cities. Many of the new houses have attached garages accessed by short driveways. As the garages came to be used for storage or living space, driveways were widened. As a result, front yards in new developments are often paved over. Frequent curb cuts have resulted in the elimination of much of the on-street parking.

A Radical Approach

It became clear to us after reviewing this material that a radical change was needed. Simply fine-tuning the existing zoning would not be enough.

We found little to guide us. Few other cities, it appears, have come up with as-of-right regulation to deal with the problem of out-of-scale development. Most rely on individual project review, a costly and time-consuming approach, or rezoning to remove development potential.

Recognizing New York's perennial housing shortage, the study team rejected out of hand proposals that would cut into housing supply. That meant, for example, saying no to the politicians and community groups that wanted a ban on any demolition of sound housing, thus preventing redevelopment of lots that are substantially underbuilt.

The key guiding principle of the rezoning effort was the notion that different zoning districts should produce different building types at different densities. A corollary was that districts that are close to mass transit should accommodate higher density development. The second principle was that all habitable floor space in a building would be counted in determining maximum floor area. Loopholes that allowed uncounted floor area would be eliminated.

Third, more parking had to be provided, especially in areas farthest from mass transit. Finally, a zoning mechanism was needed that would permit architectural creativity while providing for as-of-right approvals.

New Zoning

The researchers developed a simple matrix to characterize the distinct types of living environments they found. The axes of the matrix are based on the survey's two most significant variables: configuration (whether houses are detached, semidetached, mixed, or rowhouses) and floor area. The matrix provided the organization for new zoning designations.

In some of the lowest density districts, FAR was reduced substantially, reflecting the almost suburban character of those areas. In those districts, too, the planners established an "attic rule," which took into account the widespread use of the third-floor attics as living space. We recommended an increase of up to 20 percent of base FAR in new buildings that included attic space — which we viewed as a positive way of achieving varied rooflines. Only that portion of the attic under eight feet high and under a pitched roof qualifies for the bonus.

A key goal of our work was to encourage varied development. The best way to do this, we concluded, was by allowing more height as a tradeoff for irregular setbacks and rooflines. The setback regulations developed by Kim Schmahmann and Tom Wargo allow considerable design flexibility within the building envelope, while encouraging neighborhood compat-

ibility. In most districts, the new regulations establish a 35-foot ridge line with sloping sides. The result in many cases approximates a traditional gable-roofed house.

Other provisions seek to encourage variety in housing type. The 1961 zoning ordinance restricted detached houses to lots at least 40 feet wide. In contrast, rowhouses could be built on lots as narrow as 18 feet. Rowhouses thus became the preferred housing type in most neighborhoods—whether they were most appropriate or not.

The new zoning recognizes the differences among the city's neighborhoods. Under the old system, the lower density neighborhoods were covered by four zoning designations. The new system adds six more districts, which are designed to encourage a greater variety of small-lot houses. Several of the districts allow zero lot line, detached houses to be built on lots as narrow as 25 feet. Density may be further increased by adding small accessory apartments.

Parking is a major focus of the new zoning. In several districts, rowhouses may have only limited curb cuts, thus eliminating off-street parking on small lots and pushing the parking to the rear on larger ones, preserving planted front yards. Parking for detached and semidetached houses is limited to a 10-foot-wide ribbon along the side lot line. The idea here is to duplicate neighborhood patterns, while preserving curbside parking.

The Upshot

Responses varied widely when the planning department issued its report on the lower density contextual zoning study in December 1988. Michael Moriarty, head of Concerned Citizens of Bayside, a neighborhood advocacy group in

Queens, heralded the study as "the finest work on city planning and zoning perhaps in the entire history of the United States." Randy Lee, a builder on Staten Island, called it "planning snake oil."

In general, while many neighborhoods covered by the new zoning wanted even more restrictions, community leaders approved of the planning department's balanced approach. Ralph Lamberti, then Staten Island borough president, described it as "one of the great accomplishments of my administration." Some neighborhoods were concerned however, that the zoning would worsen an already extreme housing shortage. The Staten Island chapter of the NAACP took out a newspaper ad to that effect.

Some developers sought to include a grandfather clause that would allow projects to go forward under the old rules for two years after adoption of the new zoning. Developers also filed a lawsuit challenging the zoning on the ground that the planning department did not do an environmental impact statement. That challenge was turned down by a state trial court in August.

In June 1989, the original proposal was adopted — somewhat altered but with its guiding principles intact — as an amendment to the city zoning resolution. The new contextual zoning went into effect immediately in the four existing lower density districts, and city planners are now revising the zoning maps in accord with the amendment. The first step is to reexamine the zoning in all the neighborhoods to determine which of the new or revised zoning designations is appropriate. That process will take several years to complete.

The city planning commission also promised neighborhood groups that it would consider additional adjustments. For instance, several different community groups expressed concern that their members would no longer be able to build the large houses needed to accommodate their families. The planning department has agreed to review that situation. It will also address the concerns of residents of other neighborhoods who fear that they will be unable to add on to their small houses.

The challenge now is to use these new zoning tools to preserve neighborhood character while allowing urgently needed housing. In several areas, the planning department has joined with community groups to identify appropriate locations for both development and preservation. The ultimate success of the new zoning program is contingent upon such cooperation.

41. PHILADELPHIA USES COMMUNITY DEVELOPMENT CORPORATIONS

Steve Culbertson and Jeff Watkins

Many neighborhoods in the city of Philadelphia and throughout the United States are showing signs of revitalization and growth. Leading the efforts to foster renewal in urban neighborhoods are community development corporations (CDCs), which are nonprofit organizations based in specific neighborhoods and subject to local governance. CDCs rehabilitate and build affordable housing for neighborhood residents, foster local economic development, and provide an array of related social services, such as homeownership counseling for first-time buyers. For more than 25 years, Philadelphia's CDCs have worked to battle the decline of the city's manufacturing economy, the exodus of jobs, and the flight of nearly one million residents to the suburbs.

Philadelphia's center city has seen a remarkable renaissance during the past decade in office, retail, and hotel development. But native Philadelphians tend to regard the center city boom with skepticism — for, more than any other American city, Philadelphia has always been and re-mains a city defined by its residential neighborhoods. Many wonder whether the neighborhoods are being left behind.

The goal of the CDC movement is to ensure that the neighborhoods are *not* left behind. Just as the center city boom has its convention center and the twin Rouse towers as emblems, the neighborhood movement has its own modest monuments: the Ogontz Avenue Revitalization Corporation's Ogontz Plaza and Hardshell Café, Project HOME's renovated 48-unit special-needs residence on Fairmount Avenue, and the 54-unit Adolfina Villenueva rental complex and child-care center developed by the Women's Community Revitalization Project. *Success '96,* a report produced last October by the Philadelphia Association of Community Development Corporations, the city's trade association of community development organizations, documents the accomplishments of the CDC movement. From 1990 to 1996, CDCs in Philadelphia have generated:

• more than 1,600 units of housing

Originally published as "Rebuilding Philadelphia's Neighborhoods," Urban Land, *Vol. 56, No. 9, September, 1997. Published by the Urban Land Institute, Washington, D.C. Reprinted with permission of the publisher.*

(471 owner-occupied and 1,138 rental units);

• an additional 333 units of housing in partnership with private developers;

• 386,900 square feet of commercial, business, and incubator space;

• 116,700 square feet of daycare and social services facilities.

In addition, CDCs have organized community residents to take action to make their own blocks more livable and marketable. CDC projects have demolished derelict buildings, reduced density by creating parks and community gardens, opened desperately needed daycare centers, established community policing programs, and initiated programs to enhance neighborhood public schools (see Figure 1).

The Community Development Environment

From 1990 to 1996, the Philadelphia community development industry grew enormously. Individual organizations themselves have tripled in size, from staffs of one or two to a current average of five. The number of organizations has nearly tripled as well.

Under Mayor Edward G. Rendell, the Office of Housing and Community Development (OHCD) and the Redevelopment Authority (RDA) have provided growing support for CDCs. Through the Philadelphia Neighborhood Development Collaborative, the Philadelphia Development Partnership, and the state's Philadelphia Plan tax credit program, the city's corporations and foundations have furnished unprecedented support. The result has been a boom in CDC production. In contrast to levels of local support, however, HUD's community development block grants (CDBGs) have been shrinking. In spite of increasing demand for urban com-

munity revitalization capital, the federal retreat is likely to quicken in the future.

CDCs have responded, however, with an increasingly entrepreneurial outlook. In addition to devising ways to make CDBG-based housing production more efficient, CDCs have begun reducing the density of development projects by introducing more open, green space into development plans. After all, the labyrinthine density of many of Philadelphia's rowhouse neighborhoods originated as a temporary response to the economics and demographics of the last century. But beyond housing, CDCs now are plunging into economic development, concentrating on programs to bridge the gulf between unemployed and underemployed neighborhood residents and a regional economy with considerable job opportunities.

Increasing Housing Production

Housing development was the focus of CDCs in the first half of the 1990s, resulting in the production of 1,609 housing units during that period. CDCs increased housing production from 250 units in 1990 to more than 400 units annually by 1996.

The majority of the affordable housing produced in Philadelphia and throughout the country by CDCs has been multifamily rental housing financed with federal low-income housing tax credits, which are administered in Philadelphia by the Pennsylvania Housing Finance Agency.

The city's key nonprofit developer of multifamily rental housing is the Asociación de Puertoriqueños en Marcha (APM), an organization that also provides a range of social services in the Latino barrio of Eastern North Philadelphia. APM's director of development, Rose Gray, left a career in private construction management to oversee the production of more

FIGURE 1— PHILADELPHIA ASSOCIATION OF COMMUNITY
DEVELOPMENT CORPORATIONS PRODUCTION REPORT, 1990–1996

Type of Project	Jobs	Units or Square Feet	Project Costs
Homeownership	445	471	$29,776,814
Rental	603	1,138	$96,965,335
Rental in Partnership with Private Developer	n/a	333	$26,600,000
Commercial Development	150	36,900	$3,465,000
Facilities Development	113	116,700	$4,517,000
Business Development/ Incubation	157	350,000	$2,506,000
Greening and Gardening	n/a	30	$201,577

Gross Totals 1990–1996

Type of Project	Jobs	Units or Square Feet	Project Costs
Housing	1,069	1,967	$153,469,649
Business/Commercial Development	307	386,900	$6,512,900

Note: The housing jobs numbers are based on a calculation of part-time construction jobs generated per project. Fifty percent were earmarked for residents of neighborhoods where projects were built.

than 200 units of rental housing in the last seven years. In the process, Gray has become a master of the arcane art of packaging low-income housing tax credit deals. In contrast to the anonymous architecture of most low-income housing projects, APM's developments embody a colorful vernacular, creating buildings regarded as expressions of this reviving neighborhood's pride and hope. APM will break ground this summer on Gateway Plaza, a 100,000-square-foot shopping center in the heart of the portion of the city most affected by the past three decades of disinvestment.

CDCs increasingly are looking for market solutions to maintain housing production at current levels. The condition of the Philadelphia real estate market makes this especially difficult. There are disturbingly few Philadelphia neighborhoods where sales prices will support the cost of rehabilitation or new construction. Particularly in neighborhoods that are home to

CDCs, a large gap exists between sales prices and CDC development costs, generally of between $25,000 to $50,000. The theory behind CDC housing projects is that subsidized developments will create value where little now exists, eventually resuscitating dormant markets. Until this process evolves more fully, however, subsidies from some source will be required to continue rebuilding many of Philadelphia's neighborhoods.

Hoping to build on the strong upscale and middle-income residential tradition in the city's other northwestern communities, Chestnut Hill and Mt. Airy, the Greater Germantown Housing Development Corporation (GGHDC) is targeting deteriorated sections of its neighborhood for rehabilitation and home improvement activities. Its goal is to make the city's entire northwest section into a vibrant bedroom community. With support from the city's Redevelopment Authority and the Fund for Urban Neighborhood Development of Philadelphia-based

Pew Charitable Trusts, GGHDC plans to develop 75 to 100 new and renovated houses for ownership and rental by the end of the decade.

Preserving the Italianate style typical of much of Germantown, new houses will sell for between $40,000 and $58,000. Renovated houses will go on the market for between $25,000 and $35,000. The city's median sales price in 1995 was $58,000. All purchasers of GGHDC housing receive mortgage counseling provided by the corporation's 113-year-old parent organization, Germantown Settlement. According to GGHDC Executive Director Stephen Kazanjian, "This is an excellent opportunity for Philadelphians to acquire their own home with lower payments than renting an apartment." Taken together with GGHDC's past development of more than 100 units of affordable housing for sale and 200 units for rent, the current homeownership initiative exemplifies the balanced and powerful neighborhood impact community nonprofits can achieve.

Economic Development

The community development field is undergoing a revolution. CDCs are moving to respond to the overwhelming need within their communities for jobs. In his 1994 report, "Future of Community Development," Philadelphia's director of housing, John Kromer, recommended that CDCs pursue a portfolio approach to revitalization. CDCs have been finding new ways to create and attract businesses, create jobs, green their neighborhoods, and empower community residents, while retaining a focus on housing redevelopment. CDCs have confronted the jobs issue in four ways:

• by providing construction jobs through CDC housing production;

• by providing jobs through CDC business ventures;

• by retaining jobs through business support programs; and

• by providing jobs skills training and placement for neighborhood residents.

From 1990 to 1996, CDC housing projects generated more than 1,000 part-time construction jobs. On average these jobs lasted less than a year; taken together, however, they significantly enhanced neighborhood economies.

A 1995 mayoral executive order requires contractors to hire 50 percent of their employees from the local area and to purchase from neighborhood suppliers as well. Ten Philadelphia CDCs currently are engaged in employment projects, including the development of incubators that foster and support the formation of new neighborhood businesses.

Impact Services is the Philadelphia leader in this field. Impact's West Kensington neighborhood was once one of the world's premier industrial centers. Now littered with abandoned factories, this patch of North Philadelphia struggles with severe rates of unemployment; finding stable, legal employment along this stretch of Allegheny Avenue is in itself surely one of the hardest jobs in the country. The key to Impact's success in linking neighborhood residents with jobs is Director John MacDonald's close relationships with and intimate knowledge of the employers still remaining along what is known as the American Street corridor.

Impact has been actively involved in the American Street Business Association for about ten years, and MacDonald has been the association's vice president for the past two. Equally essential, Impact has deep roots in the community and is at ease in the worlds of the street, the shop floor, and the board room, which is what makes impact's programs bloom in this tough environment. In addition to its role as labor market intermediary, Impact has itself become an important neighborhood employer and business incubator, starting numerous business ventures in the past 23 years. The latest is its profitable archival service and its school science-kit manufacturing business. The impact Archives is housed in a formerly vacant factory, renovated by the nonprofit for controlled-atmosphere document maintenance.

Borrowing from the successful industrial retention work of the group of CDCs involved in Cleveland's West Side Industrial Retention Network (WIRENet), a few Philadelphia CDCs are beginning to focus attention on finding ways to keep neighborhood manufacturers in the area by providing them with technical assistance and back office support. In addition, a variety of job initiatives are underway to support CDCs in their efforts to retain community residents and connect them to the regional economy.

The Philadelphia trailblazer in industrial retention is the Frankford Group Ministry (FGM) CDC. The Frankford neighborhood is an aging manufacturing powerhouse, perched between the most distressed sections of North Philadelphia and the almost suburban sprawl of Northeast Philadelphia. According to Executive Director Lonnie Chafin, FGM began its industrial retention efforts with "basic organizing, only with industrial leaders and business owners." According to Chafin, "We went door to door with the manufacturing firms remaining in Frankford, learning about their businesses and listening to their problems." Chafin and the community residents on his board were shocked to find that some 3,500 manufacturing jobs were still holding on. But they also found that most of the employers were small family shops, with one overworked and nearly overwhelmed owner running the show. Most surprising to Chafin, how-

ever, was the discovery that — with a little help in back office management, marketing, basic process engineering, or finding a more appropriate neighborhood site — these businesses were poised to grow. In a short time, FGM already has seen firms benefit from their program: winning important new contracts, reaching new markets, hiring new workers, or simply reversing what seemed like an inevitable slide into oblivion. "It's been exhilarating to have ways to improve the Frankford economy quickly become so obvious to us," comments Chafin.

The national model for industrial retention is Cleveland's WIRENet. WIRENet is a joint effort by three CDCs and dozens of neighborhood manufacturers on Cleveland's west side to provide business support services directly linked to job training and placement efforts by the nonprofit organization. WIRENet's record is impressive. It has assisted in the retention or expansion of more than 35 businesses and placed 400 trained workers directly in jobs within the neighborhood.

The most promising Philadelphia CDC employment initiatives involve connecting workers to the regional economy through sophisticated analysis of emerging local economic conditions and customized skills training. The Annie Casey Foundation has funded the Philadelphia Jobs Initiative, which, with the participation of several CDCs around the Logan and West Oak Lane sections of the city, focuses on employment opportunities for minority men ages 18 to 35. A major component of the initiative is the Philadelphia Area Accelerated Manufacturing Education Program (PhAME) of the Ogontz Avenue Revitalization Corporation (OARC). Over the past decade, OARC has focused considerable energy on the extraordinary renaissance of the once moribund commercial center in this traditionally stable, mixed-income, predominantly African

American community. After completing 133,000 square feet and $17.1 million worth of retail, commercial, recreational, institutional, and residential development along Ogontz Avenue, OARC has turned to the problem of declining family income and the coming effects of welfare devolution. This pattern is spreading in Philadelphia, as CDCs that have been dedicated to housing production over the past two decades are beginning to incorporate employment projects into their community strategic plans.

The Philadelphia Jobs Initiative and OARC's PhAME borrow from the approaches of such programs as Focus Hope in Detroit and the customized industrial skills training pioneered by the Jane Addams Resource Corporation in Chicago. In this model, CDCs tailor job training and placement to the needs of the vibrant and dominant industrial clusters in their target neighborhoods. Jane Addams has developed such a fruitful, collaborative relationship with the local wire extrusion industry that employers now provide the CDC with equipment to train the industry's future workforce. In a similar vein, PhAME has developed its training and job readiness programs to teach the skills required by specific regional manufacturers.

Community Greening

The newest endeavor for Philadelphia CDCs is "greening" and open-space management. As CDCs have undertaken strategic planning initiatives in their neighborhoods, they have come to the conclusion that they will never be rebuilding at the density produced by the last century's economy and settlement patterns. There is simply no need to rebuild in the traditional Philadelphia rowhouse style when so many people have left the city. This process, which CDCs refer to as "de-densification,"

has been written about at length in the Pennsylvania Horticultural Society's 1995 report, "Urban Vacant Land." CDCs had completed some 30 greening projects by 1996 alone. With an estimated 15,000 vacant lots and an additional 27,000 vacant structures as of 1992 — and with a population rebound unlikely any time soon — CDC involvement in open-space retention and improvement will accelerate greatly in the coming years.

A recent initiative of the New Kensington CDC, in partnership with the Pennsylvania Horticultural Society (PHS), is the most ambitious example of this new thinking about land use among CDCs. From a bird's eye view, Kensington is a latticework of exceptionally narrow blocks of row homes; its density reminds one of the medieval quarters of European cities. The neighborhood still has high rates of homeownership and many stable, well-kept blocks. With the departure of 23 percent of its population over the past two decades, however, portions of the neighborhood have been increasingly abandoned. For the past ten years, the CDC has focused on housing development, building or renovating more than 50 houses for affordable homeownership. At recent community meetings, however, according to Director John Carpenter, "The most resounding message has been that the neighborhood is a terrible-looking place." These meetings made the CDC look at development differently, and it began taking advantage of vacant land to reduce density and create community green space. Last year the city RDA entered into a novel partnership with the New Kensington CDC, using its power to speed the taking of abandoned property. With organizing support from LISC and technical support from PHS's urban greening program, Philadelphia Green, the CDC will either green or transfer to residents for sideyards the majority of vacant lots in the community over the next several years. Parks, community gardens, and sub-urban-style yards will spring up where there are now trash-strewn lots.

The Future

With relatively stable CDBG financing, operating support, and working capital, CDCs will continue their steady pace toward rebuilding their neighborhoods. More than ever before, however, CDCs will be required to refocus their attention on projects that are driven by market forces. Furthermore, welfare devolution demands that CDCs focus on neighborhood employment and family income.

42. PORTLAND GUIDES GROWTH THROUGH TRANSPORTATION

Gordon Oliver

Perched in his seventh floor office in the heart of downtown Portland, Fred Hansen, director of Oregon's Department of Environmental Quality, enjoys an excellent view of the city's past successes and current challenges. He can look down on the tree-covered transit mall, symbol of Portland's efforts to pump up what had been a flagging downtown. But he can also see the suburbs spreading out all around the city.

"We've got a rare opportunity to make this city livable," Hansen said during an interview in his office. "But if we continue the breakneck growth we've had for the last five years without basic changes, we'll really have problems."

Portland has a reputation as a place that works, partly because it has attempted regional solutions to regional problems. Portland's Downtown Plan, adopted in 1972 under former Mayor Neil Goldschmidt, helped revive a struggling core and gave Portland the reputation of a city that knows how to plan for its future. In the years that followed, Goldschmidt went on to become U.S. Secretary of Transportation in the Carter administration, and the Portland metropolitan region continued to attract attention for its success in both land-use and transportation planning.

The tree-shaded transit mall, which opened in 1978 along two downtown streets, is part of a three-county transit system. That system, including a light rail line that carries 25,000 riders every weekday, delivers 40 percent of the core area's workers to their jobs.

But the region of 1.1 million people cannot rest on its laurels. Steady growth is pushing jobs and housing to the edge of a regional urban growth boundary that encompasses 234,000 acres in 24 cities and parts of three counties. Development is also spreading out — even into small towns outside the urban growth boundary dozens of miles from downtown Portland.

Moreover, despite huge investments in transit, the automobile is becoming more — not less— important in the region. On average, Portland-area residents are increasing their travel by almost four percent a year, placing a burden on the transportation system and the airshed, Hansen notes. A population growth rate of about

Originally published as "Portland Revs Up for Action," Planning, Vol. 60, No. 8, August, 1994. Published by the American Planning Association, Chicago, Illinois. Reprinted with permission of the publisher.

1.4 percent a year compounds the challenge.

Hansen is among the regional leaders seeking new approaches in a region that has shown it is open to them. His agency has broad authority under Oregon and federal law to restrict automobile use and impose industrial restrictions in order to preserve air quality. But Hansen hopes the region can avoid punishing industry and the public by gradually developing a strong transit system while establishing land-use patterns that give residents a choice in how to get around.

Hansen is optimistic. He notes that the area has a history of finding regional solutions through an obscure but powerful group called the Joint Policy Advisory Committee on Transportation — JPACT for short — which represents major political and transportation constituencies. Technically an advisory committee to the elected council of the regional government, known as Metro, JPACT calls the shots in all major transportation issues.

"Things that are very tough fights in other regions are worked out by consensus here," says Hansen, a JPACT member. "There is more of a regional ability to try to set goals."

The Clean Air Hook

Reshaping growth will be a tough battle even here, but Hansen is hoping that the federal clean air mandate will give a boost to regional planning efforts.

The Portland region is now listed as a marginal nonattainment area for ozone, although it has met federal standards every year since 1990. It's also listed as a moderate nonattainment area for carbon monoxide, although that problem has almost entirely disappeared, and downtown Portland has not violated the carbon monoxide standard since 1985.

The environmental quality department is now preparing plans to submit to the U.S. Environmental Protection Agency early next year requesting clean air status for both ozone and carbon monoxide. Those plans will include a strategy for meeting federal standards for the next decade.

The strategy will call for expanding the motor vehicle inspection program into areas outside the regional urban growth boundary, combined with implementation of a more sophisticated vehicle emission test. The environmental quality department is also preparing an "employee commute options rule" that will require companies with 50 to 100 workers to submit plans for reducing single-occupancy vehicle trips by 10 percent. The figure jumps to 20 percent for larger employers. Both programs would start next year.

Neither of these programs has aroused much opposition. Even the employee commuting rule seems likely to glide through without controversy because it is far less demanding than a similar program in neighboring Washington State.

Parking Changes Ahead

What could be controversial is the department's recommendation to lift Portland's 20-year-old downtown parking lid, which allows no more than 44,322 parking spaces in the core area. Hansen says his agency is convinced that it can keep carbon monoxide to acceptable levels without the current lid, and the city has promised to maintain a strict parking ratio downtown.

The main reason that lifting the downtown parking lid hasn't caused a furor is DEQ's proposal to impose what would be the nation's first regional parking restrictions on the Portland area. The agency's "parking ratio rule" would reduce the number of new parking spaces by requiring local governments to establish *maximum* parking ratios for new development. Its goal is a 10 percent reduction in vehicle trips generated by new retail, commercial, and industrial projects.

The parking rule, which was authorized by the state legislature in 1993 and is now being developed for implementation in 1995, parallels the statewide Transportation Planning Rule, which was adopted in 1991 by Oregon's Land Conservation and Development Commission and is being implemented in phases by local governments.

The transportation planning rule calls for a 10 percent reduction in parking spaces over the next 20 years. It also calls for a 10 percent reduction in vehicle miles traveled per capita over 20 years, and a 20 percent reduction in 30 years. The region's residents now average 12.8 miles of travel per day.

The transportation rule, which only this summer is beginning to be reflected in city and county planning codes, requires all commercial developments to be oriented to transit, bicycles, and pedestrians. In practice, that could mean that supermarkets could no longer be set back behind parking lots. And builders of fast-food restaurants would have to make them accessible by pedestrians and cyclists. Subdivision streets and bike paths would have to hook up to schools and stores.

Case Study

Portland's Lloyd District, just across the Willamette River from downtown, will be a test site for the new parking rule. In the 1960s, the former residential and warehouse district started to take shape as a suburban-style shopping and office district. In addition to the office towers, it includes the huge Lloyd Center shopping mall, the Oregon Convention Center, Memorial Coliseum, and a new arena under construction by the Portland Trail Blazers.

Many of the district's 17,000 workers commute by car, although the opening of a light-rail line in 1986 and expansion of bus service have allowed for job growth without an increase in parking spaces. Today, there are 17,600 parking spaces, but nearly half in shopping mall lots. The environmental quality department clean air strategy calls for expanding the free bus service now provided downtown by the Tri-County Metropolitan Transit District to the Lloyd District, perhaps before the end of this year.

But the biggest change will be the establishment for the first time of a maximum parking ratio. The new rule will allow two parking spaces per 1,000 square feet of office space in the district. In contrast, the city allows between 0.7 and one parking space for every 1,000 feet of office space downtown.

"In downtown," says Elsa Coleman, deputy director of Portland's Office of Transportation, "we've always had four goals: air quality, transit ridership, traffic flow, and accommodating development. By expanding to the Lloyd District, we're expanding that combination."

The LUTRAQ Approach

In the 1980s, a nonprofit land-use watchdog group called 1000 Friends of Oregon challenged a highway bypass proposed for suburban Washington County, outside Portland. That challenge raised issues about the link between land-use and transportation polices that led the state to adopt its Transportation Planning Rule.

While the bypass question is still not resolved, 1000 Friends of Oregon has broadened its effort. It is leading a $1 million study, financed by grants and federal funds, of the links between suburban land-use patterns and transportation demands.

The study is called "Making the Land Use/Transportation/Air Quality Connection"—LUTRAQ for short.

A key finding so far is that vehicle miles traveled could be reduced by 10 percent in the suburbs by creating a pedestrian-oriented environment similar to what already exists in old Portland neighborhoods. The study has also concluded that a market demand exists for 1,150 multi-family and 1,400 single-family housing units annually in transit-oriented developments in Washington County.

"When we began the study in 1989, many people were incredulous," says Keith Bartholomew, a 1000 Friends attorney who heads the study. "Nobody had thought of changing traffic by changing land-use." Today, the project is attracting attention regionally and nationally. This spring, several hundred planning professionals from all over the U.S. attended a Portland conference sponsored by 1000 Friends and the Lincoln Institute of Land Policy to consider its implications.

Metro's Take

Simultaneously, Metro, the Portland-area regional government, is working on its own long-range plan known as "Region 2040." Agency planners are examining the implications of three scenarios: continued sprawl, tightly contained development within the urban growth boundary, and controlled development of satellite cities centered around existing small towns. This fall, the Metro council is expected to make key decisions about whether to move or hold the present urban growth boundary.

Eventually, Metro will develop the nation's first regional framework plan with authority to override local plans. Over time, the huge planning effort should slowly transform the region's transportation system.

"The land-use pattern changes won't be too great in the next 10 years," says Andrew Cotugno, Metro's planning director. "In 20 to 40 years it will be more noticeable, and people will see more transit and there will be more willingness to fund more bike and pedestrian projects."

Light Rail Works

Public support is high for the region's light rail system, called MAX—the Metropolitan Area Express. The first 15-mile-long line, which opened in 1986, runs east from the downtown through the Lloyd District to suburban Gresham. A second 12-mile line to the west side suburbs is now under construction. The first phase of the project is expected to be completed in September 1997, with a six-mile extension to be finished a year later. The entire project will cost nearly $1 billion.

The Tri-County Metropolitan Transit District, which runs the light rail and bus service, expects to draw 18,900 riders in the west side line's first year of operation, increasing to 27,100 in 2005. A third line, which would run from suburban Clackamas County on the south through Portland and north into Clark County, Washington, is now under study. The transit district may ask voters this fall to approve $475 million in bonds to help pay the estimated $2 billion construction costs. The money will be collected only if the federal government approves the project in 1996.

Although light rail has helped focus development on the transit spine running east through the downtown and the Lloyd District, the transit-oriented housing developments and shopping centers visualized east of the central city haven't materialized. Still, Tri-Met has found that 36 percent of the region's residents ride transit at least once a month, double the number of occasional riders before light rail.

MAX has almost as many riders on Saturdays as the 25,000 it averages on weekdays.

"Light rail, for good or evil, has been perceived as different than transit," Fred Hansen says. "People who would never get on a bus will get on MAX."

Hoping to take advantage of light rail's popularity, Tri-Met, local governments, and the Department of Environmental Quality are engaged in an unusual public-private venture. They want to create transit-oriented developments on large undeveloped parcels near planned west side light rail stops.

They're starting with a 124-acre wooded site in suburban Beaverton. The city of Beaverton, Tri-Met, Metro, and DEQ are working with several property owners to develop a master plan, which is expected to be completed this month. Portland architect George Crandall is leading the planning effort, and Peter Calthorpe of San Francisco is a participant.

Tom Walsh, general manager of Tri-Met, is convinced that elected officials will no longer be able to sell Congress or local voters on funding light rail solely because of its value as a mode of transportation. Development patterns will also be an issue.

"The principal value of light rail is as an organizing tool," says Walsh. "It won't ever be good enough just to keep believing in it. We need to galvanize public support for what the region should look like."

Model City?

Planners and public officials from around the nation will be watching eagerly as Portland tries to strike a balance between transit and automobiles.

"Generally speaking, on land-use and parking management issues, Portland is at the top of the list," says Grace Crunican, a former official of Portland's Office of Transportation who is now the deputy adminis-

trator of the Federal Transit Administration. "People around the country have been talking about doing things that Portland takes for granted."

In the 1970s, for example, the city killed a project known as the Mount Hood Freeway — which was to run from downtown Portland through the city's east side, ending at another freeway — and instead spent the money on arterial improvements and light rail. Later in the same decade, a waterfront expressway disappeared and was replaced by the Tom McCall Waterfront Park, named for the state's environmentally crusading governor, who died in 1973.

Portland tackled its air pollution problems by imposing the downtown parking lid in 1972 and beginning a gradual phase-out of surface parking. Now, there are 11,639 spaces in surface lots, down from an estimated 15,800 two decades ago. The downtown has added over 30,000 jobs since the early 1970s while adding fewer then 5,000 parking spaces, and the percentage of downtown workers riding transit to work has doubled in that period.

Now there seems to be some slippage. Car pooling has declined by 20 percent in two years. Transit ridership has held steady for almost two years at about 200,000 trips a day, but the percentage of transit commuters has also dropped by 20 percent since 1980, according to U.S. Census figures.

In the region, less than four percent of all travel is by transit, and the percentage is declining. According to U.S. Department of Transportation 1990 statistics, Portland residents take 47 transit trips a year. That's double Houston's rate of 25 trips but less than half the San Francisco Bay Area's 109.

"Many double-wage households and single-parent households don't have alternatives to the car," says Keith Lawton, a Metro transportation planner who is leading a federally funded study of travel habits. "I don't care how good transit is; they don't have time to use it." Metro is asking 6,000

Portland-area residents and 6,000 elsewhere in the state to keep two-day diaries of all their activities, including transportation.

So far, Metro's Region 2040 plan doesn't offer a way to meet state goals for reducing vehicle miles traveled. Even if all growth were to be contained within the urban growth boundary. Metro projects just a 12 percent drop in vehicle miles traveled, far short of the state's 20 percent goal.

No one can ignore the sense of looming crisis. "There's enough evidence from everyplace else that things do get worse in a hurry," says Walsh. "We don't have the luxury of a lot of time."

Last year, however, a legislature preoccupied by a school finance crisis killed the transportation package that would have increased funding for roads and transit. JPACT members are searching for an alternative, but this summer they're busy looking for future light rail money.

Nervousness

For now, regional leaders are hoping that the U.S. EPA will approve clean air maintenance plans for both ozone and carbon monoxide. "If we can implement a plan now, we can get through until 2005," says John Kowalczyk, manager of DEQ's air planning section. "If we go over the limit, we might have to limit industrial growth."

The next step is to carry out the long-range transportation and land-use policies that are now being put on the books. But even in Portland, new ideas like the transportation planning rule won't come without controversy. "It's one thing to write rules," says Roger Millar, a consultant who represents industrial associations in discussions about the new rule. "It's another thing to change hearts and minds."

Yet Hansen believes that the region's residents will rise to the challenge. He is convinced that Portlanders place a high value on the clean air that gives them a clear view of snow-capped Mt. Hood 50 miles east of the city.

"If parking ratios become too burdensome, then people will have to come forward with alternatives," he says. "The choice we don't have is to do nothing."

43. WASHINGTON EMBRACES MIXED-USE DEVELOPMENT

Libby Howland

Development markets on the east side of downtown Washington are picking up steam. The opening in December of the MCI Center, the new multipurpose sports and entertainment arena, and the launching of a downtown business improvement district (BID) last summer are two examples of this trend. Mixed-use developments, destination entertainment attractions, and centralized management are the leitmotifs of the area's resurgence.

Though commercial real estate brokers may refer to the 120-block area — roughly bounded by 15th Street, Massachusetts Avenue, 2nd Street, and Constitution Avenue — as the East End, other real estate and civic interests are calling it Washington's "new downtown." Most of the office development now taking place in the District of Columbia is occurring here, where the vacancy rate for Class A space stands at around six percent and average Class A rents — at almost $37 per square foot — are high.

Metrorail subway access was a main reason cited by Abe Pollin, owner of the Wizards basketball team and the Capitals hockey team, for choosing a downtown Washington location for the $200 million, one million-square-foot state-of-the-art arena and destination retail/entertainment complex that many say already has sparked the revival of its down-at-the-heels neighborhood. The MCI Center is built over the Gallery Place-Chinatown Metro station, through which three lines pass — a situation that complicated construction — and it is near four other Metro stations.

According to Pollin, 70 percent of fans in the first weeks of the MCI Center arrived by Metro. Attendance at Wizards games was strong in the five weeks following the arena's opening but less so at Capitals games; however, Capitals games were not selling well earlier in the season when they were held at the US Airways Arena in suburban Landover, Maryland. Seating capacity is close to 20,000 for basketball games and slightly less for hockey. Approximately 100 Wizards, Capitals, and Georgetown University Hoyas games are scheduled annually, and it is expect that another 170 concerts and other events will be booked each year.

Crews can accomplish changeovers

Originally published as "Resurgence in Downtown Washington," Urban Land, Vol. 57, No. 3, March, 1998. Published by the Urban Land Institute, Washington, D.C. Reprinted with permission of the publisher.

from one sport to another or to other events in a matter of hours by taking up or installing floors that fit over the ice and rearranging the retractable seats. Also providing flexibility for quick transitions are ample equipment storage and staging areas, truck and bus access to the building interior, and an extensive backstage area that contains dressing rooms for performers, a special superstar suite, locker rooms, a fitness room, a family lounge for players' relatives, and production offices.

In some corporate circles, access to professional sports facilities increasingly is considered an amenity. The MCI Center therefore should have some influence on the market for office development in the neighborhood, and corporations should provide a primary market for the arena's luxury suite and club seat sales. The arena has 110 private suites, which are located at the 19th, 25th, and 31st rows and cost $100,000 to $175,000 a year, with minimum five-year leases. They are well appointed, with 12 theater-style seats, television, private restrooms, phones, wet bars, and refrigerators. Associated services include catering, underground parking, and access to a full-service business center that is still under development. Another 3,045 extrawide club seats are located between rows 20 and 31, and their ticket holders enjoy access to the Capital Club, a full-service restaurant and lounge; in-seat food service; specialty food concessions; and the business services center. The Capital Club is open to the public for private events. The arena's premium-seating food services are operated by Chicago-based Levy Restaurants.

Perhaps the most unusual aspect of the new MCI Center is its operation as a destination retail/entertainment complex. Plans call for the center to remain open from 9:00 a.m. to 11:00 p.m. daily for non-arena uses. Among the attractions are Discovery Channels' Destination: DC, the Na-

tional Sports Gallery, the Velocity Grill, and Modell's Sporting Goods Team Store:

• Destination: DC, Discovery Channel's flagship store, is a 30,000-square-foot, $20 million interactive multimedia complex that opened early this month. Owned by the Bethesda, Maryland-based cable television network, the Discovery Channel store is expected to attract a million customers during its first year. Aptly tagged a cross between a museum and an entertainment center, the store features four themed floors where visitors "explore the universe" through Discovery Channel exhibits— and retail items— in paleo world (level 1), including a 420-foot cast of a Tyrannosaurus Rex skeleton; ocean planet (mezzanine); world cultures and animal habitats (level 2); and outer space (level 3). A state-of-the-art, high-definition theater is on the top level.

• Velocity Grill, a 20,000-square-foot, upscale sports-theme restaurant on three levels, can be entered from the street or from the arena's main and club concourses. It overlooks the Wizards' practice court, which also is used by local recreational basketball leagues. It features on-site video production capabilities and ubiquitous television screens and video monitors.

• The National Sports Gallery— codeveloped by TeamWorks-Sports Consulting Group, the American Sportscasters Association, and the MCI Center — is a 25,000-square-foot sports museum and participatory activities zone. It houses the American Sportscasters Association Hall of Fame and also showcases treasured sports memorabilia. Among the activities that can be enjoyed there are pitching to on-screen major league hitters, putting at the 18th hole of the MCI Heritage Classic in Hilton Head, or tossing the football to on-screen receivers at rookie training camp.

• The 2,500-square-foot Modell's Sporting Goods Team Store features a full line of NBA, NHL, MLB, and NFL team apparel and merchandise, as well as 12 television monitors that show satellite transmissions of on-the-road Wizards and Capitals games and other sporting events.

Another draw for visitors is a behind-the-scenes, one-hour tour offered throughout the day for groups and individuals. Tour stops include team locker rooms; star dressing room; the television control room; the Zamboni ice resurfacing machine; a luxury suite; and An Insider's View — a film about the nation's capital that is shown at Destination: DC's theater.

The MCI Center features a number of other advanced technology applications. A high-speed fiber-optic network called arena Net provides tenants with Internet access, intranet capability, LAN/WAN systems, E-mail, and point-of-sales and office systems support. Seventeen interactive arena Net stations around the facility provide visitors with local tourist and MCI Center events information and also entertain them with features such as replays of great moments in sports history or digital postcards in which they appear in scenes with star athletes. A 15-ton suspended scoreboard with 12-by-16-foot video screens using LED (light-emitting diode) technology provides spectators with bright, clear images of the action on the event floor.

One clear impact that the MCI Center already has had is on development activity in Chinatown, a small area north of the arena. After years of what many consider a stagnant existence, Chinatown, with its restaurants and small shops, has become what many characterize as a boom town. Few regret the loss of some of its Chinese character as a price of transformation, although some Chinese residents and business owners fear that the area may change and drive some of them out of business as a result of high rents, huge crowds, and increasing traffic.

Downtown DC BID

Efforts to establish a downtown business improvement district began in the late 1980s, and in 1996 enabling legislation was passed. The imminent arrival of the arena provided the final push, according to Richard Bradley, the BID's executive director. Part of a burgeoning national trend, Washington's downtown BID was approved by the city last August and became operational shortly thereafter.

Directly north of the Mall, Washington's primary tourist draw, the downtown BID encompasses an area that contains 67 million square feet of office space. Fifty million square feet is in private ownership; 14 million square feet belongs to the government; and three million square feet is owned by tax-exempt organizations. There are 6,500 hotel rooms, and a slowly growing residential sector. All Metro subway lines serve the area.

More than a dozen new restaurants opened last year, and more are in the pipeline. Major attractions in the area include a number of theaters — National Theatre, Ford's Theatre, Shakespeare Theatre, and Warner Theatre; museums, among them the Museum of American Art, National Building Museum, National Museum of Women in the Arts, and National Portrait Gallery; a concentration of art galleries; the J. Edgar Hoover FBI Building; the Washington Convention Center; and now the MCI Center. The Washington Opera also has tentative plans to build an opera house in the new downtown area, possibly converting the vacant Woodward & Lothrop department store on F Street.

In addition, the city plans to construct a new, two million-square-foot, $650 million convention center on the north edge of downtown at Mount Vernon Square along New York Avenue by the year 2001. A consortium of developers has put forth a proposal to redevelop the city's current 800,000-square-foot convention center—built 15 years ago and already seen as too small to meet current demand—as an "American entertainment center" containing restaurants, retail venues, and up to 20 movie screens. The location is just three blocks away from the MCI Center.

A recently announced office project speaks to the entertainment focus of new development in the downtown district. The U.S. Mint has signed a 20-year lease with Development Resources Inc. (DRI) for a 232,000-square-foot building that DRI will develop at 801 9th Street. It is scheduled for completion at the end of next year and will occupy 140,000 square feet and lease out the remaining space. The agency is contemplating retail and entertainment uses for the first-floor space, including a historical exhibit about the U.S. Mint.

The downtown BID is a private nonprofit corporation that is run by and accountable to the area's business sector. Its stated purpose is to stabilize and improve the district's environment; retain, expand, and attract businesses and investment; and create a positive identity for the downtown. The BID's organizing effort was overseen by a coalition of area property owners, business owners, and civic and cultural organizations led by Robert Gladstone, president of Quadrangle Development and of the BID planning committee, and by Robert Carr, chairman of Carr Real Estate Development Corporation and the committee's vice president. Its business plan includes six main elements:

Public Safety. Uniformed, unarmed public safety officers have begun patrolling the area as adjuncts to regular metropolitan police patrols. They monitor street activity, provide security escorts and assistance in personal emergencies, and give directions. Together with special street and sidewalk maintenance personnel, they are know as downtown SAM (safety and maintenance) personnel.

Maintenance. Downtown SAM personnel also provide street and sidewalk cleaning services, remove graffiti, maintain street furniture and signs, and provide landscaping services.

Transportation. The BID works with other organizations to improve the district's accessibility by all modes of transportation and to improve directional signage and maps and other visitor guides. Some effort will be made to persuade Metro to extend its operating hours past midnight, especially on weekends.

Marketing. The BID is undertaking a campaign to market downtown Washington to a variety of target audiences and plans to work with local businesses to support activities to bring people downtown.

Physical Improvements. The BID plans to work with the city to implement a multiyear physical improvements program involving street lights, signage, street furniture and landscaping, and visitor-attracting uses like sidewalk cafés.

Homeless Services. Downtown SAM personnel seek to provide helpful information to homeless individuals in the area and to homeless service providers. The BID helps coordinate communication among the providers and works to find support programs for the homeless, including employment in the SAM force.

The downtown BID's budget for its first full year of normalized operations is $7.7 million, distributed as follows:

- Security Programs $2,400,000
- Maintenance Programs   1,340,000
- Transportation Programs   270,000
- Marketing   910,000
- Physical Improvements   1,150,000
- Homeless Programs   340,000
- BID Operations, including
  program overhead   1,000,000
- Contingency (four percent)   290,000

Its funds come from a BID assessment on taxable commercial real properties within the BID area and from voluntary contributions and contracts for services from tax-exempt properties. First-year assessments are $50 per room for hotels and $0.12 per square foot on net rentable square footage (calculated as 90 percent of gross building area for properties for which net rentable area is not available) and on unimproved land and parking lots. The first-year budget of $7.7 million is expected to be raised from the BID assessment ($6.1 million from 51 million square feet of commercial space); an anticipated contract with the U.S. General Services Administration to sell BID services to government-owned properties in the BID area ($1.2 million); and voluntary contributions from tax-exempt properties ($400,000).

Proceeding by fits and starts, the resurgence of Washington's new downtown has been a long time in the making. With the coming of the MCI Center, the downtown appears to have chosen mixed-use development with an emphasis on entertainment to propel itself into the future.

PART V

The Future

44. CITIES AND SUBURBS WORKING TOGETHER

Larry C. Ledebur and William R. Barnes

There is a strong economic justification for addressing the needs of central cities and for cooperation among cities and suburbs to meet the mutual economic needs of their local economic region. It can be found in the strong and consistent relationship between changes in central city incomes and changes in suburban incomes. For every one dollar increase in central city household incomes, suburban household incomes increase by $1.12.

In each of the 25 metropolitan areas with the most rapidly growing suburbs, measured by changes in median household income, central city incomes also increased over the 1979–1989 period. No suburbs in this high growth set experienced income growth without corresponding growth in their central city. This evidence indicates that cities and suburbs are interdependent. Their fates and fortunes are intertwined. Further, the evidence suggests that this interdependence of city and suburbs is becoming stronger, rather than diminishing.

This documentation of the significant relationship between cities and their suburbs is critical to the debate about whether suburbs can prosper and succeed, regardless of the fortunes of their central cities. This finding, however, should not be surprising. Cities and their suburbs are not two distinct economies. They are a single economy, highly interdependent with their fortunes inextricably intertwined.

These local economic regions are key to federal efforts to "grow the national economy." Federal efforts to "jump start" the economy through a short-run stimulus package, as well as long term efforts to increase national productivity and investment must target these local concentrations of economic activities and sources of productivity growth.

The debate over the shape of the national economic program should also recognize the diversity of circumstances and performance of these local economic regions. The breadth and depth of variations in performance of these economies, make it less likely that uniform national economic policies, administered as if there

Reprinted with permission from All in It Together: Cities, Suburbs and Local Economic Regions, *February, 1993. Published by the National League of Cities, Washington, D.C. Reprinted with permission of the publisher.*

was a single national economy, will suffice as a "national program for economic growth." There is a wide range of variation on most measures; this study presents the variation in median household income, employment change, and unemployment. This range of diversity strongly suggests that federal policies should be sensitive to these differences.

The findings of this study suggest looking at the U.S. economy as a common market of local economic regions rather than as a huge but undifferentiated "national economy." In turn, this view indicates several directions in which federal policy should develop.

• Federal economic policy should aim at improving the condition and performance of the local economic regions.
• Federal economic policy should address the variety among these local economic regions as to their circumstances and needs.
• Federal economic policy should seek to diminish city/suburb disparities within the local economic regions.

Interdependence of Cities and Suburbs

The 1990 Census provides a new focus on the critical issue of the relationship between central cities and suburbs in the United States.[1] The debate is most severely formulated in terms of whether suburbs can prosper and succeed, regardless of the fate and fortunes of their central city; or whether the prosperity of cities and suburbs are intertwined and interdependent.

This issue is critical. In the State of the Union speech President Clinton declared,"We are all in it together." If cities and suburbs are "in it together," a strong *economic* justification can be made for addressing the needs of central cities and cooperation among cities and suburbs to meet the mutual economic needs of their metropolitan area. If, on the other hand, the fate of cities and suburbs are not economically intertwined, the case for addressing the problems of central cities must be made in terms of social equity and avoidance of the longer term costs of failure to address these problems. In the current politics of the nation, the economic argument appears to be more compelling than the call for social equity.

The recently available 1990 median household income data provide new opportunities to test the hypothesis that the economic futures of cities and suburbs are interdependent.[2]

• If cities and suburbs are economically independent, rather than interdependent, then changes in suburban incomes and central city incomes should not be related or move together. A plot of these relationships will appear randomly scattered.
• If there is some degree of interdependence, changes in suburban incomes would be related to changes in central incomes and vice versa. A plot of these relationships, the scattergram, will cluster in a clear and discernable pattern.

This is clear evidence of a strong and consistent relationship between changes in central city incomes and changes in suburban incomes. The interpretation of this relationship is as follows. For every one dollar increase in central city income, suburban incomes increase by $1.12. Conversely, for every increase of $1.12 in suburban income, central city income increases by one dollar. The relationship does not imply causation, i.e., that change in one causes the change in the other. Rather, the relationship is mutual, interactive, and interdependent. This evidence strongly suggests that the economic fate and fortunes of cities and suburbs are inextricably intertwined.

Where suburban incomes are increasing, central city incomes are increasing. Conversely, where central city incomes are decreasing, suburban incomes are decreasing. Tables 1 and 2 present detailed data on these patterns of change. Table 1 focuses on the 25 largest metropolitan areas in which suburban incomes increased most rapidly between 1980 and 1990. Table 2 deals with the 18 largest metropolitan areas in which suburban incomes declined over this period.

In high growth areas, suburbs and central cities grew together. Table 1 shows that in each of the 25 metropolitan areas with the most rapidly growing suburbs, measured by absolute and percentage gains in median household income, central city incomes also increased over the 1979–1989 period. In other words, in the high growth set of metropolitan areas, no suburbs experienced income growth without corresponding growth in their central city. This also means that no central city in this high growth sample experienced income growth in the absence of suburban growth. In all but one (San Diego) of the 25 metropolitan areas, the absolute gains in suburbs exceed those in their central cities. In 10 of these metropolitan areas, however, the rate of central city income growth exceeded that of their suburbs.

	SUBURBS		CENTRAL CITY	
TABLE 1— METROPOLITAN AREAS WITH RAPIDLY GROWING SUBURBS **CHANGE IN MEDIAN HOUSEHOLD INCOME, 1979–1989**	Absolute	Percent	Absolute	Percent
1. Bridgeport-Stamford-Norwalk-Danbury, CT NECMA	$12,519	26.1	$9,196	29.8
2. Oxnard-Ventura, CA PMSA	$10,995	28.2	$8,095	26.4
3. New York, NY PMSA	$10,395	26.3	$6,464	26.4
4. San Jose, CA PMSA	$10,096	25.1	$7,620	19.7
5. Boston-Lawrence-Salem-Lowel-Brockton, MA	$9,083	26.3	$7,087	32.2
6. Middlesex-Somerset-Hunterdon, NJ PMSA	$8,906	21.4	$4,639	19.6
7. Newark, NJ PMSA	$8,669	22.9	$4,592	26.9
8. Hartford-New Britain-Middletown-Bristol, CT NECMA	$8,650	22.8	$4,790	19.4
9. Bergen-Passaic, NJ PMSA	$8,433	21.7	$6,729	33.3
10. Anaheim-Santa Ana, CA PMSA	$8,372	21.0	$4,817	14.8
11. New Haven-Waterbury-Meriden, CT NECMA	$8,286	23.2	$6,010	25.4
12. Washington, DC-MD-VA MSA	$7,315	17.1	$3,396	12.4
13. San Francisco, CA PMSA	$7,237	18.2	$6,663	24.9
14. Worcester-Fitchburg-Leominster, MA NECMA	$7,234	22.7	$5,306	21.7
15. Oakland, CA PMSA	$6,687	18.2	$3,862	16.6
16. San Diego, CA MSA	$5,914	19.7	$6,021	21.8
17. Philadelphia, PA-NJ PMSA	$5,880	16.7	$2,401	10.8
18. Raleigh-Durham, NC MSA	$5,672	18.4	$4,756	18.5
19. Honolulu, HI MSA	$5,593	14.7	$3,644	10.9
20. Los Angeles-Long Beach, CA PMSA	$5,351	16.4	$4,586	17.3
21. Providence-Pawtucket-Woodstock, MA NECMA	$5,301	17.5	$3,472	16.9
22. Riverside-San Bernardino, CA PMSA	$5,238	18.3	$3,293	12.0
23. Baltimore, MD MSA	$4,838	12.9	$2,445	11.3
24. West Palm Beach-Boca Raton-Delray Beach, MSA	$4,586	16.4	$3,950	14.0
25. Albany-Schenectady- Troy, NY MSA	$4,562	14.7	$3,297	15.6

TABLE 2 — METROPOLITAN AREAS WITH SUBURBS EXPERIENCING INCOME
DECLINES CHANGE IN MEDIAN HOUSEHOLD INCOME, 1979–1989

	SUBURBS		CENTRAL CITY	
	Absolute	Percent	Absolute	Percent
1. Fresno, CA MSA	($9)	0.0	$600	2.5
2. Cincinnati, OH-KY-IN PMSA	($24)	-0.1	($363)	-1.7
3. Portland, OR PMSA	($204)	-0.6	$669	2.7
4. Las Vegas, NV MSA	($281)	-0.9	$1,139	3.9
5. Kansas City, MO-KS MSA	($314)	-0.9	($554)	-2.1
6. Buffalo, NY PMSA	($743)	-2.2	($1,063)	-5.4
7. Tucson, AZ MSA	($755)	-2.3	($2,001)	-8.4
8. Detroit, MI PMSA	($969)	-2.4	($4,830)	-20.5
9. Tulsa, OK MSA	($1,005)	-3.4	($2,737)	-9.6
10. Louisville, KY-IN MSA	($1,050)	-3.3	($552)	-2.7
11. Oklahoma City, OK MSA	($1,327)	-4.5	($1,079)	-4.0
12. Denver, CO PMSA	($1,347)	-3.5	($1,038)	-4.0
13. Cleveland, OH PMSA	($1,380)	-3.7	($2,878)	-13.9
14. Salt Lake City-Ogden, UT MSA	($1,628)	-4.7	$224	1.0
15. Akron, OH PMSA	($1,765)	-5.0	($2,510)	-10.1
16. Pittsburgh, PA PMSA	($3,418)	-10.8	($1,859)	-8.2
17. Houston, TX PMSA	($4,667)	-11.0	($4,886)	-15.7
18. New Orleans, LA MSA	($4,913)	-14.7	($1,442)	-7.2

The interdependence between suburbs and their cities is also apparent for suburban areas experiencing income decline. Over the 10 year period, suburbs in 18 of the 78 largest metropolitan areas experienced declines in real median household incomes (see Table 2). In all but four of these, central city incomes also declined. In only one of these four did the decline in suburban income exceed one percent (Salt Lake City: -4.7 percent). The corresponding increases in central city incomes were also relatively small, ranging between one and four percent.

Of the remaining 35 metropolitan areas (not presented in the two tables above), all experienced suburban income growth. Central city median household income grew in 25 and declined in 10. In the overall sample of 78 metropolitan areas, therefore, suburban incomes grew in 60 and declined in 18. Central city incomes grew in 54 and declined in 24 (31 percent). The direction of change in suburban and central city household incomes was the same in all but 14 of these metropolitan areas (18 percent).

Furthermore, the strength of the relationship between cities and their suburbs appears to be increasing rather than declining. In 1979, the relationship between central city and suburban median household incomes was quite weak.[3] Ten years later, in 1989, this relationship had become stronger and more apparent. In other words, the degree of economic interdependence, as measured by income levels, increased over the decade.

Growing the Economies

While the documentation of the positive relationship between suburban and city household incomes is important, it should not be surprising. A city and its suburbs are not two distinct economies. They are a single regional economy, highly interdependent, with their fortunes intertwined. Given this interdependence in the regional economy, it would be surprising, indeed, if changes in city and suburban incomes were not highly interrelated. *The fate of the local economic region will dictate the fortunes of both cities and suburbs.*

Previous *Economic Reports* examined the relationships between local economic regions and the disparities between central cities and suburbs. We found that in metropolitan areas where disparity (as measured by per capita income) is high, total employment growth is lower than in metropolitan areas where disparity is lower.[4] This analysis did not find a direct relationship between the disparity and indicators of suburban economic performance. Rather, the relationship is between the city/suburb disparity and the performance of the overall local economic region.

Disparities between cities and suburbs are sharp. Some became increasingly distinct between 1980 and 1990.

• The rate of increase in employed residents was four times greater in suburbs than in cities over this decade.
• By 1990, the ratio of employed persons living in central cities to those in suburbs was .54, compared to .61 in 1980.
• Unemployment rates in 1990 were significantly greater in cities than in their suburbs (disparity ratio=1.7).
• The percent of persons in poverty was more than two and a half times greater in central cities (disparity ratio=2.4).
• The proportion of residents with high school degrees in cities was 83 percent of that of the suburbs, and the proportion of college graduates is 59 percent.

In policy terms, it appears that diminishing these disparities will strengthen the overall local economic region upon which both central city and suburb depend.

The local economic regions are not bounded by government jurisdictional lines. These local economic regions comprise city, suburb, and often nearby rural areas. Taken all together with the linkages among them, the U.S. common market of these local economic regions constitute the "national economy."

The performance of these local region economies will be crucial to the success of federal economic policies. Federal efforts to "jump start" the economy through a short-run stimulus package, as well as long term efforts to increase national productivity and investment, will inevitably target these concentrations of economic activities and sources of productivity growth. "Growing the economy," means stimulating growth in the nation's local economic regions. This essential reality should not be ignored as the President and Congress work to reach consensus on a new national economic program.

This debate over the shape of the national economic program should also recognize the diversity of circumstances and performance of these local economic regions. The breadth and depth of diversity across the many local economic regions— described in the next section — makes it less likely that uniform national economic policies, administered as if there was a single national economy, will suffice as a "national program for economic growth." Effective federal policies to "grow the economy" must recognize the importance of local economies to prospects for national growth; those policies must also be sensitive to the differences among the local economies.

Variations Among Local Economic Regions

Too often, national averages underlie federal policy and program decisions. Data, however, indicate a wide range of variation around these national averages across local economic regions. When federal policy and program decisions are driven by these national averages, therefore, the variety of circumstances and needs in local economies are ignored.

The degree of variation in the performance of local economic regions is easily demonstrated. This study examined median household incomes, employment growth and unemployment rates across the 50 largest metropolitan areas in 1990. These figures also identified the comparable national levels. These data clearly demonstrate the extent of the variation around the national average measures that underlie federal policy and program decisions.

In 1989 median household income was $30,056 in the nation. Median household incomes in these 50 largest metropolitan areas ranged from a high of $46,848 to a low of $24,442, a difference of $22,406.

Eight metropolitan areas fell below the national average and 42 were above. Of these higher income metropolitan areas, 18 exceed the national average by more than $5,000, 10 by $10,000 or more, and five by $15,000 or more. The range of variation in metropolitan median household incomes, therefore, is significant, and the national averages mask the extent of this variation. This diversity of metropolitan income performance is not related to metropolitan size, at least within the 50 largest metropolitan areas examined.

Metropolitan areas also exhibit significant variations in rates of employment growth. Among the 50 largest metropolitan areas, the rate of employment growth between 1980 and 1990 ranged from a high of 43.5 percent to a low of -1.4 percent.

The national average growth rate over this period was 18.2 percent. Twenty-six of the 50 large metropolitan areas had growth rates in excess of the national average. Of these, 10 had rates in excess of 30 percent over the 10 year period, and 10 experienced a less than 10 percent rate of growth. The rate of growth in employment was negative in three of the areas.

The unemployment rate is a primary measure of the performance of the national economy and its constituent local economic regions. In 1990, the national rate of unemployment averaged 6.3 percent. Again, the range in unemployment rates across the 50 metropolitan areas is wide, from a high of 9.2 to a low of 3.7.

The majority of these metropolitan areas (29) experienced unemployment rates below the national average, but the remaining 21 had rates in excess of the national mean. Again, there appears to be no consistent relationship between urban size and unemployment performance.

Almost all measures of economic performance reveal similar patterns of variation across local economic regions. The breadth and depth of these patterns of variations indicate that there is a need for federal policies to be sensitive to the diversity of local economic regions and their unique circumstances and needs.

Some Implications for Federal Policy

The findings of this study suggest looking at the U.S. economy as a common market of local economic regions rather than as a huge but undifferentiated "national economy." In turn, this view indicates several directions in which federal policy should develop.

• Federal economic policy should aim at improving the condition and performance of the local economic regions.

For example, the importance of infrastructure and of education and training for workers must be related to each local economic region. Also, a stimulus for job creation will work best if it is targeted and delivered locally where it is needed.

• Federal economic policy should address the variety among these local economic regions as to their circumstances and needs.

For example, an investment tax credit can be structured with an incentive for investment in local economies that need it and can use it best. Analysis of the presence and absence of this and other prerequisites for economic growth should be focussed on the local economic regions.

• Federal economic policy should seek to diminish city/suburb disparities within the local economic regions.

For example, redlining by providers of mortgages or insurance undercuts the ability of some areas to contribute to the development of the local economic region. Also, efforts to overcome the spatial mismatch of job openings and people seeking jobs will strengthen overall performance of the local economy.

Notes

1. The information in this study is based on the largest 78 metropolitan areas in 1990, (80 minus Nassau-Suffolk, NY, PMSA and Monmouth-Ocean, NJ, PMSA for which no central city is identified either in the name or by the Census Bureau). The size ranking was based on total population tabulated in the 1990 Census of Population and Housing. This ranking was performed on Primary Metropolitan Statistical Areas (PMSAs), Metropolitan Statistical Areas (MSAs) and New England County Metropolitan Areas (NECMAs). Central cities are defined as those in the name of the metropolitan area, rather than multiple central cities in the area by the Census Bureau. When no central city was in the title, the city or cities identified by the Census Bureau was used. In the case of the Kansas City, MO-KS, MSA, both Kansas City, MO, and Kansas City, KS, were used. 1980 Metropolitan Areas were reconstructed based on 1990 geographical definitions. Counties were added to, or subtracted from the 1980 SMSAs, and the variables were retabulated. 1980 Central Cities were also based on the 1990 definitions.

2. For the analyses that follow, 1979 median household incomes were adjusted to 1989 dollars.

3. The R^2, a measure of the percent of the variation explained, was a very low .07. On the 1989 data, the R^2 was .310.

4. *City Distress, Metropolitan Disparities, and Economic Growth.* Combined Revised Edition, NLC, September 1992.

45. MYTHS ABOUT DOWNTOWN REVITALIZATION

Dolores P. Palma

Since the first suburban shopping malls opened their doors, communities all across the country have been concerned with revitalizing their downtowns. Today, a large body of knowledge has been developed — the "dos and don'ts" of the trade — that can be used to guide local downtown revitalization efforts.

This body of knowledge includes myths about downtown revitalization as well as "secrets of success." The ten most common downtown revitalization myths— and the seven secrets of downtown success— are discussed below.

Myth 1: If We Build It, They Will Come

This has become known as the "Field of Dreams Approach" to downtown enhancement. It centers on the belief that a community only needs to undertake physical improvements for customers and investors to flock to downtown.

Over the last 20 to 30 years, many communities have proven this to be a myth. They have done so by implementing massive physical improvement projects that usually include new sidewalks, landscaping, street trees, planters, benches, facade improvements, etc. Thinking that their work was done, these communities then sat back and waited for customers and investors to return to downtown. Unfortunately, these communities learned that physical improvements, made on a grand scale and made in isolation, do not result in renewed downtown vitality.

Downtown and City Hall leaders in Robbinsdale, Minnesota, learned the truth — that minimalist public improvements which are combined with economic improvements yield downtown success. Mayor Joy Robb and the City Council of Robbinsdale spearheaded making downtown revitalization a priority in their community. The city's elected officials acted as the catalyst for revitalization by having a comprehensive downtown streetscape

Originally published as "Ten Myths About Downtown Revitalization," Western City, Vol. LXX, No. 6, June, 1994. Published by the League of California Cities, Sacramento, California. For information about subscribing, please call 916-658-8223 or visit the magazine's website at www.westerncity.com. Subscription information is also available by calling 1-800-572-5720 and asking for document #45. Reprinted with permission of the publisher.

project designed and implemented along West Broadway. In April of this year, the city was presented with a Merit Award for the project from the Minnesota Chapter of the American Society of Landscape Architects. The streetscape project also won broad approval from the community. In a recent survey of area residents, 87 percent of those who had seen the newly completed streetscape improvements found them attractive. But Robb and city council members knew that streetscape improvements alone — a physically driven approach — would not revitalize downtown. Instead, the city and downtown business community worked together to take a market driven approach by completing a downtown market analysis and a downtown business plan, which is being implemented by a newly formed partnership of city hall and downtowners. In fact, the entire downtown enhancement effort must be market-driven to serve customers and users, rather than physically driven, in order to succeed.

Myth 2: If We Demolish It, They Will Come

This is the flip side of Myth #1 and is known as the "Urban Renewal Approach" to downtown revitalization. This myth holds that, if old buildings are torn down and land is cleared, developers will flock to downtown. And, unfortunately, there are communities all across the country that still have vacant downtown land which was cleared in the 1960s and 1970s as part of this revitalization approach.

Since the days of the federal Urban Renewal program, community leaders have learned that clearance does not attract developers to a downtown whose market is weak. Since that time, communities also have learned that structurally sound old buildings — no matter how run-down they might look at the time — can become a

tremendous draw if they are renovated and their architectural character is preserved. In fact, older restored structures constitute the most valuable commercial real estate in this country today.

In Peabody, Kansas, (population 1410), downtown leaders have learned the truth: If we save and rehabilitate our older commercial buildings, tenants and customers are more likely to come. With help from the Kansas Main Street Program. Peabody completed a market analysis for its downtown as part of a comprehensive enhancement program which also included having downtown listed in the National Register of Historic Places. By implementing an intensive business recruitment and building preservation effort over the last four years, Peabody's downtown went from a total of eleven retail businesses in 38,400 feet to 21 retail businesses occupying 61,000 square feet of space, a 91 percent increase in retail businesses and a 59 percent increase in occupied retail square footage.

Myth 3: If We Complete One Major Project, They Will Come

This is the "Silver Bullet Approach" to downtown revitalization. It holds that if a community identifies and implements one key, major project then "everything else will take care of itself." Examples of communities that pursued the Silver Bullet Approach are those that built downtown convention centers, festival marketplaces, parking structures, or pedestrian malls — in isolation. Unfortunately, these communities learned the hard way that there is no silver bullet. Instead, successful downtown revitalization requires a multifaceted effort that addresses all of a downtown's key issues.

In Thousand Oaks, California, a private-public partnership is forming to spearhead a multi-faceted downtown enhancement program. The program, based on a shared community vision of what downtown should be like by the year 2000, addresses all of downtown's key issues and opportunities, instead of taking a silver bullet approach.

Myth 4: If We Can't Get a Department Store to Come Back to Downtown, Downtown Will Never Be Healthy Again

This is known as the "Traditional Anchor Approach" to downtown revitalization. It is true that — except for tremendously healthy downtowns — the chances of attracting a major, national department store to downtown are very slim. However, this fact does not dictate that a downtown can no longer be healthy. Instead, the most successful downtowns today are those that have redefined the concept of "downtown anchors."

All across the country, downtowns are embracing new anchors. These include cultural facilities, government complexes, entertainment facilities, tourist draws, housing units, professional office buildings, and specialty retail shops. And, communities are finding that by promoting and leveraging these anchors, their downtowns can experience renewed vitality, without a traditional department store anchor.

Elko, Nevada, named the best small town in America by Norman Crampton, author of The 100 Best Small Towns In America in 1993, has for years had nontraditional anchors in its downtown in the form of casinos. More recently, a new anchor has opened in downtown Elko. This is the Western Folklife Center, whose exhibits attract local residents and visitors all year long, and which has become known as the headquarters of the annual Cowboy Poetry Gathering.

Myth 5: We Can't Get a Department Store to Locate Downtown, So Downtown Can No Longer Support Any Kind of Retail Trade

This is the "Big Retail or No Retail Approach" to downtown revitalization. Again, it is true that the chances of recruiting a major, national department store to most downtowns today are slim. It is also true that few downtowns today can be considered to be primarily retail centers. However, these truths alone do not prove that a downtown cannot support a degree of retail trade.

In fact, many downtown professionals would argue that, by definition, a healthy downtown is one that contains some degree of retail activity. This belief holds that it is retail trade that brings pedestrians to downtown's sidewalks and, therefore, gives downtown a look of activity and health. Therefore, no matter how healthy a downtown's economy actually is, without some degree of retail trade a downtown will look dead. That is why most, if not all, downtown revitalization programs operating in this country today contain a retail retention component. And, many of these downtown programs have been successful in strengthening, and increasing, their downtown's retail base.

In Monroe, North Carolina, downtowners and community residents alike have seen this myth dispelled by young, energetic entrepreneurs who are operating specialty retail businesses in their downtown, retail businesses that are successful because they have defined their target customers and cater to the needs of those customers. A graphic example of this is a men's apparel shop call Neil Glenn, Ltd., long a part of downtown in Monroe, North Carolina. The shop recently was purchased from its retiring owner by a young entrepreneurial couple. Being customer driven, the new owners decided to target downtown attorneys, banks and business owners—a built-in, daily market—as their prime customers. This meant "retooling" the shop's merchandise from general men's wear to apparel specifically for businessmen. And, the owners realized that to truly cater to these customers, retooling must involve services that make it easy for busy businessmen to shop at Neil Glenn—opening the shop for a customer before and after regular store hours by request, special ordering for customers, tailoring, etc. Because of their entrepreneurial and customer-driven approach to retailing, Neil Glenn's new owners are proving that specialty retailers can grow and thrive in downtown, long after the traditional downtown department stores are gone.

Myth 6: Competition Is Bad for Business

This is the "Head-In-The-Sand Approach" to revitalization. The commercial districts—both old and new—that are the most successful in this country today are those in which similar and compatible businesses are located side by side in convenient groupings. There is example after example in this country of commercial districts which have proven that the clustering of compatible businesses is actually very good for business.

Rather than providing dangerous competition, the clustering of businesses expands and magnifies the market that the cluster—and each of the businesses in it—can hope to draw. This multiplier effect occurs because a cluster of businesses is more appealing to a customer—in terms of convenience and variety—than is a single, stand-alone business. Therefore, customers have a tendency to come to the clustered businesses in larger numbers, and to spend more dollars once in these clusters, than they would at a single, destination business.

Progressive small business owners in Old Town Alexandria, Virginia, have proven this myth is false by taking the initiative themselves to create several business clusters. One of these clusters, which is about three blocks long, includes a variety of home furnishing businesses—where customers can find everything from traditional rug and lamp stores to shops that offer creative home accessories, design services, and "art f/x."

In Pomona, California, private sector investors formed an antiques cluster. This is comprised of many antique vendors, located side by side, who draw customers from a great distance because of their number and variety.

Myth 7: For Downtown to Be Successful, Downtown's Retail Businesses Must Keep Uniform Business Hours

During the last several years, many downtowns across the country have included, as part of their revitalization efforts, attempts to standardize the hours of operation kept by downtown retailers. This is known as the "Let's Pretend We're a Mall Approach" to downtown revitalization. Given the independent nature of downtown business owners, and the large number of business owners in any downtown, this approach has failed dismally.

Recognizing that a single set of uniform business hours is difficult to achieve in a downtown, and possibly not advantageous to the district's retailers as a whole, the most successful downtown enhancement programs today are promoting "market-driven business hours." With this approach, retail businesses keep hours that best meet the needs of their targeted customers. By doing this, and by coordinating their hours of operation with each other, these businesses are able to accommodate and share customers.

In addition, many downtown small business owners are finding that keeping hours that are convenient for customers often means shifting to different hours rather than keeping longer hours.

In the Old Town Alexandria home furnishings cluster mentioned above, the owner of Art and Soul — a specialty retail shop offering original, high-quality art and craft items for the home — moved to smarter hours shortly after opening in Old Town. Art and Soul's original weekday hours of 10 A.M. to 6 P.M. were changed to 11 A.M. to 7 P.M., because the owner noticed:

• The hour from 10 A.M. to 11 A.M. was the slowest business time on weekdays.
• Many area tourists were on the sidewalks after 6 P.M., returning to their Alexandria hotels after a day of sightseeing.
• Both tourists and local residents heavily frequent Old Town's popular restaurants and window shop on their way to dinner.
• And, several of the shop's customers mentioned they find it difficult to get to the shop after work by 6 P.M.

By opening the same number of hours, but shifting to customer driven hours, Art and Soul enjoys the increased patronage of both visitors and residents of the area.

Myth 8: We Have to Be as Lenient as Possible with Developers or They Won't Do Business in Our Community

-and-

Myth 9: We Have to Be as Tough as Possible with Developers or They'll Take Advantage of Us

These are the twin "Play Dead or Play Hard Ball" revitalization myths. Over the last fifteen years, both of these myths have been proven false by communities all across the country. It has been proven that developers will do business in communities that demand quality projects and that take steps to ensure they obtain such projects. In fact, many developers prefer to do business in communities that demand quality projects and seek out such communities — because they know their investments will be protected in these communities.

It has also been proven that communities that are unreasonably stringent and demanding of developers will cause developers to locate their projects elsewhere. In that sense, these communities are successful in making sure that the development community does not take advantage of them! However, this attitude also makes them successful in not attracting quality developers and quality projects to their communities.

The communities that have been most successful in obtaining quality development projects in their older commercial districts are those where a partnership has been formed between the community, the city government and local developers. These efforts are commonly known as public-private partnerships. They can be highly successful in creating quality projects for the community and economically successful projects for the developer. The essential ingredient for making the partnership a success is one of attitude. All parties in the partnership must agree to cooperate so that a quality project — and one that is mutually beneficial — results.

Myth 10: If We Had More Parking, They Would Come!

This is the "Let's Find a Scapegoat Approach" to downtown revitalization. This myth holds that all of downtown's ills stem from a lack of parking. Those who believe in this myth claim that customers have left downtown for shopping malls because malls offer customers seas and seas of parking which is often (but not always) free. Therefore, the reasoning goes, "we need more parking"—this change will make downtown's businesses competitive with the malls and will make customers return to downtown.

Unfortunately, communities that have gone to great expense in creating downtown parking lots and decks, without making other needed improvements in their downtowns, have learned the fallacy of this myth. The new parking facilities remain as empty as our downtown stores. In fact, many of the more progressive downtown leaders across the country now say "we need to create a parking problem in our downtown" because this will mean that downtown stores are busy.

In fact, in the vast majority of downtowns where there is a parking problem, it is one of parking management rather than one of parking supply. This means that the number of parking spaces available is adequate. However, customers are having difficulty finding a parking spot because:

• Downtown employees and business owners are parking in spaces that are nearest to businesses and that should be reserved for their customers and clients; and
• Downtown's public parking lots are often not clearly marked.

This problem can be resolved through better management and identification of the existing parking supply and does not typically warrant creating additional parking spaces.

At the forefront of a nationwide trend, The City of Millville, New Jersey, recently improved and signed several small downtown public parking lots, making a vast dent in the issue of downtown parking.

Downtown programs which have been most successful in re-attracting customers and clients are those where business owners differentiate their businesses and give customers and clients a compelling reason to patronize that business. Successful downtown business owners have found that if they offer what customers and clients want (a specialized product, an exceptional service, a unique atmosphere, etc.), make sure customers know that this is being offered, and make existing parking convenient for their customers, then the issue of downtown parking often becomes irrelevant.

Lastly, the seven simple secrets to downtown success, which can assist in your revitalization efforts, are highlighted below.

SECRET 1: Form Partnerships—Between the business sector, the public sector, civic organizations, and community residents. The most successful downtowns are those where these sectors come together, make decisions together, and each carry their weight to reinvest and reinvent their downtown. None of these sectors can or should do it alone.

SECRET 2: Know Your Vision—Define and aggressively pursue a shared community vision of success. Waiting until the handwriting is on the wall, and then reacting to it, is the old way of doing business. The new, more successful way of revitalizing downtown is to define a clear vision of where you want your downtown to go—a vision that is realistic and that is shared by the business community, the local government and the citizens of the community—and then aggressively pursuing that vision.

SECRET 3: Be Market-Driven — Market analysis is THE critical first step for success in revitalizing your downtown; it's a tool without which downtown cannot succeed. The Field of Dreams Approach is out. Instead, the successful approach is much more business oriented — know who your customers are, who your potential customers are, what they want today, what they will want tomorrow — and provide those things. And, be flexible to keep up with the customer's changing needs and desires. This market knowledge must drive all downtown improvement actions — all of the private sector's business decisions and the public sector's governance decisions — including how to market the downtown, what business hours to keep, what types of streetscape improvements to make, etc.

SECRET 4: Create and Use a Business Plan — Businesses that operate according to a business plan are more successful than those that don't — and the same is true for business districts. Based on your shared community vision and a realistic market analysis, the downtown partnership must identify — and implement — an aggressive course of action.

SECRET 5: Dare to Be Different — Downtown must create, carve out, and become known for a particular niche in the market place. Downtown can't out-mall the mall AND it can't out-discount the discounters. However, the malls and the discounters can't out-downtown downtown. The most successful downtowns accentuate their uniqueness to make downtown stand out from the competition in the minds of its customers.

SECRET 6: Focus — Concentrate limited resources in well-defined focus areas. Downtown leaders have learned from experience that resources are too scarce to be able to successfully tackle all of a downtown's ills at once. And, our downtown areas are often too large to enhance all in one bite. Therefore, clumping downtown into focus areas has proven to be the road to success. This allows results to become more visible more quickly. And, nothing breeds success like visible results.

SECRET 7: Know the Indispensable Five M's — Management of downtown like a business; marketing campaigns for downtown and its businesses; maintenance of downtown's private and public property; market-knowledge to create a niche for downtown; and money for ongoing, quality downtown management and enhancement. While our downtowns should not try to compete head-on with shopping malls, they should learn and use these essential management techniques.

46. AN INDUSTRY APPROACH TO SUSTAINABLE DEVELOPMENT

E. S. Woolard, Jr.

When the history of environmentalism in the last quarter of this century is written, sustainable development may well prove to be the major conceptual advance in environmental thinking to have taken place during that period. The concept of sustainable development was introduced to a broad audience in 1987 by the World Commission on Environment and Development report Our Common Future, which stressed that environmental and economic issues are interrelated and that environmental issues do not respect political boundaries. It emphasized that the problems of poverty and underdevelopment cannot be solved unless we have a new era of economic growth in which developing countries play a strong role and reap substantial benefits.

The report also pointed out that the traditional model of industrial development, in which wealth was created without regard for the environmental consequences of production, had led to increasingly severe environmental disruptions around the world. The commission therefore argued for an alternative approach — sustainable development — which it defined as meeting the basic needs of all the world's people today without compromising the ability of future generations to meet their needs. There can be no doubt that industrial growth and development must continue, particularly in developing countries. But it must continue within the bounds of environmental limits.

Industry, as society's producer, has a special role to play in creating sustainable development, and some of us in the industrial community are working on ways to make sustainability a characteristic of industrial problems. In April 1991, I participated in the second World Industry Conference on Environmental Management in Rotterdam. The 700 or so industrialists at that meeting endorsed a document that we call the Business Charter for Sustainable Development. More than 200 companies have already expressed written support for it at the CEO or senior management level. In addition, several dozen prominent organizations, including the World Resources Institute, the United Nations Environment Programme, and the U.S. Environmental Protection Agency, have also expressed written support. It will

From Issues in Science and Technology, *Vol. 8, No. 3, Spring, 1992. Published by the National Academy of Sciences, Washington, D.C. Reprinted with permission of the publisher.*

become part of the international business community's contribution to the UN Conference on the Environment and Development this June in Brazil.

The chapter includes 16 principles of environmental management designed to assist businesses around the world in acquiring the features of sustainable development. But as with any such document, the real challenge will be to convert these principles into industrial practices. We should begin to show measurable progress immediately and during each year of this decade, so that we can enter the next century already firmly on the sustainable development track. To meet that challenge, industry should establish an action agenda in four areas for the 1990s:

Education and open dialogue. This effort should begin with people in industry and extend to the public in communities where industrial companies operate. There remain industrialists who take issue with sustainable development, saying that we're either giving in to the environmentalists or inviting government regulation and central planning. In my opinion, accepting the idea of sustainable development does not mean we're giving in to anyone. Rather, it means that we are working out a set of principles that will help industry live up to society's expectations around the world.

Moreover, far from encouraging government regulation, sustainable development practices should help minimize the need for regulation by demonstrating industry's willingness to take responsibility for the impact of its activities. From what I've seen in my career, the best way to invite regulation by governments is to remain idle in the face of a major social issue that directly involves industrial products or operations.

And sustainable development is not about central planning. As more information is released from Eastern European countries, we can see that central planning has been a disaster for the environment. The only way people in developing countries will have a chance to improve their health and longevity, their standard of living, and the welfare of their children will be through industrial development. But for such development to be effective and sustainable, it will have to be in the form of appropriate local solutions to local problems—which means market economics and entrepreneurial activity. Those are the opposite of central planning.

As we work to improve the awareness and acceptance of sustainable development principles by industry, we also have to communicate a similar understanding to the public. Again, the manner in which we communicate our principles and agenda to the public will vary from industry to industry and country to country. But some approaches may have the potential for broad application.

For example, the chemical industries in Canada, the United States, Europe, and Australia have adopted a program called Responsible Care, which entails a set of principles and Codes of Management Practices. The codes include specific guidelines in areas such as community awareness, emergency response, process safety, and pollution prevention. Every member company of the Chemical Manufacturers Association (CMA) must sign on to the codes and report back to the association on its progress. As long as a company is making good-faith progress in implementing the codes, other CMA companies provide assistance. Companies failing to implement the codes can be disassociated from CMA and denied the many benefits that come with membership.

Implementation of these codes can establish a continuing dialogue with representatives of the local community. We can build on those contacts to establish emergency preparedness procedures, recycling programs, and other projects.

Waste minimization and pollution prevention. In many nations, public concern about industry and the environment remains intensely focused on the generation and disposal of industrial and consumer wastes and on the environmental and public health effects of industrial emissions. Without question, getting control of waste and emissions is a vital part of any sustainable development scenario. One of the industry leaders in this regard has been the 3M Company, which in 1975 began an ambitious program to prevent pollution and eliminate the costs associated with "end-of-the-pipe" pollution controls. Employees were encouraged to contribute ideas on product reformulation, process modification, equipment design,

---

BUSINESS CHARTER FOR SUSTAINABLE DEVELOPMENT
PRINCIPLES FOR ENVIRONMENTAL MANAGEMENT

From the introduction:

… the International Chamber of Commerce hereby calls upon enterprises and their associations to use the following principles as a basis for pursuing such improvement and to express publicly their support for them. Individual programs developed to implement these principles will reflect the wide diversity among enterprises in size and function.

The objective is that the widest range of enterprises commit themselves to improving their environmental performance in accordance with these principles, to having in place management practices to effect such improvement, to measuring their progress, and to reporting this progress as appropriate internally and externally.

1. *Corporate priority:* To recognize environmental management as among the highest corporate priorities and as a key determinant to sustainable development; to establish policies, programs, and practices for conducting operations in an environmentally sound manner.

2. *Integrated management:* To integrate these policies, programs, and practices fully into each business as an essential element of management in all its functions.

3. *Process of improvement:* To continue to improve corporate policies, programs, and environmental performance, taking into account technological developments, scientific understanding, consumer needs, and community expectations, with legal regulations as a starting point; and to apply the same environmental criteria internationally.

4. *Employee education:* To educate, train, and motivate employees to conduct their activities in an environmentally responsible manner.

5. *Prior assessment:* To assess environmental impacts before starting a new activity or project and before decommissioning a facility or leaving a site.

6. *Products and services:* To develop and provide products or services that have no undue environmental impact and are safe in their intended use, that are efficient in their consumption of energy and natural resources, and that can be recycled, reused, or disposed of safely.

7. *Customer advice:* To advise, and where relevant educate, customers, distributors, and the public in the safe use, transportation, storage, and disposal of products provided; and to apply similar considerations to the provision of services.

8. *Facilities and operations:* To develop, design, and operate facilities and conduct activities taking into consideration the efficient use of energy and materials, the sustainable use of renewable resources, the minimization of adverse environmental impact and waste generation, and the safe and responsible disposal of residual wastes.

9. *Research:* To conduct or support research on the environmental impacts of raw materials, products, processes, emissions, and wastes associated with the enterprise and on the means of minimizing such adverse impacts.

10. *Precautionary approach:* To modify the manufacture, marketing, or use of products or services or the conduct of activities, consistent with scientific and technical understanding, to prevent serious or irreversible environmental degradation.

(Business Charter for Sustainable Development
Principles for Environmental Management, continued)

11. *Contractors and suppliers:* To promote the adoption of these principles by contractors acting on behalf of the enterprise, encouraging and, where appropriate, requiring improvements in their practices to make them consistent with those of the enterprise; and to encourage the wider adoption of these principles by suppliers.

12. *Emergency preparedness:* To develop and maintain, where significant hazards exist, emergency preparedness plans in conjunction with the emergency services, relevant authorities, and the local community, recognizing potential transboundary impacts.

13. *Transfer of technology:* To contribute to the transfer of environmentally sound technology and management methods throughout the industrial and public sectors.

14. *Contributing to the common effort:* To contribute to the development of public policy and to business, governmental, and intergovernmental programs and educational initiatives that will enhance environmental awareness and protection.

15. *Openness to concerns:* To foster openness and dialogue with employees and the public, anticipating and responding to their concerns about the potential hazards and impacts of operations, products, wastes, or services, including those of transboundary or global significance.

16. *Compliance and reporting:* To measure environmental performance; to conduct regular environmental audits and assessments of compliance with company requirements, legal requirements, and these principles; and periodically to provide appropriate information to the board of directors, shareholders, employees, the authorities, and the public.

---

and resource recovery. From 1975 to 1990, 3M estimates that the program saved the company $537 million by dramatically reducing all forms of waste and thus eliminating the cost of handling that waste.

Many companies now realize that they must make public commitments to reducing wastes and emissions by setting goals and then publicly measuring their progress toward those goals. In 1989, Du Pont, for example, committed to 11 specific targets as a basis for our approach to corporate environmentalism. Among these commitments was our pledge to reduce by 35 percent during this decade the total hazardous waste generated at our sites around the world. We also said that we will cut toxic air emissions by 60 percent by 1993. We will reduce emissions of airborne carcinogens by 90 percent by 2000, with continued reductions thereafter, always heading in the direction of zero emissions. We also included goals specific to our energy business, such as a decision to build only double-hulled tankers and to install double-walled tanks at all newly constructed and renovated gasoline outlets. Since 1990,

we have published environmental summaries in our annual reports that show how we are progressing toward our goals, and we will continue to do so annually.

Another important consideration in waste minimization is to be concerned about the waste we don't see as well as the waste we do. The waste we don't see is the large quantity of nonrenewable energy resources that are used inefficiently. Energy companies and industry in general should be in the forefront of developing efficient, high-value uses of our hydrocarbon resources.

This may require a reversal in the way we traditionally think about business development. Some U.S. utility companies now have aggressive programs to help residential consumers use less of their product. State regulators can make it possible for utilities to profit from such measures.

Product stewardship. We have entered an era in which industrial corporations will have to accept responsibility for the environmental impact of their materials and products from inception in the laboratory to ultimate disposition after their useful life is over.

A classic case in point is that of chloro-fluorocarbons (CFCs). Few expect the ultimate consumers of CFCs—refrigerator owners and air-conditioner users, for example—to take responsibility for the impact of these products on the earth's atmosphere. Throughout the debate over these products, responsibility has been directed to the manufacturers of CFCs and to companies that use these products in large industrial quantities. Many manufacturers of CFCs participated in the discussions that led up to the Montreal Protocol (the international agreement to reduce CFC use), have helped formulate the reduction plan, and are actively involved in the development of substitutes. If nothing else, the CFC issue was a shot across the bow, a clear indication that manufacturers will be responsible for the longterm impact of the products we produce and sell.

Similarly, concern over what to do about postconsumer plastic waste has been laid at the doorsteps of the industries that manufacture plastic resins and fabricate plastic packaging and plastic products. At Du Pont, because we are one of the world's largest producers of polymer resins, we have made a public commitment to take increasing responsibility for the plastics portion of the global solid-waste stream. We currently operate two plastics recycling plants.

Proctor and Gamble is another company that is initiating product stewardship programs, particularly with regard to the packaging of its products. P&G's approach is to seek ways to reduce solid waste throughout the product life cycle, including packaging redesign, product concentration, optimization of raw material use, and use of recycled materials.

Innovative product design and marketing. I know that for many North American companies, a traditional approach to trade was to create a product for the North American market and then look for opportunities to sell the product in other parts of the world. We will probably always have examples of this kind of marketing. But in a sustainable world economy, we can expect a new approach. Increasingly, we will have to let local needs determine the products we offer, instead of taking existing products and trying to fit them to local needs. And these needs will be defined in the context of environmental impact and resource availability, not just utility.

A simple example of this is the polyethylene pouch container, a technology developed by our Canadian subsidiary to package milk. The pouches are convenient, tamper-resistant, and, compared to competing packaging systems, reduce solid waste by up to 70 percent. As an outgrowth of this technology, we developed a similar technology to dispense cooking oil in India. Cooking oil has traditionally been sold in that country by dispensing it from a central supply, typically a 55-gallon drum, into open containers provided by the consumer. The system raises questions about contamination, adulteration, and waste from spillage.

What might seem the logical alternative, Western bottling systems, would represent a significant incremental cost to many Indian consumers. So we developed low-cost polyethylene pouches that could each hold 250 milliliters of oil, the measure for cooking a typical meal. The polyethylene film itself dissolves at cooking temperatures, is edible, and does not end up as a waste product. Consumers could buy only the amount they need and be assured of its quality. We are currently seeking to interest local firms in commercializing this technology, which we believe is an excellent example of a product that responds to local needs and lifestyles, has low environmental impact, and contributes to the standard of living in a developing nation.

If we can establish a firm base for education, waste minimization, product stewardship, and innovative product design, then we can tackle more difficult challenges. The current generation of industry leaders has the ability to see further into the future with regard to the environmental impact of our operations than any previous generation. We cannot place ourselves in the position of requiring society to choose between a strong, healthy industry and a clean and safe environment. I believe that we can have both. To do so, we have to begin by acknowledging environmental protection as a real, legitimate, and permanent factor in the planning and conduct of everything we do. If industrial growth and development cause continued environmental deterioration, then the future for industry will be an endless series of restrictions and lost opportunities. If, however, we lead industry into a new era of environmental concern and sustainable production, we can continue to reward investors, create jobs, and improve living standards in societies around the world.

47. THE END OF SPRAWL

Christopher Leinberger

Two factors—evident in virtually every metropolitan area—have defined how real estate developers and municipal agencies build commercial and residential developments and infrastructure improvements. The first is the concentration of executive housing—which tends to be located in one general area, although a few of the largest metropolitan areas claim two or three such concentrations. The second factor is the concentration of lower-income housing, which generally is located 90 to 180 degrees away from the concentration of executive housing. Since the bosses usually select a company's employment location, job concentrations tend to be driven by their proximity to executive housing, as well as their access to the regional freeway system.

These two factors have led to the emergence of the "favored quarter," where nearly all new and relocating jobs cluster and where 70 to 80 percent of infrastructure dollars are spent. This trend has pushed the fringe of the region farther and farther out, suburbanizing the rural country side at an ever-increasing pace in the favored quarter. Edge cities of one decade become inner suburbs of the next decade as new edge cities are built farther out. The last 50 years have witnessed a geometric expansion in the physical space occupied by metropolitan areas. Specifically, the land claimed by the nation's metropolises has expanded at least seven times as fast as their metropolitan population.

During the early to mid–1990s, the physical growth rate of metropolitan areas accelerated even faster than the rapid rates of the previous decades. Fringe commercial developments spring up in the hinterlands of metropolitan areas, such as the Alliance Airport area of Dallas/Fort Worth, the north Scottsdale area near Phoenix, and Cherokee and Gwinnett counties in Georgia, 40 miles north of downtown Atlanta. As sprawl has accelerated, it has emerged as a political issue that has moved from the local level—where it had simmered for years and at times boiled—to the state level and most recently to the national level.

Over the past few years, with the country's economic recovery continuing to set records and the expectation of further sprawl fueling community and political

Originally published as "The Beginning of the End of Sprawl," Urban Land, *Vol. 59, No. 1, January 1, 2000. Published by the Urban Land Institute, Washington, D.C. Reprinted with permission of the publisher.*

opposition, something entirely unexpected may be occurring — the beginning of the end of sprawl. The fringe of metropolitan areas will continue their outward push, suburban subdivisions will continue to be developed on former farmland, and huge build-to-suit offices and plants still will be sited on greenfield sites located 40 to 60 miles from downtown. However, there appears to be a small, but significant, shift in where selected new development is heading — to more infill and downtown locations. Some signs even portend a structural shift in how metropolitan areas are built and how Americans want to live. While a change in public policy — which subsidized suburban sprawl over the past 50 years — to a more balanced policy could accelerate the end of sprawl, what is really at work is a market shift that no amount of government intervention can stop.

In his book, *Metropolitics,* Myron Orfield, a member of the Minnesota House of Representatives and the advisory board of the Brookings Institution's Center on Urban and Metropolitan Policy, reports the results of recent studies he conducted that show that infrastructure improvements have been disproportionately concentrated in favored areas even though funding for the improvements comes from throughout the surrounding metropolitan area. In Chicago, for example, the tolls paid by predominantly working- and middle-class workers driving the fully paid-for Illinois Turnpike on the south side have subsidized roads built primarily in the favored quarter to the northwest and north of downtown. Given the correlation between location of employment and home values, southside commuters pay tolls to drive longer distances to work, while the value of their homes continues to decline.

However, sprawl has become a formula-driven business — reinforced by the financial markets' desire for predictability — that has led to characterless suburbs that could be located anywhere. As author Tom Wolfe wrote in his latest book, *A Man in Full* (see review in April 1999 *Urban Land*), "The only way you could tell you were leaving one community and entering another was when the franchises started repeating." In the search for answers to why children too often turn to violence, numerous writers have editorialized about the placelessness of suburbs such as Littleton, Colorado. While it is impossible to say whether characterless sprawl can play a role in the violent, antisocial behavior of youth, there is agreement that many suburbs can be described only as ugly, inhuman, and soulless.

But, anecdotal evidence suggests that lower-density, sprawling development may be changing. The first and most obvious piece of evidence is the surprising comeback of many of America's downtowns. Nearly half have rebounded or are in the process of reemerging as vibrant centers of urban life: office rents are at or above replacement levels, housing is seeing a resale market, and retail uses are reaching critical mass, putting people on the streets. Twenty years ago, only midtown Manhattan, San Francisco, Boston, and Chicago could boast viable downtowns; anyone who wanted an urban lifestyle migrated to these four cities. Today, the number of resurgent downtowns includes San Diego, Denver, Seattle, Portland, and Baltimore, among others. Even more impressive is the list of downtowns that are in the middle of the comeback process: San Jose, Phoenix, Dallas, Houston, Austin, San Antonio, Boise, Minneapolis, Memphis, Chattanooga, Nashville, Charlotte, Atlanta, Providence, Cleveland, Columbus, and Cincinnati, among others. It is not unreasonable to say that most, if not all, American downtowns will either be, or are on their way, to becoming viable real estate markets ten years from now.

The emergence of healthy urban real

estate markets is not confined to downtowns. Many "third-generation" metropolitan cores— edge cities that emerged in the 1970s but today are miles from the edge due to continued sprawl— have begun to urbanize, including West Los Angeles, Century City, Bellevue (Seattle), Buckhead (Atlanta), and the profusion of urbanizing cores (primarily due to the success of the Metro transit system) around suburban Washington, D.C., namely, Bethesda and Chevy Chase in nearby Maryland and the Ballston and Court House areas in nearby Virginia.

A recent research study conducted in Atlanta, Chattanooga, and Albuquerque by Robert Charles Lesser & Co., an independent real estate advisory firm based in Los Angeles, asked consumers a series of tradeoff questions regarding lifestyle preferences in one of three housing categories: semi-rural, suburban, or urban. Despite the prospect of smaller dwelling units with little or no yard area, over 30 percent of respondents expressed a preference for urban housing and the opportunity to walk to restaurants, shops, and work. Interestingly, not one of the three cities in the research study can point to a recent trend in urban housing. Perhaps, then, as more urban neighborhoods evolve, the percentage of consumers favoring urban housing will increase.

The underlying reason for the consumer shift is probably the aging of the baby boom generation. As baby boomers move into their 50s and many enter the empty-nest stage, some have started to question the wisdom of remaining in suburban isolation. They seem to be reevaluating how they want to live the next phase of their lives, and many report that they intend to be far more active and involved than were previous generations. An urban lifestyle may offer just the alternative they are seeking.

Apparently, many Generation Xers also prefer urban settings. The most popular Gen-X television shows—*Friends, Seinfeld, Dharma & Greg,* and *Two Guys and a Girl*—are all based in cities. The most popular shows of previous generations—*Leave It to Beaver, The Dick Van Dyke Show,* and *The Brady Bunch*—all were set in the suburbs.

A significant trend throughout the country in the past few years has been the relative price appreciation of the favored-quarter inner suburbs. Since the mid–1990s, housing prices in favored quarter inner suburbs, such as Bethesda, Buckhead, Bellevue, Palo Alto, and the Park Cities in Dallas, have increased between 10 and 20 percent per year. In contrast, the price appreciation of new housing built on the fringe of the favored quarter has barely kept pace with inflation. To avoid traffic congestion, people are willing to pay more to live in closer-in neighborhoods with history and character— neighborhoods that offer easy access to public transportation.

With bosses beginning to move back downtown and the favored-quarter inner suburbs enjoying a renaissance, it could be only a matter of time before jobs begin to return to these areas as well. In Seattle, many Gen-X software developers live downtown and have even moved their places of business downtown. Households willing to pay $200 per square foot for a downtown loft in Denver's LoDo have generated a demand for office space that now fetches rents over $30 per square foot. In addition, as bosses residing in traditional suburban executive housing concentrations have come to realize that reverse commuting is an illusion, the downtown and infill business locations hold new appeal.

Other forces at work that may, on the surface, slow sprawl appear unrelated. The first is the environmental movement, which has named sprawl "public enemy number one." Nearly all environmental organizations, from the Conservation

Fund to the Sierra Club, have endorsed major initiatives to help combat sprawl. A case in point is the open-space initiatives that appeared on ballots in 1998 and 1999 across the country asking voters to approve the use of tax dollars to buy land to protect it from development. A New Jersey ballot measure has committed the state to buy half of the Garden State's remaining undeveloped land over the next decade or so. In addition, the land trust movement has grown exponentially, using federal and state tax breaks to ensure that land remains as open space forever. The result is de facto growth boundaries around many metropolitan areas such as Miami, San Francisco, and Chicago, not to mention the growth boundaries expressly imposed by a few metropolitan areas themselves, such as Portland and Seattle.

Another force that may slow the spread of sprawl is the recognition of sprawl's cost. Recent local government fiscal impact studies demonstrate that sprawl-oriented development costs significantly more than compact development. For local governments, the difference in cost over the next 20 years between sprawl-oriented development and compact development in mid-sized metropolitan areas is measured in billions of dollars. In a special election, the citizens of Albuquerque recently passed a measure to raise taxes to pay for road improvements— but only for existing roads. Now that it is becoming known that sprawl is subsidized, imagine the effect on the sale of single-family housing located on the fringe if impact fees of $20,000 to $80,000 per dwelling unit were levied, as the fiscal impact studies conclude they should be.

Even utility deregulation may have an impact on sprawl. Before deregulation, a state utility commission would simply add up, mark up, and approve a private utility's proposed charges for a new development— without regard for unit cost by location for the delivery of electricity or natural gas.

Now increasingly deregulated utilities have every incentive to join the rest of American business in basing the price of their goods on actual costs. One preliminary utility study in Chicago indicated that the delivery of electricity to fringe developments may cost two to three times as much as to intown locations.

In most metropolitan areas, the local news media have focused on sprawl, generally painting it as a great social and environmental evil. In its weekly Horizon section, *The Atlanta Constitution* has been highly critical of sprawl. In fact, Atlanta has been considered the capital of sprawl since the early 1990s. Even major charitable foundations are now interested in combating sprawl. This past January, most of the country's largest foundations, including Packard, Hewlett and MacArthur, among others, came together to discuss how they could use their formidable resources to fight sprawl.

Given the strength of the national economy and the booming real estate market, the issue of growth management has gone beyond the local level to state and even national levels. As Tony Downs, an analyst at the Washington, D.C.-based Brookings Institution, notes in his recent book Metropolitan Visions, most observers of metropolitan growth areas now recognize that state governments need to be involved in solutions to sprawl. Over 20 state legislatures apparently agree, as evidenced by the passage of statewide growth management legislation over the past decade. The most unexpected and potentially sweeping measure in recent years has been legislation passed in early 1999 to create the Georgia Regional Transportation Authority. It is almost unthinkable that such a conservative state took the unprecedented action of directing the governor to appoint a land use and transportation regulatory body over the Atlanta metropolitan area. Historically, however, the Atlanta real estate community has been known for its progressive, forward-looking view of development trends. Accordingly, the real estate industry's reaction to the new law has been favorable.

Even more surprising has been the emergence of the sprawl issue on the national political agenda. Brought to the fore by Vice President Al Gore, sprawl has taken on the mantle of a secondary presidential issue in the 2000 election campaign. Nearly every major news weekly and opinion magazine has or will soon run a major story about sprawl.

Perhaps the hidden force influencing the sprawl debate will be Wall Street. After the 1980s real estate debacle, investment bankers became the governors of the real estate industry not only through their function as financial intermediaries for real estate investment trusts (REITs) and the secondary mortgage market but also through continuing analysis of the nation's real estate industry. The market condition that most concerns Wall Street is overbuilding, and credit markets have been proficient in restricting the flow of new money to markets and product types that show signs of overbuilding. In fact, some of the most highly regarded REITs have strategically positioned themselves to focus on "high barrier to entry" markets, building only in urban locations. Suburban development, on the other hand, is more prone to overbuilding because of an almost always ample supply of well-located land. In contrast, urban locations in metropolitan areas are few in number and pedestrian focused, imposing a natural limit on how far potential consumers will walk.

The combination of environmental, public policy, financial, and, most important, market forces will eventually put such extreme pressure on those who induce sprawl that a new approach to development will emerge. The question is how the real estate industry can adapt to it and make a profit in the process.

The most significant effect of a new approach to development will be the shift from producing a simple, formula-driven suburban product to a more complex, mixed-use urban product. This shift will require a retooling of corporate strategies, financing, tactics, and skills. With great urban places created over time, the industry will require even more patient equity than in the 1990s. Land assembly and acquisition skills will take on great importance since infill development requires developers to deal with many more landowners than development at the fringe. And teaming up with environmental groups to fight NIMBYism may be required to achieve zoning and neighborhood support. It will be much more time-consuming to get a project through the development pipeline, but the project should perform better amid less-formidable competition. Finally, given that urban land values are among the highest in the country, the chance of a major financial upside is better than in the suburbs, where real estate is becoming a mass-produced commodity.

Where will buyers and tenants get the money to pay for a more costly urban product? The answer is from the automobile industry. After taxes, the average car costs $7,000 per year to own, maintain, and operate. By locating in a pedestrian-transit-oriented community, consumers can own fewer cars. The savings realized from giving up one car frees up over $120,000 in a mortgage loan for a house ($7,000 after taxes equals $10,700 before taxes — with 35 percent in state and federal taxes. At eight percent interest over 30 years, this amount equals a mortgage of $121,200.)

If such trends portend the beginning of the end of sprawl, it will not be an easy transition for many in the real estate industry. But if the late 1990s turn out to be the high-water mark for sprawl, it would be wise to understand the implications sooner — rather than later.

MUNICIPAL RESOURCE DIRECTORY

Major professional associations and research organizations serving municipal government.

Advisory Council on Historic Preservation
Old Post Office Building
1100 Pennsylvania Avenue, N.W.
Suite 809
Washington, D.C. 20004
Telephone: (202) 606-8503
FAX:　　　 (202) 606-8647 or 8672
Internet: http://www.achp.gov

American Economic Development Council
9801 West Higgins Road
Suite 540
Rosemont, IL 60018-4726
Telephone: (847) 692-9944
FAX:　　　 (847) 696-2990
Internet: http://www.aedc.org

American Planning Association
122 South Michigan Avenue
Suite 1600
Chicago, IL 60603-6107
Telephone: (312) 431-9100
FAX:　　　 (312) 431-9985)
Internet: http://www.planning.org

American Real Estate and Urban
　Economics Association
Kelley School of Business
Indiana University
1309 East Tenth Street
Suite 738

Bloomington, IN 47405
Telephone: (812) 855-7794
FAX:　　　 (812) 855-8679
Internet: http://www.areuea.org

Asset-Based Community Development
　Institute
Institute for Policy Research
Northwestern University
2040 Sheridan Road
Evanston, IL 60208-4100
Telephone: (847) 491-3518
FAX:　　　 (847) 491-9916
Internet:
　http://www.nwu.edu/IPR/abcd.html

Association for Enterprise Opportunity
1601 North Kent Street
Suite 1120
Arlington, VA 22209
Telephone: (703) 841-7760
FAX:　　　 (703) 841-7748
Internet:
　http://www.microenterpriseworks.org

Brownfields Technology Support Center
U.S. Environmental Protection Agency
1200 Pennsylvania Avenue, N.W.
Washington, D.C. 20460
Telephone: 1-877-838-7220 (toll free)
Internet: http://brownfieldstsc.org

Building Officials and Code Administrators International
4051 Flossmoor Road
County Club Hills, IL 60478-5795
Telephone: (708) 799-2300
FAX: (708) 4981
Internet: http://www.bocai.org

Center for Compatible Economic Development
7 East Market Street
Suite 210
Leesburg, VA 20176
Telephone: (703) 779-1728
FAX: (703) 779-1746
Internet: http://www.cced.org

Center for Neighborhood Technology
2125 West North Avenue
Chicago, IL 60647
Telephone: (773) 278-4800
FAX: (773) 278-3840
Internet: http://www.cnt.org

Committee for Economic Development
477 Madison Avenue
New York, NY 10022
Telephone: (212) 688-2063
FAX: (212) 758-9068
Internet: http://www.ced.org

Community Associations Institute
225 Reinekers Lane
Suite 300
Alexandria, VA 22314
Telephone: (703) 548-8600
FAX: (703) 684-1581
Internet: http://www.caionline.org

Community Development Society International
1123 North Water Street
Milwaukee, WI 53202
Telephone: (414) 276-7106
FAX: (414) 276-7704
Internet: http://comm-dev.org

Corporation for Enterprise Development
777 North Capitol Street, N.E.
Suite 410

Washington, D.C. 20002
Telephone: (202) 408-9788
FAX: (202) 408-9793
Internet: http://www.cfed.org

Downtown Development and Research Center
215 Park Avenue South
Suite 1301
New York, NY 10003
Telephone: (212) 228-0246
FAX: (212) 228-0376
Internet:
http://www.DowntownDevelopment.com

Habitat for Humanity International
Partner Service Center
121 Habitat Street
Americus, GA 31709
Telephone: (912) 924-6935,
Ext. 2551 or 2552
FAX: (912) 924-6541
Internet: http://www.habitat.org

Interactive Economic Development Network
1730 "K" Street, N.W.
Suite 700
Washington, D.C. 20006
Telephone: (202) 223-4735
FAX: (202) 223-4745
Internet: http://www.iedn.com

International City/County Management Association
777 North Capitol Street, N.E.
Suite 500
Washington, D.C. 20002
Telephone: (202) 289-4262
FAX: (202) 962-3500
Internet: http://www.icma.org

International Conference of Building Officials
5360 South Workman Mill Road
Whittier, CA 90601-2258
Telephone: (310) 699-0541
FAX: (310) 692-3853
Internet: http://www.icbo.org

International Downtown Association
910 — 17th Street, N.W.
Suite 210
Washington, D.C. 20006
Telephone: (202) 293-4505
FAX: (202) 293-4509
Internet: http://ida-downtown.org

Local Government Commission
1414 "K" Street
Suite 250
Sacramento, CA 95814
Telephone: (916) 448-1198
FAX: (916) 448-8246
Internet: http://www.lgc.org

National Association of Counties
Joint Center for Sustainable Communities
440 First Street, N.W.
Washington, D.C. 20001-2080
Telephone: (202) 393-6226
FAX: (202) 393-2630
Internet: http://www.naco.org

**National Association of Development
    Organizations**
444 North Capitol Street, N.W.
Suite 630
Washington, D.C. 20001
Telephone: (202) 624-7806
FAX: (202) 624-8813
Internet: http://www.nado.org

**National Association of Housing and
    Redevelopment Officials**
630 Eye Street, N.W.
Washington, D.C. 20001
Telephone: (202) 289-3500
FAX: (202) 289-8181
Internet: http://www.nahro.org

**National Association of Regional
    Councils**
1700 "K" Street, N.W.
Suite 1300
Washington, D.C. 20006
Telephone: (202) 457-0710
FAX: (202) 296-9352
Internet: http://www.narc.org/narc

**National Association of State
    Development Agencies**
750 First Street, N.E.
Suite 710
Washington, D.C. 20002
Telephone: (202) 898-1302
FAX: (202) 898-1312
Internet: http://www.ids.net/nasda

National Business Incubation Association
20 East Circle Drive
Suite 190
Athens, OH 45701-3751
Telephone: (740) 593-4331
FAX: (740) 593-1996
Internet: http://www.nbia.org

**National Center for the Revitalization of
    Central Cities**
College of Urban and Public Affairs
University of New Orleans
New Orleans, LA 70148
Telephone: (504) 280-6519
FAX: (504) 280-6272
Internet: http://www.uno.edu/-cupa/ncrcc

National Civic League
1445 Market Street
Suite 300
Denver, CO 80202-1728
Telephone: (303) 571-4343
FAX: (303) 571-4404
Internet: http://www.ncl.org

**National Council for Urban Economic
    Development**
1730 "K" Street, N.W.
Suite 700
Washington, D.C. 20006
Telephone: (202) 223-4735
FAX: (202) 223-4745
Internet: http://www.cued.org

National Housing Conference
815 Fifteenth Street, N.W.
Suite 538
Washington, D.C. 20005
Telephone: (202) 393-5772
FAX: (202) 393-5656
Internet: http://www.nhc.org

National Housing Institute
439 Main Street
Suite 311
Orange, NJ 07050
Telephone: (973) 678-9060
FAX: (973) 678-8437
Internet: http://www.nhi.org

National League of Cities
1301 Pennsylvania Avenue, N.W.
Washington, D.C. 20004-1763
Telephone: (202) 626-3000
FAX: (202) 626-3043
Internet: http://www.nlc.org

**National Trust for Historic
    Preservation**
1785 Massachusetts Avenue, N.W.
Washington, D.C. 20036
Telephone: (202) 588-6219
FAX: (202) 588-6050
Internet: http://www.mainst.org

United States Conference of Mayors
1620 Eye Street, N.W.
Washington, D.C. 20006
Telephone: (202) 293-7330
FAX: (202) 293-2352
Internet: http://www.usmayors.org

**Urban and Regional Information Systems
    Association**
1460 Renaissance Drive
Suite 305
Park Ridge, IL 60068
Telephone: (847) 824-6300
FAX: (847) 824-6363
Internet: http://www.urisa.org

Urban Land Institute
1015 Thomas Jefferson Street, N.W.
Suite 500 West
Washington, D.C. 20007-5201
Telephone: (202) 624-7000
FAX: (202) 624-7140
Internet: http://www.uli.org

BIBLIOGRAPHY

A listing of books, monographs, articles, and other sources in the field of inner-city renewal.

Books

Aaron, Henry J., and Charles L. Schultze. Editors. *Setting Domestic Priorities*. Washington, D.C.: The Brookings Institution, 1992.

Bailey, John T. *Marketing Cities in the 1980's and Beyond*. Rosemont, IL: American Economic Development Council, 1989.

Barnett, Jonathan. *The Fractured Metropolis: Improving the New City, Restoring the Old City, Reshaping the Region*. New York, NY: Icon Editions, 1995.

Bates, Timothy. *Banking on Black Enterprise: The Potential of Emerging Firms for Revitalizing Urban Economies*. Washington, D.C.: Joint Center for Political and Economic Studies, 1993.

Bawden, D. L., and Felicity Skidmore. Editors. *Rethinking Employment Policy*. Washington, D.C.: The Urban Institute Press, 1989.

Birch, David L. *Job Creation in America*. New York, NY: Free Press, 1987.

Blakely, Edward J. *Planning Local Economic Development: Theory and Practice*, Thousand Oaks, CA: Sage Publications, 1989.

Bleakly, Ken. *Economic Impact Analysis: Assessing a Project's Value to a Community*. Rosemont, IL: American Economic Development Council, 1993.

Burchell, Robert W., et al. *Development Impact Assessment Handbook*. Washington, D.C.: Urban Land Institute, 1994.

Burt, Martha, and Barbara Cohen. *America's Homeless: Numbers, Characteristics, and Programs that Serve Them*. Washington, D.C.: The Urban Institute Press, 1989.

Cisneros, Henry G. Editor. *Interwoven Destinies: Cities and the Nation*. New York, NY: The American Assembly, 1993.

Clemetson, Robert A., and Roger Coates. *Restoring Broken Places and Rebuilding Communities*. Washington, D.C.: National Congress for Community Development, 1992.

Downing, Paul B. *Local Service Pricing Policies and Their Impact on Urban Spatial Structures*. Vancouver, B.C.: University of British Columbia Press, 1977.

Dryfoos, Joy G. *Full-Service Schools: A Revolution in Health and Social Services for Children, Youth, and Families*. San Francisco, CA: Jossey-Bass Publishers, 1994.

Elwood, David. T. *The Spatial Mismatch Hypothesis: Are There Teenage Jobs Missing in the Ghetto?* Chicago, IL: The University of Chicago Press, 1986.

Fosler, R. Scott. *Local Economic Development: Strategies for a Changing Economy*. Washington, D.C.: International City/County Management Association, 1991.

Harrell, Adele V., and George E. Peterson. Editors. *Drugs, Crime, and Social Isolation*. Washington, D.C.: The Urban Institute Press, 1992.

Hatry, Harry; Mark Fall; Thomas Singer; and Blaine Liner. *Monitoring the Outcomes of Economic Development Programs*. Washington, D.C.: The Urban Institute, 1990.

Herzog, Henry W., Jr., and Alan M. Schlottmann, editors, *Industrial Location and Public*

Policy. Knoxville, TN: The University of Tennessee Press, 1991.

Kemp, Roger L. *Economic Development in Local Government: A Handbook for Public Officials and Citizens*. Jefferson, NC: McFarland, 1995.

_____. *Managing America's Cities*. Jefferson, NC: McFarland, 1998.

_____. *Urban Economic Development: Successful Case Studies from American Cities*. East Rockaway, NY: Cummings & Hathaway, 1995.

Kivell, Philip. *Land and the City: Patterns and Processes of Urban Change*. London, England: Routledge, 1993.

Koepke, Robert L. *Practicing Economic Development*. Rosemont, IL: American Economic Development Council, 1993.

Kolter, Philip; Donald H. Haider; and Irving Rein. *Marketing Places: Attracting Investment, Industry and Tourism to Cities, States and Nations*. New York, NY: The Free Press, 1993.

Kolzow, David R. *Strategic Planning for Economic Development*. Rosemont, IL: American Economic Development Council, 1991.

Ledebur, Larry C., and William R. Barnes. *All In It Together: Cities, Suburbs and Local Economic Regions*. Washington, D.C.: National League of Cities, February, 1993.

Luke, Jeffrey S.; Curtis Ventriss; B. J. Reed; and Christine M. Reed. *Managing Economic Development: A Guide to State and Local Leadership Strategies*. San Francisco, CA: Jossey-Bass, 1988.

Lynn, Laurence E., Jr., and Michael McGeary. Editors. *Inner-City Poverty in the United States*. Washington, D.C.: National Academy Press, 1990.

Marshall, Edward M. *Small Business Partnerships*. Washington, D.C.: National League of Cities, 1989.

Massey, Douglas S., and Nancy A. Denton. *American Apartheid: Segregation and the Making of the Underclass*. Cambridge, MA: Harvard University Press, 1993.

McLaughlin, Milbrey W.; Merita A. Irby; and Juliet Langman. *Urban Sanctuaries: Neighborhood Organizations in the Lives and Future of Inner City Youth*. San Francisco, CA: Jossey-Bass Publishers, 1994.

McNeeley, Joseph B. *Building for the Future*. Washington, D.C.: Fannie Mae Foundation, November, 1993.

Medoff, P., and H. Sklar. *Streets of Hope: The Fall and Rise of an Urban Neighborhood*. Boston, MA: South End Press, 1994.

Milder, N. David. *Niche Strategies for Downtown Revitalization: A Hands-on Guide to Developing, Strengthening and Marketing Niches*. New York, NY: Downtown Research and Development Center, 1997.

Moe, Richard, and Carter Wilkie. *Changing Places: Rebuilding Community in the Age of Sprawl*. New York, NY: Henry Holt and Company, 1997.

National League of Cities. *Accepting the Challenge: The Rebirth of America's Downtowns*. Washington, D.C.: National League of Cities, 1994.

_____ and CH2MHILL. *Working Cities, Winning Ideas: James C. Howland Awards for Urban Enrichment, 1998*. Washington, D.C.: National League of Cities, 1999.

_____ and CH2MHILL. *Working Cities, Winning Ideas: James C. Howland Awards for Urban Enrichment, 1999*. Washington, D.C.: National League of Cities, 2000.

Norquist, John O. *The Wealth of Cities: Revitalizing the Centers of American Life*. Reading, MA: Addison-Wesley, 1998.

Palma, Dolores P., and Doyle G. Hyett. *Accepting the Challenge: The Rebirth of America's Downtowns*. Washington, D.C.: National League of Cities, 1994.

_____. *How to Revitalize Your Downtown*. Washington, D.C.: National League of Cities, 1999.

_____. *Local Officials Guide to Dynamic City Commercial Centers*. Washington, D.C.: National League of Cities, 1990.

Peck, Dennis, and John Murphy. Editors. *Open Institutions: The Hope for Democracy*. New York, NY: Praeger, 1993.

Peterson, George E. *Confronting the Nation's Urban Crisis: From Watts (1965) to South Central Los Angeles (1992)*. The Urban Institute Press, 1992.

_____, and Wayne Vroman. Editors. *Urban Labor Markets and Job Opportunity*. Washington, D.C.: The Urban Institute Press, 1992.

Probst, Katherine N.; Don Fullerton; Robert E. Litan; and Paul R. Portney. *Footing the Bill for Superfund Cleanups: Who Pays and How?* Washington, D.C.: Brookings Institution, 1994.

Rusk, David. *Cities Without Suburbia.* Washington, D.C.: The Woodrow Wilson Center Press, 1993.

_____. *Inside Game/Outside Game: Winning Strategies for Saving Urban America.* Washington, D.C.: The Century Foundation, Brookings Institution, 1999.

Schuman, Diane R., D. Scott Middleton, and Susan Giles. *Public/Private Housing Partnerships.* Washington, D.C.: Urban Land Institute, 1990.

Sklar, Holly. *Chaos or Community: Seeking Solutions, Not Scapegoats for Bad Economics.* Boston, MA: South End Press, 1995.

Snyder, Thomas P., and Michael A. Stegman. *Paying for Growth: Using Development Fees to Finance Infrastructure.* Washington, D.C.: The Urban Institute, 1987.

Squires, Gregory D. Editor. *From Redlining to Reinvestment: Community Response to Urban Disinvestment.* Philadelphia, PA: Temple University Press, 1992.

Stone, P.A. *The Structure, Size, and Costs of Urban Settlements.* Cambridge, England: Cambridge University Press, 1973.

Struyk, Raymond, and Michael Fix. Editors. *Measurement of Discrimination in America.* Washington, D.C.: The Urban Institute Press, 1992.

Sullivan, Mercer. *More Than Housing: How Community Development Corporations Go About Changing Lives and Neighborhoods.* New York, NY: New School for Social Research, 1993.

Taub, Richard P. *Community Capitalism.* Boston, MA: Harvard Business School Press, 1988.

Urban Institute, The. *Special Districts: A Useful Technique for Financing Infrastructure.* Washington, D.C.: The Urban Institute, 1992.

Vidal, Avis C. *Rebuilding Communities: A National Study of Community Development Corporations.* New York, NY: New School for Social Research, 1992.

Weston, Josh S. *Rebuilding Inner-city Communities: A New Approach to the Nation's Urban Crisis.* New York, N.Y.: Committee for Economic Development, 1995.

Wilson, William Julius. *The Truly Disadvantaged.* Chicago, IL: University of Chicago Press, 1987.

Monographs

Atkinson, Maureen; Patricia Falch; and John Williams. *Marketing Your Downtown.* Management Information Service Report, vol. 28, no. 6. Washington, D.C.: International City/County Management Association, June 1996.

Austrian, Ziona, and Henning Eichler. *Urban Brownfields Site Survey: Preliminary Analysis.* Cleveland, OH: Cleveland State University, Levin College of Urban Affairs, April 28, 1994.

Bamberger, Rita J.; William A. Blazar; and George E. Peterson. "Capital Planning." *Planning Advisory Service Report,* no. 390. Chicago, IL: American Planning Association, September 1985.

Bartik, Timothy J. *Who benefits from State and Local Economic Development Policies?* Kalamazoo, MI: Upjohn Institute, 1991.

Binger, Gary, and Janet McBride. *Beyond Polemics: A Discussion of "The Cases for Suburban Development" and "Beyond Sprawl: New Patterns of Growth to Fit the New California."* Monterey, CA: Association of Bay Area of Governments (ABAG), May, 1996.

Black, Harry. *Achieving Economic Development Success: Tools That Work.* Washington, D.C.: International City/County Management Association, 1991.

Black, J. Thomas. *Recycling Inactive Urban Industrial Sites.* Washington, D.C.: Urban Land Institute, 1994.

Bowes, David B. "Creating Globally Competitive Communities." *Management Information Service Report,* vol. 28, no. 11. Washington, D.C.: International City/County Management Association, November 1996.

Bradley, Richard H. *Building the New Framework: A Coordinated Strategic Approach.* Washington, D.C.: International Downtown Association, 1992.

_____. *The Downtown of the 21st Century.* Washington, D.C.: International Downtown Association, 1992.

Broachway, G. P. *The End of Economic Man: Principles of Any Future Economics.* New York, NY: W. W. Norton, 1993.

Canter, Larry, et al. *Impact of Growth: A Guide for Socio-Economic Impact Assessment and Planning.* Chelsea, MI: Lewis Publishers, Inc., 1986.

Case, Anne C., and Lawrence F. Katz. *The Company You Keep: The Effects of Family and Neighborhood on Disadvantaged Youths.* Cambridge, MA: National Bureau of Economic Research, 1991.

Center for Community Change. *The HOME Program: A Brief Guide for Community Organizations.* Washington, D.C.: Center for Community Change, 1992.

Darling, David L., Jr. *Setting Community Economic Goals.* Manhattan, KS: Community Development Series (No. L-714), Kansas State University, February 1988.

_____. *Strategic Planning for Community Development.* Manhattan, KS: Community Development Series (No. L-830), Kansas State University, February 1991.

_____. *Understanding Your Community's Economy.* Manhattan, KS: Community Development Series (No. L-776), Kansas State University, October 1988.

Edelstein, M. *Contaminated Communities: The Social and Psychological Impacts of Residential Toxic Exposure.* Boulder, CO: Westview Press, 1988.

Ellis, Brinille Elaine. *Strategic Economic Development.* Management Information Service Report, vol. 26, no. 2. Washington, D.C.: International City/County Management Association, February 1994.

Frank, James E. *The Costs of Alternative Development Patterns: A Review of the Literature.* Washington, D.C.: Urban Land Institute, 1989.

Gerry, Martin H. *A Joint Enterprise with America's Families to Ensure Student Success.* Washington, D.C.: Council of Chief State School Officers, 1991.

Kelly, Christine K.; Donald C. Kelly; and Edward Marciniak. *Non-profits with Hard Hats: Building Affordable Housing.* Washington, D.C.: National Center for Urban Ethnic Affairs, 1988.

Kemp, Roger L. "Clifton's Future Vision Project." *Planners' Casebook* (No. 5). Chicago, IL: American Institute of Certified Planners, American Planning Association, Winter, 1993.

_____. "Financial Productivity: New Techniques for Hard Times." *Municipal Finance Journal,* vol. 10, no. 4, April, 1990.

Kirshenberg, Seth D., and Charles Bartsch. *Brownfields: Options and Opportunities.* Management Information Service Report, vol. 29, no. 5. Washington, D.C.: International City/County Management Association, May 1977.

Kotkin, Joel. *The Future of the Center: The Core City in the New Economy.* Los Angeles, CA: Reason Foundation, 2000.

Leiterman, Mindy, and Joseph Stillman. *Building Community: A Report on Social Community Development Initiatives.* New York, NY: Local Initiatives Support Corporation, 1993.

Lichtenstein, G. A., and T. S. Lyons. *Incubating New Enterprises: A Guide to Successful Practice.* Washington, D.C.: The Aspen Institute, 1996.

Martz, Wendelyn. *Customer Service in the Planning Department.* Management Information Service Report, vol. 27, no. 5. Washington, D.C.: International City/County Management Association, May 1995.

Mayer, Virginia M.; Marina Sampanes; and James Carras. *Local Officials Guide to the CRA.* Washington, D.C.: National League of Cities, 1991.

McGrath, Daniel T. *An Investigation into the Impact of Hazardous Waste Contamination Liability on Urban Industrial Land Redevelopment in the City of Chicago.* Chicago, IL: University of Chicago, Great Cities Institute, December 5, 1995.

McLean, Mary L., and Kenneth P. Voytek. *Understanding Your Economy.* Chicago, IL: American Planning Association, Planners Press, 1992.

Melaville, Atelia I.; Martin J. Blank; and Gelareh Asayesh. *Together We Can: A Guide for Crafting a Pro-Family System of Education and Human Services.* Washington, D.C.: U.S. Department of Education and U.S. Department of Health and Human Services, 1993.

Meyer, Angela D., and Ronald J. Swager. *A Bibliography of Selected Topics in Economic*

Development Literature, 1987–1993. Rosemont, IL: American Economic Development Council, 1994.

Moore, Mark H., and Darrel W. Stephens. *Beyond Command and Control: The Strategic Management of Police Departments.* Washington, D.C.: Police Executive Research Forum, 1991.

National Council for Urban Economic Development. *Alternative Approaches to Financing Business Development.* Washington, D.C.: NCUED, 1989.

_____. *Forces in the Economy: Implications for Local Economic Development.* Washington, D.C.: NCUED, 1993.

_____. *Industrial Development Bonds: A Resource for Financing Economic Development.* Washington, D.C.: NCUED, 1994.

_____. *Neighborhood Economic Revitalization.* Washington, D.C.: NCUED, 1994.

_____. *Urban Manufacturing: Dilemma or Opportunity?* Washington, D.C.: NCUED, 1994.

National Conference of State Legislatures. *Breaking New Ground: Community-based Development Organizations.* Denver, CO: National Conference of State Legislatures, 1991.

Nowak, Jeremy, et al. *Religious Institutions and Community Renewal.* Philadelphia, PA: The Pew Charitable Trusts, 1989.

Oakland, William H., and William A. Testa. *Does Business Development Raise Taxes: An Empirical Appraisal.* Chicago, IL: Metropolitan Council and the Federal Reserve Bank of Chicago, January, 1995.

O'Connor, James, and Barbara Abell. *Successful Supermarkets in Low-Income Inner Cities.* Arlington, VA: O'Connor-Abell, 1992.

Pierce, Neil, and Carol F. Steinbach. *Corrective Capitalism: The Rise of America's Community Development Corporations.* New York, NY: Ford Foundation, 1987.

Sampson, Robert J. *Crime and Community Social Disorganization: Implications for Social Policy.* Washington, D.C.: U.S. Department of Housing and Urban Development, 1993.

Segal, Bradley; Katherine Correll; and Robert Dubinsky. *Business Improvement Districts: Tools for Economic Development.* Management Information Service Report, vol. 29, no. 3. Washington, D.C.: International City/County Management Association, March 1997.

Schmenner, Roger W. *Energy Costs, Urban Development, and Housing.* Washington, D.C.: Brookings Institution, 1984.

Stillman, Joseph. *Making the Connection: Economic Development, Workforce Development, and Urban Poverty.* New York, NY: The Conservation Company, 1994.

Swager, Ronald J. *A Bibliography of Literature in Economic Development.* Rosemont, IL: American Economic Development Council, 1987.

_____. *Economic Development Tomorrow: A Report from the Profession.* Rosemont, IL: American Economic Development Council, 1991.

Articles

Albanese, Joe, and Scott Martinelli. "Restoration Renaissance." *Urban Land*, vol. 57, no. 12, December 1998.

Andrews, Clinton J. "Putting Industrial Ecology into Place." *Journal of the American Planning Association*, vol. 65, no. 4, Autumn 1999.

Arrandale, Tom. "Developing the Contaminated City." *Governing*, vol. 6, no. 3, December 1992.

Atkinson, Maureen, and John Williams. "Managing Downtown Revitalization by District." *Urban Land*, vol. 49, no. 9, September, 1990.

Bailey, Richard. "Mall Over." *Urban Land*, vol. 57, no. 7, July 1998.

Banikowdki, J. E.; K. E. Thomas; and J. L. Zegarelli. "Cleaning Up Without Getting Cleaned Out." *American City and County*, vol. 109, no. 8, July 1994.

Barnett, Jonathan. "Shaping Our Cities: It's Your Call." *Planning*, vol. 61, no. 12, December 1995.

Berger, Renee. "Building Community Partnerships." *National Civic Review*, vol. 73, no. 2, May 1984.

Balck, J. Thomas. "Fort Worth: Maintaining Vitality Downtown." *Urban Land*, vol. 57, no. 2, February 1998.

_____. "People, Power, Politics." *Planning*, vol. 63, no. 2, February 1997.

Bogorad, Leonard. "Washington: A New Urbanist Frontier." *Urban Land*, vol. 58, no. 9, September 1999.

Bolan, Lewis, and Eric Smart. "Washington at the Millennium." *Urban Land*, vol. 58, no. 9, September 1999.

Bookout, Lloyd W. "Inner-City Retail Opportunities." *Urban Land*, vol. 52, no. 5, May 1993.

Bourne, L. S. "The Roepki Lecture in Economic Geography — Recycling Urban Systems and Metropolitan Areas: A Geographical Agenda for the 1990's and Beyond." *Economic Geography*, vol. 67, no. 3, July 1991.

Boyd, James, and Molly K. Macauley. "The Impact of Environmental Liability on Industrial Real Estate Development." *Resources*, no. 114, Winter, 1994.

Boydell, Thomas E., and Douglas R. Porter. "Building Public/Private Collaboration in Puget Sound." *Urban Land*, vol. 56, no. 9, September 1997.

Bradley, Richard H. "Vive Le Renaissance!" *Urban Land*, vol. 58, no. 9, September 1999.

_____. "Downtown Renewal: The Role of Business Improvement Districts." *Public Management*, vol. 77, no. 2, February 1995.

Bray, Paul M. "A New Tool for Renewing the Central City: The Urban Cultural Park." *National Civic Review*, vol. 83, no. 2, Spring-Summer, 1994.

_____. "The New Urbanism: Celebrating the City." *Places*, vol. 8, no. 4, Summer 1993.

Breslaw, Jon A. "Density and Urban Sprawl: Comment." *Land Economics*, vol. 66, no. 43, November 1990.

Building Association of Northern California. "Striking at the Heart of Sprawl." *BIA News*, vol. 5, no. 1, March 1996.

Carlson, David A. "Paving the Way to Economic Revitalization: 'Covenant Not to Sue' Stimulates Redevelopment in Economic Target Areas." *Massachusetts Environment*, vol. 1, no. 9, February 1996.

Coe, Barbara A. "Public-Private Cooperation." *Western Governmental Researcher*, vol. III, no. 1, Summer 1987.

Clayton, David. "Las Vegas Goes for Broke." *Planning*, vol. 61, no. 9, September 1995.

Colley, Sharon. "Housing Opens Door to Redevelopment." *American City & County*, vol. 115, no. 4, March 2000.

Cox, Robert D. "A New Approach to 'Brownfields' in Central Massachusetts." *Massachusetts Environment*, vol. 1, no. 9, February 1996.

Culbertson, Steve, and Jeff Watkins. "Rebuilding Philadelphia's Neighborhoods." *Urban Land*, vol. 56, No. 9, September 1997.

Curtis, Peter G., and Michael C. Bianchi. "Turning 'TOADS' into 'PRINCES': Financing Environmentally Impaired Properties." *Massachusetts Environment*, vol. 1, no. 3, August 1995.

Dorsett, John W. "The Price Tag of Parking." *Urban Land*, vol. 57, no. 5, May, 1998.

Drawas, Neal M. "Remediation Liability Management." *Massachusetts Environment*, vol. 1, no. 3, August 1995.

Ehrenhart, Alan. "The Trouble with Zoning." *Governing*, vol. 11, no. 5, February 1998.

Farrell, Christopher. "The Economics of Crime." *Business Week*, December 13, 1993.

Fernandez, Roberto M. "Space, and Job Accessibility." *Economic Geography*, vol. 70, no. 4, 1994.

Fondersmith, John. "Downtowns in the Year 2040." *The Futurist*, vol. 22, no. 2, March-April 1988.

Fosler, R. Scott. "The Future Economic Role of Local Governments." *Public Management*, vol. 70, no. 4, April 1988.

Foxen, Robert. "Approaching Brownfields: Public, Private Forces Combine to Develop Abandoned Property." *Massachusetts Environment*, vol. 1, no. 3, August 1995.

Frank, Lawrence D., and Robert T. Dunphy. "Smart Growth and Transportation." *Urban Land*, vol. 57, no. 5, May 1998.

Frieden, Bernard J., and Lynne B. Sagalyn. "Downtown Malls and the City Agenda." *Society*, vol. 27, no. 4, July-August 1990.

Froehlich, Maryann. "Smart Growth: Why Local Governments Are Taking A New Approach to Managing Growth in their Communities." *Public Management*, vol. 80, no. 5, May 1998.

Fulton, William. "Are Edge Cities Losing Their Edge?" *Planning*, vol. 62, no. 5, May 1996.

_____, and Morris Newman. "The Strange Career of Enterprise Zones." *Governing*, vol. 8, no. 3, March 1994.

Gallagher, Patrick. "Captivate and Educate." *Urban land*, vol. 57, no. 2, February 1998.

Gihring, Thomas A. "Incentive Property Taxation: A Potential Tool for Urban Growth Management." *Journal of the American Planning Association*, vol. 65, no. 1, Winter 1999.

Glover, Glenda, and J. Paul Brownridge. "Enterprise Zones as an Instrument of Urban Policy: A Review of the Zones in South Central Los Angeles." *Government Finance Review*, vol. 9, no. 3, June 1993.

Gubala, Timothy W. "The Difference Between Economic Developers and Planners." *Economic Development Review*, vol. 10, no. 2, Summer, 1992.

Gurwitt, Rob. "New Alliances." *Governing*, vol. 11, no. 9, June 1998.

_____. "The Rule of the Absentocracy." *Governing*, vol. 5, no. 9, September 1991.

Hahn, Kurt. "When and When Not to Use Incentives to Attract Business or to Retain Existing Businesses." *Government Finance Review*, vol. 12, no. 3, June, 1996.

Haider, Donald. "Place Wars: New Realities of the 1990's." *Economic Development Quarterly*, vol. 6, no. 2, May 1992.

Hanan, Fran, and Patricia Vaccaro. "Design 2000." *Urban Land*, vol. 59, no. 1, January 2000.

Hardy, Ruth Ellen. "Citizen Participation." *Planning Forum*, vol. 2, 1996.

Hayden, Delores. "Using Ethnic History to Understand Urban Landscapes." *Places*, vol. 7, no. 1, Fall 1990.

Harris, Robert R., and John H. Carman. "Battling the American Dream." *Urban Land*, vol. 58, no. 9, September 1999.

Hayden, Delores. "Using Ethnic History to Understand Urban Landscapes." *Places*, vol. 7, no. 1, Fall 1990.

Henning, Ed. "Business Improvement Districts." *Western City*, vol. LXIX, no. 8, August 1993.

Hill, Gary G. "Paying for New Development: The Urban Structure Program of the City of Lancaster." *Government Finance Review*, vol. 13, no. 3, June 1997.

Himmel, Kenneth A. "Entertainment-Enhanced Retail Fuels New Development." *Urban Land*, vol. 57, no. 2, February 1998.

Hoeffer, William. "Using Urban Renovation Experts." *Nation's Business*, vol. 77, no. 1, January 1989.

Hoffer, William. "Using Urban Renovation Experts." *Nation's Business*, vol. 77, no. 1, January 1989.

Holden, Alfred. "Why Toronto Works?" *Planning*, vol. 61, no. 3, March 1995.

Hollis, Linda E. "Baltimore: Washington's Neighbor to the North." *Urban Land*, vol. 58, no. 9, September 1999.

Hornick, Sandy. "Context Is Everything." *Planning*, vol. 56, no. 1, December 1990.

Houston, Lawrence O., Jr. "Downtown Managers," *New Jersey Municipalities*, vol. 67, no. 4, April 1990.

_____. "Downtown Managers." *New Jersey Municipalities*, vol. 67, no. 4, April 1990.

Howland, Libby. "Resurgence in Downtown Washington." *Urban Land*, vol. 57, no. 3, March 1998.

Huffman, Richard. "Building on Books." *Urban Land*, vol. 57, no. 5, May 1998.

Hudnut, William H., III. "Downtown: Still the Heart and the Soul of a Region." *Urban Land*, vol. 57, no. 2, February 1998.

Innes, Judith E., and David E. Booher. "Consensus Building and Complex Adaptive Systems: A Framework for Evaluating Collaborative Planning." *Journal of the American Planning Association*, vol. 65, no. 4, Autumn 1999.

Jacobson, Thomas. "Suburban Design: One Step at a Time." *Planning*, vol. 64, no. 5, May 1998.

Jensen, Peter. "San Diego's Vision Quest." *Planning*, vol. 63, no. 3, March 1997.

Jossi, Frank. "Take Me Out to the Ball Game." *Planning*, vol. 64, no. 5, May 1998.

Kay, Jane Holtz. "The Hub Is Hot." *Planning*, vol. 64, no. 3, March 1998.

Kemp, Roger L. "Economic Development: Raising Revenues Without Increasing Taxes." *The Privatization Review*, vol. 4, no. 1, January, 1988.

Knack, Ruth Eckdish. "BART's Village Vision." *Planning*, vol. 61, no. 1, January 1995.

_____. "Charleston at the Crossroads." *Planning*, vol. 60, no. 9, September 1994.

_____. "Downtown Where the Living Is Easy." *Planning*, vol. 64, no. 8, August 1998.

Labich, Kenneth. "New Hopes for the Inner City." *Fortune*, September 6, 1993.

Lassar, Terry J. "Bridging a Building Boom."

Urban Land, vol. 59, no. 2, February 2000.

_____. "On Common Ground." *Urban Land*, vol. 58, no. 10, October 1999.

_____. "Portland's On-Track Development." *Urban Land*, vol. 57, no. 3, March 1998.

_____. "Shopping in Seattle." *Urban Land*, vol. 57, no. 7, July 1998.

Lawson, Quentin R., and John N. Pannullo. "Using Marketing Strategies to Address Local Issues." *Public Management*, vol. 68, no. 6, June 1986.

Leinberger, Christopher. "The Beginning of the End of Sprawl." *Urban Land*, vol. 59, no. 1, January 2000.

_____, and Gayle Berens. "Designing for Urban Parks." *Urban Land*, vol. 56, no. 12, December, 1997.

Lewis, N. Richard. "Landmark Housing." *Urban Land*, vol. 58, no. 10, October 1999.

Lockwood, Charles. "Houston's Turn." *Urban Land*, vol. 59, no. 2, February 2000.

Lowe, Marcia D. "Alternatives to Shaping Tomorrow's Cities." *The Futurist*, vol. 26, no. 4, July-August 1992.

Luce, Thomas F., Jr. "Local Taxes, Public Services, and The Intrametropolitan Location of Firms and Households." *Public Finance Quarterly*, vol. 22, no. 2, April 1994.

Mahtesian, Charles. "Showdown on E-Z Street." *Governing*, vol. 8, no. 2, October 1995.

_____. "The Stadium Trap." *Governing*, vol. 11, no. 8, May 1998.

Marshall, John T. "Rebuilding the American City: Bonds of Friendship as Bricks and Mortar." *Planning Forum*, vol. 1, Spring, 1995.

McNeal, Alvin R., and Rosalyn P. Doggett. "Metro Makes Its Mark." *Urban Land*, vol. 58, no. 9, September 1999.

Meyer, Peter B., and Thomas S. Lyons. "Lessons from Private Sector Brownfield Redevelopers: Planning Public Support for Urban Regeneration." *Journal of the American Planning Association*, vol. 66, no. 1, Winter 2000.

Miara, Jim. "Residential Rebound." *Urban Land*, vol. 58, no. 9, September 1999.

Milder, N. David. "Crime and Downtown Revitalization." *Urban Land*, vol. 46, no. 9, September 1987.

Miller, Robert L. "Narrative Urban Landscapes." *Urban Land*, vol. 57, no. 2, February 1998.

Miller, Terry K. "Sports Venues Bring Economic Energy Back Downtown." *Urban Land*, vol. 57, no. 2, February 1998.

Moon, J. Virgil, and Tom Majors. "An Economic Incentives Ordinance in Cobb County, Georgia, Bears Fruit in a Big Way." *Government Finance Review*, vol. 10, no. 3, June 1994.

Murphy, Linda. "The Land Market: How is EPA Fostering Redevelopment of Abandoned Urban Properties?" *Massachusetts Environment*, vol. 1, no. 9, February 1996.

Nozick, Marcia. "Urban Issues Program Underway." *City Magazine*, vol. 14, no. 4, Fall 1993.

_____. "Urban Issues Program Underway." *City Magazine*, vol. 15, no. 1, Winter 1994.

Oliver, Gordon. "Portland Revs Up for Action." *Planning*, vol. 60, no. 8, august 1994.

Palma, Dolores P. "Downtown Revitalization." *Municipal Maryland*, vol. 23, no. 4, November 1994.

_____. "Effective Strategies for a Safe Downtown." *Municipal Maryland*, vol. 24, no. 7, February, 1995.

_____. "Retaining and Strengthening Existing Downtown Businesses." *Municipal Maryland*, vol. 25, no. 3, October 1995.

_____. "Ten Myths About Downtown Revitalization." *Western City*, vol. LXX, No. 6, June, 1994.

_____. "Ways to Revitalize Your Downtown." *American City & County*, vol. 107, no. 11, November 1992.

_____, and Doyle Hyett. "Born Again: Downtown Revivals Offer Salvation for Cities." *American City & County*, vol. 122, no. 8, July 1997.

Peiser, Richard B. "Density and Urban Sprawl." *Land Economics*, vol. 65, no. 3, August 1989.

Pender, Robert B., and Frank C. Shaw. "Public-Private Partnerships." *Texas Town & City*, vol. 78, no. 6, June 1990.

Perlman, Ellen. "Downtown: The Live-In Solution." *Governing*, vol. 11, no. 9, June 1998.

Platt, Roger. "Recycling Brownfields." *Urban Land*, vol. 57, no. 6, June 1998.

Ressler, Thomas. "Business Incubators." *Western City*, vol. LXIX, no. 7, July 1993.

Robinson, Brian. "Curbing Urban Sprawl." *civic.com*, vol. 3, no. 5, May 1999.

Rodne, Kjell. "Diversifying the Local Economy." *Public Management*, vol. 73, no. 3, March 1991.

Roeder, David H. "Organizing for Economic Development." *Planning*, vol. 59, no. 4, April 1993.

Rosen, Martin J. "Reviving Urban Parks." *Urban Land*, vol. 56, no. 11, November 1997.

Rosenfeld, Jordan M. "Designing Urban Public Plazas." *Urban Land*, vol. 56, no. 12, December 1997.

Roy, Roger. "Orlando: Too Much of a Good Thing." *Planning*, vol. 62, no. 3, March 1996.

Rubin, Herbert J. "Community-Based Development Organizations." *Public Administration Review*, vol. 53, no. 5, September-October, 1993.

Russell, Charles. "Environmental Equity: Undoing Environmental Wrongs to Low Income and Minority Neighborhoods." *Journal of Affordable Housing & Community Development Law*, vol. 5, no. 2, Winter 1996.

Russell, Peter. "Brownfields Redevelopment: A Developer's Nightmare or a Dream Come True?" *Massachusetts Environment*, vol. 1, no. 9, February 1996.

Rypkema, Donovan D. "Preserving for Profit." *Urban Land*, vol. 57, no. 12, December 1998.

Salvesen, David, and Craig Richardson. "Keeping Up with Growth." *Urban Land*, vol. 58, no. 9, September, 1999.

Schweiger, Renate. "Seattle Revitalized." *Urban Land*, vol. 58, no. 10, October 1999.

Serrao, Gregory. "Ghost Towns or Downtowns? Saving the Cities." *Journal of Housing*, vol. 48, no. 5, September 1991.

Sink, David. "The Political Role of City Managers in Economic Development Programs: Theoretical and Practical Implications." *State and Local Government Review*, vol. 15, no. 1, Winter 1983.

Smith, Mark. "Civano: Lessons for a Region." *Urban Land*, vol. 57, no. 7, July 1998.

Starger, Steve. "Reinventing Downtown Hartford." *CT Business*, vol. 1, no. 4, November-December 1998.

Stinson, Shauna. "The Air Up There." *Urban Land*, vol. 58, no. 10, October 1999.

Stokley, Jan. "Community-based Economic Development." *Economic Development & Law Center Report*, vol. 15, no. 2/3, March-June 1985.

Sweazey, John, and Robert Schwartz. "Urban Community Housing." *Urban Land*, vol. 56, no. 11, November 1997.

Tabak, Lawrence. "Wild About Convention Centers." *Atlantic Monthly*, vol. 266, no. 2, April 1994.

Taebel, Delbert A. "Economic Development: The New Kid on the Block." *Texas Town & City*, vol. 82, no. 4, April 1994.

Taylor, Marilyn J. "Newark Turning the Corner." *Urban Land*, vol. 57, no. 2, February 1998.

Turner, Robyne S. "Growth Politics and Downtown Development: The Economic Imperative in Sunbelt Cities." *Urban Affair Quarterly*, vol. 28, no. 1, September 1992.

Ward, Janet. "Cities Engineer Train Station Revivals." *Urban Land*, vol. 114, no. 6, June, 1999.

Warson, Albert. "Toronto's Waterfront Revital." *Urban Land*, vol. 57, no. 1, January 1998.

Wassmer, Robert W. "Can Local Incentives Alter a Metropolitan City's Economic Development?" *Urban Studies*, vol. 31, no. 8, August 1994.

Wiewel, Wim; Joseph Persky; and Daniel Felsenstein. "Are Subsidies Worth It?: How to Calculate the Costs and Benefits of Business." *Government Finance Review*, vol. 11, no. 5, October 1995.

Woolard, E. S., Jr. "An Industry Approach to Sustainable Development." *Issues in Science and Technology*, vol. 8, no. 3, Spring, 1992.

Voith, Richard. "*City and Suburban Growth: Substitutes or Complements?*" *Business Review*, Federal Reserve Bank of Philadelphia, September/October, 1992.

Voorhis, Scott Van. "Betting on Boston." *Urban Land*, vol. 57, no. 12, December 1998.

Wolf, Virginia L. "General Planning." *Missouri Municipal Review*, vol. 51, no. 2, February 1986.

York, Jim. "Miamians at the Gate." *Urban Land*, vol. 56, no. 5, May 1997.

Other

Bendick, Marc, Jr., and David W. Rasmussen. "Enterprise Zones and Inner-City Economic Revitalization" in George Peterson and Carol Lewis, *Reagan and the Cities*. Washington, D.C.: The Urban Institute, 1985.

Bonnell, Barbara. "Inner-Harbor Development." *Lawyers Title News*. Richmond, VA: Lawyers Title Insurance Corporation, May-June 1986.

Farr, Cheryl. "Encouraging Local Economic Development: The State of the Practice." *Municipal Year Book*. Washington, D.C.: International City/County Management Association, 1990.

Gugliotta, Guy. "Rebuilding a Community from the Bottom Up." *Washington Post*, January 24, 1993, p. A1.

Lemann, Nicholas. "Four Generations in the Projects." *New York Times Magazine*, January 13, 1991, pp. 14, 16–21.

Office of Technology Assessment, United States Congress. *The Technological Reshaping of Metropolitan America*. Washington, D.C.: United States Government Printing Office, September, 1995.

Partners for Livable Communities. *In Pursuit of Livability: A Strategic Planning Cooperative*. Washington, D.C.: Partners for Livable Communities, Preliminary Report, 1996.

Prager, Adam J.; Philip Benowitz; and Robert Schein. "Trends and Practices in Local Economic Development." *Municipal Year Book*. Washington, D.C.: International City/County Management Association, 1995.

Reisch, Mark. *Brownfields Program: Clean Up Urban Industrial Sites*. Washington, D.C.: The Library of Congress, Congressional Research Service, April 3, 1995.

United States General Accounting Office. *Report to the Chair, Committee on Small Business, House of Representatives — Community Development: Reuse of Urban Industrial Sites*. Washington, D.C.: United States General Accounting Office, June, 1995.

ABOUT THE CONTRIBUTORS

Affiliations are as of the time the articles were written.

Joe Albanese, Vice President of Operations, Shawmut Design and Construction, Boston, Massachusetts.

Maureen Atkinson, Senior Partner, Urban Marketing Collaborative, Inc., Toronto, Ontario, Canada.

Richard Bailey, Director, Chattanooga News Bureau, Sponsored by the Chattanooga Chamber of Commerce and the City of Chattanooga, Chattanooga, Tennessee.

William R. Barnes, Director of the Center for Research and Program Development, National League of Cities, Washington, D.C.

Renee Berger, President, Teamworks, Inc., San Francisco, California.

Gayle Berens, Senior Director, University Education and the Inner-City, Urban Land Institute, Washington, D.C.

David B. Bowes, Chief Researcher-Writer, Modern Communities and Modern Manufacturing Project, cosponsored by the Manufacturing Institute and Partners for Livable Communities, Washington, D.C.; and President, Oakleaf Associates, Keedysville, Maryland.

Richard Bradley, Executive Director, International Downtown Association, Washington, D.C.

Paul M. Bray, Private Attorney, and Senior Counsel, New York State Legislative Bill Drafting Commission, Albany, New York.

J. Paul Brownridge, City Treasurer, City of Los Angeles, California.

Sharon Colley, Assistant Editor, *American City & County Magazine*, Intertec Publishing Corporation, Atlanta, Georgia.

Steve Culbertson, Executive Director, Philadelphia Association of Community Development Corporations, Philadelphia, Pennsylvania.

John W. Dorsett, Principal, Walker Parking Consultants, Indianapolis, Indiana.

Alan Ehrenhalt, Executive Editor, *Governing Magazine*, Congressional Quarterly, Inc., Washington, D.C.

Daniel Felsenstein, Assistant Professor, Geography Department, Hebrew University, Jerusalem, Israel.

Maryann Froehlich, Director, Office of Policy Development, Department of Planning, Policy, and Evaluations, U.S. Environmental Protection Agency, Washington, D.C.

Patrick Gallagher, Senior Vice President, Douglas Gallagher, Houston, Texas, Washington, D.C., and Nashville, Tennessee.

Glenda Glover, Assistant Professor, Department of Accounting, School of Business, Howard University, Washington, D.C.

Al Gobar, President, Alfred Gobar Associations, Placentia, California.

Timothy W. Gubala, Director of Economic Development, County of Roanoke, Roanoke, Virginia.

Kurt Hahn, Director, Department of Financial and Economic Services, City of Healdsburg, Healdsburg, California.

Gary G. Hill, Director of Finance, City of Lancaster, Lancaster, California.

Sandy Hornick, Director of Zoning, Planning Department, City of New York, New York.

Libby Howland, Freelance Editor and Writer, Tacoma Park, Maryland.

Roger L. Kemp, Author, Editor, Futurist, and City Manager, Meriden, Connecticut.

Terry J. Lassar, Communications Consultant and Writer about Development, Architecture, and Planning Issues, Portland, Oregon.

Larry C. Ledebur, Director, Center for Urban Affairs, Wayne State University, Detroit, Michigan.

Christopher Leinberger, Managing Director, Robert Charles Lesser and Company, Santa Fe, New Mexico.

Charles Mahtesian, Staff Writer, *Governing Magazine*, Congressional Quarterly, Inc., Washington, D.C.

Edward M. Marshall, President, Marshall and Associates, Inc., Washington, D.C.

John T. Marshall, Candidate, Juris Doctor Degree, College of Law, University of Florida, Tallahassee, Florida.

Scott Martinelli, Project Manager, Shawmut Design and Construction, Boston, Massachusetts.

Gordon Oliver, Writer of Transportation and Regional Land-Use Issues, *The Oregonian*, Portland, Oregon.

Dolores P. Palma, President, HyettPalma Inc., Alexandria, Virginia.

Ellen Perlman, Staff Writer, *Governing Magazine*, Congressional Quarterly, Inc., Washington, D.C.

Joseph Persky, Professor of Economics, University of Illinois, Chicago, Illinois.

Thomas Ressler, Freelance Writer, Athens, Ohio.

Craig Richardson, Ph.D. Candidate, City and Regional Planning, University of North Carolina, Chapel Hill, North Carolina.

Brian Robinson, Freelance Writer, Portland, Oregon.

David H. Roeder, Editor, *Chicago Enterprise Magazine*, Commercial Club of Chicago, Chicago, Illinois.

Herbert J. Rubin, Professor of Sociology, Northern Illinois University, DeKalb, Illinois.

Donovan D. Rypkema, Consultant, Real Estate and Economic Development, Washington, D.C., specializing in downtown revitalization and the redevelopment of historic buildings.

David Salvesen, Ph.D. Candidate, City and Regional Planning, University of North Carolina, Chapel Hill, North Carolina.

Steve Starger, Freelance Writer, Portland, Connecticut.

Marilyn J. Taylor, Partner; Skidmore, Owings & Merrill, New York, New York.

Janet Ward, Associate Publisher and Editor, *American City & County*, Intertec Publishing Corporation, Atlanta, Georgia.

Jeff Watkins, Policy Analyst, Philadelphia Association of Community Development Corporations, Philadelphia, Pennsylvania.

Josh S. Weston, Chairman, Research and Policy Committee, Committee for Economic Development, New York, New York.

Wim Wiewel, Professor of Urban Planning and Policy, and Special Assistant to the Chancellor, University of Illinois, Chicago, Illinois.

John Williams, Senior Partner, Urban Marketing Collaborative, Inc. Toronto, Ontario, Canada.

E. S. Woolard, Jr., Chairman, DuPont Co., Inc., Wilmington, Delaware.

INDEX